D1522433

Generic Histories of German Cinema

Screen Cultures: German Film and the Visual

Series Editors:
Gerd Gemünden (*Dartmouth College*)
Johannes von Moltke (*University of Michigan*)

Generic Histories of German Cinema

Genre and Its Deviations

Edited by Jaimey Fisher

 CAMDEN HOUSE

Rochester, New York

First published 2013
by Camden House

Camden House is an imprint of Boydell & Brewer Inc.
668 Mt. Hope Avenue, Rochester, NY 14620, USA
www.camden-house.com
and of Boydell & Brewer Limited
PO Box 9, Woodbridge, Suffolk IP12 3DF, UK
www.boydellandbrewer.com

ISBN-13: 978-1-57113-570-4
ISBN-10: 1-57113-570-7

Library of Congress Cataloging-in-Publication Data

Generic histories of German cinema : genre and its deviations / edited by
    Jaimey Fisher.
        pages cm. — (Screen cultures: German film and the visual)
    Includes bibliographical references and index.
    ISBN-13: 978-1-57113-570-4 (hardcover : alk. paper) —
    ISBN-10: 1-57113-570-7 (hardcover : alk. paper)
    1. Motion pictures—Germany—History and criticism. 2. Film genres—
Germany. I. Fisher, Jaimey.
    PN1993.5.G3G3573 2013
    791.430943—dc23
                                                                2013019461

This publication is printed on acid-free paper.
Printed in the United States of America.

Contents

Acknowledgments

I WOULD LIKE to express my gratitude to Jim Walker, editorial director at Camden House, for his steady support and expert guidance, as well as to Gerd Gemünden and Johannes von Moltke for their encouragement and advice throughout the project.

An earlier version of Eric Rentschler's essay appeared in *Weimar Cinema, 1919–1933: Daydreams and Nightmares*, edited by Larry Kardish (New York: Museum of Modern Art, 2010), 44–59.

Introduction: Toward Generic Histories— Film Genre, Genre Theory, and German Film Studies

Jaimey Fisher

WITH THE DEATH OF "Promi-Produzent" Bernd Eichinger in January 2011, many obituary writers, media commentators, and film-industry luminaries, such as Wolfgang Petersen and actor Til Schweiger, took the occasion to revisit the last forty years of German cinema.[1] Eichinger's oeuvre ranges from works now canonized as part of New German Cinema, such as *Falsche Bewegung* (Wrong Movement, 1975) and *Hitler—Ein Film aus Deutschland* (Hitler: A Film From Germany, 1977), to some of the biggest blockbusters of 1990s genre cinema such as *Der bewegte Mann* (The Moved Man, released in English as *Maybe . . . maybe not*, 1994) and *Ballermann 6* (1997), to the post-2000, globally marketed historical dramas *Der Untergang* (Downfall, 2004) and *Baader Meinhof Komplex* (2008). Although Eichinger's star rose more in the later phases of New German Cinema, he worked with New German Cinema luminaries as varied as Wim Wenders, Alexander Kluge, and Doris Dörrie, as well as, more recently, a director who has positioned himself as a second-generation inheritor of that cinema's often provocatively political project, Oskar Roehler. On the other, more mainstream hand, he was the producer of films such as the Berlin-shot *Resident Evil* series: made in English, based on a video game, and starring a former Ukranian supermodel, it is one of the highest-earning film cycles made outside the United States and United Kingdom.[2] Beyond his involvement at the level of the film or film series, Eichinger was also a force at the studio level:

---

[1] Petersen talked about Eichinger's death in a number of interviews, including "Wolfgang Petersen: Eichinger war ein Freund," accessed 21 Jun. 2011, http://www.dw.de/wolfgang-petersen-eichinger-war-ein-freund/a-6420125; a more conventional eulogy was Schweiger's much-quoted and somewhat bitter piece, Til Schweiger, "Nachruf: Bernd Eichinger? Die coolste Sau von allen," *Die Welt*, 26 Jan. 2011, http://www.welt.de/kultur/kino/article12352484/Bernd-Eichinger-Die-coolste-Sau-von-allen.html.

[2] See Brandon Gray, "Resident Evil resurrected for a fifth time," http://www.boxofficemojo.com/news/?id=3103&p=s.htm, 3. Mar. 2011. By way of comparison,

he took over Constantin-Film in 1979 and built it into the biggest studio player in German cinema. Moreover, reminiscent of old Hollywood moguls, he was often thoroughly involved in the content of the films, both at the casting and at the script level. In these and other ways, his career can be said not so much to reflect, but rather to have helped define the vicissitudes of German cinema for almost half its history.

Such a career is worth bearing in mind when considering the evolution of German film studies. It is worth noting that there are, at least at the time of writing, virtually no scholarly works on Eichinger's impact on the German film industry, despite the widespread testimony upon his death that he was, perhaps like Erich Pommer in the 1920s or Artur Brauner in the 1950s and 1960s, the dominant film figure of his time. This lack of scholarship on Eichinger has largely to do, I think, with the conventional perspectives of film scholarship within German studies, which has tended to separate art and auteur cinema from popular movies. But like Pommer and Brauner before him, Eichinger's highly varied career emphasizes how, from the perspective of the film industry, the conventional barrier between art cinema and popular cinema is not impassable and is, in fact, deliberately and profitably traversed all the time. For instance, one article commemorating Eichinger noted how successful he was at securing the sort of public monies that were a crucial factor in New German Cinema, but he effectively obtained them for both his art and his popular projects.[3] In German film studies, although more attention has been paid to popular cinema in the last fifteen years, the notion that popular film is distinct from art and auteurist cinema persists, despite the fact that Eichinger's career, and Pommer's and Brauner's for that matter, call it into question.[4]

So why the persistence of this duality between art and popular cinema, why this kind of industry blind spot in German film studies? I would submit that the persistence of this notion of a gap between art and popular cinema has to do, at least in part, with the almost complete lack of genre studies in German film studies; the notion of genre, as I shall detail below,

---

the *James Bond* franchise has averaged $69 million per film, while the *Resident Evil* franchise has earned an average of $50 million per film.

[3] Rüdiger Suchsland, "Der Riese unter den Zwergen," *Berliner Zeitung*, 25 Jan.2011, http://www.berlinonline.de/berliner-zeitung/kultur/328541/328542.php.

[4] See, for example, Tim Bergfelder, *International Adventures: German Popular Cinema and European Co-productions in the 1960s* (New York: Berghahn Books, 2005); Christine Haase, *When Heimat Meets Hollywood: German Filmmakers and America, 1985–2005* (Rochester, NY: Camden House, 2007); Randall Halle and Margaret McCarthy, eds., *Light Motives: German Popular Film in Perspective* (Detroit: Wayne State University Press, 2003); and Leonie Naughton, *That Was the Wild East: Film Culture, Unification, and the "New" Germany* (Ann Arbor: University of Michigan Press, 2002).

has become for film studies elsewhere an important means of negotiating between the individual filmic text and the industry more generally. In German film studies, where genre has received almost no sustained attention, two basic sorts of works have defined the field until now. First, there have been important auteurist studies focusing on the specific career of a given director (such as Thomas Elsaesser's work on Fassbinder or Gerd Gemünden's study of Billy Wilder). Second, and even more prominently, there are studies based on familiar historical periods: in fact, most of the major works in the field have been based on conventional historical periodization—Anton Kaes's *Shell Shock Cinema* and Eric Rentschler's and Sabine Hake's works on cinema under the Nazis, for example, as well as Elsaesser's *New German Cinema*. This has added to the emphasis on conventional historical periodization in analyses of German cinema in general, as can be seen in the volumes edited by Noah Isenberg and Christian Rogowski on Weimar cinema, Hake and John Davidson on the 1950s, and Fisher and Brad Prager as well as Paul Cooke and Chris Homewood on post-1989 cinema, among others. Of course, given the vicissitudes of Germany history in the twentieth century, the tendency to focus on historical periods is certainly understandable and warranted. But these two main areas of German film scholarship do also leave a lacuna in transperiod genre criticism; one, however, that the present volume addresses.

Recently, as noted above, German film studies has witnessed the emergence of a third sort of work, that is, studies of popular cinema in Germany, including works by Johannes von Moltke, Tim Bergfelder, Randall Halle, Margaret McCarthy, Leonie Naughton, and Christine Haase. It is remarkable, however, that even as film studies scholars manifest more interest in popular cinema in Germany, their works (with the exception of von Moltke's and, to a certain extent, Bergfelder's) largely neglect the study of genre, which has been so influential for film studies generally. As Timothy Corrigan and Patricia White observe in their recent, massive anthology of film theory, there has never been a concept more central to both film theory and history than genre.[5] Yet German film studies, even those works that consider popular films, generally neglect the substantial scholarship on the history and theory of film genres, something that the present volume aims to remedy. And, as noted above, any investigation of the history of genre should not focus solely on popular cinema but rather reconceptualize film history in a way that can pertain to both popular and art cinema. And so in this volume we deploy theories of genre to reconsider and refigure foundational notions about German film history, as well as looking at transperiod genres. In these

---

[5] Timothy Corrigan and Patricia White with Meta Mazaj, *Critical Visions in Film Theory: Classic and Contemporary Readings* (Boston: Bedford/St. Martin's, 2011), 443.

ways we aim to offer a fundamental reconsideration of where German film studies has been and where it will now go.

In *Generic Histories* we argue that the many recent theories and histories of genre can illuminate German film studies anew, in both popular and art cinema—in fact, it can help develop a broader context in which the links and relations among art and auteur and popular cinema become clearer and more illuminating. In addressing genre in German cinema, we foreground one central aspect of recent genre theory: we explore genre and genre theories for their potential for rethinking film history as well as cultural history more broadly. *Generic Histories* maintains that reading generically will allow and invite the investigation of genre across conventional historical periods (1919–33, 1933–45, 1945–61, 1961–89, and so on). In reconsidering these traditional divisions, the collection is not, in any way, a- or antihistorical but rather intends to open up history in different ways: it indexes and tracks history within genres via continuities as well as ruptures. Reading against the grain of traditional periodization, the essays foreground the historical consolidation and trajectories of genres—genre studies should, as scholars such as Rick Altman and Steve Neale suggest, emphasize the ongoing histories of film genres and their ever mutating forms.[6] To give a sense of both the trajectories of genres and their particular instantiations, each essay offers a general history of a genre as well as a specific case study of a key film. The essays in this volume read genre historically and do so in a German context that has starker caesurae than does US film history, and thus allow the volume to make an explicitly German contribution to genre theory.

The Vagaries of Postwar Theories of Film Genre

Although scholarship on German cinema has tended to neglect genre, film genre theory has not forgotten the Germans. German theorists, especially Adorno, Horkheimer, and Kracauer, have played surprisingly prominent roles in film genre theory and histories: they, particularly the former two, tend to be cited at one end—unsurprisingly, the negative one—of the wide spectrum of theoretical perspectives on genre. In the view of many genre theorists and historians, their work usefully serves up the unequivocal condemnation of popular genres as symptomatic of the stultifying and soporific effects of modern mass culture. The relation, indeed association, of genre with mass culture is one of the most important developments in modern genre theory (versus ancient theories of genre, as with Aristotle). For marquee genre theorists such as Rick Altman and Barry

---

[6] Rick Altman, *Film/Genre* (1999, repr., London: BFI, 2002). Henceforth cited as *F/G*; Steve Neale, *Genre and Hollywood* (1999, repr., New York: Routledge, 2000).

Langford, Adorno and Horkheimer articulate, along with Althusser, the emphatically ideological reading of genre, in which genre-inclined mass culture veils the deeper, more insidious aspects of capitalism. For Altman, such theorists see the "narrative situations and structural relations" of such cultural products deliberately misrepresenting social and economic contradictions, obscuring material realities, and thereby conjuring false consciousness (*F/G*, 27). In his history of genre, Barry Langford likewise rolls out Adorno and Horkheimer's culture-industry chapter as influential on those genre critics (such as Judith Hess Wright) who understand genre films as symptomatic of mass cultural standardization, distraction, and indoctrination.[7]

Although Kracauer's approach to cinema was clearly quite different—it is difficult, though perhaps fun, to imagine Adorno writing *From Caligari to Hitler*—some genre historians, such as Mark Jancovich, have tended to associate Kracauer's work with Adorno and Horkheimer's culture-industry analysis, ignoring the strong historical element that Kracauer introduced to his (admittedly reductive) analysis of Weimar cinema and mass culture more generally.[8] In fact, it is also this historical element in Adorno and Horkheimer's work that these portrayals tend to omit and that can, I think, open up the kind of approach this volume takes. For instance, there is little mention of the culture-industry chapter's place within *Dialectic of Enlightenment* or of the project's formative context of Nazi-coerced emigration to the United States and its industrial capitalism. Moreover, and likewise unhelpfully ahistorical, Altman, Langford, Jancovich, and others overlook later reconsiderations of these earlier overwhelmingly negative assessments, including Adorno's reconsideration of film historically in his "Transparencies on Film" or those in Kracauer's *Theory of Film*.[9] Thus despite consistently playing the bêtes noires of these scholars of genres, the German theorists point emphatically to a more historical approach, and so overlooking or downplaying this historical aspect of their work seems a particularly stark oversight, given where genre theory, as I shall explore shortly, has ended up. The short overview of film genre theory that follows aims to demonstrate how, in the most recent phase of genre theory, a focus on history has returned full force, even as contemporary genre theory absorbs sundry elements from earlier theoretical moments. This overview seeks to explicate the arc

[7] Barry Langford, *Film Genre: Hollywood and Beyond* (Edinburgh: Edinburgh University Press, 2005), 21. See Judith Hess Wright, "Genre Films and the Status Quo," in *Film Genre Reader III*, ed. Barry Keith Grant (1974, repr., Austin: University of Texas Press, 2003), 42–50.
[8] Mark Jancovich, *Horror: The Film Reader* (London: Routledge 2002), 11.
[9] Theodor Adorno, "Transparencies on Film." *New German Critique* 24/25 (1981): 199–205; and Siegfried Kracauer, *Theory of Film* (Oxford: Oxford University Press, 1960).

of theories of genre that inform the basic approach of *Generic Histories* as well as to give some context to some of the theories and historians of genre cited in the essays in the present collection.

Many theorists and historians of film genre start with the long history of theories of literary genre, ranging from Aristotle and Horace to Warren and Wellek, Todorov, and Frye, the earlier ones mostly taking the measure of how successful works were in mimicking generic models, the later ones largely lamenting how the undue influence of a genre could maim works aiming at originality and creativity. It is beyond the purview of this introduction to give a detailed analysis of such theories of literary genres, but the longer-term effects of such literary studies on studies of film genre have, I think, not been great, despite the homage ubiquitously paid. This is not least because, as discussed below, theories of film genre were products of an increasing focus on the film industry at a specific historical moment. In literary theories of genre there is nothing convincingly analogous to the generic interests and complex operations of film production and the industry in which it is housed. Two aspects of these literary theories of genre, however, are worth noting and at least anticipate (if not openly influence) aspects of the theory of film genre: the long-term interest (from Aristotle on) in genre's effect on audiences, and the historical contingency and variability of the aesthetic value of originality. The interest in genre's textual effects has increasingly tended toward an interest in the audience's role in genre operations. On the other hand, the historical rise of originality (versus aesthetic fidelity to generic models) intersects, I think, the art-versus-popular-cinema duality mentioned above, the vacillating valuation of artistic originality as against generic models. Acknowledging the relevance and power of generic models gives us new understanding of how all media interrelate and therefore function intertextually. Such intertextuality is built on audience expectation, recognition, and reaction surrounding the text.

This greater attention dedicated to the readership or audience underscores what I regard as perhaps the central contribution of genre theory to film studies: the consistent balancing of the particular (filmic) text with other aspects of a text's function for readers and in broader society. Genre theory has consistently foregrounded and illuminated the text, its effects, and its affects, but it has also extended these by way of both audience and institutional contexts (the latter including both the film industry and its ancillary institutions, such as criticism). In fact, I would say that this kind of contextual reading of the individual text, analyzing the text in relation to audience and institutional aspects, forms a sort or triangle that can replace the one of "artist/film/audience" that Steve Neale cites from Tony Ryall in his *Genre and Hollywood*.[10] The whole history of genre the-

---

[10] Neale, *Genre and Hollywood*, 12.

ory underscores how such theory has analyzed the particular filmic text but simultaneously put it into the wider context of its audience and its institutional framework. There had been, of course, from early on, interest in the sociological makeup of film audiences (for example, in Emilie Altenloh's 1914 study), but genre theory investigates and illuminates the way in which these three aspects of cinema writ large—filmic text, audiences, and industry institutions—operate at their points of intersection, interaction, and influence.[11] In fact, I attempt here to analyze the history of film genre theory for its alternating emphasis on certain aspects of this triangulated genre model: at various moments in that history, theorists of genre have given more weight to one or two of these relative to the others. With this triad in mind, the following account aims to illuminate not only the various terms and concepts central to film genre studies, but also to elucidate the rise of historical analysis within that genre theory.

Auteur and 1950s Genre Theory

The first significant wave of critical writing about film genre, that of the mid-1950s and 1960s, was primarily concerned with something for which it became much more famous, namely, the auteur. As a number of scholars (especially Langford and Neale) have pointed out, it took 1950s auteur theory to bring sustained interest in, and lend consistent credibility to, the study of genre.[12] As is often pointed out, *Cahiers du cinema* critics, such as the young Truffaut, Rohmer, and Godard, under the tutelage of *Cahiers* editor Bazin, famously elevated directors to the status of authors by focusing on films that expressed (putative) individuated and personal visions.[13] It has been less often recalled, however, that this elevation of auteurist expression requires familiarity with the recurring elements of the genres in which these directors were operating. Despite the marquee value of the auteur, it took no little attention to genre to identify the pertinent auteurist aspects of a filmmaker's work, especially because the *Cahiers* critics tended to apotheosize directors known for what were regarded as genre films (figures such as John Ford, Howard Hawks, and above all Alfred Hitchcock). As Neale notes, this allowed for much more serious and systematic engagement with Hollywood productions than before and moved these innovative analyses beyond content considerations into

---

[11] Discussed in Miriam Hansen, "Early Silent Cinema: Whose Public Sphere?" *New German Critique* 29 (Spring 1983): 147–84.

[12] See Langford, *Film Genre*, 9–10, and Neale, *Genre and Hollywood*, 10.

[13] For an overview of the concept of auteurism/authorship, see the section in *Film Theory: Critical Concepts in Media and Cultural Studies*, ed. Philip Simpson, Andrew Utterson, and K. J. Shepherdson, 4 vols. (London: Routledge), especially vol. 2, part 4.

issues of "form, style, theme, and mise-en-scène."[14] Given that many of these directors' works had been received as mainstream genre films, distinguishing them then occasioned detailed, often innovative analysis of genres' visual elements.

For our purposes (in the German context), then, it is worth emphasizing that auteurism and film-genre criticism, in fact, emerged in entwined fashion, such that auteur theory emerged along with that of genre and was by no means defined, as it would be in German *Autorenkino*, primarily in opposition to popular genre.[15] This interweaving of auteurism and genre, one that both complicates and questions the notion of an auteur, is something realized in a number of essays in the current volume, including those by Lutz Koepnick (on Fritz Lang's science-fiction films), Jaimey Fisher (on Bernhard Wicki, a now forgotten but once ubiquitously celebrated auteur), and Marco Abel (on the self-referential *policiers* of one of Germany's most prolific auteurs, Dominik Graf). The films of all these directors make clear the thin, and co-constitutive, line between auteurism and genre cinema.

The interweaving of auteurism and genre also illuminates the distinction between genre and popular cinema, overlapping at times as they may: in the view of many of these early critics of genre, most significant auteurs self-consciously utilized genre within the studio system to realize their own individualistic visions. For the *Cahiers* critics, then, even the most auteurist films could be genre films, as there was no abiding opposition between auteurist work and popular work. This perhaps surprising development was true as well when the thinking and writing of the *Cahiers* critics influenced Anglo-American film studies at a crucial moment of its own development in the 1960s and early 1970s. Critics Andrew Sarris and Pauline Kael became the highest profile proponents of such theories, but scholars introduced them into their research on film genre, too. For example, in 1969 in his influential book, *Horizons West*, Jim Kitses emphasized that directors should not be defined against genre, but rather see genre as a resource to draw upon.[16] Even into the mid-1970s, Cawelti would be emphasizing in an auteurist vein how certain directors can artistically exploit the most hackneyed genre clichés through "stereotype vitalization."[17]

There were, however, clear shortcomings to this association of genre theory with auteurism, shortcomings brought into stark relief if

[14] Neale, *Genre and Hollywood*, 11.

[15] Ian Garwood, "The *Autorenfilm* in Contemporary German Cinema," in *The German Cinema Book*, ed. Tim Bergfelder, Erica Carter, and Deniz Göktürk (London: bfi, 2002), 202–10.

[16] Jim Kitses, *Horizons West* (London: Thames & Hudson, 1969), 26.

[17] John G. Cawelti, *Adventure, Mystery and Romance: Formula Stories as Art and Popular Culture* (Chicago: University of Chicago Press, 1976), 11.

one invokes the three aspects (text, audience, institutional context) that I am highlighting in this brief history of film genre theory. An emphasis on the self-expressive auteur occasions primarily close analyses of individual texts created by that individual. It does little to highlight how viewers or institutions relate to and help form genres. In fact, even though such an approach might highlight some aspects of the operations of a given genre, it would tend to focus on those aspects exploited by auteurist directors instead of explaining how the genres function more generally. For example, the sort of stereotype vitalization of which Cawelti writes would occasion analysis of prevailing stereotypes, but it would likely do little to explain why that stereotype had become dominant or how it functioned in multiple contexts. In a related fashion, such an approach would also, as Barry Langford has argued, leave marked historical lacunae:[18] focus on the auteurist aspects of genre films only partially elucidates why certain genres burgeon or wither at particular moments in what Cawelti and Schatz would come to call, in a more structuralist phase of genre criticism that I discuss below, the life cycle of a given genre.

1960s Generic Iconography and Conventions

One early and influential departure from auteurism imported a critical discourse not so much from literary studies as from art history. "Iconography" has become one of the most-cited aspects of film genre, one that illuminates what viewers see on the screen and in their mind's eye when they conceive of a genre. In the late 1960s and early 1970s, scholars like Edward Buscombe and Lawrence Alloway borrowed (quite selectively) from art historian Erwin Panofsky and took iconography to refer to images in genre films whose meaning is derived not only (or even so much) from the specific context of a given film, but rather from other films and media, usually other texts in the same (putative) genre. For the most-cited examples (and these genres are particularly well suited to such an analysis), the cowboy kit, saddled horse, and wide-open landscapes belong to the iconography of the Western, while long coats, machine guns, and city streets mark the gangster film. For critics like Colin McArthur, such iconographies typically comprise three constellations of images: mise-en-scène elements directly relating to the actor, to the contexts in which the actors operate, and to technologies exhibited in the film generally.[19] Buscombe used the term "visual conventions" in describing iconography, which implies nonvisual conventions as well, although

---

[18] Langford, *Film Genre*, 10.

[19] Colin McArthur, *Underworld USA* (London: Secker & Warburg, 1972), 23.

ultimately these theories conspicuously tend to the visual aspects of films in addressing iconography.[20]

Beyond lending to genre study the legitimacy of a more established academic discipline and influence, this iconographic focus, that is, the focus on such genres' visual recurrences, advanced the trend away from the content-oriented (narrative/thematic) analyses of literarily inclined critics. Investigations of iconography corresponded well to an intuitive sense of film genre as different from literary genre, to an intuitively visual basis for a (largely) visual medium. Moreover, and perhaps more importantly, iconography refocused analysis not so much on genre as a tool for extraordinary auteurist directors but rather on the creation of meaning in any individual text by the wider field of generic texts. Iconography helped genre studies refocus on the centrality of the intertext: it was only by way of such an intertextual understanding and analysis that one could understand how any single genre film worked. And with an emphasis on intertexts' recurring elements (rather than on auteurism's differentiating aspects), scholars turned their attention to the most popular films of a genre (rather than its critically most exceptional works).

The shift from the content of the single picture—or the career of the single auteur—to the importance of iconography in the many intertexts comes into focus in a number of essays in the volume. Horror is a genre probably most easily identifiable by its iconography and, indeed, in both Gerd Gemünden's essay on Edgar Ulmer's *Black Cat* and Kris Vander Lugt's on various postwar horror films, such as *Nekromantik* (1987), iconography is the key to identifying and tracking the genre in all its gory vagaries. Science fiction is another genre perhaps most marked by its iconography, as the imagery and its context almost invariably have to convey a sense of futurity in the narrative. Lutz Koepnick traces a number of such iconographic aspects of science fiction, including their first deployment in Lang's *Frau im Mond* (Woman in the Moon; for example, the ship's tortured path to the launching pad or in the countdown sequence—imagery then adopted by NASA, of course, in a notable example of life imitating art). In many other essays as well, genres' iconographies are discussed as a core part of their generic mechanisms, even if not explaining the specific films in question entirely (for example, in Paul Cooke's small-town iconography of the Heimat film, or mine of the war film).

These essays confirm a shift in the iconographic approach in the triad of cinematic aspects I sketched above: there is a high degree of familiarity that an audience must bring to the individual text for such iconographic intertextuality to function, and that familiarity of the audience, especially

---

[20] Edward Buscombe, "The Idea of Genre in the American Cinema," *Screen* 2, no. 2 (Mar.-Apr. 1970): 30–45. Reprinted in Grant, *Film Genre Reader III*, 12–26.

in its visual forms, became an increasing focus of scholarly research on genre.[21] Iconography helps shift the theoretical emphasis away from texts that differentiate themselves from genres (auteurism's strength) to the audiences that support them. For an example of a genre phenomenon that such audience-focused intertextuality and iconography elucidate well, one might consider the importance of casting, including particular stars who overlap with a genre's specific iconography (*F/G*, 34–35). The phenomenon of stardom is fundamentally iconographic and intertextual, requiring attention to audience familiarity well beyond the single text if its ubiquitous and influential operations are to be understood.[22] This formative intersection of iconography and casting recurs in a number of the essays in the volume.

Genre as Myth, Ritual, and/or Archetype: Structuralist Approaches to Popular Film

Despite shifting attention to the audience, such an iconographic approach quickly demonstrates its shortcomings when one considers it across a wide variety of genres. One abiding problem with emphasizing the iconography of a genre is that even as it corresponds well to viewers' intuitive senses of genres such as Westerns and gangster, horror and science-fiction films, its explanatory power is severely limited for other important genres such as the musical, the romantic comedy, or even drama more generally. Obviously, these are generally easily identifiable genres—one knows a musical when one hears it—but even those films belonging to a generally acknowledged canon of such films (say, *Singing in the Rain* or *Moulin Rouge*) do not demonstrate a consistent iconography or even consistent narrative conventions. This limitation, along with broader academic trends, helped another trend in genre theory to gain purchase, namely, structuralist approaches that tend to focus on genre's deeper layers of cultural ritual, archetype, and myth. Structuralist approaches were part of a wider and influential theoretical trend in the late 1960s and 1970s, one whose key influences across academic disciplines included Ferdinand de Saussure, Vladimir Propp, Claude Lévi-Strauss, Roland Barthes, Louis Althusser. and Jacques Lacan. With these important theorists, the structuralist trend in genre theory clearly brought film studies into the academic world, a move that the importation of iconography from art history had anticipated.

---

[21] Even some of the earliest iconographic criticism foregrounded this kind of intertextual familiarity; see Lawrence Alloway, "On the Iconography of the Movies," *Movie* 7 (1963): 4–5. Discussed in Neale, *Genre and Hollywood*, 14.
[22] Langford, *Film Genre*, 2.

Structuralism lent itself well to genre theorists, because structuralists such as Propp and Lévi-Strauss took as an object of study a culture's
recurring narratives—for Propp it was folk-narratives, and for Levi-Strauss
it was a culture's myths, but the success of such recurring narratives
shares a clear affinity with the repetitive and abiding success of genres.
Moreover, structuralism sought in these recurring folk and myth narratives a more profound social function and meaning with which genre
critics and theorists were happy to vest products that had often been
dismissed as stupefying and superficial. Linking genre to myth, archetype, and ritual affirmed its importance and located it at the center of
a culture's collective self-expression. Finally structuralism, influenced by
Saussure's famous distinction between *langue* (the underlying structures
of language) and *parole* (the particular instance of speech), offered a kind
of bifurcated model that circumvented the problems of genre iconography and became influential for later genre theory. The structuralist model
suggests that genres share certain deeper (and therefore not necessarily
iconographic) structures—usually a society's central oppositions and/or
contradictions—that shape the underlying constellation of the film, while
the individual films manifest those deeper structures in a variety of ways,
just as the individual instance of *parole* can vary within *langue*. Such a
bifurcated model for genre thus locates the deeper structures in social
oppositions that structure a given narrative, as Levi-Strauss did in myth,
but also allows for the individual text's articulation and working through
of that structuring opposition.

The basics of this approach—recurring narratives as collective self-
expressions of a culture's deepest contradictions, the bifurcated model of
deep structure and particular instantiations—informed many of the most
important studies of film genre of the late 1960s, 1970s, and into the
1980s. A number of studies sketched the deeper, structuring social oppositions in established genres, like the Western working through the opposition between wilderness and civilization, which Jim Kitses famously
charted as part of a grid of structuring oppositions.[23] Will Wright made
an explicit comparison revealing of this trend: "the Western, though
located in a modern industrial society, is as much a myth as the tribal
myths of the anthropologists."[24] For horror and science fiction, the preferred opposition seemed to be, at least in the work of Bruce Kawin, in
the known versus the unknown.[25] One of the most-cited writers on genre,
Robin Wood, proves quite structuralist in his influential theory of horror

---

[23] Jim Kitses, *Horizons West*, 11. Reproduced, for instance, in Neale, *Genre and
Hollywood*, 134.

[24] Will Wright, *Sixguns and Society: A Structural Study of the Western* (Berkeley:
University of California Press, 1977), 187.

[25] Bruce Kawin, "The Mummy's Pool," in *Planks of Reason: Essays on the Horror
Film*, ed. Barry Keith Grant (Metuchen, NJ: Scarecrow, 1984), 3–20.

as operating in the opposition between the repressed and its spectacular return.[26] Wood was, however, able to read subtly in many of his analyses, avoiding an obvious pitfall offered by this approach, that of reducing the text to its (putative) underlying oppositions. His work shows how psychoanalysis, particularly in its semiotic/Lacanian inflection (the one particularly influential for film studies at that time), might also be regarded as structuralist: this was also true of the long-running melodrama debate in the work of Mary Ann Doane, Thomas Elsaesser, and Peter Brooks, among others. Altman locates a number of genre histories and theories of the late 1960s through the early 1980s in what he terms the ritual camp, including those by Braudy, McConnell, Sobchack, Wood, Wright, and his own earlier work on the musical (*F/G*, 26–27).

Although fewer and fewer—including in this volume—cite these structuralist theorists, structuralism has certainly had an important afterlife in genre theory and history. Whenever one foregrounds the social function or reflection of a genre, the echoes of structuralism can be heard: in many ways, the structuralist emphasis on genre's links to society's subterranean structures has been absorbed into contemporary understandings of genres. This is true of many of the essays in the volume, which in some ways extend, but also emphatically update, these structuralist approaches, especially by putting them into their historical context. In discussing musical comedies in the late 1920s and early 1930s, Eric Rentschler elaborates on Kracauer's notion of distraction for the masses, phenomena (both distraction and masses) that, although here linked to specific moments of modernity, nevertheless rest in the deeper structures of industrial society. Steve Choe takes up the social structures evoked and exploited by the thriller, including the notion of a secret state within a state and a political *Ausnahmezustand* (state of emergency) that recurs from German democracy's earliest to latest days, from early Weimar to postunification. As noted above, the Heimat film is the German genre *par excellence* related to social ritual and society's opposition of inside/outside, even if, as Paul Cooke explores in his essay in this volume, the later iterations of Heimat take up these inside/outside oppositions to knowingly question them. Finally, Antje Ascheid's engagement with recent romance and postromance films tracks historically an immensely popular genre's foundations in love and sexuality, both timeless and historically conditioned, registering the impact and function of the singles' society in genre.

In these ways, the essays in the volume reflect a self-conscious historicizing of the repeatedly recurring narratives foregrounded in structuralist analyses of genre. This matches the turn to the historical that emerged in the later phrases of structuralist theory. Two of the most influential genre

---

[26] Robin Wood, "The American Nightmare: Horror in the 1970s," in Jancovich, *Horror: The Film Reader*, 28.

theorists of this period, John G. Cawelti and Thomas Schatz, advanced the mythic/ritual theory of genre in different ways, although both foreshadow the growing importance of a more historical approach. Largely in line with the mythic analysis—Cawelti writes that genre, "can be defined as a structural pattern which embodies . . . a myth in the materials of language"[27]—Cawelti emphasized what he termed certain recurring popular "formulas," which include the hard-boiled detective or gangster film and comprise conventions expressing the collective fantasies of US audiences over many decades. Such formulas expressed dominant fantasies while also resolving tensions endemic to the culture's various deeper attitudes. On the other hand, particularly in his slightly later work, Cawelti also suggested how these recurring formulas could change in accordance with "audience response," such that "new themes and symbols" could emerge.[28] The persistence of fantasy and subsequent formulas and their ability to change suggests a certain tension around history in his work, a central issue, as we shall see, in structuralist criticism in general.

Dovetailing with this tension around myth and history was the work of Thomas Schatz, who offered some of the most influential histories and theories of genre in this period. Schatz is credited with emphasizing the evolution of genre, but he also certainly saw it as mythic and ritual. For example, in his much-cited 1981 work *Hollywood Genres: Formulas, Filmmaking and the Studio System*, he emphasized that genres constitute a form of "collective cultural expression."[29] Schatz, however, did go further than many structuralist critics in thematizing the very fact of generic diversity (as opposed to merely discussing individual genres): he explicitly addressed the simultaneous coexistence of many genres (their synchrony), but nonetheless argued that the diversity of genres demonstrates the wider range of myths in a given culture. Extending the bifurcated model I foregrounded above, Schatz even theorized two different types of genres, one determinate (and more iconographically based, with its central conflicts over physical space, such as the Western or gangster film), and one indeterminate (less iconographic, more abstract and working more within narrative convention, with conflicts more internal and psychological, such as the social melodrama or screwball comedy).[30] By foregrounding and theorizing the diversity of genres, Schatz could deduce that each genre has what he called (in a much-cited passage) a "generic community," a constellation that corresponds to the deeper myths or issues that the genres are collectively expressing.[31]

---

[27] Cawelti, *Adventure, Mystery and Romance*, 30.
[28] Cawelti, *Adventure, Mystery and Romance*, 34.
[29] Thomas Schatz, *Hollywood Genres: Formulas, Filmmaking and the Studio System* (New York: McGraw-Hill, 1981), 13.
[30] Schatz, *Hollywood Genres*, 27.
[31] Schatz, *Hollywood Genres*, 20.

Cawelti's consideration of audience response as a factor in creating genres underscores the audience dimension of the triad I sketch above. These structuralist approaches extend and elaborate iconography's engagement with the audience by more precisely querying how films functioned for audiences. In aiming to locate deep collective forms in societies and its audiences, structuralism was part of a broader theoretical trend that emphasized the social function of culture and especially of cultural narrative, a trend reflecting a growing concern with the social context of art and culture in the 1960s and 1970s. In viewing society as a more collective and unified entity, this development dovetailed with social and political currents of the time, as well as with the broader critique of celebration of the genius creator, of which auteurism was doubtless a part. Like iconography's emphasis on audience familiarity and its shift away from auteurs, but extending beyond it, structuralism's focus on such deep structures in societies shifted from single texts and their individual creators to recurring patterns and the audience that is attracted to them. Of particular importance to many of these scholars, as Cawelti's work suggests, was the system of commercial feedback that audiences offered mainstream cinema, compelling filmmakers and the studios to adapt films to genres that were constantly honed by those paying audiences, a system that made genres especially reflective of a culture's central ideals and conflicts. Cawelti, for instance, focuses on how audience response produces a genre by offering constant feedback and in effect conditioning it to accord with the deeper attitudes and tensions of a society.[32]

Post-Structuralism and the Rise of Historical-Discursive Analyses

With its greater attention to audience and its sociocultural underpinnings, structuralism indelibly influenced genre theory in the late 1960s and 1970s, and into the 1980s, but critiques of these genre theories manifested myriad dissatisfactions with it as early as the 1970s, dissatisfactions that dovetailed with the rise of post-structuralism. The concurrence of these critiques underscores how, even while certain theoretical perspectives may predominate, competing critiques also vie for explanatory purchase—for instance, although I have organized many of these ideas into discrete sections, many, in fact, coexisted and were mutually influential. Post-structuralism highlighted the limitations and blindspots of much of the above, particularly the reductive homogenization that positing deep structures in a putatively unified society would entail. In particular, post-structuralism questioned whether one can really speak of deep structures that reflect fundamental aspects of a society or culture

[32] Cawelti, *Adventure, Mystery and Romance*, 34.

and, indeed, whether there really is "a" society or "a" culture at all. In this way post-structuralism fragmented the notion of a unified whole, be it social or cultural, and its concomitant master narratives, highlighting instead a multiplicity of often conflicting and contradictory voices. Such approaches were also highly skeptical of tales of origins, and they consistently found, in what might at first have seemed a stable, teleological narrative, a cacophony of contestations.

These critiques of structuralist positions inform three influential ideas that recur in the present volume. First, Andrew Tudor, the author of, among others, *Theories of Film* (1974) and *Monsters and Mad Scientists: A Cultural History of the Horror Film* (1989), uncovered the now-often-cited notion of an "empiricist dilemma" in most genre theories and histories.[33] Tudor observed that scholars analyzing a genre invariably begin by examining a given set of films to ascertain what "indefinable 'X'" the films share that qualifies them for a particular genre.[34] In this way genre studies—be they auteurist, iconographic, or structuralist—build their theories inductively upon a body of works that are more or less unproblematically regarded as belonging to the genre. Scholars would then draw a general conclusion (namely, that indefinable X) from a body of works selected, if not arbitrarily, intuitively. But Tudor emphasized that the initial choice of the body of works would inevitably limit and even determine the conclusions that could and would be drawn, something Altman also points to as a recurring corpus problem in genre studies (*F/G*, 216–17). For Tudor, and implicitly for Altman, then, the attempt to isolate the genre's essence, its indefinable X, is the wrong approach, because it invariably relies on an unconvincing, even suspect, selection process. Although Tudor is contemporaneous with the structuralists, his intervention directs genre away from individual films and even groups of films and instead toward a broader classificatory network interwoven into the culture, something, as I shall detail below, that has had a lasting impact on genre studies and its growing historical and discursive concerns.

Tudor observed that even though critics concentrate more on audiences' roles in genre definition, audience members are not nearly as troubled as critics by the precise genre classification of a given film. This question of the discreteness of genre classification and its categories foreshadows another series of critiques of the structuralist approach, namely, the increasing acknowledgement of pervasive generic hybridity (sometimes termed, somewhat disturbingly, "impurity"). In its focus on deep structures, structuralism tended to prefer discrete genres, since they would more simply and convincingly reflect and articulate fundamental

---

[33] See Andrew Tudor's chapter, "Genre," in Tudor, *Theories of Film*; also in Grant, *Film Genre Reader III*, 5.
[34] Tudor, "Genre," 3.

social oppositions, but as scholars such as (the later) Cawelti, Janet Staiger, and Steve Neale, among others, have observed, a great number, or even the majority (according to Staiger), of films fall between the cracks when genres are seen as discrete entities.[35] As a matter of fact, many films rely on a deliberate hybridization for their most powerful effects, as Gemünden, Alter, and Fisher explore in this volume. Some of these most critically acclaimed effects include, as Cawelti in particular outlines, the self-conscious and self-reflexive manipulation, often ironicization, of genres in genre films themselves.[36] If genres are the honed formulas that reflect the dearest myths of a culture, then this self-conscious, ironic, and often openly parodic distance from those genres would seem to undercut the centrality and depth of those structures. Cawelti demonstrates how a genre can move rather quickly through a series of different phases, including a period of parody, of the baroque, of the burlesque, and of demythification of the genre, often through hybridization (as Fisher and Gerhards discuss in their essays).[37] This variety of relationships to the genre, as well as diversity in its hybrid forms, would not be expected if the genre's primary function were to work through a society's deepest myth and oppositions.

Third, one of the most cited theories of genre grew out of a dissatisfaction with, but then, I would argue, a kind of sublation of structuralism. In a widely cited argument, Rick Altman links and critiques the ritual and ideological theories of genre discussed above, both of which he regards as animating genre with some deeper but highly speculative agency (*F/G*, 26–28). In the ritual approach, as noted above, the mythic oppositions of a society's deep structures form the genre, while in the ideological approach of Jean-Louis Comolli, Jean-Louis Baudry, and the *Screen* critics, it is the deceptive but nonetheless deep contradictions of capitalism that manifest themselves in surface symptoms of the very same genres. But it seems to me that one of Altman's own most influential theories of genre, that of a generic semantics and syntax, simultaneously critiques, but also incorporates, the structuralist approach in a sublating mode not so often remarked upon. In Altman's much-cited linguistic analogy for genre, a genre's semantics refers to "shared plots, key scenes, character types, familiar objects or recognizable shots and sounds" and thereby seems quite close to the iconographic theories sketched above (*F/G*, 89). Altman himself mentions iconography in this context and says that one can judge a film's semantics in part through still images from the film, an assertion underscoring its proximity to iconography. On the

---

[35] See Janet Staiger, "Hybrid or Inbred: The Purity Hypothesis and Hollywood Genre History," in Grant, *Film Genre Reader III*, 185–201.

[36] John G. Cawelti, "*Chinatown* and Generic Transformation in Recent American Film," in Grant, *Film Genre Reader III*, 243–61.

[37] Cawelti, "Chinatown," 254–56.

other hand, a genre's syntax refers to the "building blocks" of a genre such as "plot structure, character relationships, or image and sound montage" (*F/G*, 89). These notions arise in a number of essays in the current volume, but I think it is important to be mindful that Altman's very notion of syntax underscores the deeper structures of language, and he cites, in sketching a genre's syntax, both the "deeper structures underlying generic affiliation" and the above-mentioned structuring oppositions in the Western that Kitses outlines. In these ways Altman has certainly made room in his much-cited theory for at least some of structuralism's insights, although he is skeptical of locating genre solely within social ritual or ideology critique (*F/G*, 49). His emphasis on a concurrent generic semantics and syntax thus deliberately integrates the iconographic and structural approaches. As he makes clear, certain genres will operate more by a semantic approach, some more by syntax, but both ought to be seen to operate simultaneously. These concurrent operations occasion what Altman emphasizes as a "coordinated" approach to analyzing genre, one acknowledging and incorporating the two traditions (*F/G*, 90). This later iteration of a bifurcated model, one that sublates two dominant strains of genre theory by incorporating and encompassing both, echoes post-structuralism's rejection of a single, unifying theory: this theory foregrounds its openness to multiple causes and concurrent, competing explanations.

History and Discourse in Contemporary Theories of Film Genre

If Altman's notion of generic semantics and syntax sublated structuralism into a broader approach, his other most-cited concept, that of "genrification," hints at what has largely replaced structuralist understanding in the wake of these critiques, namely, a historical-discursive approach. By this I mean not only how discourse defines genre but also how these discourses unfold diachronically and therefore constitute an ongoing system and process, as Altman puts it. Altman's notion of genrification summarized and advanced a trend clear from the late 1970s and 1980s, namely, a concern with the historical development of genres, including their formation, consolidation, and vicissitudes. This interest in the historical character of genres can also be seen as a reaction to structuralism, which both Steve Neale and Altman (two of the leading proponents of the historical-discursive approach) criticized for its tendency to dehistoricize genre. Neale points out that structuralism tended to regard all films in a genre as functioning synchronically to symptomatize a society's timeless oppositions, while Altman cited its tendency to "surround" genres with "pagan rituals, native ceremonies, undated traditional texts, and descriptions of human nature," to render genre a "rabbit hole" to archetype and myth

(*F/G*, 49). For him, stating it starkly, "two generations of genre critics have done violence to the historical dimensions" of genre (*F/G*, 49–50). These points have helped steer genre study in a new direction, although it should be observed that both the later Cawelti and Schatz did address the evolution of genres, so it is not really fair to consign all structuralist criticism to the scrap heap of ahistory.

This historical critique of structuralism serves as the foundation for two theories of genre that inform the current volume, both emphasizing the historical and discursive dimensions of genre. For Altman, the historical critique of structuralism's approach is a precursor to the notion of genrification, that is, the historical and discursive process by which a genre is instituted, maintained, transformed, and eventually abandoned. Instead of querying the deep structures a certain set of films allegedly share (echoing Tudor's critique of an indefinable X), he investigates when certain forms win out, even for the time being; which forms were (at least temporarily) abandoned to clear the field for the (ephemeral) victory; and which changes, both historical and generic, were instituted to consolidate the (provisional) triumph (*F/G*, 50). To paraphrase his own memorable metaphor (one discussed by Choe in his essay), Altman is committed to investigating not so much the "mighty genre river," but rather its many "tortuous tributaries," as well as its "riverbed-defying floods" (*F/G*, 50). Above all, he emphasizes the process character of genrification: it is not so much the search for the historical origins of a genre (though it may include that) as, much more, a charting of its ongoing unfolding (*F/G*, 65). But this process aspect of genre is, Altman emphasizes, not linear, and tracing the history of a genre entails tracking its retreats as well as its advances, its downs as well as its ups. For example, to invoke the linguistic process in genrification that he foregrounds: the shift from an adjectival use of a type (say, the Western railroad film) to its noun usage (the Western) not only reflects but helps institutionalize a genre: certain types, and their substantives with them, can fall out of fashion and usage, although some may be revived (and then abandoned and then revived, and so forth) later.

Tracing such vicissitudes—the formation and fates of certain types—through linguistic usage foregrounds the discursive and thus (nonfilmic) textual aspect of genrification. Altman's analyses are full of references to studio memos, marketing campaigns, and critics' reviews, sometimes even more than to the films themselves. Such a discursive analysis of a film's genre reveals, for instance, that many marketing campaigns avoid associating a film with a single genre, just as critics regularly do (something, as noted above, that Janet Staiger has emphasized). Such insistence on generic hybridity (something with which structuralism was poorly equipped to deal) shows how studios are constantly experimenting with production differentiation until a new genre takes hold—at which time they would then typically try to differentiate again, to their commercial advantage.

Altman's adamantly discursive theory of genre—that is, to consider when the discourse of a genre consolidated itself and but then morphed in untold ways—was one shared with some innovative histories of genre in the mid-1990s, including two about film noir: Charles O'Brien's "Film Noir in France" (1996) and James Naremore's *More than Night: Film Noir in Its Contexts* (1998), which Altman discusses in a two-page insert box in his *Film/Genre*.[38] In a much-quoted passage affirming this discursive turn in genre studies, Naremore said that "[film noir] has less to do with a group of artifacts than with a discourse—a loose, evolving system of arguments and readings helping to shape commercial strategies and aesthetic ideologies."[39] This assertion of discursivity would seem particularly true of the notoriously difficult-to-define genre of film noir—if it even is a genre—but Naremore's argument has been generalized in the literature to genre more broadly.

To revisit the triad of variables with which I started, it is clear that, in Altman's, O'Brien's, and Naremore's accounts, the focus is discursive and so as much on the studios/production companies and critics as on the films or even audiences—we are indeed a long way from the theories of literary genre of the 1950s and 1960s. In fact, when Altman's *Film/Genre*, in set-off and emphatic formatting, sketches the three necessary developments before a "full genrification could take place," he outlines the contributions from the above-mentioned three corners of cinema (*F/G*, 53–54): studios had to initiate a move away from preexisting substantive genres with "transgeneric adjectival material" (such as "musical comedy"); second, the films in question had to develop new aesthetic positions that negotiate between a substantive deployment of the conventional material and a simultaneous differentiation by departing from or innovating that same material; and, third, audiences had to become aware of these processes, such that the new genre differentiated and consolidated itself in the minds of the public. Such a model allows for a useful distinction between a film genre and a genre film (a recurring question in the scholarship): for Altman, a genre had to achieve these kinds of steps and consolidate into a genre before a genre film in that genre can be imagined (*F/G*, 53). It is noteworthy that this tripartite development for full genrification incorporates the three areas I have been tracing throughout this overview: there is still a role, if somewhat diminished, for the filmic text and audience in Altman's genrification, but it builds in entirely new ways on studios' seeking to develop new types for the purposes of (product) differentiation.

---

[38] Charles O'Brien, "Film Noir in France: Before the Liberation," *iris* 21 (Spring 1996): 7–20; and James Naremore, *More Than Night: Film Noir in Its Contexts* (Berkeley: University of California Press, 1998). See also *F/G*, 60–61.

[39] Naremore, *More than Night*, 11.

This negotiation of three aspects of the film industry intersects the work of another prominent scholar in these recent phases of genre theory, Steve Neale. Neale foregrounded and popularized a now much-cited phrase, the genre as "inter-textual relay," a notion that he credits to Lukow and Ricci.[40] He arrives at this definition by commencing with a more audience-oriented inquiry: he follows John Ellis in asking what the "narrative image" of a genre is, that is, what do people imagine when they hear the name of a given genre.[41] Although this notion is more audience-oriented and vaguely reminiscent of generic iconography, Neale goes on to unfold a distinctly discursive perspective on genre, as he underscores how a wide field of multiple media and messages forms a narrative image among the public. This wide field would include, at the least, the "public discourse of press, television, radio";[42] critics who use genre terms; exhibitor habits and patterns, such as programs that emphasize one genre over others; and, above all, according to Neale, studios' publicity and marketing campaigns, including advertisements, press releases, posters, trailers, and even credit sequences. The multiple and diverse origins of this narrative image emphasize the way in which such terms circulate in wider society: among industry institutions, critics, audiences, and the filmic text, all contributing to an approach that can only be termed discursive.

Both Altman's genrification and Neale's "inter-textual relay" emphasize a broader circulation that incorporates the three aspects of the triad with which I started, while addressing their individual shortcomings. For example, Neale, like Barry Langford in a recent book on film genre, views these sorts of discursive analyses as, at least partially, circumventing the recurring problem of what Langford terms the elusiveness of the audience.[43] Even though, as I argued above, theories of genre have, long foregrounded the role of the audience more and more, both Neale and Langford lament how elusive audience reactions remain and how difficult, then, it is to pin one's analytical hopes on them. This recognition of the elusiveness of the audience dovetails, I would suggest, with the growing interest in production trends or cycles rather than genres: a production trend or cycle is a set of films that demonstrates (usually owing to commercial success) recurring visual and narrative patterns in a specific place (often, but not limited to, one production company or studio or a series of directly competing ones) over a specific, usually relatively brief, period.[44] Such trends or cycles are something that can more easily be tracked by attending to institutions' producing, distributing, and

[40] Neale, *Genre and Hollywood*, 39–40.

[41] Neale, *Genre and Hollywood*, 30.

[42] Neale, *Genre and Hollywood*, 39.

[43] Langford, *Film Genre*, 11.

[44] See Tino Balio, *History of American Cinema*, vol. 5, *Grand Design: Hollywood as a Modern Business Enterprise* (New York: Scribner, 1993), 179–80.

exhibiting via the discursive documenting of such processes. Theorists of genre have also increasingly underscored the phenomenon and both its importance for and difference from conventional genre. The films of a specific cycle are clearly related to each other (by the discourses of those institutions) rather than by the vaguer notion of a transhistorical genre, which tends to rely on a putative model of the audience as much as on a highly selective set of films. This distinction is something taken up in a number of the essays in this book, including those by Gerd Gemünden, Sascha Gerhards, and myself. In addressing both cycles and the broader genres of which they are part, such historical-discursive approaches can more convincingly draw inferences about the audience from the prevailing discussion of the films: presumably studio employees, critics, and so on, know something about the audiences with which they are dealing (at the very least, they probably know more than scholars).

Generic Histories of German Cinema

These two concepts, genrification and intertextual relay, resonate with the focus of the present volume, namely, a primarily historical-discursive approach to film genre in Germany. This approach emphasizes the broader circulation of genre terms, the vagaries in the histories of those terms, and the operations of specific texts within them. But the essays also locate these myriad themes in a historical framework even if they transcend conventional periodization, so the essays are loosely grouped chronologically. The first section, "Weimar and Beyond," reconsiders the Weimar period as one not only comprising the well-known high-art films but also popular genres. In his essay on 1920s and 1930s horror films, Gerd Gemünden addresses an important chapter in German film history that also illuminates generic questions in transnational fashion: he analyzes the career of a German auteurist director, Edgar G. Ulmer, who emigrated to Hollywood and, in many ways, to its genre system. Gemünden reviews the development of auteurist horror in the Weimar period, but then turns to US productions from prewar and wartime Los Angeles, where expectations for genre cinema clearly predominated. In her chapter on the essay film in the Weimar period and beyond, Nora Alter underscores one of the important lessons of Anglo-American genre criticism: that genre and its operations are relevant not only to commercial and popular cinema but also to what is usually considered art or art house film. The essay film offers Alter an opportunity to engage with another of the recurring themes of US genre criticism, as exemplified in the work of Rick Altman and Linda Williams, namely, its literary links and even its origins. Richter's 1929 *Inflation* (about the troubled 1920s economy and its impact on everyday life) proves to be an important early milestone, because of its distance from both documentary and avant-garde film.

Lutz Koepnick reflects on how Fritz Lang's *Frau im Mond* (Woman in the Moon, 1929) has failed to have a strong influence on the science-fiction genre, particularly in contrast to his monumental and monumentalist *Metropolis*. This issue seems particularly relevant in a volume on genre, since *Frau im Mond* bequeathed to science fiction much of the genre's recurring iconography. This failure of an early film to exert influence in an enduring genre offers Koepnick an occasion to contemplate how science fiction works with time: how it must stage a futurity doomed to become obsolete almost as soon as the film is released. In his contribution, Eric Rentschler considers how a full third of the films made during the Weimar Republic were comedies. With close readings of some of the most popular films of this era, including *Drei von der Tankstelle* (Three from the Filling Station, 1930) and *Der Kongreß tanzt* (The Congress Dances, 1931), Rentschler demonstrates how musical comedies took a sophisticated approach to their subject matter, approaches that diverged from those in art cinema while nonetheless addressing the prevailing uncertainty of the time.

Generic Histories' second section, "Generic Decades?," engages three decades (the 1940s, 1950s, and early 1960s) that are normally associated with genre films and therefore have attracted relatively modest scholarly attention. My contribution to this volume considers the war film, a genre that has been largely neglected in German film studies, but one that, along with the Heimat film, dominated the 1950s. It takes up a film that is widely acknowledged to be one of the artistically most accomplished films of German film history—Bernhard Wicki's *Die Brücke* (The Bridge, 1959)—and argues that the relative neglect of the film in scholarship is due to its very clear, if hybrid, generic aspects. Likewise attending to the late 1950s, Sascha Gerhards analyzes one of the most successful cycles in global film history, the wave of thirty-eight filmic adaptations of Edgar Wallace's crime novels. Gerhards examines this particular cycle within the larger context of the crime genre since the 1920s. While he endorses the only other major analysis of the cycle—Tim Bergfelder's, which concentrates on transnational escapism inherent in the films— Gerhards also argues that attending to what Thomas Schatz and John Cawelti have called the life cycle of a genre can illuminate these films' often ironic mechanisms. In her chapter, Kris Vander Lugt follows up on Gerd Gemünden's aforementioned essay on horror prior to the Second World War by tracing its post-1945 trajectory. While Gemünden explores how the genre is usually seen as having emerged in Germany during the Weimar era, Vander Lugt recounts how it largely disappeared during the Third Reich and then reemerged in the 1950s. He argues that, in its postwar forms, the genre operated in a kind of kitsch crucible between a recurring (national) theme of coming to terms with the past and the global horror boom from the 1950s into the 1970s.

The third section: "Genres of Consensus?" takes up postreunification cinema to demonstrate how what Eric Rentschler has termed a "cinema of consensus" does not constitute any kind of radical break but rather is engaged with the long history of German genre. Hester Baer's essay on Bernd Eichinger's career and his impact in the 1980s, especially through the quasi-genre of literary adaptation, shows how the famously generic cinema of the 1990s had clear antecedents in the 1980s and even earlier. Commencing with Rick Altman's emphasis on genrification and the historical aspects of genre, Steve Choe traces the genre cues that have been mobilized around the German (psycho) thriller over the course of German film history. Beginning with the sensation film in the late 1910s and early 1920s, Choe demonstrates how these thrillers depict societies and polities under exceptional circumstances, in which different kinds of governance and sovereignty reign. Lang's Mabuse films deliberately exploit Mabuse's formation of a "state within a state" for its thrilling aspect, something picked up much later in the popular and acclaimed thriller *Das Experiment* (Oliver Hirschbiegel, 2001). Engaging another generic remnant from an earlier era, Paul Cooke analyzes the post-2000 rebirth of the Heimat film. After giving an overview of what Rick Altman calls the syntax and semantics of the Heimat genre in the 1950s and then its refiguration in the 1960s and 1970s, Cooke turns to hugely successful films like *Wer früher stirbt, ist länger tot* (He Who Dies Sooner is Dead for Longer, released in English as *Grave Decisions*, 2006), *Das Wunder von Bern* (The Miracle of Bern, 2003), and *Nordwand* (Northface, 2008). These films retool the basic narrative trajectory (the syntax) of the Heimat genre to demonstrate their self-conscious distance from the films of the 1950s as well as from the deliberately anti-Heimat films of New German Cinema.

In her essay Antje Ascheid analyzes one of the commercially most successful German genres of the post-Wall era, the romantic comedy. Ascheid considers three romance films, two of which function as what she calls postromantic films and one as a classic romantic comedy. Ascheid argues that the postromantic films straddle popular and art cinema: with their familiar themes of the heart, they are addressed to a wider audience, but nonetheless seem auteurist and artistic in their realist engagement with the socioeconomic context around the lovers. In the volume's concluding essay, Marco Abel considers a key figure of the contemporary German genre film, Dominik Graf, whose unique career allows Abel to reflect on the demise of 1970s and early 1980s *Autorenkino*. Graf has been an outspoken critic of that kind of *Autorenkino* and emphasizes his admiration for directors who deliberately rework genres, including Sam Peckinpah and the early Martin Scorsese, as well as directors such as Nicholas Roeg, Mike Figgis, Sam Fuller, and Jean-Pierre Melville. Graf's career also offers Abel (and the volume) an opportunity to address one of the fundamental aspects of genre in contemporary German film, namely, the relationship between the film and television industries. In his film *Die Sieger* (The Victors, 1994) Graf manages, within the apparent confines of the genre, to offer comment on German political culture, the architecture of Germany's many medium-sized cities, and the unnecessarily high priority German society gives to maintaining its standard of living. His work underscores once again how genres and their histories are interwoven not only with fluctuations in the film and television industries, but also with the vicissitudes of German culture more generally.

1: Parallel Modernities: From Haunted Screen to Universal Horror

Gerd Gemünden

> *For an exile habits of life, expression, or activity in the new environ-*
> *ment inevitably occur against the memory of these things in another*
> *environment. Thus the new and the old environments are vivid,*
> *actual, occurring together contrapuntally.*
>
> —Edward Said

> *[My father was] a European intellectual who had based most of*
> *his thinking on the great minds of the German language, only to*
> *find that it led to a stupid monster of an Austrian painter named*
> *Hitler. For the rest of his life he tried to understand how civilization*
> *could end up in barbarism.*
>
> —Arianné Ulmer Cipes

Edgar G. Ulmer and German Horror Legacies

IN AN EXTENSIVE INTERVIEW with filmmaker Peter Bogdanovich in 1970, Edgar G. Ulmer made references to two German sources that gave shape to his famous horror film *The Black Cat*, which he directed for Universal in 1934: "Junior [Laemmle] gave me free rein to write a hor-ror picture in the style we had started in Europe with *Caligari*," only to add a few moments later that the film "was very much out of my Bauhaus period."[1] This puzzling double reference to two very different and aes-thetically even incompatible sources holds an important clue to what Ulmer wanted to achieve with his first film produced by a major studio. Most obviously, this can be read as a typical Ulmerian gesture to establish cultural capital.[2]

---

[1] Edgar G. Ulmer, "Interview with Peter Bogdanovich," in Peter Bogdanovich, *Who the Devil Made It: Conversations with Legendary Film Directors* (New York: Ballantine, 1997), 575–76.

[2] To be sure, such claims of having been associated with the movements that made Germany famous in the early 1920s were a survival strategy for émigrés

Fig. 1.1. Das Cabinet des Dr. Caligari *(1920). Screenshot.*

Robert Wiene's 1920 classic of German silent cinema and the Bauhaus school of architecture and design are among the shorthands for "German culture" that must have held the biggest name recognition in 1930s Los Angeles, and by invoking them Ulmer obviously laid claim "to being part" of the traditions that gave rise to them. Not that he did not have some justification—after all, Ulmer began his career as set designer on *Der Golem und wie er in die Welt kam* (The Golem and How He Came Into the World; Paul Wegener, 1920), where he served as apprentice under Hans Poelzig, the name-sake for Hjalmar Poelzig in the film, who together with Gropius and Mies van der Rohe was among Germany's great architects.[3] At the same time, and unlike most other exiles and émigrés working in Hollywood in the 1930s, Ulmer *can* claim to have collaborated on many significant Expressionist films, particularly through his work for F. W. Murnau, while his first German feature, *Menschen am Sonntag* (People on Sunday), which he codirected with Robert Siodmak, counts as a masterpiece of the New Sobriety with which the Bauhaus had much in common. Yet the over-

---

and meant as passe-partout to Hollywood's studio doors, but particularly Ulmer pushed the limits. Elsewhere in the same interview Ulmer makes the completely unsubstantiated claim that he designed the sets for *Caligari*, and the long list of films in which he says he was involved includes virtually everything done by Murnau as well as Lang's *Die Nibelungen* and *Metropolis*. It was claims like these that had Lotte Eisner call Ulmer "the greatest liar in the history of cinema." Quoted in Deborah Lazaroff Alpi, *Robert Siodmak* (Jefferson, NC: McFarland, 1998), 20.

[3] On Poelzig's contribution to film architecture, see Claudia Dillmann, "Die Wirkung der Architektur ist eine magische: Hans Poelzig und der Film," in *Hans Poelzig: Bauten für den Film* (Frankfurt: Deutsches Filmmuseum, 1997), 20–75.

all project of *The Black Cat* as captured by the catchwords "Caligari" and "Bauhaus" clearly goes beyond this biographical dimension. Here Ulmer combined two key examples of Weimar culture that despite their differences stood for the promise, the achievements, and, ultimately, the failure of modernism. Both had been heralded as a radical new beginning in literature, the arts, architecture, and design, and both had been highly influential for German cinema of the 1920s, often appearing in hybrid form in films such as Fritz Lang's *Metropolis* or *M*. With the Nazis' rise to power both movements fell into disrepute, with their main protagonists forced into exile. Recalling them in the American context of 1934 is thus not only a gesture of preservation and commemoration but also an attempt to harvest their progressive energy at a moment of political crisis.

What is at stake in Ulmer's 1934 horror film—and in German exile cinema in Hollywood in general—has to be understood in light of the parallels experienced by so many émigré and exile filmmakers between the modernity of Weimar Berlin and that of prewar and wartime Los Angeles. The failure of Weimar modernity and democracy must have provided the exiles with a dubious moment of historical recognition, an uncanny déjà vu of sorts, when the Depression-ridden United States of the early 1930s, with its large-scale unemployment and political radicalization of the left and the right, replayed scenarios of the political, economic, and social crises of the late Weimar years.[4] In hindsight, it must have become clear to Ulmer that in particular the failure to overcome the aftermath of the First World War, with its tremendous war reparations, the shame and humiliation associated with the Versailles Treaty, and the myth of the German army being stabbed in the back cleverly exploited by right-wing groups ultimately had paved the way for the National Socialists. Particularly the specter of the past war clearly brought into focus the very real possibility of a new and even greater armed conflict, and, as Ulmer biographer Stefan Grissemann has stated, Ulmer himself professed to fear the coming of a war that he was convinced the United States would lose.[5] As I will argue in this essay, it was this specter that motivated Ulmer's decision to draw on the haunted screen of Weimar cinema for his directorial debut at Universal, and recast the horror film as a war film.

---

[4] American observers concurred. See, for example, the widely discussed essay by J. B. Matthews and R. E. Shallcross, "Must America Go Fascist?" *Harpers Magazine*, Jun. 1934, 1–15; or a symposium titled "Will Fascism Come to America?" in *The Modern Monthly* of September 1934. One year later Sinclair Lewis's bestselling novel, *It Can't Happen Here*, was published, which answers the question of whether America might become fascist in the affirmative.

[5] Stefan Grissemann, *Mann im Schatten* (Vienna: Paul Zsonlay, 2003), 139.

Ulmer and Universal Horror

In order to understand what I call Ulmer's recasting of a certain genre, we must first trace that genre's prominence and significance in German cinema of the 1920s, which for Ulmer and most other émigrés served as stepping stone and enduring point of reference for their work in the Hollywood film industry. Seen in this light, my reading of *The Black Cat* may serve as a multilayered case study. An example of the "translation" of a genre from one national cinema into another, the film raises important questions, not only about the transnational dimension of genre cinema, but also about genre cinema's relation to auteurism, and about the possibility of political filmmaking within the Hollywood studio system, particularly under the duress of exile.[6] Ultimately, I claim, the film is emblematic for German exile filmmaking in the Hollywood studio system of the 1930s.

Ulmer's contribution to the American horror genre of the 1930s could build, of course, on the strong affinities between Weimar's haunted screen and Universal Horror, which also explain why the émigrés did particularly well in this genre. As we now know, the horror genre gained prominence in Weimar because of calculated efforts to wed popular filmmaking to artistic aspirations, in order to overcome the bourgeoisie's distaste for the medium of film.[7] Equally important was Erich Pommer's stated goal to break into the international market by creating films with a decidedly "German" flavor, something in which Hollywood had no interest. Robert Wiene's *Das Cabinet des Dr. Caligari* (The Cabinet of Dr. Caligari; Robert Wiene, 1920), to cite the most influential example driven by these imperatives, thus couched a sensationalist crime story with the caché of German Expressionist art and literature, carefully ignoring the fact that by 1920 this artistic movement had basically run its course, and many of its most prominent representatives had died on the battle fields of the First World War. It was the critical *international* success of *Das Cabinet des Dr. Caligari, Der Golem, wie er in die Welt kam,* and *Nosferatu* (F. W. Murnau, 1922) that made Hollywood first take the horror film seriously.

While the particular German context of the "Kino-Debatte" played no role in Hollywood's decision to take the genre seriously, the considerable artistic and technological innovations that accompanied the above-cited films did make a lasting impression. The horror film came to be

---

[6] Even though Ulmer arrived in Hollywood long before Hitler's rise to power, Goebbels's anti-Semitic restructuring of the German film industry and the subsequent Nuremberg laws made it impossible for Jews like Ulmer to return to Germany, turning many erstwhile émigrés into exiles.

[7] Anton Kaes, ed., *Kino-Debatte: Texte zum Verhältnis von Literatur und Film, 1909–1929* (Munich: DTV, 1978).

Figs. 1.2a and 1.2b. Der Golem, wie er in die Welt kam *(1920)* *and* Nosferatu *(1922). Screenshots.*

considered a genre that was especially well-suited for the innovative use of special effects, camera work, set design, makeup and costume, and even musical scores, because these innovations could be easily justified as motivated by the plot line and the subjectivity of its protagonists.

In the United States it was Universal that specialized in the genre, as a means of finding a niche in the first-run market, producing thirteen of the roughly thirty horror films made by the eight majors in the 1930s, and hiring a lot of European talent for this purpose. Paul Leni, who had directed *Das Wachsfigurenkabinett* (*Waxworks,* 1924), was signed by Carl Laemmle to adapt the Broadway comedy *The Cat and the Canary* (1927), followed by *The Man Who Laughs* (1928), starring Conrad Veidt. Murnau's *Sunrise* for Fox of the same year, for which Ulmer was credited as assistant art director to Rochus Gliese (already a collaborator of Wiene's and Murnau's in Germany), inflected motifs from the Weimar "street film" with the horror narrative of the intrusion of the outsider. These films distinguished themselves by employing trademarks of German Expressionist cinema such as chiaroscuro lighting, set design, and makeup. The premature deaths of Leni in 1929, horror star Lon Chaney in 1930 (who starred in *The Phantom of the Opera,* on which Ulmer worked as set designer), and Murnau in 1931 ended the era of silent horror, but the stage had been set for the genre's future growth. That same year, *Dracula* became the founding film of the horror sound-film cycle. Universal's biggest moneymaker of the year, it was filmed by Karl Freund under Tod Browning's direction. Freund went on to film *Murder in the Rue Morgue* (Robert Florey, 1932), before debuting as director with *The Mummy* that same year, while Karl Struss, who had shot *Sunrise,* did the camera work on Rouben Mamoulian's *Dr. Jekyll and Mr. Hyde* (1931). Between 1931 and 1936 the studio made nineteen horror features, first specializing in product differentiation (ever-new monsters) before turning to sequels with *The Bride of Frankenstein* (1935). With the stricter enforcement of the Production Code beginning in 1934, horror films became a particular target for censorship—of which *The Black Cat* is a prime example—and two years later the interest in the genre declined, the A-budget devotion to horror concluded, and the Universal empire toppled.

The majority of films in the cycle credited European-born professionals in key positions, most notably, of course, Boris Karloff and Bela Lugosi. The Hungarian-born Lugosi can in fact also be seen as a German import of sorts: he fled Budapest for Vienna for political reasons in 1919 and starred in Berlin one year later in Murnau's *Januskopf* (Janus Head, a variation of the Jekyll and Hyde story), soon followed by *Die Teufelsanbeter* (The Devil Worshippers, Marie-Louise Droop and Muhsin Ertugrul, 1920), playing in both the kind of fare that became his specialty at Universal.[8] Particularly Lugosi's Caligari figure in *Murders in the Rue Morgue* is an avid example of the cut-and-paste technique of some of Universal's films in this genre. Yet no matter the quality or originality of these forms of transfers and translations, it must be said that the participation of German émigrés in horror films was higher than in any American genre until the advent of the anti-Nazi film, and often paved the way for long-lasting careers.[9]

While personal continuities marked the entirety of the cycle, the stylistic affinities were more pronounced in Universal's silent pictures than in the talkies, as the transition to sound stifled the fluidity of the camera, a trademark of Murnau's films in particular, and the novelty of Expressionist design and lighting wore off. The dialogue-heavy *Dracula* and *Frankenstein* betrayed their proximity to the stage adaptations that had popularized Bram Stoker's and Mary Shelley's novels, further enhanced by the fact that Lugosi and others who had acted in Broadway productions also starred in the films. References and allusions to German films such as *Nosferatu* became confined to plot elements and individual ideas and lacked their predecessors' visual elegance and stylistic flamboyance. Not until *The Black Cat* would German Expressionism be revisited by Universal in more than just a perfunctory or clichéd manner, clearly demonstrating that the pull of Weimar cinema in Hollywood extended well into the 1930s.

---

[8] On Lugosi's career, see Arthur Lenning, *The Count: The Life and Films of Bela "Dracula" Lugosi* (New York: G. P. Putnam's Sons, 1974). Ulmer claims to have known Lugosi "since the time he was Minister of Culture in the communist government of Bela Kuhn in Hungary." Quoted in Bernard Eisenschitz and Jean-Claude Romer, "Entretien avec Edgar G. Ulmer," *Midi-Minuit Fantastique* 13 (1965): 4.

[9] As William K. Everson writes, "even some of Universal's "B" Westerns of these years [the second half of the 1920s] had a Germanic look to them." Everson, *Classics of the Horror Film* (Seacaucus, NJ: Citadell, 1974), 26. Other prominent exiles and émigrés who worked on horror films include Peter Lorre, Robert and Curt Siodmak, and Joe May; even William Dieterle tried his hand at the genre once and scored a major success with *The Hunchback of Notre Dame* (1939).

Among Ulmer's films, *The Black Cat* stands out for its creative fusion of German and American film traditions and genre conventions, providing a careful balance in which the film's many more trivial or faulty aspects, such as the ellipses in the script, the disappointing secondary cast, and the crude attempts at comic relief, are offset by an innovative use of a classical score, an extraordinary set design, and a nuanced, against-character casting of the co-stars Karloff and Lugosi. The plot revolves around a deadly conflict between Poelzig and Werdegast, former friends whom a wartime betrayal has turned into bitter enemies, and a young American couple on their honeymoon, the Allisons, who are unwittingly drawn into this. They narrowly escape from Poelzig's modernist edifice before Werdegast, in a final self-destructive gesture, blows everything to smithereens.

Like many Universal horror films of the 1930s, *The Black Cat* hovers at the border of A-level production and B-film. Apart from certain directorial choices, which I will discuss later, this must be attributed to purely monetary reasons. While Universal thought of its horror films as A-films meant to break into the first-run market (and were associated with significant cost for sets, makeup, costumes, and major stars), Universal A-films still often resembled a different studio's B-productions. They were often afforded fewer setups and fewer takes, and they had to rely on stock footage for locations and the talent of minor stars. *The Black Cat*, which was shot in fifteen days for a budget of exactly $91,125, was a significant scale-back from *Dracula* and *Frankenstein* (which cost $355,000 and $262,000 respectively), apparently because Universal thought that pairing Karloff and Lugosi would by itself bring in the audience. It nevertheless made a $140,000 profit for Universal, proving that the horror cycle was still going strong and giving Ulmer his first real recognition as director. In light of this success it is ironic that Ulmer chose to direct the independent low-budget Western *Thunder of Texas* (1934) as his next project, rather than another Universal production. Soon thereafter his affair with Shirley Castle, the wife of Carl Laemmle Sr.'s nephew Max Alexander, would become public, putting an end to any possible employment at Universal.

Critics have uniformly agreed that Ulmer's move away from the big studios must be seen as a conscious strategy to retain a sense of uncompromised artistic freedom. In this they followed the director's own assessment; Ulmer famously told Bogdanovich that he "did not want to be ground up in the Hollywood hash machine."[10] While the means at his disposal were much more limited for his subsequent Yiddish-language films around New York, his work at the PRC film studio, and his later European coproductions, artistic control, so the argument goes, remained largely in his own hands provided he stayed within the budget and the

---

[10] "Interview with Peter Bogdanovich," 592.

films turned a profit—thus allowing the director to retain a "personal" touch and develop an individual style. Building on the "discovery" of Ulmer the artiste by French cinephiles such as François Truffaut and Bertrand Tavernier, American critics such as John Belton and Andrew Sarris admired how Ulmer turned economic constraint into a virtue and an art, and his ultra-pragmatic mise-en-scène of problem solving was celebrated as the sign of a true auteur. As Sarris states, "[Ulmer] is one of the minor glories of the cinema. Here is a career, more subterranean than most, which be signature of a genuine artist. . . . That a personal style could emerge from the lowest depths of Poverty Row is a tribute to a director without alibis."[11] Belton is even more emphatic:

> Ulmer is clearly an auteur: his films all bear the stamp of a single and consistent narrative personality, but the raw material with which he works—scripts and performers especially—varies tremendously in quality from film to film. His set design, lighting, editing, and camera technique frequently transcend the banality of his scripts and the weakness of his actors' performances.[12]

Perhaps the biggest single factor attributing to Ulmer's auteur status is his long interview with Bogdanovich, true to the motto that behind every great auteur (Hitchcock, Fuller, Sirk) there stands a great interview. Apart from embellishing his contributions to the great German films of the 1920s, Ulmer here strives to give his cinematic output a coherence and unity that is all but invisible to the naked eye.

As has been pointed out by numerous critics, there are, of course, serious problems with this notion of auteurism.[13] On the most obvious level, the quality of Ulmer's films is not argued but simply asserted; one quickly notes that the same quotes, the same tropes, and the same biographical criticism get rehearsed again and again, and any careful argument is ultimately short-circuited. In the end, auteurist criticism becomes an unstoppable machine of aesthetic valorization. What is more troubling for our context is that auteurism seems to imply a transcendence of history, an assertion that cannot be upheld for Ulmer. Since *The Black Cat* was an A-film made for a major studio, it is particularly problematic to claim it as an auteurist work, precisely because its conception, production, and execution were fraught with controversy and compromise, involving

---

[11] Andrew Sarris, *The American Cinema: Directors and Directions, 1929–1968* (New York: Dutton, 1968), 143.

[12] John Belton, "Edgar G. Ulmer: A Reassessment," in Belton, *Cinema Stylists* (Metuchen, NJ: Scarecrow, 1983), 147.

[13] Dana Polan, "*Detour*'s History/History's *Detour*," in *Edgar G. Ulmer: Essays on the King of B's*, ed. Bernd Herzogenrath (Jefferson, NC: McFarland, 2009), 137–49.

censorship issues, extensive rewriting and reshooting demanded by studio brass, and divergent marketing strategies that are typical of large-scale studio productions. To call *The Black Cat*, as Bernd Herzogenrath has done, "a personal work of art, an underground avant-garde film" is, to misquote one of the film's hokiest lines, not just "perhaps baloney" but most certainly so.[14] Instead, it is precisely the negotiation of different national film traditions and their respective genre conventions that caters to and frustrates audience expectations, ultimately making this production so rich and rewarding. While I would claim that Ulmer's political concerns do find a voice in this film, it must be reiterated that those concerns were refracted both by what studio executives considered to have commercial potential with contemporary audiences and by what was acceptable to the Hays office, which enforced the Production Code. The concept of auteurism becomes even more questionable under the duress of exile, which for filmmakers meant the experience of loss of control and authorship over their lives and careers. As Lutz Koepnick has argued, "the question of authorship in exile film studies . . . is less a question of material practices and creative self-realization than it is a question of reading narratives, mise-en-scènes, set designs, acting patterns, and sound tracks against the grain of mainstream interpretations in order to make them speak about the exile's experience of rupture."[15]

The Black Cat

When Edgar G. Ulmer's *The Black Cat* premiered in Hollywood on 3 May 1934, the film was anticipated as the latest installment in Universal's highly successful cycle of horror films. In advertising campaigns and promotional materials much had been made of Universal's first-time pairing of its two biggest draws of the series, Boris Karloff and Bela Lugosi (which Ulmer claims was his idea).[16] By double-teaming the stars who had embodied Dracula and Frankenstein's monster, as well as numerous only slightly less scary abominations, audiences were led to expect a double-whammy of fright. But *The Black Cat* proved to be distinctively different. Unlike its famous predecessors, it was not based on nineteenth-century British novels and their highly successful Broadway adaptations but on an original screenplay by Peter Ruric after a story by Ulmer and Ruric (though Ulmer claimed later to have worked on the script as well), and

[14] Herzogenrath, "Ulmer and Cult/ure," in *Edgar G. Ulmer: Essays on the King of B's*, 28.
[15] Lutz Koepnick, "Mad Love: Re-Membering Berlin in Hollywood Exile," in *Caught By Politics: Hitler Exiles and American Visual Culture*, ed. Sabine Eckmann and Lutz Koepnick (New York: Palgrave MacMillan, 2007), 197.
[16] Eisenschitz and Romer, "Entretien avec Edgar G. Ulmer," 4.

the plot had only the faintest connection to the famous story by Edgar Allan Poe.[17] It was furthermore one of the few films in the cycle to have a contemporary setting, even if the location, the Carpathian mountains, at first evoked the remoteness and otherworldly quality of *Dracula*. But most distinctive was the fact that *The Black Cat* was the only film from the 1930s horror cycle to explicitly foreground the connection between the horror genre and the trauma of the First World War. Devoid of the monsters that had appeared in the previous Universal films, it focuses on the monstrosity of humans under the extreme conditions of modern warfare and its aftermath. The film therefore refrains from the graphic horror associated with some abominable other and instead only hints at acts of terror, the full extent of which has to be imagined by the viewer. The film successfully blurs the line between the fantastic and supernatural elements of a horror film and the unsettling, dream-like and nightmarish realism of an (anti-)war film.

While Lugosi's and Karloff's characters in other films of the horror cycle are mostly remembered for their respective costumes, makeup, and scary looks, *The Black Cat* features the two actors in their psychologically most complex roles. The Hungarian psychiatrist Dr. Vitus Werdegast and the Austrian engineer Hjalmar Poelzig are old friends whom a wartime betrayal has turned into arch enemies, yet the different war neuroses from which they suffer serve as a mutual bond. Both suffer the fate of spiritual death that befalls those who physically survive the war, turning them, as Poelzig astutely observes, into the "living dead," who lead zombie-like existences. While Werdegast has survived fifteen years of internment as a prisoner of war only because of his desire for revenge, Poelzig has become a necrophiliac who embalms his female victims and exhibits them in large glass cases, while also practicing devil worship. It is highly significant—and emblematic for the repetition compulsion that Freud diagnosed in shell-shocked war veterans—that both need to return to the site of prior torment to settle their final score. And while the film features an unprecedented array of crimes and abnormalities, including sadism, torture, incest, murder, revenge, Satanism, necrophilia, ailurophobia (the fear of cats), voyeurism, and—in an earlier draft of the screenplay—rape, the master narrative is clearly one of betrayal and the final reckoning with wartime trauma.

Always a highly efficient narrator, Ulmer wastes little time introducing the trauma of the bygone Great War as the central motif of terror in *The Black Cat*. The film opens on a bustling Budapest train station, where

---

[17] Originally E. A. Dupont was slated to direct *The Black Cat*, based on a different story outline, which was, however, never turned into a full script. It remains doubtful whether Ruric and Ulmer actually read Poe's story; on the script housed in the Margaret Herrick Library of the Academy of Motion Pictures (AMPAS) in Los Angeles, the American author's name is misspelled as Edgar Allen [*sic!*] Poe.

Fig. 1.3. The Black Cat *(1934). Screenshot.*

a young American couple on their honeymoon, identified by a close-up of
their papers as Mr. and Mrs. Allison, settle into their seats. Their intimate
privacy is soon interrupted when another traveler is placed in their com-
partment. He introduces himself as Dr. Vitus Werdegast, the literal meaning of which ("to become a guest") is not only an ironic comment on his
badly timed intrusion on the honeymooners, but also foreshadows the
more sinister and consequential intrusion on his wartime friend Hjalmar
Poelzig. This intrusion provides the central conflict of the film, in which
the Allisons will get caught up as innocent bystanders. Yet Werdegast is
not the sinister outsider we may expect him to be given Lugosi's previous
roles in horror film, but rather a victim himself, as we soon learn. Having
commented to Peter Allison how much Allison's wife, sleeping at his side,
resembles Werdegast's own before he had to leave her to go to war "for
Kaiser and country," Werdegast reveals his past: "Have you ever heard of
Kurgaal? It's a prison below Omsk on Lake Baikal. Many men have gone
there. Few have returned. I have returned. [Pause.] After fifteen years, *I*
have returned."[18] Peter Allison, and the viewer, can only imagine what

_____

[18] The spelling of locations mentioned in the film follows the script housed at
AMPAS. It should be noted that the script contains some inconsistencies—we
find, for example, alternate spellings of "Vishegrad" (scene A3) and "Vızhegrad"
(scene A33)—that can be attributed to the great haste under which Ulmer and
Ruric worked. I have reconciled the inconsistencies here for clarity.

Werdegast must have endured there, and what he may hope to find upon his return.

As befits the ominous tale of the intruder, a torrential rainfall greets the travelers in Vishegrad, from where they continue on by bus. As if on cue, the bus driver picks up on the theme of the Great War, telling his passengers of the war casualties in the hills they are driving through:

> "All of this country was one of the greatest battle fields of the war. Ten thousands of men died here. The ravine down there was piled twelve deep with dead and wounded men. The little river below was swollen red, a raging torrent of blood. The high hill yonder, where engineer Poelzig now lives, was the site of Fort Marmaros. He built his home on its very foundation. Marmaros, the greatest graveyard in the world."

A close-up of Werdegast, listening with his eyes closed, suggests how the past is replayed in his mind, having the atrocities he lived through come alive at the very moment he traverses the battlegrounds again after fifteen years. For the first time we see him in the trance-like state that will grip him for much of the remainder of the film. And the war continues to claim its victims—immediately after the driver has finished his sentence about the greatest graveyard of the world, he loses control over his vehicle and dies at the very same place ten thousand soldiers found their death before him. The Allisons, Werdegast, and his servant survive without great harm and in the rain make their way to Mr. Poelzig's house, introduced by a painted establishing shot (one of Ulmer's trademark money-saving devices) as a gleaming and unworldly modern fortress atop a hill ringed by the white crosses of the graves of the war dead.[19]

In his interview with Bogdanovich, Ulmer explained that the setting and the plot of *The Black Cat* were inspired by an idea of the Prague writer Gustav Meyrinck, who had written the novel on which Wegener's *The Golem* was based, a film on which Ulmer claims to have worked even though he was only fifteen years old at the time (there is some evidence that he actually did):

> Meyrinck at that time was contemplating a play based on Doumont [*sic*], which was a French fortress the Germans had shelled to pieces during the First World War; there were some survivors who didn't come out for years. And the commander was a strange Euripides figure who went crazy three years later, when he was brought back to Paris, because he had walked on that mountain of bodies.[20]

---

[19] Interestingly, the script does not include this shot.
[20] "Interview with Peter Bogdanovich," 576.

If one takes a closer look at the real battles surrounding Douaumont, a fortress near Verdun considered impregnable and of utmost significance for the French defensive system, one quickly realizes that reality bred even stranger stories than Meyrinck's. Douaumont was a huge fortress constructed of steel and concrete, with vaults that could house an entire battalion of infantry, but when the Germans attacked and conquered it on 25 February 1916, it was manned by only fifty-seven men, a fact unknown to the Germans. The French later mounted a counterattack, which would eventually degenerate into the drawn-out trench warfare that was already a feature of the Western front; they finally recaptured it on 24 October, but only after incurring huge losses.

The inability to escape a cycle of repetition informs not only the personal history of the two antagonists but also the overall image of history portrayed in the film, as becomes evident in the structure of its main setting. Poelzig's Bauhaus-style edifice is a modernist marvel of chrome and glass, replete with sliding doors, intercom system, a striking staircase, and an open floor plan. Residing on top of the former fortress's formidable foundations, it stands in complete contrast to its dark bowels, which feature an impenetrable system of corridors and chambers that serve Poelzig's sinister purposes. Here, behind huge steel doors, Poelzig keeps his cabinet of embalmed women in glass cases, next to the gun turrets and calculating charts still intact from the war. Adjacent is the large room where he holds his satanic masses and performs his ritual murders, with the embalming rack nearby where he kills his second wife and where he will find his own death at the hands of Werdegast. One level lower are the left-over explosives that will blow up the entire structure after Werdegast has flipped the "red switch," providing a befitting apocalyptic ending that will claim the lives of these last two surviving soldiers and that emulates the battles of the Great War. While ostensibly separated as three independent layers, it is telling that the septic and sterile modern edifice cannot cover the odor of death and decay that lies beneath; repeatedly Werdegast remarks that throughout the house he can still "sense death in the air," and even Peter Allison quips that if he were ever in need of someone to build him "a nice, cozy, unpretentious insane asylum, [Poelzig] would be the man for it." Madness pervades the ultra-rational functionalism of the glass and chrome modernism, because at the very foundation of reason, the film suggests, lies an irrationalism that cannot be repressed. Ulmer's critique of culture is clearly indebted to that of his fellow Viennese, Sigmund Freud: underneath a thin veneer of refined culture lurk sexual deviations and dark religious fanaticism that can hardly be kept in check, ever threatening to be self-destructive as they do in the climactic and all-consuming violence that ends the film.

It is striking that the three levels of Hjalmar Poelzig's edifice symbolize key moments of Austro-German wartime and postwar history:

while the deepest one, holding the buried explosives, obviously represents the destructive power of war, interspersed with the graves of its victims, the Expressionist chapel where Poelzig celebrates Lucifer calls to mind the Expressionist sets of *Caligari*, *Wachsfigurenkabinett*, and *Warning Shadows*; the Bauhaus-style fortress on the top, finally, evokes the cold, detached modernism that emphasized the functionality, transparency, and visual clarity of this new architecture, while also hinting at the New Sobriety, or "Neue Sachlichkeit," a movement in the arts and literature meant to leave behind what it perceived to be the extreme subjectivity and irrationalism of Expressionism. By showing these layers to be fatefully connected, *The Black Cat* refutes any view of history that promises progress or a certain teleology.

The landscape that surrounds the fortress is also saturated with history, as the previously quoted lines by the bus driver make clear. Ulmer's Carpathians are the location of very real violence, not the otherworldly horror of *Dracula*. The scene of two policemen arguing over whose hometown is more beautiful—one of few meant to provide comic relief—fits in here. While it pokes fun at the rivalry of local patriots and their provincialism, it also highlights the desire to emphasize the beauty of a country that is otherwise shown as scarred by war (and thus explains to some degree why the Allisons would choose this location over Niagara Falls for their honeymoon). More importantly, *The Black Cat* employs a concept of foreignness that is different from most horror films of the period. Lugosi and Karloff are still typed as the ethnic others they portrayed in virtually all films in this genre, but the conflict here is *between* those others (with the Allisons thrown in as pawns) and not between an American (or British) citizen and an outside threat. Thus while Karloff's character still denotes the sexual deviance and decadence typically associated with the Old World, Lugosi gets to undo that stereotype by playing his most sympathetic role in a horror film, even if that role was originally conceived by Ulmer to be far more menacing and ambiguous.[21] What is

---

[21] After the filming was completed, the studio brass considered the film too vile for the public and ordered alterations to the script and consequent reshooting. Originally, the script had Werdegast almost as menacing as Poelzig, but after objections from the studio executives several scenes were cut and new ones added to make Lugosi's role less ambiguous and far more sympathetic. Other changes included the cutting of Poelzig's rape of Joan Alison, and depicting Karen as a benign and innocent beauty rather than as the cat-woman she was originally meant to be. Also toned down were the script's graphic depictions of Poelzig's skinning. For a detailed account of the production history, including alterations to the script, see Gregory William Mank, *Karloff and Lugosi: The Story of a Haunting Collaboration* (Jefferson, NC: McFarland, 1990), 45–83, and Paul Mandell, "Edgar Ulmer and *The Black Cat*," *American Cinematographer* (Oct. 1984): 34–47.

more, it is suggested that Karloff's perversity, however strange and bizarre it may be, stems from his wartime experience and is not an inherent character trait. The Carpathians emerge as the location of past and present conflict, a conflict that is grounded in history and not myth or legend, and that conflict has bearings on outsiders only because they happen to be in the wrong place at the wrong time. How saturated with real tragedy this very location would turn out to be would become evident only ten years later, in 1944, when the Germans entered Hungary and built one of the biggest concentration camps in Hungary in the Carpathian town of Mateszalka, close to the Jewish district of Marmaros.[22]

The importance of the topicality of the First World War for Ulmer becomes further evident if we consider some of the changes between the script and the released film.[23] Originally Werdegast was to explain his participation in the war by saying, "For God and country," not "For Kaiser and country," a change that was presumably added to highlight the alliance between the Austro-Hungarian Empire and the German monarchy. The bus driver was far more explicit in listing historical detail, pointing out that the thousands who died here included "Austrians, Hungarians, Russians," thereby pointing to Ulmer's belief that war knows only losers, no winners. And it was emphasized in the script that the horror of trench warfare, which is mostly associated with the Western front, had also occurred in the East: "That hill over there was taken by the Russians twenty-two times—and retaken by our brave men." The omission of these lines must be attributed not to the Hays office but to studio executives who felt audiences might get bogged down with historical detail that is of little meaning to them.

Equally revealing are the instances in which Ulmer sought to link the aftermath of the First World War with the rise of Nazism, arguably one of the main projects of the film. Much more was made in the script of the arrival of the guests to the Black Mass, who were to be greeted by Werdegast while Poelzig readied himself for his duties. The list of names suggests members of a decadent Austrian nobility (with some typical Ulmerian in-jokes thrown in). Among them we find Hauptmann Eichel, Fräulein Krug, Graf Trivers, Count Windischgraetz and his sister, Count Hauptmerde, and Herr Sternberg, most likely a jab at the phony nobility of Josef von Sternberg; the implication is that their loss of prestige and power after the collapse of the empire has made them susceptible to devil worship, much like the disenfranchised German petit bourgeoisie of the late Weimar Republic who had voted Hitler into power. Most startling

---

[22] Herzogenrath, "Ulmer and Cult/ure," 30.

[23] The most extensive discussion of these changes is found in Mank, *Karloff and Lugosi*, 45–83. However, many of the changes listed below are not mentioned by him.

in this group are a certain "Herr and Frau Goering," the latter spotting a slight, Hitler-esque mustachio on her upper lip that provides a linking of Nazism with androgyny and homosexuality (possibly an allusion to Roehm's widely known homosexuality)—a daring coupling of fascism with sexual deviancy that would not be more fully explored until Visconti and Cavani pursued the issue in Italy many decades later.

The Black Cat and Spaces of Modernity

The foregrounding of the topicality of war attests most profoundly to the exilic dimension of Ulmer's use of the horror genre, but of course any translation of genre conventions worked as much *within* as *against* the grain of studio conventions, budget restrictions, and audience expectations. Thus many aspects of *The Black Cat* should not be seen simply as a subversion or radicalization of a given material but as an extending or inflecting of it. This process is very much informed by the topicality, location, and social context of Ulmer's host country and its newly adopted cultural heritage.

As noted above, one of the most striking features of *The Black Cat*, apart from the pairing of the two horror superstars Karloff and Lugosi, is certainly the set, which provides an allegorical expression of the legacy of German modernism. But as is typical for the plurality of vision of exile filmmaking, Poelzig's Bauhaus of horror invokes not only the culture of the abandoned homeland but also that of the adopted new home. Thus critics have cited Frank Lloyd Wright's Ennis House in the Hollywood Hills as a concrete inspiration for Ulmer's set.[24] Built in 1924, and thus still a comparative novelty at the time of *The Black Cat*'s production, Wright's modernist, fortress-like private home was (and still is) an imposing structure, the key building component of which was concrete that had been poured into blocks. Given its imposing look and prominent location perched high above the Los Angeles freeways, it is perhaps not surprising that the Ennis House has by now become a popular setting for horror and science-fiction films, including *The House on Haunted Hill*, *Blade Runner*, and *The Day of the Locust*. California earthquakes and mudslides of the past decade have made the house uninhabitable for the moment, turning it into a modernist ruin that sits vacant. The Ennis House thus stands (at least for now) in the long tradition of the abandoned house, a staple of the British gothic novel which itself is another important source on which *The Black Cat* draws. In this literary genre decaying castles, manors, or towers figure prominently not only as the main location but as larger symbols for the clash between the present and the dark secrets of the past. Like Ulmer's critique of rationalism, these novels often meant to show that in an increasingly secular and skeptical age some remnants of a

---

[24] Grissemann, *Mann im Schatten*, 70; Mank, *Karloff and Lugosi*, 59.

pagan and mythical past could not be as easily rejected as some contemporaries believed. Horace Walpole's *The Castle of Otranto* (1764), often considered the founding text of the genre, became a major influence for Edgar Allan Poe's "The Fall of the House of Usher" (1838). "House of Usher" itself is a far more significant source for Ulmer's film than "The Black Cat," which was invoked by Universal for box-office purposes only. Poe's tale of the Usher dynasty and Ulmer's film share a sense of futility and oppressiveness within a closed-in universe from which there is no escape. Just as Poelzig's compound explodes in the end, the climax of Poe's tale has the titular mansion split and sink into the bog; while no concrete explanation for this is supplied, there are strong allusions to incest and murder that render this ending inescapable. These allusions find a direct resonance in Ulmer's film, which is deeply disturbing precisely because of its suggestiveness; unlike in other films of the genre, which often feature a particular monster's bestiality, here violence happens offscreen or is alluded to by sounds (when Poelzig kills Karen) or shadows (when Werdegast skins Poelzig alive like a cat, as if to rid himself of his own cat phobia). What is not said in *The Black Cat* is far more unsettling than what is spelled out. Lastly, much attention is given in Poe's story to "preserving her [Usher's deceased sister's] corpse," much like the female corpses on display in Poelzig's cabinet of necrophilia, and both tales are driven by narratives of the return of the repressed that cannot but end in complete annihilation.[25]

What distinguishes the house of Poelzig from the house of Usher and other gothic domiciles is the startling contrast between the ultra-modern décor and architecture of the villa and the torture chambers and dungeons of bygone times below, which creates a disturbing spatial and temporal asynchronicity. As Donald Albrecht has observed, the attention to detail in something as ephemeral as a film set is truly extraordinary in Ulmer's film:

> Each of the set's individual rooms exhibits an impressive formal and spatial complexity. The bedrooms, for example, are vertically divided by cantilevered projections supported along one wall by freestanding, wedge-shaped piers. Every room is sparely furnished with chrome tubular chairs polished to a high sheen. Luminous walls and ceilings, light fixtures, sliding doors, and digital clocks are among the electrically driven devices that serve the inhabitants of this elegant Corbusian *machine à habiter*.[26]

Yet despite the open floor plan and clean, angular lines, this is a closed world. The painted backdrops behind the windows emphasize the feeling

---

[25] Edgar Allan Poe, *Selected Writings* (Baltimore: Penguin, 1967), 150.

[26] Donald Albrecht, *Designing Dreams: Modern Architecture in the Movies* (New York: Harper & Row, 1986), 101.

of being locked in, reiterating a sense of claustrophobia that the whole film emanates. As in a wartime siege or a trench, there is an all-pervading sense of entrapment and hopelessness, and the Allisons's escape at the last moment has the feeling of a happy ending tagged on to a tale that really allows for no survivors.

A formidable iron spiral staircase connects Poelzig's villa with the former fortress below on which it is built. Its gun turrets and calculating charts are also the products of a rationalist architecture, this time one of steel and concrete in the service of modern warfare; the cultured, refined side of modernism of the above, this film suggests, cannot exist without its destructive, death-embracing other below. No shrieking doors or cobwebs, the staple of the genre, are found here, only the remnants of clinical and cynical tools of mass destruction. Only the room where Poelzig celebrates his Black Mass and plans to sacrifice Joan Allison is dominated by the kind of Expressionist set design that *Dracula* and *Frankenstein* relied on, reinforced by Poelzig's and his followers' theatrical robes and makeup, and an overly dramatic use of light and shadow.

The Black Cat infuses the supernatural elements of classic horror with a dream-like, nightmarish realism. It seems that not only Joan Allison has gone "mediumistic" (as Werdegast calls it, after he has given her a powerful narcotic), but also Poelzig and Werdegast themselves. Karloff's and Lugosi's somnambulist movements underscore their respective characters' hypnotic state of mind, yet another of the many allusions to *Caligari*, and throughout the film Poelzig is seen in the black, silken nightgowns and pajamas of a waking dead. The very first shot of him has him rise in his bed like Nosferatu from his coffin or Cesare summoned by Dr. Caligari, the silhouette of his dark, chiseled body appearing like a statuette against the indirect light of the window behind him, with his lifeless wife horizontally stretched out in front of him—a composition that emphasizes the calculating and inhuman nature of this military traitor–turned-high-priest-of-rape-and-murder.

Perhaps the most startling scene in the film, however, is one driven not by action or dialogue but by the roaming camera of John Mescall, which detaches itself from the characters and inspects the dark underworld of Poelzig's villa, beginning at the calculating charts and carefully tiptoeing along the thick concrete walls of fortress Marmaros, before climbing up the long spiral staircase that connects the two levels. William K. Everson has criticized the film's modernist camerawork as "sometimes too tricky for its own good," but he concedes that "the striking, pictorial quality of the film creates a decidedly non-Hollywood and nonstereotyped horror film."[27] In this particular scene the camera becomes its own

---

[27] Everson, *Classics of the Horror Film*, 122. On Universal's overall production in the period, see Clive Hirschborn, *The Universal Story* (New York: Crown, 1983).

Fig. 1.4. The Black Cat *(1934). Screenshot.*

independent character. Separated from the point of view of any character, and thus violating the norms of classic storytelling, Poelzig's words
to Werdegast in this one-minute sequence cease to be part of a dialogue
and become the voice-over commentary of an omniscient narrator that
accompany the unfettered camera:

> "Come, Vitus. Are we men or are we children? Of what use are all
> these melodramatic gestures? You say your soul was killed, that you
> have been dead all those years. And what of me? Did we not both
> die here in Marmaros fifteen years ago? Are we any less victims of the
> war than those whose bodies were torn asunder? Are we not both
> the living dead? And now you come to me playing an avenging angel
> childishly thirsting for my blood. We understand each other too
> well. We know too much of life. We shall play a little game, Vitus. A
> game of death, if you like."

This is the only scene in the film where such a prolonged effect is created,
and Poelzig's comments about the deathly bond of two undead survivors
become the central metaphor for the entire film.

Finally, no discussion of how *The Black Cat*'s negotiation of genre
conventions pushed the envelope of the 1930s horror film would be

complete without attending to its innovative use of music. Unlike any other Universal film from the cycle, *The Black Cat* has a fully orchestrated score that provides music for fifty-five of the film's sixty-five minutes of running time. It combines an impressive original score by Heinz Roemheld, a 32-year-old Berlin-trained composer, with his arrangement of classical music by Tchaikovsky, Chopin, Schubert, and Liszt. If Ulmer can be trusted (and Roemheld actually confirms this), the classical score was the director's idea and meant to express the refined taste of Poelzig. As William Rosar has shown in an essay on the scores of Universal's horror movies, what was particularly innovative in this film was not only to have music underlying almost the entire film (including scenes with dialogue) at a time when music was typically confined to the opening and closing credits, but also to have certain characters be associated with certain passages that serve as leitmotifs.[28] As Rosar notes, the film opens with Liszt's "Hungarian Rhapsody" for the scenes on the Budapest train station. The brooding *Tasso* theme then becomes Werdegast's leitmotif, while Tchaikovsky's *Romeo and Juliet* serves as the Allison's theme. Poelzig is introduced with a flurry of Liszt's Sonata in B Minor, the so-called "Devil Sonata" (as is well-known, Liszt himself had a fascination with Satan), while Brahms' *Sapphic Ode* is Karen's theme. The film also cleverly switches between diegetic and nondiegetic music, first having a futuristic device that looks like a clock but turns out to be a radio play Chopin's second piano prelude, while later Poelzig himself plays Bach's Toccata, Adagio, and Fugue in C on the organ. At the Black Mass we hear diegetic music for the last time when the organ is again played, this time by an unidentified guest (played by John Carradine, who would star in *Bluebeard*, Ulmer's second foray into the horror film in 1944).

The decision to have the film scored almost in its entirety harks back to the era of silent cinema, but the innovative use of leitmotifs for individual characters also heightens psychological depth and directs the emotions of the viewers. Stefan Grissemann has rightly observed that music in Ulmer's films tends to "dictate our feelings a little too much," but in relation to *The Black Cat* that criticism seems overstated.[29] Here the music underscores the trance-like acting of Karloff and Lugosi or the uncanny, self-propelled exploration of the camera discussed earlier, where Poelzig's self-reflective monologue about the living dead is underscored "by the hymn-like allegretto movement of Beethoven's Seventh Symphony."[30] How controversial and daring this use of music was at the time can be seen by the fact that studio head Carl Laemmle Sr. objected more vehe-

---

[28] William H. Rosar, "Music for the Monsters: Universal Pictures' Horror Film Scores of the Thirties," *Quarterly Journal of the Library of Congress* 40, no. 4 (1983): 391–421. The following remarks are indebted to Rosar's insightful analysis.
[29] Grissemann, *Mann im Schatten*, 285.
[30] Rosar, "Music for the Monsters," 404.

mently to it than to any other of the many controversial aspects of the film (including its depiction of violence, critique of religion, and so on) and at one point even threatened to completely bar the film from release.[31] Yet when the film turned out to be Universal's biggest moneymaker of the year, those concerns were quickly forgotten.

---

[31] Tom Weaver, "An Interview with Shirley Ulmer," in *The Films of Edgar G. Ulmer*, ed. Bernd Herzogenrath (Metuchen, NJ: Scarecrow, 2009), 269.

2: The Essay Film and Its German Variations

Nora M. Alter

ONE OF THE MOST popular genres within nonfiction cinema today is the so-called "essay film." These audiovisual productions are literary or philosophical meditations on a variety of topics, including self-reflective explorations on the nature of image- and sound-making, social critiques and histories, and introspective investigations plumbing the depths of human nature. As varied as the form and topics of these films are, there is common agreement on their definition. The essay film has generally been characterized as an in-between genre that moves freely from fiction to non-fiction, part documentary, part fantasy, made for television viewing and for gallery or museum exhibition. One of the characteristics of the essay film is that it is not predictable, since it does not follow the conventional rules. Moreover, essay films are both informed by and produce *theory*. To that extent, they constitute part of a body of experimental films, which Edward S. Small identifies as a genre and refers to as "direct theory."[1]

The contemporary essay film is international, and many of its producers have a transnational or diasporic identity. At the same time, however, there are national variations of the essay film. When one traces a history of the genre, it is evident that several national cinemas have a clearly developed brand of this hybrid form that identifies them as being part of a larger national cinematic tradition. Thus there are the French, British, Italian, North American, Latin American, and German essay films. It is difficult to identify a point of origin for these essay films, for evidence of cinematic essays may be found throughout early cinema. These instances, however, not marked by a clear conceptualization of the visual essay, appear rather as experiments, or possibly accidents. The essay film as a self-conscious category, I suggest, appears first in the vibrant German avant-garde film milieu of the 1920s. It surfaces there from the rich territory of educational, cultural, instructional, and other nonfiction films, including newsreels, that dominated the cinematic landscape. Seemingly in hibernation during the 1930s and through the immediate postwar period, the genre

---

[1] See Edward S. Small, *Experimental Film/Video as Major Genre* (Carbondale: Southern Illinois University Press, 1994).

reemerged in the 1960s, reaching its apex in the 1980s. Though the production of essay films has not abated, the terrain has shifted significantly, including its venues for distribution and exhibition.

When and why essay films emerged is difficult to answer. Writing about Hans Richter in 1964, film critic Jay Leyda laments in a footnote "Today the 'film essay' form is almost totally, and incomprehensibly, ignored. The only modern filmmaker who employs a witty variation of it is Chris Marker."[2] Leyda's remark makes two important observations: first, he implies that the essay film was recognized and practiced by a prewar and even presound generation of filmmakers, and, second, he draws attention to the fact that at the time of his writing, an otherwise vibrant time for film development, experimentation, and exploration, the essay film was largely ignored. In the late 1960s and 1970s, however, the form was revived by two different types of filmmakers. On the one hand, there were those such as Rainer Werner Fassbinder, Ulrike Ottinger, Helke Sanders, Hans Jürgen Syberberg, Werner Herzog, Wim Wenders, referred to today as the giants of New German Cinema. That they are better known for their feature films is not coincidental, although many used these shorter, more theoretical films as sketches or means by which to work out aesthetic problematics. On the other hand, roughly parallel to the rise of these filmmakers was an alternative group of nonfiction filmmakers that included Alexander Kluge, Hartmut Bitmosky, Harun Farocki, Rosa von Praunheim, Peter Nestler, Jean-Marie Straub and Danielle Huillet. These essayists tended to eschew commercial feature productions and relied instead on other media, such as television. Generally, low-production aesthetics, a shorter length than feature films, and a presentation of material that demands concentrated thought and focus on the part of the viewer mark their films. During the past two decades the most significant change that has transpired within the genre for both groups has been a shift in exhibition venues from television and cinemas to museums, galleries, and biennales; from single-channel distribution to three-or-more-channel installations.

The essay film is linked historically to the literary form of the essay and can be traced back to Montaigne's *Essais* (1580). These essays are considered by many to initiate this self-reflective, subjective, and hybrid genre between fiction and nonfiction, literature and philosophy. Critics, scholars, and media makers are also draw to later practitioners of the essay, including Francis Bacon, Giacomo Leopardi, Ralph Waldo Emerson, Friedrich Nietzsche, and, more recently, twentieth-century essayists to guide their analyses and interpretations. Those who are interested in probing personal subjectivity and constructions of the self tend to turn to the writings of figures such as Jean Starobinski or Robert Musil. Those who seek to draw a

[2] Jay Leyda, *Films Beget Films* (London: George Allen & Unwin, 1964), 30.

connection between form and expression often cite Georg Lukács, Theodor Adorno, or Roland Barthes. Walter Benjamin and Siegfried Kracauer are sources for those interested in a sociohistorical problematic. And the theories of Hans Richter and Alexandre Astruc are mobilized by those whose concern is the aesthetics of representation. Max Bense is evoked as a proponent of the essay as an experimental form of critique. As indicated by the above, there is a decidedly *German* bent to those theorists whose work underpins many audiovisual essays. Indeed, Lukacs's seminal "On The Nature and Form of the Essay" (1910), Adorno's response, "The Essay as Form" (1954), some forty years later, and Bense's "On the Essay and Its Prose" (1947) are considered by many to be foundational texts.

Historically, essays often appear at a time of crisis. Thus Lukacs's treatment of the essay ties it to a modernist crisis affecting traditional literature such as the novel, drama, poetry, and the arts of painting, sculpture, music, and the like. Not surprising then that Lukacs's meditations on the contemporary essay situate it between scientific and aesthetic production, and that he defines it as "criticism as a form of art."[3] Approximately two decades and one world war later, writing in a context of social, political, and economic upheaval, Robert Musil's explorations of the essay are marked by the increasingly unstable contemporary intellectual landscape and the search for an alternative genre for the production of sociopolitical critique. In the same spirit, Bense's "On the Essay and Its Prose," written immediately following the horrors of the Second World War, seeks to find a possibility for critical writing in a postapocalyptic landscape. Adorno's, "The Essay as Form," in the mid-1950s projects the essay as a politico-philosophical genre fighting an increasingly reified world. Like its literary philosophical antecedent, the audiovisual essay also surfaces during periods of social, political, aesthetic, and/or technological crises.

Whereas the German thinkers referred to above focus on the written essay, the essay as a genre was also developed within the realm of audiovisual production. Leyda locates the emergence of the modern essay film in Hans Richter's *Inflation* (1928).[4] Richter's film predates by a dozen years his "Der Filmessay: Eine neue Form des Dokumentarfilms" (The film essay: A new form of documentary film, 1940), a short text in which he formally introduces and describes the new genre.[5] Richter, like Leyda,

---

[3] Georg Lukacs, "On the Nature and Form of the Essay" (1910), in *Soul and Form* (Cambridge, MA: MIT Press, 1980), 2.

[4] "With his *Inflation*, made in 1928 to introduce a forgotten commercial film, he began a series of 'film essays', partly dependent on the same stock-shot libraries that Ruttmann employed. Kracauer describes Richter's film essays as 'sagacious pictorial comments on socially interesting topics.'" Leyda, *Films Beget Films*, 30.

[5] Hans Richter, "Der Filmessay: Eine neue Form des Dokumentarfilms," in *Schreiben Bilder Sprechen: Texte zum essayistischen Film*, ed. Christa Blümlinger and Constantin Wulff (Vienna: Sonderzahl, 1992), 195–98.

retrospectively cites his own film, *Inflation*, as an early example of what an essay film might look like. Following *Inflation*, in the 1930s, Richter made several related sketches for cinematic projects including his *Super Essay Films* (1941). Practice and experiment came prior to formalizing ideas in writing and, in its filmic incarnation, *Inflation* constituted the first concrete conceptualization of an alternative cinematic form, one that was neither pure aesthetics nor simple reportage. In "Der Filmessay," Richter proposes a new genre that will enable filmmakers to make the "invisible" world of ideas visible on the screen. Unlike documentaries that present factual information, the essay film produces complex thought that at times is *not* grounded in *reality* and can be contradictory, irrational, and fantastic. The essay film, according to Richter, no longer binds the filmmaker to the rules and parameters of traditional documentary practice. Rather, the imagination with all of its artistic potentiality is now to be given free rein. A decade later Bense stresses that the essay should above all be a form of experimentation. Moreover, Richter explains that he is employing the term "essay" because it signifies a genre in between genres, one that merges documentary with experimentation and art. Richter's theories not only resonate with Lukacs's formulation of the literary essay, in which the latter postulates that the essay originates from the science of art but then radically departs from the constraints of "dry matter" into "free flight" (13); it also resonates with Benjamin's concept of translation, which was a manipulation of "modes," that is, different expressions in a new arrangement or form.[6] The "task of the translator" was to enable the movement of thoughts and ideas across national and cultural borders. Although Benjamin refers exclusively to written texts, he does not exclude the possibility of translation from one medium into another. Indeed, in a later essay, "The Author as Producer," he argues that "we have to rethink our conceptions of literary forms or genres, in view of the technical factors affecting our present situation," and thereby indicates his keen awareness that new media such as cinema and photography will transform established genres and produce new forms.[7]

In order to better understand the significance of *Inflation* and Richter's later essay, it is necessary to briefly sketch out the cinematic landscape at that time. In the space of one year between 1921 and 1922, along with better-known cinematographic works such as F. W. Murnau's *Nosferatu* and Charlie Chaplin's *The Kid*, two films came out, each of which helped to shape and define a new strand of nonfiction cinema: Robert Flaherty's *Nanook of the North* (1922) and Richter's *Rhythmus*

---

[6] Walter Benjamin, "The Task of the Translator," in *Illuminations*, trans. Harry Zohn, ed. Hannah Arendt (New York: Schocken Books, 1969), 70.
[7] Walter Benjamin, "The Author as Producer," in *Reflections*, ed. Peter Demetz (New York: Schocken Books, 1986), 224.

21 (1921). The former was hailed by British documentary theorist and filmmaker John Grierson as the seminal inspiration of documentary film-making. In his oft-quoted essay "The First Principle of Documentary" (1932) Grierson differentiated *Nanook* from other earlier forms of non-fiction films such as actualities, newsreels, and travelogues, because it initiated a change "from the plain (or fancy) descriptions of natural material to arrangements, rearrangements, and creative shapings of it" (83). From that perspective, *Nanook,* and later, Flaherty's *Moana* (1926) constituted significant interventions in a field dominated by superficial facts. For as Grierson articulated in an early lecture,

> in documentary we deal with the actual and in one sense with the real. But the really real, if I may use that phrase, is something deeper than that. The only reality which counts in the end is the interpretation which is profound. . . . But I charge you to remember that the task of reality before you is not one of reproduction but of interpretation.[8]

Equally as significant as *Nanook,* but for a different public, was Richter's *Rhythmus 21.* Ushering in the school of abstract filmmaking, the film offers a black and white study of Suprematism (Malevich), squares and rectangles that change in size and depth through a series of rhythmic evolutions. ("Twenty-one" refers to the year it was made.) In 1920 Richter had already collaborated with fellow artist Viking Eggeling to produce a pamphlet, "Universelle Sprache" (universal language), in which, as he recalls in 1965, they tried to defend the thesis "that the abstract form offers the possibility of a language above and beyond national frontiers."[9] Therefore, an art that is based on national or cultural identification should be shunned in favor of productions that achieve transcendent or noncommunity-specific communication. Richter continues that "the basis for such a language would lie in the identical form of perception in all human beings and would offer the promise of a universal art as it had never existed before." *Rhythmus 21* ushered in a series of abstract studies in film by Richter (*Rhythmus 23* [1923], *Rhythmus 25* [1925], *Fuge in Rot und Gruen* [Fugue in Red and Green, 1923]), Walther Ruttmann (*Opus I–IV* [1921–25]), Oscar Fischinger (*Wax Experiments* [1921–26], *Orgelstabe* [Staffs, 1923–27], *Stromlinien*

---

[8] Grierson, in an untitled lecture on documentary from somewhere between 1927 and 1933, reprinted in Ian Aitken, *Film Reform: John Grierson and the Documentary Film Movement* (London: Routledge, 1990), 76–77. For his part, Grierson pushed his agenda to "arrange," "rearrange" and "creatively shape" the documentary tradition. His calculated creation of the myth of origin not only secured a historical past but it also proleptically cast a future and determination for nonfiction film as "documentary" that extended over half a century.

[9] Viking Eggeling and Hans Richter, *Universelle Sprache* (Fort in der Lausitz, Germany: Eigenverlag, 1920), no pagination.

[Flow Lines, 1925]), and others, who constitute what is now known as the classical filmic avant-garde of Weimar cinema. The overriding structure of these works was determined by the motion of the filmed objects in time and space, rather than by any physical referential materiality. The movement and editing were often choreographed to music scores that determined the overall rhythm.[10]

Approximately twenty years after the initial release of *Nanook* and *Rhythmus 21*, that is, in 1939 and 1940, the Museum of Modern Art in New York organized two important film events. The first was entitled "The Nonfiction Film: From Uninterrupted Fact to Documentary" in which *Nanook* was screened, and the second was a festival centered on abstract European films that featured Richter's *Rhythmus 21*, in addition to films by Man Ray, Fernand Léger, and Marcel Duchamp. The fact that a major institution for modern art saw nonfiction films as part of its purview is significant in and of itself, but within that area, to divide the field between works primarily based on facts and those rooted in abstract art is of further import, for it reinforced and historically located a fundamentally misleading split in nonfiction film. MOMA's film programs thus institutionally produced a skewed dual lens through which to understand European nonfiction production of the 1920s. Of even more concern is that it proleptically cast into the future a division between two types of filmmaking that came to dominate the postwar landscape of nonfiction cinematographic production: documentary and art films. (Bense observes a similar split in writing between the two primary tendencies: creative [Erschoefpung] and recording [Erziehung or Tendenz]). The problem with such a dual vision is not that it is wrong, or even too polarized, but that it does not account for the concrete exceptions that produced another type of cinema that does not strictly adhere to either of these two categories but falls between the two, namely, the essay film.

The fact that the postwar 1920s coincided with a period of high modernism within the arts is not coincidental. The early essay films are concomitantly reacting to and with new visual arts and the aesthetic avant-garde, as well as to what might be called a documentary impulse or a trend toward realism in the literary arts. This tendency was no doubt related to the popularity of photography and film with their increasingly high degree of concern with verisimilitude. In addition, within film production proper, it is generally assumed that this process began around

---

[10] Accompanying the film *Opus I*, for example, was a musical score composed by Max Butting. Following the success of *Opus I*, Ruttmann made three other "Opus" films, *Opus II* (1923), *III* (1924), and *IV* (1925). Richter's *Rhythmus 23* and *25*, and *Fuge in Rot and Gruen* set into motion a complex interplay of shapes and forms arranged according to the musical composition of a fugue, in which several motifs of polyphonic composition are repeated as voices and parts that enter and exit in succession.

1908 with the streamlining narrative film production that was firmly consolidated by the 1920s. Noël Burch has termed this the Institutional Mode of Representation, which he defines as "that set of (written or unwritten) directives which has been historically interiorized by directors and technicians as the irreducible base of 'film language' within the institution and which has remained a constant over the past fifty years, independently of the vast stylistic changes which have taken place."[11] The Institutional Mode of Representation "has also of course been interiorized by all spectators as they learn (generally at a very early age) to read the films of the institution."[12] As the production of feature films increased and became more mainstream, certain genres became part of the staple fare: these included melodrama, detective stories, comedy, historical fiction, horror, and the like. However, in parallel, just as genres became solidified in the feature film, so too, I argue, in the nonfiction film. On the one hand there were newsreels, science films, ethnographic films, colonial films, travel films, *Lehrfilme*, or instructional films, culture films (*Kulturfilme*) and the like, films whose purpose was primarily informative and educational. On the other, there were the art films such as the abstract experiments mentioned earlier of Richter, Ruttmann, and others. These were often produced in response to commercial feature films. Thus early on Ruttmann penned a short proclamation entitled "Kunst und Film" (Art and film, 1913–17) in which he argued against narrative films, proposing instead that cinema was an inherently visual art form and therefore should be most closely aligned to painting and dance.[13] A couple of years later he revised his theory and instead declared that because successive movement of frames was such an integral part of film, the new medium should be situated between painting and music.[14] From these explorations there emerged a cinematic avant-garde or art cinema. Within this grouping were Impressionistic filmmakers such as Delluc, l'Herbier, Germaine Dulac, Able Gance and Jean Epstein; German Expressionists

---

[11] Noël Burch, *Theory of Film Practice* (New York: Praeger, 1973), 50.

[12] Burch, *Theory of Film Practice*, 100.

[13] The exact date of this short text is not known. "Denn die Kinematographie gehört unter das Kapitel der *bildenden Künste*, und ihre Gesetze sind am nächsten denen der Malerei und des Tanzes verwandt." Walter Ruttmann, "Kunst und Kino," in *Walter Ruttmann: Eine Dokumentation*, ed. Jeanpaul Goergen (Berlin: Freunde der Deutschen Kinemathek, 1990), 73.

[14] "Eine Kunst für das Auge, die sich von der Malerei dadurch unterschneidet, dass sie sich zeitlich abspielt (wie Musik), und dass der Schwerpunkt des Künstlerischen nicht (wie im Bild) in der Reduktion eines (realen oder Formalen) Vorgangs auf einem Moment liegt, sondern gerade in der zeitlichen Entwicklung des Formalen. Dass diese Kunst sich zeitlich abwickelt, ist eines ihrer wichtigsten Elemente der Zeit-Rhythmus des optischen Geschehens." Walter Ruttmann, "Malerei mit Zeit," in Goergen, *Walter Ruttmann: Eine Dokumentation*, 74.

like Robert Wiene; Surrealists such as Louis Bunuel, Salvador Dali, Antonin Artaud, and Robert Desnos; and Dadaists, including Hans Richter, Viking Eggeling, Walter Ruttmann, Marcel Duchamp, Rene Clair, Francis Picabia, and Fernand Léger. Whatever the variations, there was a significant body of films that René Clair termed "pure cinema" or what Richter called "absolute cinema." The borders between these various groups, especially Dadaists and Surrealists, are in no way clean and clear, and there are many overlaps.

These instances of alternative cinema are known as the cinematic avant-garde. In his well-known thesis, Peter Bürger proposes that the avant-garde fundamentally provides a critique of "the category *art as institution*" (liii). During the 1920s a series of confluences brought this about, when a group of artists assumed that "when art is institutionalized as ideology in developed bourgeois society . . . its critique must engage its most developed exemplification" (98). Extending Bürger's theory to the specific domain of filmmaking, one may propose that avant-garde cinema emerged as a parallel response to the burgeoning popularity and influence of the institution of cinema.[15] For Burch, the "Cinema Institution" meant

> not simply the film industry, whose function is to fill cinemas, not to empty them; it also refers to the mental machinery—that other industry—which spectators "accustomed to the movies" have historically interiorized, and which enables them to consume films (the Institution is outside and inside us, it is indiscriminately collective and private, sociological and psychoanalytical).[16]

The avant-garde films radically challenged an institutionalization of cinema as a commercial mass medium produced for entertainment, and sought instead to create an art form that by its very existence constituted a critique. However this critique was not just directed against the institution of cinema but, because it was using film as an aesthetic and/or an artistic medium—like painting—concomitantly challenged the very institution of art and its traditional forms of expression. Avant-garde cinema, I would argue, thus constituted a double form of institutional critique.

What I want to suggest in this brief overview is that, despite the fact that the cinematic landscape of the 1920s was dominated by spectacular commercial large-scale fictional productions, there was a thriving parallel industry in nonfiction cinema—a category which was already perceived of

---

[15] There are several film historians who argue that the development of film and its relatively short history by the 1920s make this definition inadequate. As quoted by A. L. Rees, "Foreword," in Hans Richter, *The Struggle for the Film: Towards a Socially Responsible Cinema*, trans. Ben Brewster, ed. Jürgen Römhild (New York: St. Martin's, 1986), 3–10.

[16] Burch, *Theory of Film Practice*, 100.

as consisting of two branches: one based on facts, science, and what would be called in the 1930s documentaries; and the other, avant-garde art. In other terms, by 1928 (the year of Richter's *Inflation*), Burch's theories of the institutionalized mode of representation (IMR) of commercial films may be applied to two branches of nonfiction cinema at the time: fact films and art films, in that there was a predictability and pattern-like approach to these productions similar to that found in feature films. These productions, aside from technological innovations, did little to advance and broaden the field conceptually. As Grierson observes, "The rebellion from the who-gets-who tradition of commercial cinema to the tradition of pure form in cinema is no great shakes as a rebellion. Dadaism, Expressionism, symphonies are all in the same category. They present new beauties and new shapes; they fail to present new persuasions." Richter expresses a similar discontent with nonfiction cinema when he declares that a beautiful film of a rural landscape or a "romantic" village is highly problematic, because it reveals nothing of the history and sociopolitics of the region. "Outwardly everything looked quite picturesque, and there were plenty of opportunities for marvelous shots. But such a manner teaches one nothing about the object represented. And yet this is the "documentarian usual style, this superficial reportage."[17] Richter quotes directly from Brecht's now notorious statement that "A photograph of Krupps or the AEG yields hardly anything about those industries." The category of nonfiction, as it was then understood, was becoming increasingly bankrupt. Indeed, in 1930 at the second Avant Garde Film in Brussels, it was declared that "the Avant Garde as a purely aesthetic movement has passed its climax and is on the way to concentrating on the social and political film, mainly in the documentary form."[18] As a result, at the same time that there was an institutionalization of fictional narrative cinema, other types of filmic productions developed within the nonfictional realm with a similar consolidation of genre and form. By the late 1920s there was mounting frustration, and what even might be called an aesthetic "crisis," regarding alternative cinema. Now nonfiction films also constituted a cinematic category to be critiqued and explored. And it is precisely at this juncture that the essay film originates—to echo Lukacs—between science and art. In other words, I propose that the German essay film emerged not only in response to the institutionalization of feature films but also to the institutionalization of nonfictional documentary-like films and to avant-garde filmmaking as well.

In 1928 Hans Richter sought to make a film that would relate to the one question that remained central to him: "What social purpose does

[17] Hans Richter, *The Struggle for the Film: Towards a Socially Responsible Cinema*, trans. Ben Brewster, ed. Jürgen Römhild (New York: St. Martin's, 1986), 46–47.
[18] As quoted by A. L. Rees, "Foreword" in *The Struggle for the Film*, 9.

cinema serve?"[19] After seven years of making films in which formal experimentation dominated over any social content, Richter was ready to pursue a new tack. *Inflation* constituted the first concrete conceptualization of an alternative cinematic form, one that was neither pure aesthetics nor simple reportage.[20] As he wrote, shortly after completing *Inflation*, "the path of theater-freed film follows two directions: one in the pursuit of so-called unstaged shots, which are the technical base of weekly recordings of reality, the main proponent and director of this type of cinema is Dsiga Werthoff [*sic*]; the other type of film is that without plot, theme or narrative—the so-called 'absolute film.'"[21] Although he oversimplifies Vertov's project, Richter's statement indicates his awareness of how limited the genre of nonfiction was by the late 1920s.

Like other nonfiction films at the time, *Inflation* was commissioned by UFA as a short to precede the commercial feature, Wihelm Thiele's *Die Dame mit der Maske* (The Lady with the Mask, 1928). For Richter, the potential to reach a mass audience cannot be underestimated; it pushed him into thinking how best to pursue his social goals, since this production would not be screened for a like-minded public but rather for the average filmgoer. The film would have to cut a fine line between being artistic, while at the same time remaining critical and accessible. To that end, Richter pushed his use of montage to a new level. As marked by the subtitle: "A Counterpoint of Declining People and Growing Zeros," the short consists of a rapid flow of superimposed images of abstract circles in motion against a black screen. As they gradually come into focus, they are recognized as coins, replaced by ever-increasing quantities and values of banknotes juxtaposed with their equivalent in US dollars. As the notes multiply, images of consumer goods such as a sewing machine, an automobile, food, types of shelter, and the like crowd the screen, followed by a series of close shots of human faces bearing anguished expressions and suggesting poverty. The film then cuts to figures of wealthy businessmen, who are shot from a low angle, thereby increasing both their stature and dominance. Clearly, they are engaged in high-end trading of goods and stocks. The next sequence presents a well-dressed man who, viewers presume, is reading about his loss of fortune in a newspaper. In a brilliant montage of images, Richter transforms him from his position of bourgeois respectability to that of a beggar asking for handouts. Shots of "faceless masses" that lose their individuality to poverty increase, and the final minutes are filled with images of nihilist revolution as buildings collapse in a paroxysm of destruction and violence.

---

[19] Richter, *The Struggle for the Film*, 24.

[20] Hans Richter, "Der Filmessay," 195–98.

[21] Hans Richter, "Film von morgen," in *Hans Richter Film ist Rhythmus*, ed. Ulrich Gregor, special issue of *Kinemathek* 95 (July 2003): 56. All translations in this essay are my own except where otherwise credited.

The rapid-fire cascade of images symbolically corresponds to the crisis brought on by the uncontrolled inflation in which Germany found itself. Thus Richter formally underscores a relationship between his film style and his subject. The essay as a literary/philosophical form often emerges during periods of crisis, and in *Inflation,* the correlation is dual: on the one hand, materialistic socioeconomic collapse, on the other a self-reflectively conceptual confusion leading to the condition of nonfiction film. A factual news report of the same length—eight minutes—could not convey the utter destruction, registers of despair, and agonizing anxiety caused by the mental and physical collapse. A feature film would run the risk of turning a tragedy into melodrama, with excessive attention to the stars who would personalize and outweigh the real crisis at hand. What makes Richter's film so effective is that it condenses, through cinematic tools and language of montage, superimposition, and stop-motion, a complex historical drama, delivering its message in a single punch. Richter here parallels Benjamin's theory that history is conceptualized in dynamic image. To go back to Richter's comment about the misleading effects of the photograph of the bucolic village; images alone do not reveal the problematic relationships below the appearance. In contrast, he posits film as the medium capable of revealing the other side:

> The cinema is perfectly capable in principle of revealing the *functional* meaning of things and events, for it has *time* at its disposal, it can contract it and thus show the development, the evolution of things. It does not need to take a picture of a "beautiful" tree, it can also show us a growing one, a falling one, or one swaying in the wind—nature not just as a view, but also as an element, the village not as an idyll, but as a social entity.[22]

Inflation, by using fast-motion images, provides the spectator with a complex critical commentary on the crisis of inflation; it offers both a brief history and a projected future: full collapse of the socioeconomic and -political state. As such, it is a cinematic essay that does not pretend to be a news report based on facts, a commercial feature, or an abstract art film: it stands as an impressionist meditation encoding a sharp social critique.

Like many artists, Richter's career in Germany was interrupted in the 1930s and was only picked up a decade later across the Atlantic in New York. There he joined the community of other exiles and resumed both his filmmaking and his teaching practice. In 1947 he made the ambitious collaborative essay film, *Dreams That Money Can Buy,* and influenced a whole generation of North American film essayists, who would expand

---

[22] Richter, *The Struggle for the Film,* 47.

the genre in the 1960s.[23] However, in Germany essay filmmaking did not end in the 1930s but continued to be practiced by Walter Ruttmann, Willy Zielke, and others.

One of the most profound developments affecting the essay film at that time was the advent of sound. The addition of a sound track often composed of multiple tracks complicates and adds to the essay film in several different ways. Relevant to this discussion are primarily three types of sound: noise, music, and human utterances. By *noise* I refer to audible signs that are attached to objects that fill the screen space, such as the noise of traffic, the rhythmic pounding of a jackhammer, or a dog barking—noises that help locate the spectator in the diegesis, or conversely, serve to dislocate and confuse. Similarly, music may emanate from an obvious source within the filmic narrative space, or it may be nondiegetic, or it may be purposefully intertwined. Finally, at the most basic level sound gives a voice to filmed subjects and thereby obviates the need for dialogue or intertitles. For example, certain types of documentaries with lengthy interviews are inconceivable without sound. However, perhaps one of the most prevalent and (over) used strategies of sound in the essay film is the voice-over. This nondiegetic commentary may take the form of the reading of a diary or of personal letters, as in Chris Marker's *Sunless* (1983) or Chantal Akerman's *News from Home* (1977), or it may be a "neutral," relatively toneless voice delivering a lecture to the viewer, as in Harun Farocki's *Bilder der Welt und Inschrift des Krieges* (Images of the World and the Inscription of War, 1989). Usually there is a direct correspondence between the commentary and the images and other sounds projected on the screen, with the former illustrating, commenting on, or in some way relating to the latter. In some instances, however, the connection between the visual and the audible is intentionally not related, as in Yvonne Rainer's *Journeys from Berlin/1971* (1980). More often than not, voice-over commentaries hold a special place in nonfiction film, where they are often granted an authority that is readily accepted and rarely challenged. And indeed, many essay filmmakers consciously play with this false authority, beckoning the viewer not to accept it, but instead to find contradictions, errors, and other strategies of manipulation. Thus Walter Wippersberg's *Festival of Chickens* (1992) constitutes an essay film in the form of a mock anthropological-ethnographical documentary in which the voice-over plays the key role in delivering the subversive, irreverent punch line. In short, the addition of a voice-over commentary adds another layer of meaning to an essay film, one that vies with the subtitles and written text layered onto the screen and that delivers even

---

[23] See Nora M. Alter, "Hans Richter in Exile: Translating the Avant-garde," in *Caught by Politics*, ed. Sabine Eckmann and Lutz Koepnick (New York: Palgrave, 2007), 223–43.

more information and produces additional meaning. Overall then, the addition of sound to film imbues the essay film with a myriad of possible new threads for weaving in a dense audiovisual text. Adorno has likened thought and by extension the essay to a woven carpet that does not "progress in a single direction; instead, the moments are interwoven as in a carpet. The fruitfulness of the thoughts depend on the density of the texture" (13).

Returning now to the essay film in Germany in the 1930s, the form did not disappear but rather continued to thrive. Indeed, factors such as the mixing of fact and fiction, and its inherently subjective nature, made it a particularly suitable genre for the rewriting of history, the production of myth, and the manipulation of information. Indeed, in Britain Humphrey Jennings composed nationally inspired essays, as for example, *Words for Battle* (1941) and *Listen to Britain* (1942), whose aim was to bolster the British war effort. In Germany Ruttmann made cinematic essays focused on cities such as *Stuttgart* (1935) and *Düsseldorf* (1936), whose goal was to instill feelings of pride and nationalism, and *Deutsche Panzer* (German Tanks, 1940), which celebrated military technology. Zielke's remarkable *Das Stahltier* (The Steel Animal, 1935) constitutes a complex audiovisual essay that purports to construct the history of the German steam engine. While seeking to make a film that champions German technology and superior engineering, Zielke is confronted with a number of historical facts that contradict the dominance of the German model, such as the uncomfortable "actuality" that the engine actually originated in Britain. Zielke undercuts the brilliance of the initial invention by demonstrating that period of historical invention with a series of highly comical reenactments in which the British appear more as hapless blundering fools who inadvertently stumble on a creation rather than as systematic, cool, rational thinkers who are masters of science and technology. *Das Stahltier* then focuses on a young German engineer, Klaassen (Aribert Mog), who seeks to perfect the engine into the ideal modern locomotive. He bears all the characteristics of the romantic genius inventor who ultimately achieves his dream. The final scenes of the film are marked by a fantastical journey of the engineer "riding" the machine, driving it faster and faster. In its frenzied journey it comes to resemble a human, the headlights are eyes, the grill, a mouth. The high-speed journey is matched visually by a series of very sharp cuts and edits that alternate from shots of Mog's face to the engine, to the instrument panel measuring the speed. Once climax is achieved, the entire film and engine slow down with a shot of the engineer lying on the grass in front of his now static engine, smoking a cigarette. Whereas *Das Stahltier* is a humorous piece akin to more recent films by Peter Watkins, such as *La Commune (Paris 1871)* (2003); later cinematic essays, such as Franz Hippler's *Der ewige Jude* (1940), constitute a dangerous and insidious vitriolic rant in the form of an essay. The essay film thus at that time was still a form of critique—however, one that was marked by right-wing rather than the left-wing or liberal politics with which it is associated today.

If there is a time when essay films in Germany were relatively dormant, it is the postwar period—a time marked by a conscious reconstruction of the German cultural landscape (East and West). In particular, the film industry was systematically examined and overhauled, given the prominent role it had played during the Third Reich. Not only were the programs of German theaters dominated by foreign films, many of which had been banned during the war, but foreign film delegations participated in reeducation programs. Among these efforts were the French film theorist and critic André Bazin and essay filmmaker Chris Marker. Marker, in a 1951 essay, "Croix de bois et chemin de fer," recalls a conversation he had while traveling in Germany with a former Nazi train conductor:

> My best friend died in a concentration camp, and I have been active in the education of Germans for the last five years—because I harbor no hatred for the German people. But it is precisely by not forgetting anything, by recalling together the concentration camps that we shall perhaps succeed in working together for a world without concentration camps.[24]

In 1949 Bazin and Marker organized the first of a series of annual retreats held in different locations throughout Germany.[25] Sponsored by the left-wing cultural organization "Travail et Culture" (Work and culture), these seminars included film screenings, lectures, and discussions. They were attended by future German film critics, such as Frieda Graf, Ulrich Gregor, and Enno Patalas, as well as by filmmakers Wolfgang Staudte, Paul Rotha, and others. This cultural initiative was significant, not only because it provided an alternative to the Hollywood staple offered by the US government's cultural affairs division, but more importantly because it operated from a perspective that viewed film as a seventh art—parallel to the other arts. From that point of view, then, cinematic practice not only encompassed production but included the active construction of a public sphere consisting of alternative exhibition venues such as ciné clubs and cinématheques, which provided spaces not only for screenings but also for debates fostering a loyal public that was actively involved in an ongoing critical cinematic dialogue. Further, in France there were several serious film journals, such as *Cahiers du Cinéma*, *Regards neufs sur le cinéma*, and *Cinéma*, that sought to provide the space for debate and

---

[24] Chris Marker, "Croix de bois et chemin de fer," *Esprit* 175 (Jan. 1951): 88–90.
[25] The first took place in the Black Forest, then it was held at Titisee (1949), Schluchsee (1950), Bacharach am Rhein (1951), Lindau am Bodensee (1952), and Bad Ems (1953).

whose contributors included critics, historians, theoreticians, and film-makers. According to Tim Corrigan, it was precisely from this charged and engaged milieu that the French essay film emerged; Noël Burch identifies Georges Franju's *The Blood of the Beasts* (1949) as the first of these. At the time, Marker was working with Alain Resnais on their remarkable "pamphlet" (essay) film, *Statues Also Die* (1953). What I suggest is that this cultural initiative actively sought to promote and encourage a type of filmmaking that was not based on entertainment and the dream-factory model, but rather had a rigorous intellectual spine that served as a network through various institutional systems. Thus, for example, in 1957 Gregor, Patalas, and Grafe founded *Filmkritik*, the seminal journal in German for film studies, the first volumes of which included texts by Benjamin and Adorno. Two years later Patalas was involved in organizing "DOC 59," a collective of young documentary filmmakers. Various film clubs, museums, alternative screening sites, and festivals opened up throughout the Federal Republic, and a new film academy, the DFFB, was established in Berlin in 1966. West German directors, influenced by the French New Wave and "auteur theory," referred to themselves as "Autoren." A series of manifestos, such as the Oberhausen Manifesto, were penned by young directors and critics who sought to do away with 'Papa's Kino." It is in this vibrant environment—one perhaps analogous to that of the 1920s—that the critical essay-film project begun by Richter resurfaced in full force.

Eric Rentschler rightfully singles out Alexander Kluge and Peter Schamoni's 12-minute short *Brutalität in Stein* (Brutality in Stone, 1961) as "Young German Film's earliest sign of life."[26] Rentschler refers to the work as a documentary and reads it primarily as an anti-*Kultur* film, albeit one marked by *"experimentation,* intervention, and reinterpretation" (35). With this designation he clearly places it as part of the trajectory of short *Kultur* films that were shown before features and flourished during the Third Reich (32). While this reading is not inaccurate, it generically limits conceptually what Kluge and Schamoni's film achieves. For, I would posit, *Brutalität in Stein* constitutes an essay film, a text that seeks to actively engage in a public dialogue. As noted above, Marker codirected *Statues Also Die*, an essay film that investigated the brutality of colonialism through statues, sculptures, and other cultural projects left behind. The story is told through the objects, as the voice-over commentary explains, "When people die they enter into history; when statues die, they enter into art. This botany of death is what we call culture." Marker and Resnais's text is concerned with the problem-

---

[26] Eric Rentschler, "Remembering Not to Forget: A Retrospective Reading of Kluge's *Brutality in Stone*," special issue on Alexander Kluge, *New German Critique* 49 (Winter, 1990): 23–41.

atic of a history that continues to inform and shape the present, even
though it has been disavowed. Much of the film is made up of still shots
of inanimate objects such as sculptures and masks. However, the interplay between camera, commentary, and music serves to reanimate these
objects and imbue them with a narrative, a social history that many would
prefer to forget. In a similar fashion, Kluge and Schamoni's *Brutalität
in Stein* comprises a series of shots of Nuremberg with its monumental
architectural ruins from the Third Reich, a voice-over, quotations from
a variety of sources—public and private—including songs, radio recordings, and reminiscences. The horrific past that haunts the now desolate
structures emerges through the soundtrack. The voices co-mingle in a
disjointed dialogue, reminding the viewer of the deadly course taken by
Germany. As Rentschler astutely observes, "The authentic concern with
Brutality in Stone is with the past, with the images and self-images of
that past and their unacknowledged place in present discourse" (34). In
some instances, Kluge and Schamoni seem to take the philosophy directly
from Adorno and Horkheimer's *Dialectic of Enlightenment* and translate
it into audiovisual images. The film's experimental form—its meditative
soundtrack and poetic visual style—places it at odds with the information
imparted on the soundtrack, exceeds the generic limits of a documentary
or *Kulturfilm*, and locates it firmly within the essay genre.

Brutalität in Stein* emerged during a dual crisis for film and culture.
The film, poised at the beginning of the 1960s, ushered in a period of
the experimental in the realm of aesthetic and cultural production as
well as radical politics. In response to this crisis, basically two branches
of filmmakers emerged, each of which produced essay films. On the
one hand there was a group based primarily in Berlin, which included
Farocki, Straub and Huillet, Holger Meins, Bitmosky, Sanders, and others who sought to formally and thematically transform cinema. Their
films are marked by the blurring of fact and fiction, self-awareness of the
medium, and an explicit politics. Some works, such as Farocki's *Nicht
löschbares Feuer* (Inextinguishable Fire, 1969), called directly for an end
to the war in Vietnam, whereas others, such as Sanders's REDUPERS—
Die allseitig reduzierte Persönlichkeit (REDUPERS—All-around Reduced
Personality, 1977) dealt with feminist gender politics and the medium
of photography and film. These filmmakers operated on the fringe of
popular media, driven more by politics than entertainment. During the
1970s the main venue for support for such alternative forms was German
television, with distribution limited to a national public. On the other
hand, at the same time mainstream German film enjoyed a renaissance in
the international spotlight with the emergence of New German Cinema.
Directors such as Wenders, Herzog, Fassbinder, Hans Jürgen Syberberg,
Volker Schloendorff, and Margarethe von Trotta produced competitive
feature films. Often overlooked is the fact that alongside their narrative

successes they made shorter, experimental essays that functioned as work-ing sketches and drafts, addressing problems of aesthetic and cultural rep-resentation and the role of the German filmmaker. Thus in 1971 Herzog made *Land des Schweigens und der Dunkelheit* (Land of Silence and Darkness) a meditative essay about deaf-mutes, which was immediately followed by *Aguirre, der Zorn Gottes* (Aguirre, Wrath of God, 1972). Wim Wenders in 1977 released *Der amerikanische Freund* (*The American friend*, 1977) and in 1980 produced *Lightning over Water*, an essay about the tension between film and video and the death of Nicholas Ray. Fassbinder's *Warnung vor einer heiligen Nutte* (Warning about a Holy Whore, 1971), a scathing critique of the film industry, is sandwiched between *Whity* (1970) and *Die bitteren Tränen der Petra von Kant* (The Bitter Tears of Petra von Kant, 1972).

Following the radicalized 1960s, the 1970s in West Germany were marked by divisive domestic politics, including the presence of an increas-ingly violent relationship between the state and the RAF (Red Army Faction). Holger Meins died during a hunger strike in 1974, and Ulrike Meinhof allegedly committed suicide in 1976, followed by the presumed suicides of Gudrun Ensslin, Andreas Baader, and Jan Carl Raspe on 18 October 1977 in the Stammheim maximum-security prison outside Stuttgart. The "German Autumn" of 1977 provoked a series of responses within the Left-leaning West German cultural milieu. Most significant for the development of the essay film was the 1978–79 omnibus production *Deutschland im Herbst* (Germany in Autumn), produced in the immedi-ate aftermath of the Stammheim deaths.[27] *Deutschland im Herbst* is a series of loosely-pieced-together audiovisual sketches comprising fictional segments, archival footage, and interviews by nine filmmakers, including Kluge, Fassbinder, and Schlöndorff, who each respond to the "crisis" of violent state power directed against its citizens, the media blackout, and the escalating terrorism by young activists. The crisis, nearly a quarter of a century after the end of the Second World War, provides a situation for West Germans to directly confront and examine the past, which in turn leads to a series of traumatic confrontations. *Deutschland im Herbst* com-bines both fiction and nonfiction; it mixes documentary fact and footage with staged scenes and mini-dramas. It does not provide answers or con-clusions but is an open-ended inquiry, a film meant to provoke thought. As Adorno writes about the essay, it "finds its unity in and through breaks and not by glossing them over" (16). And Lukacs remarks that "the essential, the value-determining thing about [the essay], is not the verdict [at which it arrives] . . . but the process of judging" (18).

---

[27] For a detailed analysis of *Germany in Autumn* see Nora M. Alter "Framing Terrorism: Beyond the Borders," in *Projecting History: German Nonfiction Cinema, 1967–2000* (Ann Arbor: University of Michigan Press, 2002), 43–76.

Institutionally, in terms of the development of the German essay film, the late 1970s proved in many ways to be a watershed. The journal *Filmkritik* continued to play a seminal role as a venue for film theory and critique. From 1974 to 1984 Farocki and Bitmosky assumed editorship of the journal and focused fully on creating a counter public sphere for film criticism and reception. In 1979, the Hamburg Declaration of German filmmakers acknowledged the need for a synthesis between "feature film" and "documentary . . . films that reflect on the medium," recalling the much earlier appeal to the essay film outlined by Richter as a form that would bring together documentary and art cinema for social ends. During the 1980s the German essay film flourished with works such as *Reverse Angle* (Wenders, 1982), *Tokyo-Ga* (Wenders, 1985), *Bilder der Welt und Inschrift des Krieges* (Images of the World and the Inscription of War; Farocki, 1988), *Reichsautobahn* (Federal Autobahn; Bitomsky, 1986), *VW Komplex* (Bitomsky, 1990), *Die Macht der Gefühle* (The Power of Emotion; Kluge, 1983), and *Der Angriff der Gegenwart auf die übrige Zeit* (*The Assault of the Present on the Rest of Time*, also released in English as *The Blind Director*, Kluge, 1985). One of the main venues for funding and distribution was West German television. Indeed, the openness of television broadcasting networks was such that after 1985 Kluge abandoned filmmaking in favor of television production and even piloted his own television series, "Fact and Fiction" and "Cultural Window." Although essay filmmakers were producing work throughout Europe and North America, they were working in isolation or on the cultural margins without the sense of being part of a coherent movement or group. In contrast, in West Germany the essay film was consciously recognized and identified as an independent genre that was neither documentary nor art film.[28]

The year 1989 proved pivotal for many reasons. In terms of filmmaking it marked the revolution from analog to digital production. Anxiety about the loss of the negative and its attendant "truth" value was a recurring theme for several filmmakers. Wenders sought to make sense of this transformation and its implication for film production in his essay film, *Notebooks in Cities and Clothes* (1989). As important as the conversion from analog to digital was the "revolution" of the postwar world order—the collapse of the former Soviet Union, the alleged "death of Communism," in the Western world, and the triumph of capitalism. Films such as Andrei Ujica and Farocki's *Videogrammes of a Revolution* (1992) use found footage to reconstruct and comment on the official media reports of the final hours of Rumanian dictator Nikolai Ceaucescau and

---

[28] One of the earliest publications on the essay film was in German. See Christa Blümlinger and Constantin Wulff, *Schreiben Bilder Sprechen: Texte zum essayistischen Film.*

his wife. Their compilation of material attests to the role that the average citizen played in protesting the regime and enabling change to occur. Of course, in Germany the end of the former Soviet Union and its satellite states was particularly significant, because it ended the status of Germany as a divided country. All the events coalesced and were condensed into the powerful image of the fall of the Berlin Wall on 9 November 1989 (that now celebrated date conveniently replacing as a national marker another not so popular one from 1938). Films such as Ulrike Ottinger's *Countdown* (1990) trace the final days leading to the monetary unification of the two countries; Marcel Ophüls's *Novembertage* (November Days, 1991) presents reunification as a scathing musical comedy; and Jean-Luc Godard's *Germany Year 90 Nine Zero* (1991) is a nostalgic philosophical piece of mourning and lament. Nearly a decade later, Hito Steyerl examined contemporary Berlin involved in a process of reconstruction in *Die leere Mitte* (The Empty Center, 1999). In this film she focuses on the rebuilding of the Potsdamer Platz, once a vibrant center of Weimar activity, destroyed during the war, and left as an empty wasteland in the middle of the divided city. The rush to fill the empty space that serves as a scar and constant reminder of a past all too many want to forget becomes a thematic thread, filled with references to the Weimar past and the Third Reich, and with citations from Kracauer and Benjamin. In particular, Steyerl is concerned with the rising xenophobia and racism in the new Germany, which has led to attacks on foreigners and on Germans of Turkish and Asian origins. Her cinematic essay rings an alarm bell and signals a serious social and political crisis that the dominant media wish to bulldoze over. Through images and sounds, she brings together the past and present in a discomfiting constellation.

With the end of the Cold War, a new geopolitical alignment took place. The 1990s and the 2000s have been marked by increasing globalization. Gone are the postwar divisions of first world, second world, and third world. East and West have been replaced by "Central." Most significant for the development of the German essay film, however, is the formation of the European Union in 1993, followed by the implementation of the Euro as the currency for the majority of its members. The economic significance of a unified Europe for national cultural products cannot be underestimated. Various nationalist policies that previously supported individual artists were dismantled in favor of funding structures directed toward transnational or multinational projects. National and regional television support dried up, leaving many filmmakers stranded. With new regulations imposed through GATT and other treaties, cultural productions had to be increasingly trans- or multinational. Projects that involved several nations would be supported by the European Union. Instead of making films designed for a distracted and mobile spectator, often miniaturized on a small screen, some filmmakers embraced film as the entire institution of cinema. Ottinger has made extraordinary epic historical and ethnographic essays, such as the 501-minute German-Mongolian coproduction *Taiga* (1992), the Israeli-German four-hour *Exil Shanghai* (1997) and the Korean-German coproduction *Die koreanische Hochzeitsruhe* (The Korean Wedding Peace, 2009). Bitmosky, too, focuses on large-theater formats, making the 35mm *B-52* (2001) and *Staub* (Dust, 2007), two cine-essays that in their visual and aesthetic style are far removed from the low production quality of his earlier television essays such as *Reichsautobahn*. Bitmosky and Ottinger celebrate the medium of film, while concomitantly acknowledging that it is becoming an increasingly rarified "last machine."

However, the move into the art world was a totally new direction that all but abandoned traditional cinema. This new venue emerged because of changes within the visual arts and the art world. Film and video practice expanded and became accepted as an aesthetic medium along with painting, sculpture, and the like. New sources of funding for production, exhibition, and distribution were thus discovered by filmmakers who had previously relied on state sponsorship and television programming, as they increasingly turned toward and were picked up by galleries, large-scale exhibitions such as the Venice Biennale or Documenta, and eventually museums. However, this introduced a change in identity from "filmmaker" to "artist." It also meant a radical rethinking of a practice that was previously conceived of as single-channel projections of a preconceived size in a movie theater. Not only were multiple channels and screens encouraged, but also new ways of thinking about space—a space that contained mobile spectators who could walk around a screen, take in several projections at the same time, and be distracted by other variables in the space, and might only spend a couple of minutes on each projection—a far cry from the ritual of going to a theater to sit in the dark in silence for two hours, immersed in a concentrated, focused experience. Essayist Farocki addresses this transformation in his first two-screen installation, *Schnittstelle* (Cutting Point, 1995)—films are no longer screened in museums but actually staged for them. Farocki employs two separate screens within one viewing space to create what he refers to in a dialogue with Kaja Silverman focusing on Godard's *Numero deux* (1975) as a "soft montage." This unique form of montage comprises a "general relatedness" of images, "rather than a strict opposition of equation" produced by a linear montage of sharp cuts.[29] Soft montage therefore allows for an increased flexibility and openness of the text for the spectator—associations are suggested but not formally mandated. This form of montage is essentially a filmic parallel to Adorno's essayistic schema in

---

[29] Kaja Silverman and Harun Farocki, *Speaking about Godard* (New York: NYU Press, 1998), 142.

which "discrete elements set off against one another come together to form a readable context . . . [as] the elements crystallize as a configuration through their motion. The constellation is a force field, just as every intellectual structure is necessarily transformed into a force field under the essay's gaze."[30] In a recent work, *The Silver and The Cross* (2010), made for the exhibit *The Potosi Principle: How Shall We Sing the Lord's Song in a Strange Land*, curated by Alice Creischer, Andreas Sieckmann, and Max Jorge Hinderer, Farocki's work is exhibited as one film split between two sets of images. Each set of images contains either sequences from present-day Potosi, Bolivia, or details from Gaspar Miguel de Berrio's *Description del Cerro Rico e Imperial Villa de Potosi* (1758), a panoramic painting depicting the wealth, citizens, and laborers of the colonial city of Potosi, in Bolivia. During the sixteenth century Potosi was one of the wealthiest and largest cities in the world, with a population exceeding that of London. Not only was it the capital of silver production, but it also served as the first conduit for the global transportation of slave laborers from Africa, and later China. In the initial years the Spanish exploited the native population of Indians, who died by the thousands because of mercury poisoning; followed by Africans, and later Asians, who died from working in poor conditions at high altitude and from the ongoing mercury poisoning. The exact number of deaths has never been recorded, nor does any evidence remain today of that genocide. Farocki meticulously examines every square inch of the painting, performing an elaborate iconographical analysis in order to expose precisely that which is not shown or is left invisible. The painting depicts Potosi during its economic heights as a lively and vibrant city full of commerce, religious icons, and ceremonial processions. Also included are details of the waterworks constructed around the city to help in the production of the silver. However, what is omitted in this otherwise extremely thorough tableau is any sign of the exploitation of the various slave populations used to produce this enormous wealth. This conspicuous absence speaks of the massive violence—described by the voice-over as "large-scale genocide" wrought upon both the indigenous population and the foreign slave laborers. If the original painting seeks to capture a history that at the time of its production was already two hundred fifty years old, Farocki, another two hundred and fifty years later, produces an audiovisual history painting that à la Benjamin restores the "losers of history." The double-screen projection with its images from the past and the present, one set derived from the medium of painting, the other from digital photography, allows for a dialogue, a commentary. The narrative voice-over is performed by the same person (Cynthia Beatt) who delivered the text some

---

[30] Adorno, "Essay as Form," in *Notes to Literature*, vol. 1, trans. Shierry Weber Nicholsen (New York: Columbia University Press, 1991), 13.

twenty years earlier in Farocki's signature essay film, *Bilder der Welt und Inschrift des Krieges*. Her voice is factual, neutral, and without emotion as she delivers the counter-history of Potosi. The political critique of this audiovisual essay emerges in the contradictory imagery of the two screens, the black voids that provide the viewer with the time to pause, to think, and to contemplate.

The shift to a digital world created an unlimited audiovisual databank easily accessible for downloading. Indeed, Farocki's 2006 *Respite* is drawn from archival footage taken by an inmate in the Dutch Westerbrok transit camp. Farocki arranged and reedited the material and inserted explanatory intertitles. As in much of his earlier work (and in this he differs completely from Ottinger), the images are not his own but are drawn from other sources—found footage. At the same time, just as downloading is easy, so too is the posting of material. In order to reach a public, actual exhibition sites are no longer necessary. Individual audiovisual essays can be posted on You-Tube or Facebook. New mobile technologies allow for immediate accessibility wherever one is. What does this mean for the genre of the essay film? Only that it continues to change with the times. To conclude, let us return to Richter. Writing in 1955, he observes, "The progressive cinema can no longer be identified simply with artistic cinema."[31] In other words, there has to be a social and political dimension. In an era where making audiovisual images has become easier than ever before and the audiovisual essay has become a preferred form, one that eschews rules and regulations, a plea for a politics of the genre is still necessary. For Adorno, after all, the essay constitutes the political form par excellence—and so too it should be for essay films.

---

[31] Richter, *The Struggle for the Film: Towards a Socially Responsible Cinema*, 29.

3: The Limits of Futurity: German Science-Fiction Film over the Course of Time

Lutz Koepnick

Count Down

FRITZ LANG'S 1929 *Die Frau im Mond* (The Woman in the Moon) is rightly known for its invention of the so-called "countdown" practice and hence for how science-fiction cinema has the ability to envision and shape our use of various technologies long before their actual arrival. Lang's film abounds with images and procedures later generations came to associate primarily with the sober ingenuity of the NASA space program, whether we think of the slow passage of the rocket to its launch pad, the travelers' intricate preparation for take-off, or the capturing of the experience of weightlessness. A product of Lang's well-known preoccupation with space travel, *Die Frau im Mond* thus seems to do what science-fiction cinema does at its best, namely mobilize elaborate special effects for engineering a credible preview of coming technological attractions. And yet today's audiences may find it quite difficult to sit through an entire screening of *Die Frau im Mond* for reasons other than mere curiosity. The film's historical achievement, its ability to prefigure a future that has become a future generation's past, has also contributed to the film's relative oblivion. Precisely because history has proven Lang's imagination right, *Die Frau im Mond* no longer holds our attention. The film's posthumous fate is representative of the unique dilemma of both science-fiction filmmaking and the critical writing about this genre. Dedicated to visions of futurity that are both stunning and believable, science-fiction features have to risk rapid aging and forgetting in order to keep believably ahead of reality. Any attempt to write the history of science-fiction cinema has to reckon with this problem—the fact that science-fiction films inhabit multiple times at once and, in their very historical meaning, are not immune to the historian's present itself.

While *Die Frau im Mond* might count today as one of Fritz Lang's most forgotten films, Lang's other science-fiction film of the 1920s, *Metropolis* (1927), continues to occupy every cinephile's list of top

Fig. 3.1. Die Frau im Mond *(1929). Screenshot.*

favorites. Though its staggering production costs almost wrecked the entire German film industry, the film has kept its ability to fascinate viewers and stun our imagination. Its set designs—futuristic high-rise buildings, fancy laboratory settings, multilevel transportation systems, menacing factory halls, and functionalist underground housing—have lost little of their visual appeal, while the its narrative, in spite of all its flaws and convoluted economy, has remained powerful enough to bond the viewer's identification and encourage ever-new interpretations. As it envisioned a seemingly distant future of dehumanizing machines and acute social antagonism, *Metropolis* was very much able to address and rework the anxieties of an age—the turbulent years of the Weimar Republic—deeply torn about the meaning of past, present, and future. It proudly displayed the work of newest special effects, yet it also provided ample fodder for viewers perceiving the course of Weimar modernization as deeply unsettling and threatening. *Metropolis* had (and continues to have) something for everyone: romance and action, heroism and malevolence, emotional drama and social commentary. As importantly, however, the film developed its visual and narrative energy, not by turning its back on the present, but by probing into the present's very hopes, confusions, and fears. It reached out for something timeless by embracing rather than opposing its own contemporaneity. It thus excelled in what critics like J. P. Telotte understand as one of the key ideological operations of mainstream science-fiction filmmaking: humanizing the abstracting thrust of technological change and thus rendering more moderate how modern (and postmodern) societies project themselves into the future.[1] Lang never shied away from charging his vision of futurity with eclectic mythological clichés, and *Metropolis*'s unique status as a cult classic results in large measure from how the film blended different generic modalities and historical temporalities—how it inscribed the future in the past and defined tomorrow's struggles as echoes of mythological, historical, or present-day conflicts.

The exceptional longevity of Lang's *Metropolis* illuminates why *Die Frau im Mond*, though often considered one of the first "serious" science-fiction films in the history of (German) cinema, has failed to command viewers' attention in the long run. Consider the launch sequence in the first part of *Die Frau im Mond*, stretched out over almost ten minutes and offering more detail than narrative filmmaking in most cases can really tolerate. We begin with a public lecture, audience members laughing callously at Professor Manfeldt's plan to travel to the moon so as to mine its presumed gold resources. We cut forward in time to witness Professor Manfeldt's dream come true. An extended shot presents the rocket in all its impressive design, including its dual cameras engineered to picture the moon during the rocket's approach. An animation sequence illustrates the planned flight trajectory from earth to moon. We see various shots of crew members approaching and entering the rocket, applauded by the ground crew and then chased by a mob of photographers. We have to endure the very slow transfer of the rocket to its launch pad. We witness the travelers' elaborate anticipations of take-off. We read about the successful separation of mothership and start rocket, and then cut to close-ups of a speedometer and of the astronauts' faces reflecting the space ship's enormous speed. What stitches all these images together is the presence of a radio announcer who is repeatedly shown on a special viewing platform supplying his listeners as much as the film's viewers with explanatory commentary. This choice, of course, is surprising, given the status of Lang's work as a silent film that was shot and released when synchronized sound was about to become the new standard of cinematic pleasure. Yet far from reading the role of Lang's announcer as a nod to the newest hype in filmmaking itself, we must see it as a symptom of the film's curious and often quite paradoxical overdetermination, of structural ambivalences quite paradigmatic—as we will see later—for much of what can be considered as German science-fiction cinema.

Silent as it is, the voice of Lang's announcer in *Die Frau im Mond* might be in need of textual representation to be heard. But his primary function in the film is to produce an excess of discourse able to

[1] J. P. Telotte, *A Distant Technology: Science Fiction Film and the Machine Age* (Middletown, CN: Wesleyan University Press, 1999).

simultaneously fire up and frame the viewer's attention as much as that of the diegetic listener. The role of the announcer, as master of ceremonies, is, on the one hand, to pronounce the technology of space travel to be a self-fulfilling prophecy and self-contained spectacle. In lockstep with the role of media representatives in many science-fiction films, his principal function is to authenticate the film's vision of futurity, presenting space travel as a wonder whose miraculous thrust cannot be questioned, as a special effect taking on the brute force of a natural presence, as a sublime attraction firmly thrusting us into the future. On the other hand, however, in choosing the impossible, namely, in visualizing a radio announcer's address in a silent feature and thus visually severing voice from body, Lang works really hard to ensure that the viewer's fantasy will not get too much ahead of itself. He deliberately splits the operations of speech: his principal goal here is to celebrate the purity of his futuristic vision and stress his film's pedagogical value—to make us both feel awe for the future's rationality and soberly reflect about the wonders of tomorrow. Imaginative technologies, in science-fiction film, need persuasive special effects to bond the viewer's attention and affect, but Lang's film at the same time hesitates to grant the future too much apparent reality, so as to make it clear that this future is meant to be a product of scientific reason rather than blind emotion. What here is intended to open science fiction's window onto tomorrow is words, not bodily action; arguments, rather than speechless identification; reason and discourse, instead of spectacle and melodramatic emotion.

Unlike Lang's *Metropolis*, then, which freely mixed different narrative tropes, generic elements, and historical myths so as to offer a richly embodied vision of the future, *Die Frau im Mond* turns out to be too pedagogical and explicatory in detail, too much concerned with the "science" in science fiction, too little dedicated to the materiality of telling tales of the future to serve as a lasting vehicle of fantasy. In this, *Die Frau im Mond* prefigures what would come to haunt many of the relatively few German science-fiction productions ever since: an authoritative tone of sobriety and rationalist restraint, not simply privileging dispassionate images over both affective narratives and bedazzling special effects, but also continually expressing deep-seated anxieties about the genre's most fundamental task of conjuring alternative life worlds, of conjoining fantasy and futurity. One of the most underrepresented genres in the history of German filmmaking, German science-fiction cinema has frequently more to tell than to show, to explicate rather than to engross. Its representative films tend to be descriptive rather than full of dramatic action; they seek to produce discourse about the future and to frame our understanding of things to come instead of creatively borrowing from various narrative and visual inventories to project gripping stories and unexpected visions of tomorrow. With the exception of *Metropolis*, the majority of German science-fiction films lack strong narrative drives and inventive self-confidence. Like the radio announcer in Lang's *Die Frau im Mond*, they have a propensity to teach (and preach), to lecture and elucidate, as if trying to outdo their own scientists, space travelers, and engineers with forms of rationalist reflexivity that afford no narrative space for the unpredictable messiness of desire. What German science-fiction cinema often tends to ignore is the fact that the mere attempt to offer believable previews of both the possibilities and the dangers of tomorrow does not necessarily make good science-fiction cinema.

It is no exaggeration to say that science fiction works at its best whenever it allows viewers to thread fantasy and desire into the images (and sounds) presented on screen—to desire the future in all its precariousness and in this way to explore the unsettled nature of the present. Science fiction cannot do without effective elements of affect, understood here as film's ability to move the viewer and set our imagination in motion. As *Die Frau im Mond* exemplifies, however, German science-fiction cinema all too often is quite reluctant to move viewers in ways that could cloud their rationalism. This cinema tends to envision futures in which technology and science seem to deplete the very resources that make narrative and popular filmmaking tick. If science-fiction film in many respects is always also about the future of cinema itself, about its ability to involve ever-new technologies to shape our fantasies, desires, and daydreams, German science-fiction films overwhelmingly picture the future as if it no longer required or allowed for what we expect from cinema, as if the world of tomorrow and the grounds of cinematic pleasure were mutually exclusive. It is my task in the following pages to chronicle and explore this rather impossible position and course of German science-fiction film through time in further detail.

Science Fiction and/in German Culture

The body of work belonging to German science-fiction cinema is so lean that the term itself appears to be somewhat of a misnomer. To speak about the development and presence of a certain genre requires our ability to identify a rich tradition of representatives referenced and reworked in each and every of its instantiations, defined by a discrete set of narrative or audiovisual elements, and discussed by producers, critics, and audiences alike as fitting an identifiable corpus of film. Yet no matter how we tweak the conceptualization of generic identity, it does not take much to question whether science-fiction cinema in Germany ever really consolidated into a genre in the first place. And even if we stress the historical, cultural, and hence pragmatic inflections of specific genre formulas (rather than operating with a universalizing concept of individual genres as transcultural archetypes or unifying myths), the relative dearth of what may count as German science-fiction film remains stunning. To write about science-fiction cinema in Germany, as a result, always also means to engage with the presence of an absence and contemplate possible reasons for why the rockets of German science-fiction cinema—in spite of some notable exceptions—never really took off.

This is not to say, of course, that German filmmakers other than Fritz Lang completely stayed away from projecting the future and telling tales of marvelous science or unheard-of engineering. In the immediate wake of the First World War and the impact of Expressionist art on Weimar filmmaking, German cinema experienced a brief first swell of science-fiction themes, funneled through that era's predilection for fantastic horror and its uncanny distortions of the real. Though set in some seemingly distant past, Paul Wegener's *Der Golem, wie er in die Welt kam* (The Golem and How He Came Into the World, 1920) deserves as much mention here as Eugen Illés's *Alraune* (Mandragora, 1918) and Robert Wiene's two features *Genuine* (1920) and *Orlacs Hände* (The Hands of Orlac, 1924), films that drew in varying degrees on Expressionist cinema's penchant for the figure of the mad scientist. Starting with Lang's *Metropolis* and *Die Frau im Mond*, a second wave of domestic science-fiction productions stretched from the last years of silent-film technology across the final troubles of the Weimar Republic into the early moments of the Nazi era. Georg Wilhelm Pabst's *Die Herrin von Atlantis* (Queen of Atlantis, 1932) and Karl Hartl's *F.P.1 antwortet nicht* (F.P.1 doesn't answer, 1932) belong to this group, as they brought synchronized sound to German science-fiction cinema, as do films such as Kurt Bernhardt's *Der Tunnel* (The Tunnel, 1933) and Hartl's *Gold* (1934), films released after the inauguration of the Nazi regime but not necessarily to be counted as integral moments in Joseph Goebbels's "ministry of illusion."[2]

Whereas the films of the early 1920s relied heavily on the romantic motif of the sorcerer conjuring forms of life that turn against their own creators, the science-fiction productions of the early 1930s time and again revolve around the figure of the modern engineer trying to establish networks of traffic and connectivity across expansive geographies. In accord with the Expressionist focus on uncanny doubles and fantastic shape shifters, the films of the 1920s repeatedly articulated profound concerns about the authenticity of the corporeal, the spiritual, and the human vis-a-vis the technological possibilities of simulating life; these films often found their present's future in the past, poetically triangulating the role of the inventor or (mad) scientist with that of both the artistic genius and

---

[2] Eric Rentschler, *The Ministry of Illusion: Nazi Cinema and Its Afterlife* (Cambridge, MA: Harvard University Press, 1996); for an extended analysis of Bernhardt's *Der Tunnel*, see Lutz Koepnick, "Screening Fascism's Underground: Kurt Bernhardt's *The Tunnel.*" *New German Critique* 74 (Spring/Summer 1998): 151–78.

Fig. 3.2. Clockwise: Die Herrin von Atlantis *(1932);* F.P.1 antwortet nicht *(1932);* Der Tunnel *(1933);* Gold *(1934). Screenshots.*

the divine creator. In the films of the 1930s, by contrast, modern technologies of transport and communication play an important role to fortify a troubled (male) body against the very modernity it so eagerly wants to inhabit. Future technologies here might unsettle bourgeois understanding of home, subjectivity, and identity, but they also provide ample redemptive resources to reshape the subject and his body and in so doing build new postbourgeois communities.

Although it is tempting to explore possible correlations between the role of technology in the science fiction of the early 1930s and the rise of Nazi power and its reengineering of the body politic, it is important to note that neither science-fiction motifs nor the horror genre or the fantasy film had much staying power during the later 1930s. Nazi cinema tried to massage minds and coordinate desire, but unlike Hollywood in the 1930s it had little tolerance for transporting its audiences to unknown places and times, for scaring viewers with wacky scientists and gruesome monsters, or for contemplating the future as a site of either utopian or dystopian energy. The fact that it took German cinema until the late 1950s to launch the next series of science-fiction vehicles, and that this new series initially originated from East Germany's DEFA studios rather than its West German counterparts, should in addition make us wonder whether strictly political brackets are really the most useful tools to periodicize the scattered presence of science-fiction cinema in Germany. In spite of its deepening political alliance with the United States during the 1950s and Hollywood's quite successful pursuit of science-fiction formulas during the same period, West German film studios did virtually nothing at all to emulate the role of science-fiction films in Hollywood as a means to play out Cold War tensions, nuclear anxieties, and the pressures of the space race. Aside from a few mad scientists populating West-German films of the 1960s, the only notable exception was the TV miniseries *Raumpatrouille: Die phantastischen Abenteuer des Raumschiffes Orion* (Space Patrol: The Fantastic Adventures of the Spaceship Orion, 1966), which was broadcast in fall 1966 on West Germany's ARD channel in seven installments and—like World Cup soccer and various films of the Edgar Wallace TV series—succeeded in emptying German streets, with viewing rates of up to 56 percent. East German audiences, on the other hand, during the same period had considerably more luck in viewing domestic science-fiction productions on cinema screens, even though some of the most prominent films of the time resulted from complex collaborations with other East bloc nations. Kurt Maetzig's *Der schweigende Stern* (Silent Star, 1960) and Frank Vogel's *Der Mann mit dem Objektiv* (The Man with the Camera, 1961) are early representatives of DEFA science-fiction productions, whereas Hermann Zschoche's 1972 *Eolomea* and Gottfried Kolditz's 1976 *Im Staub der Sterne* (In the Dust of the Stars) provide later examples. Although shot at the height of both the Cold War and the GDR's dictatorial attempts to restrict the mobility of its population, most of DEFA's science-fiction films not only capitalized on themes of space and time travel, but—like their West-German counterpart *Raumpatrouille*—regularly featured highly international sets of characters; that is, research and space-flight collaboratives whose emphatic diversity moved viewers beyond the factual division of the world after the construction of the Berlin Wall.

In its preoccupation with special effects, and with the special effect that is cinema itself, science-fiction productions lend themselves ideally to probe cinema's ability to conjure semblances of the real, animate fantasy, and mesmerize the spectator. Some of the most memorable films of Georges Méliès, in their very early effort to explore the visual possibilities of moving pictures around 1900, resulted from direct engagements with science-fiction themes. It should therefore come as no surprise that a number of West-German filmmakers associated with the New German Cinema of the late 1960s and 1970s alluded to the science-fiction genre in their effort to free German cinema from the burdens of the past and to experiment with alternate and active forms of viewership. Alexander

Fig. 3.3. Upper row: Raumpatrouille: Die phantastischen Abenteuer des Raumschiffes Orion *(1966). Lower row:* Der schweigende Stern *(1960). Screenshots.*

Kluge's 1971 *Der große Verhau* (The Big Mess) could be named here as much as Werner Herzog's *Fata Morgana* of the same year, Rainer Werner Fassbinder's TV miniseries *Welt am Draht* (World on a Wire, 1973), and Wim Wenders's highly self-reflexive *Der Stand der Dinge* (The State of Things, 1982) and—somewhat later—*Bis ans Ende der Welt* (Until the End of the World, 1991). But to think of these films, including even more recent work by Werner Herzog such as *The Wild Blue Yonder* (2005) and *Encounters at the End of the World* (2007), as viable contributions to the genre of science-fiction films would grossly miss the point, not simply because these films primarily engage science-fiction elements as a vehicle for exposing the seductive power of the cinematic image, the commercial aberrations of the film industry, and the circularity of mainstream viewership, but because in so doing they seek to defy the very condition of popular filmmaking and its essential reliance on genre formulas. Kluge's, Wenders's, or Herzog's films of the period used science-fiction elements in order to situate themselves outside the very bounds of commercial filmmaking and its genre system. While much could be said about the aesthetic and intellectual merits of, for instance, *Der große Verhau* or *The Wild Blue Yonder*, such a discussion has no real place in an essay seeking to trace the commercially mediated pleasures of formulaic repetition and variation that are at the core of genre filmmaking.

In the absence of any real sense of formal continuity and domestic viability, German science-fiction cinema since the early 1980s has had little opportunity to improve its public visibility and market share. On the contrary, in the wake of Hollywood blockbuster productions such as the original *Star Wars* trilogy (1977–83), the *Terminator* sequels (1984, 1991), the critically acclaimed *Blade Runner* (1982), and other large-scale science-fiction productions, German cinema has been unable to mobilize the resources in order to meet audience expectations. Some critics and viewers may have welcomed Roland Emmerich's 1984 *Das Arche Noah Prinzip* (The Noah's Ark Principle, 1984) and *Moon 44* (1990) as viable entries to the genre, but in retrospect these films largely document the extent to which science-fiction filmmaking today has become Hollywood-bound, evidenced not least of all by Emmerich's own move to Los Angeles and his consequent success with films such as *Stargate* (1994), *Independence Day* (1996), *The Day after Tomorrow* (2004), and *2012* (2010). The only notable exception in this respect is Michael Herbig's 2004 *(T)Raumschiff Surprise—Periode 1* (Dreamship Surprise—Period 1), which attracted almost 10 million viewers to German theaters (twice as many as Emmerich's *The Day after Tomorrow* during the same year). But in spite of all the film's references to the *Star Wars* and *Star Trek* franchises, its futuristic setting and (moderately persuasive) special effects, it is difficult to argue that German viewers embraced it because of its science-fiction setting—rather than primarily because of Herbig's signature style of parody and trash, his over-the-top gags and ridicule, his sexual innuendos and consistent staging of utter foolishness. Just as his previous feature *Der Schuh des Manitu* (Manitou's Shoe, 2001) relied on selected motifs of the Western genre in order to parody, not so much the genre itself, but a whole gamut of contemporary things German, in *(T) Raumschiff Surprise—Periode 1* science-fiction elements are a mere pretense, deliberately transparent, to crack jokes about pretty much all and everything. The film dared to do what science fiction in Germany had rarely done, namely to hybridize the generic elements of science fiction with those of other successful genres, but it did so to such as degree that critics, producers, and viewers alike were hard-pressed to recognize this film as science fiction in the first place—rather than primarily as comedy.

Failures to Launch

In his *Hollywood Genres* Thomas Schatz emphasizes the extent to which the pleasures of genres result from cumulative viewing processes whose stress on ritualistic repetition operates as a vehicle of social integration:

> The first viewing of a Western or musical actually might be more difficult and demanding than the viewing of a non-genre film, due

to the peculiar logic and narrative conventions of a genre. With repeated viewings, however, the genre's narrative pattern comes into focus and the viewer's *expectations* take shape. And when we consider that the generic pattern involves not only narrative elements (character, plot, setting) but thematic issues as well, the genre's *socializing* influence becomes apparent.[3]

Science-fiction filmmaking in Germany never really achieved what Schatz considers the quasi-contractual power of cumulative patterns and shared expectations. Though German audiences have clearly enjoyed viewing science-fiction films imported from Hollywood, the products of German science-fiction filmmakers often look and sound as if they are made for viewers who are watching science fiction for the first or perhaps even the last time. Rather than appealing and reshaping the audience's expectations, science-fiction films in Germany tend to struggle with their own lack of tradition and hence self-assuredness. They provide stories, settings, and protagonists constantly engaged in trying to persuade the viewer that they are dealing with science fiction to begin with. They evoke the category of genre, not as a rich source of patterns, formulas, conventions, and variations, but as something in need of being defined and reinvented with each and every film. German science-fiction cinema, in other words, is best described as a cinema continually searching for, while also shying away from, its status as genre. It enunciates rather than assertively draws on existing formulas; it explains in great detail the peculiar meaning of its narrative turns and special effects instead of trusting viewers to bring into play their familiarity with other examples. As if haunted by the assumption that science fiction, because of its ethos of inventing the unknown, would call for radical newness in each and every of its instantiations, German science-fiction cinema has shown considerable anxiety about the genre's logic of repetition and as a result has come to offer films that, by and large, frustrate the viewer's own meaning-making and hence the socializing function of cinematic viewing.

It is not difficult to identify some of the basic reasons for the relative dearth of German science-fiction productions since the 1920s and hence for the fact that German science-fiction films never really coagulated into a proper genre in the first place. Other reasons, however, are of a more complex nature and—because they seek to conceptualize the presence of an absence—may involve some more speculative activity. Let me, in the remainder of this essay, develop five possible explanations for the failure of science-fiction films to achieve some sense of generic identity in Germany, reasons that range from industry-related aspects all the way to long-standing anxieties about the relationship between technology and culture in modern German society.

---

[3] Thomas Schatz, *Hollywood Genres: Formulas, Filmmaking, and the Studio System* (New York: McGraw-Hill, 1981), 11.

First, like no other genre, the fantastic extravaganzas of science-fiction filmmaking are deeply tied to the health and optimism of a particular film industry. Making science-fiction films is an expensive business; it requires considerable costs for futuristic set designs and elaborate special effects, as it needs to display future life worlds without drawing too much attention to their artifice. Just as space-travel programs are spearheads of technological innovation, science-fiction cinema plays an essential role in moving the present state of filmmaking into the future. It stimulates the development of innovative technologies and mechanisms so as to attract the viewer's attention, and it requires this industry to be willing to abandon current technological inventories and assemblies so as to dominate the film industry in the future. If the narratives and spectacular images of science-fiction films wrestle with the issue of technological progress, successful science-fiction filmmaking requires an industrial base eager to embrace technological progress for the sake of progress—eager to introduce costly new special effects that make yesterday's effects seem to belong in the realm of immature fancy.

As the developments of the last thirty years indicate, the primary base for mainstream science-fiction filmmaking today is Hollywood, precisely because local film industries such as that in Germany find it increasingly difficult to marshal the necessary production costs and to move confidently into the future. This trend, however, is not an entirely new one. As is well known, ever since the end of the First World War German filmmaking has found itself in a curious love-hate relationship with Hollywood cinema, trying to emulate Hollywood formulas while at the same time seeking to churn out popular products of its own. Science-fiction filmmaking in Germany, understood as the film industry's litmus test for commercial viability and technological innovativeness, suffered more than any other genre from this rivalry; this was amplified by the fact that strong periods of German mainstream film production such as the later 1930s and the 1950s coincided with periods in which larger ideological exigencies sidelined futurity and instead highlighted the dynamic of the present or hoped to revamp this present in the image of the past. Though national film industries such as the British, the French and, at times, also the German have often actively participated in Hollywood's drive toward technological and economical self-reinvention, science-fiction filmmaking today is rather at odds with the realities of national cinemas. The overt use of flat irons as space-ship controls in *Raumpatrouille* may have produced many laughs and smirks among contemporary German viewers, but it was indicative of the fact that chronic budget limitations put national film industries in a rather disadvantageous position when they were trying to engineer a future whose design could compete with the seamless pleasures Hollywood has been able to project onto international screens since at least the 1950s.

Second, the total dearth of West-German science-fiction produc-tions in the immediate postwar period, when compared with Hollywood's contemporary preoccupation with alien takeovers and even with East German cinema's sporadic forays into space travel in the early 1960s, sug-gests another reason for the want of futurity on German screens at least since the end of the Second World War: the lasting burdens of a violent past haunting the present in each and every one of its moments. As is well known, in the late 1940s and 1950s West-German popular cinema took flight into rural picture-postcard settings, whose preindustrial, anti-urban, and often in fact quite unhistorical veneer invited viewers to block out memories of the immediate past and encounter the Now in disguise borrowed from a much older historical moment. Though West-German popular filmmaking was perhaps not as escapist as critics and filmmak-ers of previous decades regularly assumed,[4] it certainly was not ready to turn its gaze toward the future, be it to celebrate some utopian other-ness or express anxieties about where coming technological developments might take the nation. If genre filmmaking involves a triangulated con-tract between filmmakers, film producers, and audiences, the contracts of West-German postwar cinema did not include screening the future's seeds in the present. West-German cinema throughout much of the postwar period was largely engaged in catching up with the present while fending off various specters of the past; people were troubled by repressed memo-ries and eager to stabilize their place amid the new mise-en-scène of rela-tive prosperity, burgeoning consumer culture, and social and geographical mobility. That DEFA studios, on the other hand, were much more willing to project images of tomorrow may, among other reasons, also reflect the existence of a considerably different memory culture in the GDR, one according to which the ideological dogmas of anti-fascism consid-ered the present to have mastered the troubling remnants of the past and thus cleared the ground for more confident gestures of moving into the unknown. Rather than feeding on (Hollywood's) Cold War paranoia of the late 1950s and early 1960s, DEFA science-fiction features such as Maetzig's 1960 *Der schweigende Stern* allowed internationalist crews of scientists to travel space collaboratively precisely because their Soviet bloc members allegedly had long triumphed over and contained the violent particularism and imperial aspirations of fascism. The spectacular flatness of narrative and character development in these films, however, may also be seen as a direct expression of the extent to which DEFA science fiction owed its existence to stifling processes of ideological overdetermination,

---

[4] For more differentiated accounts, see Johannes von Moltke, *No Place like Home: Locations of Heimat in German Cinema* (Berkeley: University of California Press, 2005), and John Davidson and Sabine Hake, eds., *Framing the Fifties: Cinema in a Divided Germany* (New York: Berghahn, 2007). See also Jaimey Fisher's essay on 1950s war films, chapter 5 in the present volume.

a dogmatic repression of the past not so much different from the West's attempts at forgetting after all. In face of the divided memory culture of the immediate postwar era, West-German genre filmmakers shunned futuristic scenarios altogether, whereas East-German screens exhibited tomorrows whose listless absence of drama, depth, and passion hinted at nothing so much as the fervor by which GDR ideologues sought to emancipate the present from the past and considered the future as a vacuum to be filled solely by the unclouded rationalism of socialist engineers.

Third, science-fiction filmmaking, in Hollywood and elsewhere, thrives heavily on the proliferation of science-fiction motifs in other arenas of cultural production: the sparks of fan communities, widely read novels, serialized fiction, Popular Science magazine, and so on. It thus comes as no surprise that the brief heyday of German science-fiction cinema in early and late Weimar Germany as well as during the middle years of the GDR coincides with periods in which science-fiction writing and fandom was able to garner some attention: the often quite conservative fantasies of Hans Dominik during the 1920s represent one end of the spectrum of science-fiction writing, while the socialist realist projections of East-German writers during the 1950s are representative of the other.[5] But for each moment in which science-fiction writing in twentieth-century Germany was able to claim some respectability and legitimacy, many other moments could be named in which futuristic fantasy was largely denigrated as trash and idle diversion—a denigration that in turn deeply affected the film industry's willingness to risk the production of quality products. The reasons for the strikingly low status of science fiction in German culture even beyond the domain of film are manifold, and much older than the twentieth century itself. Unlike the French or British literary scene, in whose context authors such as Jules Verne and H. G. Wells were able to develop science-fiction writing into a reputable genre prior to or around 1900, science-fiction writing in Germany at the same time largely suffered from the German intelligentsia's refusal to bridge the gap between the rise of modern technology and civilization on the one hand, and on the other, the realm of aesthetic pleasure and cultivation. Because, for Germany's highbrow elite, aesthetic culture and modern technology inhabited different planets, tales of space flights, alien encounters, and time travel had little chance in garnering any artistic merit. In spite—or perhaps precisely because of—of the international success of German scientists in the late nineteenth and early twentieth centuries, fictional versions of future science were disparaged as both a vilification of scientific rationalism and a debasement of the true spirit of poetic culture, as a genre of writing void at the same time of both true content and form.

---

[5] For more on science fiction writing in the GDR, see Sonja Fritzsche, *Science Fiction Literature in East Germany* (Oxford: Peter Lang, 2006).

Imperial Germany's privileging of aesthetic cultivation over technological civilization had a profound impact on the way in which German
cinema engaged with what is at the core of science-fiction fantasy, namely,
the belief in the transformative power of future technology. If the so-
called *Kino-Debatte* during the early decades of film production was eager
to rescue the German project of high culture from cinema's foray into
the commercial and the popular,[6] it simultaneously defined strict limits
for an active development of science-fiction motifs within filmic representation as well, science fiction in the specifically German context being
understood as one of the popular cinema's most vacuous and commercially degraded layers. Much more willing to understand technological
achievements as cultural artifacts, Germany's French neighbors enjoyed
science-fiction writing long before it received any attention in Germany.
Early film pioneers such as Georges Méliès actively engaged with science-
fiction elements in order to explore the power of the cinematic apparatus,
its ability to displace ordinary structures of time and place, its capacity to
foster a fascinated gaze and thus make us suspend our disbelief, and its
unprecedented capability of celebrating motion and indexing the passing
of time. In light of the initial absence of any strong efforts to integrate
modern aesthetic and technological culture, the German cinema of the
early 1900s never really witnessed the likes of pioneers such Méliès. As
a result this cinema largely failed to explore the curious kinship between
filmic technology and science fiction—the extent to which cinema itself
in its entire apparatical setup is a special effect that lends itself ideally to
tell stories about unknown times, spaces, and futures. Whereas for Méliès
the popular genre of science fiction revealed the truth about cinema's
abilities, the technological bias of German culture in the early 1900s
sought to curb such associations and to remake cinema in the guise of
more esteemed, older aesthetic traditions. Science fiction, in the peculiar German context, represented what intellectuals and ideologues feared
most about cinema. It was seen as offering a medium for mind-numbing
diversion and facile pleasure, consuming the viewer with images of inau-
thentic artifice and the presentation of technology as spectacle.

Film genres cannot function without drawing on internal traditions
and strategies of variation. However, they do not thrive unless they are
also able to rework semantic elements and syntactic narrative patterns that
circulate outside the cinema at any given point in time. German cinema,
far beyond the early decades of the twentieth century, has set aside comparatively little space for science-fiction filmmaking, because the traditional breach between technology and culture remained open for many
years to come and thus led to a striking marginalization of science-fiction

---

[6] Anton Kaes, *Kino-Debatte: Texte zum Verhältnis von Literatur und Film,
1909–1929* (Munich: dtv, 1978).

writing and fandom in the larger domain of culture. Continually haunted by the anti-technological legacies of modern Germany, German film culture and its critics have always felt much more comfortable about seeing its auteurs expose the technological wonders of the cinematic medium rather than observing commercial genre filmmakers—however critically—in their effort to mirror the appeal of the cinematic apparatus and the power of science fiction in each other.

Fourth, as Janet Staiger has argued persuasively, Hollywood, even at its most classical, never pursued pure structures of generic conventions and hence never produced films that appealed to one category of genre only. For both theoretical and historical reasons, genres have always been more messy and internally varied than critics have assumed, in spite of their legitimate desire to find patterns of identity and order amid factual variety and abundance. Fordian as much as post-Fordian cinema thrived on the power of incorporating—of inbreeding and hybridizing—multiple generic formulas and allusions. Staiger wants us to reserve the term "inbred" for intra-cultural and "hybrid" for cross-cultural forms of recombination.[7] Though in her argument she does not address the genre of science fiction, its history both during and after the classical studio area neatly illustrates her thesis, given the critical importance of other generic conventions—horror, fantasy, the Western, film noir, action, road movie, disaster film, melodrama, and others—for the development of the genre at different times. In all likelihood, we know instantly how to identify a science-fiction film as such when we see it, but the dynamic and popularity of Hollywood science-fiction films has in large measure rested on their ability to serve as a vehicle of generic inbreeding and thus of recombining familiar narrative patterns and audiovisual inventories for their own cause. No genre is ever as pure and autonomous as its producers, critics, and fans want it to be, including the often seemingly antiseptic and highly ordered universe of science-fiction.

As if the relative absence of a viable and respected science-fiction tradition in German literary culture was not enough, German science-fiction filmmaking has simultaneously suffered throughout the entire twentieth century from the relative weakness of other generic modalities able to inbreed with domestic products and provide them with narrative energy and attraction. With the brief exception of Expressionist filmmaking, in which science-fiction productions such as *Der Golem*, *Orlacs Hände*, and *Metropolis* actively drew on horror and melodrama, German science-fiction filmmaking has always found itself in a comparatively hostile position precisely because of the severe limitations to generic cross-fertilization within the space of a film industry in which action, disaster, and fantasy

---

[7] Janet Staiger, "Hybrid or Inbred: The Purity Hypothesis and Hollywood Genre History," in *Film Genre Reader III*, ed. Barry Keith Grant (Austin: University of Texas Press, 2003), 185–201.

have historically had comparatively little currency. The effect of this structural dilemma for science-fiction filmmaking in Germany has been twofold. Unable to achieve productive inbreeding, German directors on the one hand pursued the making of science-fiction films not only as if representatives of this genre would be shot and seen for the first or for the last time ever, but also as if it was the filmmaker's task to define this putatively new genre as a pure and autonomous entity—as something that didn't need other generic elements in order to inspire its plots and appeal to the viewer's desire. German science-fiction productions, from *Die Frau im Mond* to *Silent Star* and *Space Patrol Orion*, have largely failed to draw on action, horror, crime, or even melodrama to make their stories and characters tick, a failure that is due to filmmakers' pursuit of generic purity. As a result, their narratives tend to be dull and their psychology forced. On the other hand, overcompensating for the absence of ample domestic sources of generic crossover, German science-fiction films have often chosen to double their efforts in pursuing what Staiger, with some reservation, would call generic hybridization. They have, with great conspicuousness, borrowed from or alluded to the futuristic films and stories developed elsewhere (Hollywood, the Soviet Union), hoping to exploit strategies of intercultural transfer as a film's primary attraction. While in *Dreamship Surprise—Period 1* this overdetermined grasp for hybridity results in rather juvenile inanity, the prominent internationalism of early 1930s and of later DEFA features rarely masks the fact that the mere presence of English techno-language or Soviet cosmonauts is not enough to produce compelling science fiction. Whether they actively defied the idea of generic inbreeding or overcompensated for the lack of domestic traditions with forced transculturalism, German science-fiction filmmakers had limited resources to remedy the adverse conditions for successful production processes. This weakness of science fiction in German film history also reflects the weakness of all kinds of other genres in German filmmaking. We would therefore be mistaken to fault individual directors for films marked and marred by the overarching structural restrictions of German cinema.

Fifth, in spite of its often deep-seated dystopianism, science-fiction filmmaking actively inscribes futurity into the present. It might warn the viewer about the perils of tomorrow, of a future in which machines destroy the bonds of community, and excesses of technological reason obliterate the foundation of meaning and humanity. But it rarely does so without celebrating the ability of cinematic technology to project this future on screen, thus fusing technophobic anxieties about the present and the future with a technophilic admiration of the extraordinary power of filmmaking to capture the unknown.[8] Unlike any other category of genre filmmaking,

---

[8] Michael Ryan and Douglas Kellner, "Technophobia," in *Alien Zone*, ed. Annette Kuhn (London: Verso, 1990), 58–65.

science fiction projects unknown futures as much as it relies on proven syntactic or semantic conventions. Each film is called upon to develop new special effects able to envision the future as we have never been able to see it before. It must subscribe to a formalized logic of progress in whose context the hunt for innovative techniques of representation constantly marks today's standards and conventions as unrealistic and hence outmoded. In this, science-fiction filmmaking occupies one of the last bastions of the project of Enlightenment and its belief in ongoing development and perfectibility. Notwithstanding its often pessimistic and quite conservative concern about the future of humanity, science fiction is, as a mode of industrial filmmaking, deeply optimistic. It designates and constantly discards the present as the future's past, driven by what strikes producers and audiences alike as an irresistible rhetoric of transformative newness.

There are good reasons for arguing that German twentieth-century culture has largely lost this sense of technological progressivism, of cultural history as a project of linear progress and automatic transformation to something better. Adorno and Horkheimer's infamous ruling—"the wholly enlightened earth is radiant with triumphant calamity"[9]—may not exactly be on every moviegoer's favorite reading list. But Adorno and Horkheimer's critique of the dialectical entwinement of enlightenment and domination, of cultural progress and mythic regression, has clearly come to occupy an important position amid the entire landscape of twentieth-century German thought and self-understanding. Deeply skeptical about any further progressivist vision of newness and advancement, this critique defines strict limits as to what drives mainstream science fiction in the first place. It cannot but disparage science fiction's magic of technological innovation and transformative rationality as helplessly naive and undialectical, including the genre's often paradoxical duality of technophobia and technophilia. Science fiction, as seen from the vista of German critical culture's disenchanted and despairing reason, wants to have its cake and eat it too. It entertains viewers with technologically innovative visions of the hazards of technology, whereas the true challenge would be to show how the logic of science-fiction filmmaking itself produces the very specters its narratives seek to exorcize. In its undialectical belief in the transformative nature of technological progress and abstract rationality, science fiction thus belies whatever Germans could and should have learned from the disastrous course of rationality in their own history. Although such Adornonian stances may no longer be shared by many Germans today, an underlying skepticism about the future of progress remains pervasive and clearly corrodes any self-confident pursuit of science fiction as a project of situating the

---

[9] Theodor W. Adorno and Max Horkheimer, *Dialectic of Enlightenment: Philosophical Fragments*, trans. Edmund Jephcott (Stanford, CA: Stanford University Press, 2002), 1.

future in the present. As a result, science fiction has become German film culture's perhaps most guilty pleasure. Hollywood's ever-growing dominance in the global science-fiction market answers to a peculiarly German need: it allows German audiences to revel in pleasures that, if produced by German film companies themselves, would strike critics and viewers alike as deeply problematic and illegitimate.

Rotwang Reloaded?

The two single most iconic and famous images of German science-fiction cinema no doubt stem from one and the same sequence of Fritz Lang's *Metropolis:* the image of the scientist Rotwang as he manipulates all kinds of fantastic machinery in the hope of transferring the flesh, heart, and life from Maria, the saintly preacher of the catacombs, to Maria the robot, a figure meant to seduce and discipline the unruly masses while at the same time embodying Rotwang's frustrated male desire; and the image of Maria the robot in Rotwang's laboratory, light rings wandering up and down her metallic exterior, special effects finally supplying her mechanical body with the real Maria's bodily features and thus seemingly consummating the triumph of science over the exigencies of the real.

As is well known, Rotwang's victory is not meant to last, as the robot's simulated surfaces will eventually unravel and both the city's leaders and its proletarian population will learn to recognize and embrace the authenticity of the heart. Like Rotwang's fleeting exuberance, the success of German science-fiction filmmaking also proved to be fleeting, never again managing the visual and narrative energy that propelled *Metropolis* to international triumph. Successful genre filmmaking, as Rick Altman has influentially argued, requires the competent deployment of both syntactic and semantic dimensions. As a "concatenated series of events regularly repeated according to a recognizable pattern,"[10] genre cinema needs iconographic building blocks (such as certain props, atmospheric settings, plot situations, and character types) shared across an extended body of work as much as it necessitates identifiable structures (such as predictable forms of plot and character development; specific principles of editing and montage) stitching these building blocks into relatively predictable textual orders. In mixing diverse narrative, visual, and stylistic inventories, *Metropolis* uniquely managed to organize syntactic and semantic elements into an effective constellation, one that was clearly able to resonate, not only when it was released but also over decades to come, with what Altman calls genre's pragmatic dimension—the way in which audiences respond to, appropriate, contest, and thus co-constitute what we can call genre in the first place. The majority of German science-fiction films,

---

[10] Rick Altman, *Film/Genre* (1999; repr., London: BFI, 2002), 84.

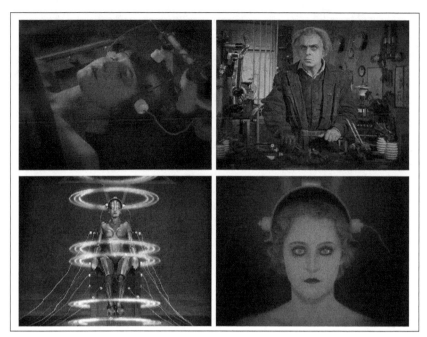

Fig. 3.4. Metropolis *(1927). Screenshots.*

whether produced prior to or after *Metropolis*, whether produced on the western or eastern side of the Wall, before its construction or in its aftermath, have never fared as well as Lang's unwieldy work. The reasons for Rotwang's final defeat are also at the heart of the dilemma of German science-fiction film. Like Lang's at once medieval and hypermodern magician-scientist, German science-fiction cinema may at times have engaged complex special effects and technologies, not simply to invent new futures, but in so doing to recuperate the dreams of the past. Yet rarely, in this effort, have science-fiction filmmakers in Germany been able to do what genre filmmaking requires most: to participate actively in an ongoing and therefore quasi-transhistorical dialectic of repetition and variation; to self-confidently tap into and contribute to a recognizable stream of meanings, images, narrative structures, and spectatorial expectations. Like the inventor-cum-genius Rotwang, whose lab is isolated from the rest of the world and whose inventions primarily serve his own private needs, German science-fiction film as a whole has never really succeeded in galvanizing sharable patterns and recurring meanings across an extended stretch of time. Science fiction thus figures as German cinema's most spectral genre. In most of its discontinuous instantiations, it haunts a past that never was and projects—mostly from scratch—near or distant futures that are not destined to be.

4:   The Situation Is Hopeless, but Not Desperate: UFA's Early Sound Film Musicals

Eric Rentschler

Beyond the Haunted Screen

"THE WEIMAR CINEMA has never been a particularly popular cinema," writes Thomas Elsaesser. "It has always been something of a film-maker's or a film scholar's cinema."[1] In this assessment, the films made in the Weimar Republic stand out above all by dint of the formal accomplishment and intellectual appeal of "individually authored art films."[2] Commentators who share this persuasion applaud the masterpieces of Ernst Lubitsch, Fritz Lang, F. W. Murnau, and G. W. Pabst and focus on the mean streets, dread spaces, and eccentric narratives of what Lotte Eisner called "the haunted screen," from *Das Cabinet des Dr. Caligari* (The Cabinet of Dr. Caligari, 1920), *Nosferatu* (1922), and *Dr. Mabuse, der Spieler* (Dr. Mabuse, the Gambler, 1922) to *Metropolis* (1927) and *Die Büchse der Pandora* (Pandora's Box, 1928) along with other films of the fantastic, street films, chamber room melodramas, and big-city symphonies.[3] The hallmarks of the silent era have without a doubt played a much more estimable role in the history of German cinema than the productions made after the coming of sound and the Nazi takeover. Despite its unquestionable veracity, this argument has also unwittingly helped to foster a partial and occluded view.[4] A more inclusive approach would

---

[1] Thomas Elsaesser, "Film History and Visual Pleasure," in *Cinema Histories, Cinema Practices,* ed. Patricia Mellencamp and Philip Rosen (Frederick, MD.: University Publications of America, 1984), 81.

[2] Thomas Elsaesser, "Film History and Visual Pleasure," 71.

[3] See Lotte H. Eisner, *The Haunted Screen: Expressionism in the German Cinema and the Influence of Max Reinhardt,* trans. Roger Greaves (Berkeley: University of California Press, 1973).

[4] To this day many observers persist in equating Weimar cinema with Expressionist film—a mighty feat of abbreviation, both reductive and inaccurate, given that of the more than 3,500 German features that premiered during that era only a handful of them bear the earmarks of the period style. For a detailed

want to consider, along with the period's canonized productions, its less well-known genre films.

At first blush, most German sound features from the late 1920s and early 1930s seem to be decidedly out of synch with the harsh and harried *Zeitgeist*, a time of mass unemployment, economic instability, political unrest, and existential disquiet.[5] Indeed, the vast majority of genre films from the Weimar Republic's last years, especially the many musical comedies, would seem best characterized as *ungleichzeitig*, or out of keeping with the times.[6] Here we behold performers who move with grace and ease, language that is perky and insouciant, and lavish set designs that bear few traces of grim realities. There is an intrepid vitality and an abundance of good cheer, even in the midst of crisis; despite imposing odds, the denizens of these fantasy worlds remain chipper and unflappable. Produced in a country that was dancing on a volcano, these films provide light fare for hard times. The situation may be hopeless, they suggest, but it is not desperate.[7]

In Weimar film musicals, which for the most part are operettas, bodies and spaces are constantly in motion; these symphonies of silliness celebrate mobility and transport. At the start of *Die Drei von der Tankstelle* (The Three From the Filling Station, 1930), a car hurtles down a country lane; the top is down, and its male occupants are in the finest of fine fettles. Trees zoom by, and the camera alternates between a whirring front wheel and a rear view from a side mirror. The entire scene unreels to the accompaniment of a spirited song:

---

and differentiated account of German Expressionist film, see Jürgen Kasten, *Der expressionistische Film: Abgefilmtes Theater oder avantgardistisches Erzählkino? Eine stil-, produktions-, und rezeptionsgeschichtliche Untersuchung* (Münster: MAkS, 1990).

[5] The philosopher Karl Jaspers, in his important 1931 diagnosis of the precarious final years of the Weimar Republic, wrote that people have "been uprooted . . . It is as if the foundations of being had been shattered . . . The foundations of life quake beneath our feet." Jaspers, *Die geistige Situation der Zeit* (Berlin: de Gruyter, 1931); in English, *Man in the Modern Age*, trans. Eden Paul and Cedar Paul (New York: Anchor, 1957), 2.

[6] *Ungleichzeitigkeit* is the key concept of Ernst Bloch's seminal analysis *Erbschaft dieser Zeit* (Zurich: Oprecht & Helbling, 1935); in English, *Heritage of Our Times*, trans. Neville Plaice and Stephen Plaice (Berkeley: University of California Press, 1991).

[7] The phrase is a variation of Karl Kraus's often quoted adage, "Die Lage ist hoffnungslos, aber nicht ernst," here "verzweifelt, aber nicht hoffnungslos." See Kraus, *Erlaubt ist, was missfällt: Karl Kraus zum Vergnügen*, ed. Günter Baumann (Ditzingen, Germany: Reclam, 2007).

Fig. 4.1. Die Drei von der Tankstelle *(1930). Screenshot.*

Sunny day, lovely day
Heart aflutter and the motor running!
Agreeable goal, agreeable start
And a most pleasant journey[8]

and a spunky score. *Quick* (1932) begins in an exclusive spa with state-of-the-art fitness machinery devised to make muscles taut and faces firm. The resort's fussy guests, fixated on the state of their health, devote their abundant leisure time to the pursuit of diversion. Echoing the dramatic prologues from Arnold Fanck's mountain films, *Die verliebte Firma* (The Company's in Love, 1932) commences with some dissolves over breathtaking panoramas. As the light musical treatment intimates, however, this first impression is illusory; after measuring the sublime immensity of the Alpine landscape, the camera narrows in on a singing romantic couple. This film about the making of a film quickly takes leave of the authentic location and moves to a big-city studio setting.

These sound fantasies are time machines as well. *Das Flötenkonzert von Sanssouci* (The Flute Concert of Sanssouci, 1930) spirits us away to Dresden in 1756, sampling conversations among a gathering of emissaries from countries conspiring against Prussia. The opening tracking shot lasts a full four minutes, granting us ample occasion to school our gaze in the play of signs and signals. Everything is coded here, we learn, even the musical accompaniment, so that seemingly innocuous phrases ("Isn't politics also a matter of not talking about politics?") assume political

---

[8] The German original is "Sonniger Tag! Wonniger Tag! / Klopfendes Herz und der Motor ein Schlag! / Lachendes Ziel!" All translations are my own, except where otherwise credited.

Figs. 4.2a and 4.2b. Der Kongreß tanzt *(1931). Screenshots.*

meanings. In *Der Kongreß tanzt* (The Congress Dances, 1931), cannons mark the start of a new day in 1814 at the Congress of Vienna. A voyeuristic camera sidles through a room full of people eagerly awaiting the latest developments. The most recent arrivals to the conference confirm that all of Europe is represented at the event; meanwhile, cannons continue to resound as nervous officials sneeze with equal loudness. From this antechamber we move to Count von Metternich's bedside where, in a touch reminiscent of Ernst Lubitsch, world history takes place behind closed doors.[9] Over breakfast, the statesman monitors the vast proceedings via an elaborate network of minions and machines.

With great emphasis, these features implement the means of audiovisual reproduction, putting gramophones, radios, and projectors on conspicuous display. *Das Lied einer Nacht* (One Night's Song, 1932) opens with the sound of a voice and the shadow of a microphone, which yield to the shadow of an announcer and then the shadow of a performer. A dissolve to a long tilt up radio towers is followed by another dissolve to an antenna on a building top and a pan across a window and into a living space. The mediated voice has, we see, found an audience, a dog sitting in front of a radio and listening to a loud male singer. The camera cuts seamlessly to a man with his mouth wide open—not a performer, but a patient at the dentist's office. There is an inordinate energy and irreverence in the subsequent cuts between places, faces, and spaces, as the film catapults from Vienna to Budapest to Bucharest; as a train travels through the night, we track the path of a telegram over the wires.

Einbrecher (Burglars, 1930) takes us behind the scenes and offers a hands-on view of a technology that creates artificial worlds. The first shot provides a close-up of a singing torero, an animated figure redolent of a tale by E. T. A. Hoffmann, and opens up to a gathering of costumed cyborgs, stand-ins for the make-believe beings who inhabit the film we are about to see. A Walt Disneyesque *metteur en scène* directs the proceedings

---

[9] The comparison with Lubitsch comes from Karsten Witte, "Too Beautiful to Be True: Lilian Harvey," trans. Eric Rentschler, *New German Critique* 74 (Spring–Summer 1998): 38.

in a laboratory for mechanical puppets. Later in the film a song reiterates the imaginary trappings of the world before us:

The dog looks alive,
The child speaks,
A world of simulations.
Everything moves in turns.
Inside her is only clockwork,
Not a heart.

The Cultivation of Distraction

One might say, as Weimar contemporaries often did, that most early German sound endeavors were vapid and formulaic, indeed clockwork constructions without a heart.[10] Film studios certainly realized that this thought was on many critics' minds—and did not hesitate to acknowledge it. Toward the end of *Die Koffer des Herrn O. F.* (The Suitcases of Mr. O. F., 1931), for instance, two executives from OTAG (Ostend Feature Film, Inc.) reflect on how their studio's new features might best respond to the strained economic climate. Their recipe for success is standardized light fare with only the most modest variations. The studio head gestures proudly to posters of coming attractions, images of romantic pairs who will appear in future operettas: *Ich liebe, Du liebst, Er liebt, Wir lieben, Ihr liebt*—and, finally, to fill out this grand ensemble of six films, *Alle lieben*. And that is not all. There are also plans for similar productions with a martial aspect, as we see in a further profusion of posters: *Kasernenduft: Eine Tonfilm-Operette* (The Aroma of the Barracks: A Sound Film Operetta), *Kasernenzauber* (The Magic of the Barracks), *Es ist lustig zu marschieren* (It's Fun to March), and *Kasernenluft* (The Air of the Barracks). In this economy, revue films coexist cozily with military reviews.[11] "A film with deeper meaning," maintains the studio boss, facing the camera in a close-up, "is of interest to no one. A film without deeper meaning is what a big city needs."

German features of the early sound era, apart from a few notable exceptions, have indeed been seen as lacking deeper meaning. Weimar cinema, by and large, is equated with the silent era before 1929; it has

---

[10] See Rudolf Arnheim, "Escape into the Scenery (1932)," in *Film Essays and Criticism*, trans. Brenda Benthien (Madison: University of Wisconsin Press, 1997), 190. Speaking of recent German features, he says "there is little of note as regards the development of sound film—as is the case everywhere in contemporary film production."

[11] Cf. Witte's seminal essay on German revue films, "Visual Pleasure Inhibited: Aspects of the German Revue Film," trans. J. D. Steakley and Gabriele Hoover, *New German Critique* 24–25 (Fall–Winter 1981–82): 238.

gone down in film history as a site of modernist endeavor that contributed substantially to international understanding of the medium's expressive potential and exercised an indelible influence on the very notion of what constitutes a film. Its chief significance for the scholars who established its critical reputation abides in its status as a "motor of modernity," as an entity that in crucial ways fueled Germany's belated and conflicted attempts to become a modern nation.[12] Features of the era at once enact and embody the tug and pull within this national body between the old and the new, between modern and antimodern initiatives. German films of the early 1930s, apart from unquestioned masterpieces such as Lang's *M* and *Das Testament des Dr. Mabuse*, seemed in comparison devoid of substance and seriousness. If there is anything modern about early German sound films, it would seem to be their industrialized uniformity.

Even though comedies constituted a full one-third of the features produced during the Weimar era, they invariably take a back seat to German films of the fantastic and surely suffer when placed beside contemporary generic counterparts made in France and the United States. No German director of the 1920s, beyond the young Lubitsch and, on occasion, Reinhold Schünzel and Ludwig Berger, has received particular recognition; discussions about German film comedies more often than not focus on performers.[13] Early German musical comedies do not hold up well when compared with works by René Clair, Lubitsch, or Rouben Mamoulian: *Die Drei von der Tankstelle* pales next to *Sous les toits de Paris* (1930) and *Der Kongreß tanzt* is surely no *Love Parade* (1932). And the only German filmmaker who could rival Busby Berkeley's masses in motion would be Leni Riefenstahl. The popular early musical comedies, especially those produced by UFA's Erich Pommer, were frequently charged with being escapist and negligible.[14] There were, to

---

[12] Anton Kaes, "Film in der Weimarer Republik: Motor der Moderne," in *Geschichte des deutschen Films*, ed. Wolfgang Jacobsen, 2nd rev. ed (Stuttgart: Metzler, 2004), 39–98.

[13] See Georg Seeßlen, "Das Unterhaltungskino II: Das Spiel mit der Liebe—Aspekte der deutschen Stummfilmkomödie," in *Die Perfektionierung des Scheins: Das Kino der Weimarer Republik im Kontext der Künste*, ed. Harro Segeberg (Munich: Fink, 2000), 95–96.

[14] UFA's early sound musicals include *Melodie des Herzens* (Hanns Schwarz, 1929), *Liebeswalzer* (Wilhelm Thiele, 1930), *Die Drei von der Tankstelle* (Thiele, 1930), *Einbrecher* (Schwarz, 1930), *Ihre Hoheit befiehlt* (Schwarz, 1931), *Nie wieder Liebe* (Anatole Litvak, 1931), *Bomben auf Monte Carlo* (Schwarz, 1931), *Der Kongreß tanzt* (Erik Charell, 1931), *Zwei Herzen und ein Schlag* (Thiele, 1932), *Das Lied einer Nacht* (Litvak, 1932), *Quick* (Robert Siodmak, 1932), *Ein blonder Traum* (Paul Martin, 1932), *Ich bei Tag und Du bei Nacht* (Ludwig Berger, 1932), *Ich und die Kaiserin* (Friedrich Hollaender, 1933), *Ein Lied für Dich* (Joe May, 1933), *Walzerkrieg* (Ludwig Berger, 1933), *Saison in Kairo* (Reinhold Schünzel, 1933), and *Viktor und Viktoria* (Schünzel, 1933).

be sure, several realist films that addressed social circumstances and confronted unresolved political problems; *Kameradschaft* (Comradeship,
1931) and *Westfront 1918* by Pabst (1930) and Bertolt Brecht and Slatan
Dudow's *Kuhle Wampe* (1932) are noted exceptions to the rule. Josef
von Sternberg's *Der blaue Engel* (The Blue Angel, 1930) had musical
numbers, but no one would mistake it for a comedy. The much larger
ensemble of films, it was—and often still is—said, sought to transform
the gravity of reality into a kinder and gentler unreality. Lightweight fare
(which did not necessarily have a light touch) was a preferred approach:
operettas and revues, social comedies, romances, and farces with a folksy
flair. "Again and again," Rudolf Arnheim wrote about German film
releases of 1931, "we note with dismay that we must flee into a void
when we want to amuse ourselves."[15]

Three concerns have strongly inflected discussions of early German
sound comedies. First, contemporary commentators met the coming of
sound in general with suspicion, claiming, as did Arnheim, that it would
mean the death of cinema as an art because its higher level of realism
threatened to undermine "all the exceptional qualities of silent film
that we had loved."[16] In a retrospective assessment, Siegfried Kracauer
elaborated on how the presence of sound divested the image of its sug-
gestive and evocative power. Verbal statements, he submitted, tend to
articulate intentions whereas camera shots apprehend the unintentional
and the unspoken. Silent films probed "levels below the dimension of
consciousness, and since the spoken word had not yet assumed control,
unconventional or even subversive images were allowed to slip in. But
when dialogue took over, unfathomable imagery withered and intentional
meanings prevailed." He went on to note that both talkies and silent films
contain ideological inscriptions, "although analysis of these attitudes is
hampered rather than facilitated by the addition of spoken words."[17] Béla
Balázs was hopeful that sound films might "teach us to analyse even cha-
otic noise with our ear and read the score of life's symphony"—in short,
that they might train the human ear, just as silent films had trained the
human eye.[18] Unfortunately, he later admitted, these great hopes would
rarely find fulfillment in the sound era.[19]

A second complaint was that the sound comedies intensified film's
powers of distraction. The UFA musicals of the early sound era were seen,

---

[15] Rudolf Arnheim, "Hans Albers (1931)," 220.

[16] Arnheim, "Sound Film Gone Astray (1932)," 42.

[17] Siegfried Kracauer, *From Caligari to Hitler* (1947; repr., Princeton, NJ:
Princeton University Press, 2004), 205.

[18] Béla Balázs, *Theory of the Film*, trans. Edith Bone (New York: Dover, 1970),
204. First published in 1945.

[19] Béla Balázs, *Theory of the Film*, 194.

in Arnheim's words, as film confections.[20] They appeal to "what is bad and stupid in man" and ensure "that dissatisfaction shall not burst into revolutionary action but shall fade away in dreams of a better world." These industrial commodities legitimate the status quo and stultify the possibility of collective resistance;[21] they fortify belief in the church and the power of capital; they also propagate the sanctity of marriage and the home.[22] According to Ernst Bloch, writing in 1929, distraction fuels emotion without creating momentum and "dams life back to nothing but youth, to inflated beginnings, so that the question concerning the Where to never arises."[23] Distraction is evasion, a deception "which is supposed to conceal the place and ground on which it occurs"; life becomes fully determined by the interests that govern the status quo: tedium by day, escape by night.[24] People come to regard their material limits and experiential lacks through the eyes of the powerful and big business. "In the evening, when lit, the dust of the day looks really colourful and alluring. This entices, but does not fulfil, does not create the desire for more genuine things, but for things that are always new."[25]

A third objection was even more emphatically political. The most prominent escapist sound comedies issued from UFA, a studio taken over in 1927 by the media mogul Alfred Hugenberg and dominated since then by his right-wing agenda. These productions colluded with nationalist and reactionary designs, increasingly so after Hugenberg, as chairman of the supervisory board, allowed political dictates to determine the studio's direction. In 1930 the critic Hans Sahl spoke out against Hugenberg's upbeat panegyrics for the German military, his *Zapfenstreiche*, saying that they agitated against reflection, transforming the sound film into "a German tragedy." Hugenberg, Sahl elaborated, "is fortunate in his control of a contingent of cinemas that permit him to add these films to

---

[20] In his scathing review of *Der Kongreß tanzt*, Arnheim calls it "a gumdrop" and mockingly cites approving words about the film that appeared in the *Lichtbildbühne*: "What's been concocted is a confection that will tickle the palates of the unknown millions to whom this film is dedicated, like manna from heaven." Rudolf Arnheim, "Partly Expensive, Partly Good (1931)," in *Film Essays and Criticism*, 175.

[21] Rudolf Arnheim, *Film*, trans. L. M. Sieveking and Ian F. D. Morrow (London: Faber & Faber, 1933), 171. In 1931 two influential analyses of the commercial film apparatus's regressive workings appeared in German translation: Ilja Ehrenburg's *Die Traumfabrik: Chronik des Films / The Dream Factory* (Berlin: Malik, 1931) and René Fülöp-Miller's *Die Phantasiemaschine / The Fantasy Machine* (Berlin: Zsolnay, 1931).

[22] Arnheim, *Film*, 176.

[23] Bloch, *Heritage of Our Times*, 25.

[24] Bloch, *Heritage of Our Times*, 26.

[25] Bloch, *Heritage of Our Times*, 36.

the repertoire without drawing any attention."[26] The films that stirred the masses and provided emotional sustenance during the last years of Weimar, observes Klaus Kremeier, were not leftist productions by Pabst or Brecht or Willi Münzenberg, but rather UFA's melodramas, comedies, films about Prussia, waltz fantasies, and barracks comedies. The progressives simply failed to understand collective dispositions and thus remained unable to address the masses' inner cravings.[27]

While still sensitive to the objections of critics such as Arnheim, Balázs, and Kracauer, recent commentators have suggested that we might approach the early sound films in less dismissive ways and regard them as integral parts of the Weimar legacy.[28] In reconsidering the significant exemplars of UFA sound operettas made before the Nazi ascent to power, we in fact gain a sense of critical acumen and a decided self-consciousness; the films are very much self-aware products of their times and not just regressive and, as such, symptomatic texts. If we put these works into dialogue with films of other genres, we encounter different answers to similar dilemmas: diverse strategies for dealing with times of crisis and the crises of the times. In the process, we can comprehend the diversity of ways in which the Weimar Republic was both experienced and cinematically represented.[29] The seeming antagonisms of apparently nonsynchronous film

---

[26] Hans Sahl, "Zapfenstreich bei der Ufa," in *"Und doch . . ." Essays und Kritiken aus zwei Kontinenten*, ed. Klaus Blanc (Frankfurt am Main: Luchterhand, 1991), 99.

[27] Klaus Kreimeier, *Die Ufa-Story: Geschichte eines Filmkonzerns* (Munich: Hanser, 1992), 208.

[28] Notable endeavors in this vein include contributions on UFA operettas by Thomas Koebner, Jörg Schweinitz, and Corinna Müller in *Diesseits der "Dämonischen Leinwand": Neue Perspektiven auf das späte Weimarer Kino*, ed. Thomas Koebner (Munich: edition text + kritik, 2003), 341–408; Michael Wedel's well-researched and comprehensive monograph *Der deutsche Musikfilm: Archäologie eines Genres, 1914–1945* (Munich: edition text + kritik, 2007); and Corinna Müller, *Vom Stummfilm zum Tonfilm* (Munich: Fink, 2003). In English, see Elsaesser, "It's the End of the Song: Walter Reisch, Operetta, and the Double Negative," in Elsaesser, *Weimar Cinema and After: Germany's Historical Imaginary* (London: Routledge, 2000), 330–58.

[29] The bicycle race between two window washers in *Ein blonder Traum* recalls the opening sequence of *Kuhle Wampe*, but with a decided tonal difference: the friends are having fun, which cannot be said of Bertolt Brecht's desperate jobseekers. Villa Blitz, the country squatter's hut in *Ein blonder Traum*, likewise brings to mind the homeless community called Kuhle Wampe. The life of the disfranchised in the UFA feature was decidedly at odds with the situation presented in Slatan Dudow's short documentary, *Zeitprobleme: Wie der Arbeiter wohnt* (Contemporary Problems: How the Worker Lives, 1930).

artifacts, as Karsten Witte once observed, "can in fact produce historical insights."[30]

Communities of Circumstance

In 1930 the German Reich was 1.7 billion Reichsmarks in debt, and four million people were unemployed. An article in the trade paper *Film-Kurier* in July 1931 posed a question very much on the minds of UFA studio executives: "What then would be more needed now than an offering of films that might lead audiences out of this spiritual vacuum and offer something that is both uplifting and distracting?"[31] *Die Drei von der Tankstelle*, produced by Erich Pommer, put this upbeat resolve into practice and became the most successful film of the 1930–31 season.[32] A trio of friends (Willy Fritsch, Heinz Rühmann, and Oskar Karlweis) return from a long vacation to find their servants gone and their belongings impounded. "Something very unpleasant happened during your absence," says their lawyer. An earthquake? they wonder. Or maybe a change of government in Lippe-Detmold? This was after all a seismic time full of unpleasant surprises, particularly in Lippe-Detmold, where two years earlier the Nazis had won their first regional election. And in the state elections on 14 September, a day before the film's premiere, the Nazis had scored a decisive breakthrough. Asked if his wife perhaps might have had a blond child, the lawyer (played by a German Jew, Kurt Gerron) says no; things are "even worse than that: you're bankrupt."

The production registers the state of economic emergency and political turmoil, all the better to make light of it. Nonetheless, the rise of the Nazis along with a tweak of Jewish anxiety do not go unacknowledged. The bankrupt trio remains unmoved by the challenge to their financial status; they bounce about in unison, cheerfully contemplating all the things they will have to do without, singing "Great God, we're bankrupt." Werner R. Heymann's five songs bring an undeniable vigor to the film, as does Franz Planer's intimate lighting (for instance, in the romantic duet, "Liebling, mein Herz lässt Dich grüssen"/"Darling, my heart sends its love to you"), fine touches that make up for Wilhelm Thiele's often clunky mise-en-scène (particularly his maladroit blocking and circus-ring staging) and the sometimes-less-than-fluid editing. Hoping to recoup

---

[30] Witte, "Wie Filmgeschichte schreiben?" *epd Kirche und Film* 34, no. 12 (December 1981): 12.

[31] Described in Kracauer's article, "Not und Zerstreuung: Zur Ufa-Produktion 1931/32," *Frankfurter Zeitung*, 15 Jul. 1931.

[32] The titles of several films from 1932 were even more unabashed in their attempt at uplift: *Man braucht kein Geld* (You Don't Need Money) and *Es wird schon wieder besser* (Things Will Get Better Again).

Figs. 4.3a and 4.3b. Die Drei von der Tankstelle *(1930). Screenshots.*

their losses, the three comrades sell their car and buy a filling station on a heavily trafficked road in the boonies. Sharing the chores of attendant, all three become enamored by Lilian (Lilian Harvey), a sprightly blonde in a shiny convertible, though only one of them (as casting policy dictated, her steady romantic partner Fritsch) will gain her favor.

Through it all, what the film speaks of as "the three meshugge musketeers" never break a sweat; by no fault of their own, the sunny boys become executives in the Gas Station Corporation owned by Lilian's father. Even if reality intrudes in a brief documentary glimpse of the working day in a factory, this drab prospect is tempered by its protagonists' free-and-easy perspective:

> We've seen work from the distance
> And even from the distance it was not a pretty sight.

As in many contemporary UFA features, the pleasures of the male bond seem more compelling than the obligatory romantic union.[33] In the final moments, Willy (Fritsch) shakes hands with his friends and carries Lilian away from the scene. They pass through a curtain and suddenly stand before a spotlight. Looking into the camera, Lilian is astonished. There are people out there, she says, an audience! "Yes, indeed. A bunch of total strangers!" What are they doing there? What are they waiting for? Lilian quickly comes up with an answer: an operetta is not over until after the finale; to that end, the film offers a closing extravaganza in a protracted take that unites the entire cast of players.

---

[33] Lilian Harvey and Willy Fritsch, the German dream couple, appeared together in a dozen films between 1926 and 1939. As stars, however, their popularity did not extend beyond Germany. And without question the chemistry between them was not exactly explosive. When they come together at the end of films, their union is invariably sealed with a kiss, but the viewer remains hard pressed to imagine that it might lead to further intimate activity. More than anything, they are comrades, very much along the lines of Ben Barr Lindsey's *The Companionate Marriage* (1927), an American guide to domestic designs that was quite popular at the time in Germany.

An altogether different "bunch of total strangers" occupies a shabby rooming house in Robert Siodmak's *Abschied* (Farewell), of the same year; here the impact of hard times becomes far more palpable and poignant. In this anti-Grand Hotel people live at close quarters; intrusions by strangers into private spheres and personal affairs are common occurrences. Everyone is at loose ends, albeit hopeful that things will get better. The film's key romantic couple sustain a candid conversation about their prospective monthly income, minutely calculating how, if all goes well, their savings will accrue over time and what that accumulated amount will mean for their future well-being. Siodmak's drama, which grants nary a glimpse of exterior spaces, presents a claustrophobic community of circumstance that negotiates dire straits. In the end, we see Brigitte Horney, who has just been left high and dry by her lover, sitting alone in a darkness of emotional devastation. This finale is anything but a celebration:

> Everything in life is also like a song
> Fading and vanishing, a farewell.[34]

Too Lovely to Be True

The haunting theme song of *Abschied* evokes the ephemeral and precarious nature of human endeavor:

> How quickly we forget what once was
> Nothing remains of everything that once was.[35]

The signature tune of *Der Kongreß tanzt* does something similar in a far more reassuring fashion:

> Today all fairy tales become true
> Today one thing is clear to me
> That only happened once
> That never happens again
> That's too lovely
> To be true.[36]

The catch phrase "Das gab's nur einmal" has now become the incarnation of the nostalgic embrace of precious moments and past delights, a

---

[34] German original: "Alles im Leben ist auch wie ein Lied / Verklingt und entflieht, ein Abschied."

[35] German original: "Wie schnell vergißt man, was einmal war / Nichts bleibt zurück, alles war einmal."

[36] German original: "Heut' werden alle Märchen wahr, / heut' wird mir eines klar: / Das gibt's nur einmal, / Das kommt nicht wieder, / das ist zu schön, um wahr zu sein."

yearning for yesteryear's hit tunes or cinematic evergreens.[37] The past on view in this "superoperetta" (which cost a hefty 4 million Reichsmarks), directed by the master showman Erik Charell, is a simulacrum of Vienna, a site of court intrigue, balls, and waltzes, of sentimental schmaltz over Heuriger in Grinzing, and of Wiener Mädln and snappy marching cavaliers.[38] A love affair between the shop girl Christel (Harvey) and Czar Alexander (Fritsch) unfolds while the congress convenes. Hoping to distract Alexander from decisive deliberations, Metternich hires a seductive agent to waylay him; the czar in turn engages the dimwitted Uralsky (also played by Fritsch) as a body double.[39] Christel and Alexander thus have time for assignations while the gathered nations plot Europe's future. Upon learning that Napoleon has returned to France, however, Alexander puts an end to the whirlwind affair and bids farewell.

Although the film was the uncontested box-office hit of the season, it met with the extreme displeasure of influential critics. Kracauer deemed it "a senseless gathering of decorations"; in the name of amusement, the historical revue diverted attention from the true state of crisis and awakened "illusions and desires that can only serve the forces of reaction, and whip up a dust storm that totally blinds the audience."[40] Arnheim's assessment was every bit as harsh. It was a pity, he remarked, that members of the audience lacked the czar's power to deputize doubles: "I can think of people who would have liked to have sent stupid Uralsky to the film" in their place.[41] And yet, if *Der Kongreß tanzt* is an illusory concoction, it is one that makes no bones about its creation of illusions. Doubles stand in for characters in this fiction just as the film actors play their roles. The first view of Christel shows her responding to a foreigner's question: "Do you speak English?" No, she replies, which of course belies the contemporary spectator's better knowledge that the film star Harvey grew up in London. Metternich is a master surveiller, akin to Dr. Mabuse or the Frederick the Great of *Das Flötenkonzert von Sanssouci,* who at once oversees comings and goings and puts things in motion. In that way his interventions enable the spectator's own sensory ubiquity; as a guiding hand, he also figures as an onscreen surrogate for the director. His panoptic point of view is primarily aural; from his bedside control center he moni-

---

[37] Film critic Curt Riess's voluminous panegyric about the stars and productions of classical German cinema echoes the song's title. See *Das gab's nur einmal: Das Buch der schönsten Filme unseres Lebens,* 2nd ed. (Hamburg: Verlag der Sternbücher, 1957).

[38] Kracauer, *From Caligari to Hitler,* 208.

[39] Fritsch would also play double roles in UFA's *Walzerkrieg* (Battle of the Waltzes, 1933) and *Amphitryon* (1935).

[40] Siegfried Kracauer, "Kunst und Dekoration," *Frankfurter Zeitung,* 13 Oct. 1931.

[41] Arnheim, *Film Essays and Criticism,* 176.

tors what is going on in a room, and we then see what he hears—and in this way both share and exceed his access to the flow of information.

The film's famous theme song exalts a lovely moment that has passed and will not return. This might be read as a celebration of nostalgia, but if one considers the lines more carefully, it would seem to be nostalgia for something that perhaps never really happened, for an experience that was "too lovely to be true"—much like the film we are watching, which glorifies cinema's powers of illusion and makes them transparent. Sights and sounds unreel in an unceasing flow of motion that seems real but is of course imaginary. Precisely at the moment when Harvey sings of things being "too lovely to be true," memorializing, in Karsten Witte's words, the "glorious promise of the *status quo ante*," costumed cable carriers enter the image.[42] The song describes this profusion of light and movement as "ein goldner Schein," which in German has a double meaning. This "golden gleam" renders things bright and brilliant, so much so that it sometimes blinds us. In the film's rousing setpiece, the song itself exerts a contagious appeal during its performance in and passage through a number of social spaces, from the city to the countryside, with a changing cast of social classes singing the catchy lyrics and confirming the tune's irrepressible popularity. In the process, the film shows us the mediation of a self-conscious mass culture as well as revealing its illusory and false constitution, a dream machinery that openly acknowledges the spurious quality of its productions—"zu schön, um wahr zu sein" (too lovely to be true).

The Limits of Make-Believe

As a fictional artifact that reveals its own sense of potential and discloses its production of meaning, *Der Kongreß tanzt* was anything but unique. A number of UFA operettas laid bare the cinematic apparatus and, in so doing, made it apparent just how self-consciously the studio's talented and sophisticated creators had crafted their productions. Ludwig Berger's *Ich bei Tag und Du bei Nacht* (I in the Day and You at Night, 1932, released in English as *Happily Ever After*), in fact, could be said to ironize UFA operettas. In this regard, it was hardly an anomaly, for features that poked fun at film conventions, as Jörg Schweinitz has argued, abounded during the Weimar era.[43] Nonetheless, for all his critical awareness, director Berger was surely no Brecht who espoused anti-illusionism in the name of political enlightenment. Indeed, Berger first gained notoriety as a filmmaker enamored of fairy tales, as his whimsical Cinderella adaptation,

---

[42] Witte, "Too Beautiful to Be True," 38.

[43] Jörg Schweinitz, "'Wie im Kino!': Die autothematische Welle im frühen Tonfilm," in Koebner, *Diesseits der "Dämonischen Leinwand*," 373–92.

Fig. 4.4. Ich bei Tag und Du bei Nacht *(1932). Screenshot.*

Der verlorene Schuh (The Lost Shoe, 1923), attests. He crafted escapist scenarios endowed with *Stimmung*, hoping to shed light on the "golden gleam" of UFA's fantasy worlds and to provide a kind of enchantment in which spectators might find refuge without being blinded.

After his return to Germany from a disappointing three-year sojourn in Hollywood, Berger declined UFA's offer to direct *Der Kongreß tanzt*. *Ich bei Tag und Du bei Nacht*, shot also in English and French, would become his masterpiece. Two denizens of Berlin share a bed in the same rooming house, but in shifts. Grete (Käthe von Nagy) works as a manicurist by day; Hans (Fritsch) waits on tables in an upscale night club. (If the disposition were reversed, quipped critic Willy Haas, "this would not be an operetta, but rather a moral tragedy.")[44] Grete and Hans meet by chance on the street, each mistaking the other for someone of a higher-class station. The narrative's obvious destination, of course, is the resolution of this confusion of identities, so that the two can sleep next to—rather than after—each other.

The narrative of *Ich bei Tag und Du bei Nacht* contrasts escapist fantasies with everyday pursuits and shows how they interact. Each morning on his return to his part-time lodgings, Hans walks past a cinema and talks to the projectionist, Helmut. The film's opening sequence shows the start of *Dies alles ist Dein* (All of This is Yours), a Bombastik-Film production that outdoes any UFA extravaganza (even *Der Kongreß tanzt*) in its excessive escapism and opulent over-the-topness. Helmut is enthusiastic about the new release, quoting an approving critic on how this "real-life fairy tale" makes it clear that "the golden moment" will one day come to all of us. Grete, likewise, repeatedly compares her everyday life

---

[44] Willy Haas, "*Ich bei Tag und Du bei Nacht*," *Film-Kurier*, 29 Nov. 1932.

to what she sees at the cinema and seems happiest when the two overlap so that things "are just like the movies." Hans is not smitten by screen fantasies and, suspicious of being taken in by anything or anyone, considers films to be lies (*Schwindel*). Negotiating between these poles of naive acceptance and cynical reason, Berger's feature presents a modern world in which the media is an integral part. We hear popular songs emanate from projectors and phonographs as well as radios, so incessantly that we readily understand a landlady's complaint that "hit tunes are spreading like the plague." In their waking encounters, characters carry the movies with them. During an outing to Sanssouci, Hans and Grete manage to get locked in the music room of Frederick II. They hear a flute being played, as if the ghost of the Great King were present, albeit in the form of a reprise from UFA's Prussia film of several seasons back with Otto Gebühr, *Das Flötenkonzert von Sanssouci*. While in the castle, the couple also sees Expressionist shadow plays straight out of Murnau or Lang. The reality of their world (and this film) reminds them (and us) of other films.

The reality that *Ich bei Tag und Du bei Nacht* represents, however, is also that of contemporary Berlin. Although the film was shot almost without exception in the Babelsberg studio, it provides a primer for the navigation of modern times and urban spaces. Characters dwell in part-time quarters that are anything but cozy or commodious. We see a glimpse of Hans's wallet, which is all but empty. Again and again we view price tags and hear characters talk about how much things cost and how people cannot afford them.[45] We encounter a swank bar from the perspective of a waiter who works there rather than that of its well-heeled patrons. Berger depicts the uneasy facts of everyday life that give rise to fantasies; he also shows various ways in which the producers of mass culture respond to and capitalize on collective dreams of a better world. The film legitimates the necessity for imaginary spaces that take people away from their vicissitudes and dissatisfactions.

Many Weimar films, both sound and silent, insistently and persistently interrogate the medium of cinema and disclose the constructive capacities and abusive powers of a nascent mass culture. In the final shot of *Das Cabinet des Dr. Caligari*, we quite literally see double and cannot determine whether the figure of authority is a benevolent doctor or a homicidal lunatic. *Die Strasse* (The Street, 1923) revels in the enticements of urban life in the form of a cinematic experience and at the same time demonstrates the perils of such seductive spectacles. Ironic epilogues leave us with all too happy endings in *Der letzte Mann* (The Last Man, 1924) and *Geheimnisse einer Seele* (Secrets of a Soul, 1926). Lang's *M* exhibits how urban subjects apprehend increasingly abstract living spaces through

---

[45] In UFA's *Ein blonder Traum* there is a long scene in which the protagonists calculate the cost of a better life in minute detail.

visual and verbal mediations—which as the film itself makes apparent are usually inconclusive and, as such, quite often unreliable. UFA's early sound musicals, to varying degrees, represent self-conscious exercises in wishful thinking, where a yearning for distraction coexists, not always amicably, with the reality principle.

Ich bei Tag und Du bei Nacht ends where it starts: at the movies. During the pyrotechnic finale of *Dies alles ist Dein,* the camera tracks down rows of delighted viewers and fixes on a smiling Hans and Grete; they kiss as the lights come up and the audience rises to leave. We cut back to the screen and, while the curtains close, see *Ende* before the image darkens. If you are looking for succor, this UFA comedy suggests, one can find it in cinema's illusions, but only for a moment; for lasting happiness, look elsewhere. In these late-Weimar productions, fantasies of a better life gained fulfillment in the form of conciliatory reveries that were, however, clearly marked as fictions and therefore not meant to be taken seriously. For all its regressive properties, observed Kracauer, distraction possesses a truth potential: it has the power to expose the world's true state of disarray and fragmentation rather than masking it.[46] These early sound comedies surely do not go quite that far in their pursuit of distraction; they do, however, mark the limits of make-believe and caution the spectator about the downside of confusing cinematic illusions with social solutions.

---

[46] Kracauer, "Cult of Distraction: On Berlin's Picture Palaces," in *The Mass Ornament: Weimar Essays,* trans. and ed. Thomas Y. Levin (Cambridge, MA: Harvard University Press, 1995), 328.

5:   Resisting the War (Film): Wicki's "Masterpiece" *Die Brücke* and Its Generic Transformations

Jaimey Fisher

ONE HESITATES TO START with any sort of polled survey, but such surveys both illuminate and constitute the wider film culture that the present volume's generic approach foregrounds. In a 1995 survey celebrating the centennial of cinema, Bernhard Wicki's *Die Brücke* (The Bridge, 1959) was named by industry personnel, critics, and scholars the thirteenth most significant work of German cinema's first century, placing it between *Der Student von Prag* (The Student of Prague, 1913) and *Abschied von Gestern* (Yesterday's Farewell, released in English as *Yesterday Girl*, 1966); even more impressively, this remarkably high ranking rendered it the list's third highest postwar film (the top of the list is dominated by films of the celebrated Weimar era). Critics placed it ahead not only of all the works of the so-called New German Cinema but even of Weimar classics such as Lang's *Dr. Mabuse, der Spieler* (Dr. Mabuse, the Gambler, 1922); Murnau's *Der letzte Mann* (The Last Man, released in English as *The Last Laugh* 1925); and Pabst's famously controversial *Die 3-Groschen-Oper* (Three-Penny Opera, 1931). Although this survey hardly proves quality, it underscores a contradiction within the broader film culture of which *Die Brücke* and this kind of survey are both part: despite this dignified company on the survey's list, *Die Brücke* has received very little scholarly attention, which is all the more surprising given that *Die Brücke* is also the most highly placed war film in the survey.[1] This lack of later scholarly engagement seems to be a peculiarity largely due to the status of the war film and film genre in general in German film scholarship—a status that has subsequently led to a marked neglect of genre films, of 1950s cinema, and of *Die Brücke* in particular.

There can be little doubt that *Die Brücke* was an important film, both on its own merits and in terms of Germany's wider film culture, which subsequently celebrated its Swiss-Austrian director, Wicki, as one

---

[1] Reprinted in Robert C. Reimer and Carol J. Reimer, *A Historical Dictionary of German Cinema* (Lanham, MD: Scarecrow, 2008), 333–37.

of its most important figures. The film won more than fifteen international prizes, including the Golden Globe for foreign film in 1960, was Germany's foreign-language Oscar nominee (*Black Orpheus* won), and established actor-turned-director Wicki as one of German cinema's best-known and most beloved figures. The popularity of the film, along with its international success, brought Wicki considerable renown around the world, something in fairly short supply for German cinema in the 1950s. As Stephen Brockmann recounts, the UN praised the film for its promotion of peace, and, in the USSR, it was dubbed into fifteen local languages.[2] Wicki had studied art at the Bauhaus in Dessau and then acting under Gustaf Gründgens, the former of which led to his internment in the concentration camp Sachsenhausen outside Berlin from 1938 to 1939. After *Die Brücke*, he worked on international, including Hollywood, productions, such as codirecting Daryl Zanuck's omnibus film *The Longest Day* and acting in Michaelangelo Antonioni's *La Notte* (The Night, 1961). *Die Brücke* was also remade for TV in 2008 as part of the post-1989 wave of quasi-heritage films, viewed by over 3.5 million viewers. Today the legacy of Wicki and the stature of the film is confirmed by another aspect of the wider film culture cited above: the "Bernhard Wicki Prize—The Bridge—Peace Prize for German Film" is given annually for the promotion of "humanity, tolerance, and education" at Germany's second-most-important film festival, the Munich Film Festival (recipients have included, among others, Volker Schlöndorff for the *Der neunte Tag* [The Ninth Day, 2004] and Florian von Donnersmarck for *Das Leben der Anderen* [The Lives of Others, 2006]). As the survey and these awards confirm, *Die Brücke*'s long-term place in German film and media culture seems to be indelible.

So why this sort of scholarly neglect of such a popular and renowned film? Conventionally, the 1950s were, as Johannes von Moltke puts it memorably in his *No Place like Heimat*, the decade of the "quintessentially 'bad object' of German film historiography,"[3] with critics like Joe Hembus famously condemning its quality (*Der deutsche Film kann gar nicht besser sein*) and the 1961 Berlin Festival refusing even to grant a prize to any of the eighty West German features.[4] In the last fifteen years, however, scholars have begun to reexamine the culture and cinema of the 1950s; important studies include von Moltke's own monograph on the Heimat film, but also the work of Heide Fehrenbach, Norbert Frei, Robert Moeller, and Ute Poiger, as well as an edited

---

[2] Stephen Brockmann, *A Critical History of German Film* (Rochester, NY: Camden House, 2010), 303–4.

[3] Johannes von Moltke, *No Place Like Home: Locations of* Heimat *in German Cinema* (Berkeley: University of California Press, 2005), 21.

[4] Joe Hembus, *Der deutsche Film kann gar nicht besser sein* (Bremen: Carl Schünemann, 1961).

volume by Hanna Schissler and another by John Davidson and Sabine Hake.[5] None of these important reconsiderations of the 1950s discusses *Die Brücke*, which the centennial survey named as the most important film of the 1950s, at any kind of length. The neglect of the war film in general and *Die Brücke* specifically is especially surprising given their intersection with discourses about memory of the Third Reich and of coming to terms with that past, certainly two of the most important cultural themes for the early postwar period.

The film has been neglected in part, I think, because it does not correspond to the prevailing image of the "bad object" of that period and so does not fit the dominant scholarly schemata for the 1950s. As I shall discuss below, there has been universal praise of *Die Brücke*'s cinematic artistry and achievement since its premiere. On the other hand, the film does not conform to the type of European art film frequently given attention in conventional film histories, including some of its contemporaries, such as works by Ingmar Bergman, Michaelangelo Antonioni, or Jean-Luc Godard. It has fallen between the critical cracks, I think, because it functions quite clearly as a genre film, a film open about genre operations of the sort that film scholars, especially German film scholars, have tended to neglect. *Die Brücke* was not so much a radical break from its cinematic context (the 1950s war film), as some contemporary art films, such as *L'avventura*, were from theirs, but rather a deliberate engagement with a mainstream genre and a contemporary production trend (a trend in which Wicki was already involved via his acting). And it so happens that the genre within which this film operates, the war genre, is one that has been afforded a relatively low level of theoretical sophistication in both German and Anglo-American film studies, especially when compared to melodrama, the Western, film noir, or even the musical/musical-operetta, all of which have had numerous and major works written about them.

I argue that, in its conspicuous and deliberate genre workings, the film is a key forebear of a certain type of later 1960s/1970s art film that, as John G. Cawelti has shown, deliberately manipulates and demythifies

---

[5] Heide Fehrenbach, *Cinema in Democratizing Germany: Reconstructing National Identity after Hitler* (Chapel Hill: University of North Carolina Press, 1995); Norbert Frei, *Vergangenheitspolitik: Die Anfänge der Bundesrepublik und die NS-Vergangenheit* (Munich: DTV, 2003); Robert G. Moeller, *War Stories: The Search for a Usable Past in the Federal Republic of Germany* (Berkeley: University of California Press, 2001); Ute Poiger, *Jazz, Rock, and Rebels: Cold War Politics and American Culture in a Divided Germany* (Berkeley: University of California Press, 2000); Hanna Schissler, ed., *The Miracle Years: A Cultural History of West Germany, 1949–1968* (Princeton, NJ: Princeton University Press, 2001); John Davidson and Sabine Hake, *Framing the Fifties: Fifties Cinema in Divided Germany* (New York: Berghahn Books, 2007).

the mainstream genre it exploits.[6] Such art films require an awareness and appreciation of their generic contexts to understand just how cannily each film operates within its chosen genre. To demythify the war film genre within which it is conspicuously working, *Die Brücke* deploys another genre that was important in early postwar Germany, the so-called youth film, a genre that had already become central for the issue of coming to terms with the past in the late 1940s. The film's deployment of the so-called "youth film" (the *Jugendfilm*, which was common in the late 1940s) allows for a dismantling of a dominant discourse in many of the 1950s war films, namely, the canny, older soldier-citizen who was never (completely) complicit with the Nazi regime.[7]

War Films in a War-Making and Recovering Nation

The war film had been an important genre in German cinema since the 1910s. As is well documented, the First World War resulted in the coordination of cinema to the war effort, something that actually led the vast majority of narrative entertainment films to deliberately avoid representations of the war. The war was largely left to newsreels, which also tried to forego the larger and increasingly troubled context of the war for the more limiting and limited point-of-view shots of the trenches. Nonetheless, it eventually yielded combat films, with both military farces and full-blown war films, including Paul Leni's *Das Tagebuch des Dr. Hart* (The Diary of Dr. Hart, 1917), which Sabine Hake sees as standing out "through a surprising realism in its presentation of the daily life in the military."[8] Hake's observation underscores the long-term association of the war genre with (putative) realism. Otherwise, however, films made during the war tended to avoid representations of the war, which would likely only have reminded viewers of the hardships that those at the front and at home were enduring because of the war effort.

In the early postwar period, war films largely disappeared from German screens—at least at the level of manifest content, for, as Anton

---

[6] John G. Cawelti, "*Chinatown* and Generic Transformation in Recent American Film," in *Film Genre Reader III*, ed. Barry Keith Grant (1979; repr., Austin: University of Texas Press, 2003), 243–61.

[7] Erica Carter, "Men in Cardigans: *Canaris* (1954) and the 1950s West German Good Soldier," in *War-Torn Tales: Representing Gender and World War II in Literature and Film*, ed. Danielle Hipkins and Gill Plain (Oxford: Peter Lang, 2007), 5–29; Jennifer Kapczynski, "Armchair Warriors: Heroic Postures in the West German War Film," in *Screening War: Perspectives on German Suffering*, ed. Paul Cooke and Marc Silberman (Rochester, NY: Camden House, 2010), 17–35.

[8] Sabine Hake, *German National Cinema* (London: Routledge, 2002), 23.

Kaes has argued in his *Shell Shock Cinema*, signs of the war might well have been everywhere.[9] For this reason, I will use the term combat films for films in which combat scenes and sequences play central, often climactic narrative roles. Some ten years after the First World War, there was an explosion of interest in the combat film, including most famously Pabst's *Westfront 1918* and *Kameradschaft* but also, from a less critical perspective, *Stoßtrupp 1917*. As Kracauer emphasizes, there was also at this time the considerable popularity of so-called "barrack comedies" (discussed briefly in Eric Renschtler's essay in the present volume). Although the decade-long delay in the arrival of such films—both combat and comedy—is usually cited as evidence of a belated cultural working-through, it is also an example of how a technology, namely, the advent of sound, was inextricably connected to the rise of a film genre (the musical operatta being the other obvious one). For example, in *Westfront 1918*, the innovative use of sound, especially offscreen sound, was repeatedly cited as a central aspect of its putatively radical realism.[10]

This production trend at the end of the 1920s and early 1930s also underscores another important aspect of the workings of film genre, namely, its transnational aspects: as has been well researched, *Im Westen nichts Neues* (Nothing New in the West, released in English as *All Quiet on the Western Front*), a German novel by Erich Maria Remarque, was made, in 1930, into a celebrated US film by Lewis Milestone, which in turn created a sensation when it opened in Germany and various right-wing groups, including the Nazis, held protests. The protests against it remind us that cinema was part of a widespread transnational memorialization and memory culture of the war in the 1920s as well as a flashpoint for politics to come. In fact, during German cinema's most infamous period, the period under the Nazis, war films not only became an important part of the "total war" but also a top-grossing cinematic form (for example, in the blockbusters *Wunschkonzert* [Request Concert, 1940] and *Die große Liebe* [The Great Love, 1942], which both have important combat sequences). Despite this importance in the 1940s, it is noteworthy that the influential histories of cinema under the Nazis, including those by Eric Rentschler, Sabine Hake, and Linda Schulte-Sasse, do not foreground the war film (for example, in none of those histories does "war film" appear in the indexes, although genres like melodrama, comedy, and romance all do)—part of a broader pattern of neglect of the war film, even in its most popular and influential forms.

---

[9] Anton Kaes, *Shell Shock Cinema: Weimar Culture and the Wounds of War* (Princeton, NJ: Princeton University Press, 2009).
[10] See Jaimey Fisher, "Landscapes of Death: Space and the Mobilization Genre in G. W. Pabst's *Westfront 1918* (1930)" in *The Many Faces of Weimar Cinema: Rediscovering Germany's Filmic Legacy*, ed. Christian Rogowski (Rochester, NY: Camden House, 2010), 268–85.

A Generic Decade? Genre Cinema in the 1950s

Despite the negative critical reception and scholarly legacy, the 1950s proved a golden age in at least one filmic sense—ticket sales. This commercial success was due in no small part to historical conditions that led to the dominance of genre cinema. By the early 1950s the German film industry (insofar as one can even refer to "a" German film industry at that point) was highly decentralized, even fragmented, because of its specific historical context. Allied controls, licensing procedures, and above all determined decartelization that forbade vertical integration of the film industry resulted, by the late 1940s, in a myriad of small and generally undercapitalized production companies. Given their chronic undercapitalization and subsequent modest commercial prospects—especially in light of copious foreign competition on postwar German screens—production companies almost invariably made feature films at a loss, usually a loss of about 25 percent of production costs, something that bankrupted many of the small production companies that had burgeoned in the heady decartelization of the early postwar period.[11] These bleak financial prospects were due not least to a local entertainment tax, which, in some places, ran as high as 30 percent on box-office revenue ("Vergnügensteuer").[12] This led to an unusual degree of control for the distributors, since their capital (usually through loans and guarantees) was required for production companies to finance films, while these same distributors could, on the exhibition side, force theater owners to block-book film programs (as many as twenty films in a block until legal regulations set it at six).

This very challenging financial climate yielded a robust genre system that could minimize these frequently crushing financial risks of film production. The companies that stumbled upon a successful genre product (as Berolina did with the Heimat film, with such films as the wildly popular *Schwarzwaldmädel* [Black Forest Maid, released in English as *Black Forest Girl*, 1950] and *Grün ist die Heide* [Green is the Heather, released in English as *The Heather is Green*, 1951]) had a considerable competitive advantage that resulted in the repetitive production of very similar films. In this way, because of the fragmented character of the film industry, genre cinema became particularly dominant in this rather dire financial climate. As is well known and famously documented by Elsaesser in his *New German Cinema*,[13] such industry conditions obtained until the early 1960s, when changes in the state subsidy system and television transformed the financial prospects for film producers. Knut Hickethier points

---

[11] Knut Hickethier, "The Restructuring of the West German Film Industry in the 1950s," in Davidson and Hake, *Framing the Fifties: Fifties Cinema in Divided Germany*, 196–97.

[12] See Hickethier, "Restructuring of the West German Film Industry," 197.

[13] Elsaesser, *New German Cinema* (Basingstoke, UK: Macmillan, 1989).

out that such changes were afoot already in the later 1950s, although it was the Oberhausen Manifesto in 1962 that became the marquee event in these ongoing changes.

Although there were clear historical and economic reasons for the predominance of genre film in the 1950s, the question persists of why certain genres were successful and how these genres evolved in this particular context. Among the most popular genres in this 1950s context was the war film, generally seen as the decade's second-most-important genre behind the much more cited and discussed Heimat film. The production of movies about the war quadrupled in West Germany between 1952 and 1958, and the war film established itself as the second-best commercially performing genre in the last era of massive cinema-going audiences. As Robert Moeller puts it: "In the decade where more Germans went to the movies than ever before—or ever since—some 10 percent of the movies they could see were about the war."[14] Many critics see the surfeit and popularity of war films resting at the intersection of West Germany's complicated and ambivalent memory culture as well as the unfolding debate about German military tradition and rearmament. As Erica Carter argues, for instance, the popularity of the war genre in the 1950s indicates the abiding presence and acknowledgement of memories of the war as well as of the Nazi past more generally, but the films also reveal how it might not have been the sort of memory marked by heartfelt remorse that would seem appropriate in light of Germany's recent war crimes. Films such as *Canaris* and *Der 20. Juli* negotiated that recent past in largely self-serving ways that offered the audience opportunities to empathize with characters whose behavior suggested that not all Germans were the same kind of perpetrators and, indeed, some might even have resisted Nazi crimes.

The 1950s war film was, moreover, not only a locus for German national discourse; in fact, a number of reviews of *Die Brücke* mention not only the German war genre but also the significance of non-German-war films for the understanding of the genre in the German public sphere. These non-German-war films provide important evidence (like that of *All Quiet on the Western Front*, as noted above) that almost all genres circulate and operate globally. For one very relevant example, in the year before Wicki's *Die Brücke*, David Lean's British-US coproduction *Bridge on the River Kwai* was the second-to-top grossing film in West Germany and, as Ann-Marie Scholz has shown, galvanized a heated discussion among German critics, who were perplexed by a film that did not seem as clearly antiwar as Columbia Pictures's publicity department had

---

[14] Robert Moeller, "Victims in Uniform: West German Combat Movies from the 1950s," in *Germans as Victims*, ed. Bill Niven (Basingstoke, UK: Palgrave MacMillan, 2006), 44.

claimed in the German marketing of the film.[15] Some critics grudgingly agreed that the film could be understood as antiwar; some thought it was, at best, ambivalent and ambiguous about the hostilities; and surprisingly many unmasked, in rather histrionic fashion, the film as actually prowar—an argument in which some German critics would have been invested at a moment when NATO (with the United States and UK, who had coproduced the *Kwai*, at its head and helm) was solidifying its position against the newly formed Warsaw Pact. Scholz argues convincingly that *Bridge on the River Kwai* and these conflicted responses underscore the transnational character of memory culture in postwar West Germany. For our purposes, *Bridge on the River Kwai* and the public sphere debates it galvanized emphasize how genre is always transnational, often in rich and complicated ways.

Die Brücke weighs in on these myriad generic trends—both as a war film but also as a film self-consciously distancing itself from those very same trends, including those that were transnational, in postwar memory. Set in a small Bavarian town in April 1945, *Die Brücke* recounts the desperate moment when the home front became the combat front in Germany's wartime collapse. Despite the defeat that was clearly coming, seven teenaged boys are, with differing levels of enthusiasm, drafted into the German army. With their fathers largely absent because of the war, their mothers manifest a range of reactions, from dogged commitment to despairing resignation. One vociferous skeptic of their late conscription is their middle-aged male teacher, Stern, who was exempted from service for health reasons. This teacher attempts to intervene with their commanding officer, a captain who is a former teacher himself but who apparently ignores their current teacher's entreaties. The boys are given a mere one day of training before being shipped off to the front, but this stone-faced captain abruptly orders a corporal to take the boys to defend their own hometown bridge, primarily to keep them away from the combat front and from almost assured death. This apparently merciful plan falls apart, however, when the corporal is shot by the town's military police, who are convinced, given that he is hanging around a small town of little strategic importance, that he is one of the many deserters at this late stage of the war. His death leaves the boys without an actual commander who could call off their senseless defense of a bridge that is, in any case, slated for demolition by the Wehrmacht. When US tanks roll into the town, the boys fight bravely but senselessly until the German demolition team shows up and informs them that they are blowing the bridge to halt the US advance. The boys are incredulous that they could have sacrificed so

---

[15] Anne-Marie Scholz, "The *Bridge on the River Kwai* (1957) Revisited: Combat Cinema, American Culture and the German Past," *German History* 26, no.2 (2008): 219–50.

Fig. 5.1. Die Brücke *(1959). Screenshot.*

much for nothing, and one of them ends up shooting the leader of the Wehrmacht demolition team. Only one of the seven boys survives, underscoring the senseless loss and the squandered idealism of their generation. The final shot returns to the very beginning of the film, to the bridge, still standing at that point, that was then the center of small-town life and is now a memento mori of searing, senseless sacrifice.

The film was greeted with immediate as well as lasting accolades. Some of its first reviews pronounced it an utterly new achievement, an unprecedented triumph, in postwar German film, and declared that Wicki, with this film alone, had catapulted himself into the elite of German-speaking directors[16] while another declared him a "Spitzenregie";[17] that review managed to call it both a high point of German film production (noticeably omitting "postwar") and a masterpiece.[18] Multiple critics called it the "hardest" war film of the decade, and another said that no other German film had ever spoken in this kind of language about the war[19]—a reference both to other war films' modes of representation and this film's innovation in such representation. The Berlin Filmkommision encouraged only children over 16 to see it, and then only with their parents, in

[16] "Triumph der Brücke: Abend-Interview mit Bernhard Wicki," *Der Abend*, 26 Oct. 1959; Karl-Heinz Krüger, "Ein Höhepunkt der deutschen Filmprodukution: Bernhard Wickis Meisterwerk, Die Brücke," *Der Abend*, 14 Nov. 1959.

[17] Mato Weiland, "Bernhard Wickis großer Regieerfolg: Nur einer kehrt aus der Kriegshölle zurück," *Abendpost*, 26 Oct. 1959.

[18] Weiland, "Bernhard Wicki's großer Regieerfolg."

[19] Weiland, "Bernhard Wicki's großer Regieerfolg," and Helmut Haffner, "Das Nein zum Krieg: Uraufführung des Films 'Die Brücke' von Bernhard Wicki," *8 Uhr-Blatt*, 23 Oct. 1959.

light of the many "untrue and falsified" war films of recent years.[20] One piece that appeared in *Der Abend* offered over 15 quotes from various cinemagoers who were leaving the Zoo cinema after its Berlin premiere, with most finding it the hardest and most brutal war film they had seen.[21] The piece ends with another generic comment, but one from an atypical audience member, namely, the well-known director Helmut Käutner, who said: "Ist das nicht ein großartiger Film von dem Berni [Wicki]? Danach sind weitere Kriegsfilme hierzulande tatsächlich überflüssig" (Isn't that a great film from Bernie [Wicki]? After this, further war films will be superfluous in this country).[22]

The Generic Operations and Transformations of *Die Brücke*

In its engagement with both the national and the transnational genre, *Die Brücke* offers a very early example of a generic mode engaged in later by the directors of the New German Cinema (as well as other 1960s and 1970s art-cinema directors around the globe), one that John G. Cawelti has termed the demythification of an established genre. In their studies of genre, Thomas Schatz and Cawelti discuss how genres enter periods of self-reflexivity, some time after their appearance and consolidation.[23] Such self-reflexivity can yield, among other things, what Norman Kagan has called "genre commentaries" (which he traces in Robert Altman's films, for example, on the war genre in *M*A*S*H*, 1970). Cawelti sketches out, in elaborate detail, four modes of "generic transformation" of such self-reflexively generic films, including those of the burlesque, the nostalgic, and the reaffirmative. But, for him, the "most powerful mode of generic transformation" is that of demythologization, which requires a sense of both a genre's history and its parameters.[24] In such demythologization, I would argue, the director self-consciously deploys the themes, motifs, and iconographies of genres—what Rick Altman has termed the semantics of the genre—while also varying the deeper narrative structure, or what Altman would call the syntax.[25] This is something certainly

[20] Karl-Heinz Krüger, "Ein Höhepunkt der deutschen Filmprodukution: Bernhard Wickis Meisterwerk, Die Brücke," *Der Abend*, 14 Nov. 1959.

[21] "Und was sagen die Berliner? ABEND-Blitzumfrage vor dem Zoo-Palast-Portal," *Der Abend*, 14 Nov. 1959.

[22] "Und was sagen die Berliner? ABEND-Blitzumfrage vor dem Zoo-Palast-Portal," *Der Abend*, 14 Nov. 1959. All translations in this essay are my own, except where otherwise credited.

[23] Thomas Schatz, *Hollywood Genres: Formulas, Filmmaking and the Studio System* (New York: McGraw-Hill, 1981), 36–41. Cawelti, "Chinatown," 250–51.

[24] Cawelti, "Chinatown," 254.

[25] Robert Altman, *Film/Genre* (1999; repr., London: bfi, 2002), 88–89.

both Altman and Arthur Penn achieved again and again, Altman not only in *M*A*S*H*, but (as Kagan details) also in his Western *McCabe and Mrs. Miller* (1972), his detective film *The Long Goodbye* (1973), and his show-business film *Nashville* (1975). For his part Penn (as Cawelti details) reworked the gangster film in *Bonnie and Clyde* (1967), the detective film in *Night Moves* (1975), and the Western in *The Missouri Breaks* (1975). In a German context, one could speak of a similar demythification of the Heimat genre around the same time (late 1960s, early 1970s) in films such as Peter Fleischmann's *Jagdszenen aus Niederbayern* (Hunting Scenes from Lower Bavaria, 1969), Volker Schlöndorff's *Der plötzliche Reichtum der armen Leute von Kombach* (The Sudden Wealth of the Poor People of Kombach, 1970), and Werner Herzog's *Herz aus Glas* (Heart of Glass, 1976). In these anti-Heimat films (discussed in Paul Cooke's essay in this volume), the generic demythification parallels a demythification that is historical as well as political, both dynamics doubtlessly at work in the films of Altman and Penn.

Such genre demythification is tied to what Cawelti calls the "life cycle characteristic" of genre, something that, for the purposes of this volume, helps us think about the way in which the histories of genre are interwoven with the cultural history of Germany. For Cawelti, there are various periods within this life cycle of the genre:

> [Genres] move from an initial period of articulation and discovery, through a phase of conscious self awareness on the part of both creators and audiences, to a time when the generic patterns have become so well known that the people become tired of their predictability. It is at this point that parodic and satiric treatments proliferate and new genres gradually arise.[26]

In suggesting this kind of life cycle to a genre, Cawelti is describing the arc of popular genres in 1970s US cinema. Rick Altman has, however, critiqued this influential notion as overly organic, particularly as the life part of life cycle points not so much to a cyclical as to linear and progressive development. Indeed, *pace* Altman, with the trends of German war films since the 1920s, the story is not so simply linear or progressive. Some skepticism toward the war genre, even a demythifying project, can be found as early as Pabst's *Westfront 1918* and *Kameradschaft*, a self-conscious questioning and dismantling that was then abruptly suspended during the Nazis' reign.[27] Similarly, then, at a much earlier moment, the genre's cycle was indelibly impacted by the culture and cultural politics of postwar Germany. But if one takes this kind of demythification occurring not over the entire life cycle of a genre, but within a particular and

---

[26] Cawelti, "Chinatown," 260.
[27] Fisher, "Landscapes of Death."

more historically defined production trend, then such a demythification tendency late in the particular trend does seem highly relevant. Works later in any specific cycle display a kind of generic exhaustion with their predictability, and there is a sense that the cycle of genres can reflect a general discontent with the prevailing cultural myths of any given historical moment.

These various aspects of generic exhaustion and subsequent demythification are certainly manifest in the reception of *Die Brücke*: much of the praise for Wicki's film provided an occasion for critics to complain about the surfeit of war films throughout the 1950s, critically acclaimed though some were.[28] Various reviews referenced the clichés of the war film and emphasized, in their extravagant praise, how *Die Brücke* was able to avoid them.[29] One particularly interesting example is a *Tagesspiegel* column on war films by Karena Niehoff from mid-November 1959 on the occasion of *Die Brücke*'s Berlin premiere (about a month after it had premiered in Mannheim, a month during which, as noted above, there had been overwhelmingly positive press about the film). Niehoff begins her piece with the 1950s trend of war films mentioned above, but her sarcasm about these films (some of them, such as *Hunde, wollt ihr ewig leben?*, which won the German Film Prize in gold that year, had received glowing critiques) symptomatizes precisely the kind of generic exhaustion of which Cawelti writes:

> Kriegsfilme, pardon, Antikriegsfilme hatten wir seit Kriegsende die Fülle: Von der "08/15"-Welle und dem prangenden "Stern von Afrika" über die freundliche Erinnerung an die "Blitzmädel," nicht zu vergessen "Stalingrad" und "Taiga" und "Hunde, wollt ihr ewig leben"—alles im Grunde der mehr oder weniger gleiche Teig, in dem die Hefe des deutschen Traumas aufging.[30]

> [Since the end of the war, we've had our fill of war movies, oh, sorry, anti-war films: from the *8/15* wave and the resplendent *Stern über Africa* to the friendly reminder of the *Blitzmädel*, and don't forget *Stalingrad* and *Taiga* and *Hunde, wollt ihr ewig leben?*—all basically the same dough in which the yeast of the German trauma rises.]

---

[28] See, for example, Karl-Heinz Krüger, "Kinder unterm Stahlhelm: Wickis 'Brücke' wurde ein erschütterndes Meisterwerk," *Der Abend*, 23 Oct. 1959, or Egon Stadelman, "Die Brücke, ein Antikriegsfilm: Ein grosser deutscher Filmerfolg," *Sonntagsblatt*, 29 Nov. 1959.

[29] Helmut Wittkowski, "Die Brücke, ein Meisterwerk von Bernhard Wicki: Der Beste Nachkriegsfilm gegen den Krieg," *Deutsche Woche* 44 (1959); Klaus Norbert Scheffler, "Ein offener Brief an Bernhard Wicki: Ist "Die Brücke" ein Antikriegsfilm?" *Deutsche Woche*, 30 Dec. 1959.

[30] Karena Niehoff, "Blick auf die Leinwand: Die Jungen fressen sich selber auf," *Tagesspiegel*, 15 Nov. 1959.

Within this well-kneaded dough of the genre, she then reviews some of the repeating clichés of the genre as it played out over the 1950s, including: "Ehrenrettung des deutschen Landsers, der diskrete Hinweis darauf, daß eigentlich Soldaten doch bessere Menschen sind; selbst manche starren Nazis, tapfer jedoch, wurden im rechten Moment als falschgeführte Pflichtnaturen der Nachsicht im Kinoparkett empfohlen" (the rescue of the honor of a German soldier, the discreet hint that soldiers really are better people; even some of the rigid Nazis, brave nonetheless, were afforded, as misled followers, leniency in the cinema hall). Confirming the transnational character of the well-worn genre, she sees US films like *From Here to Eternity* participating in the "Gleichschritt" (march step) of the genre. In her sketch of the genre as it existed at the end of the 1950s, Niehoff references another war film, *Die letzte Brücke*, by a key figure of 1950s West German cinema, Helmut Käutner, but she then distinguishes between Käutner's image of a bridge and Wicki's. Like all the war films above that she mentions, Käutner's allows for the persistence of humanity amid the carnage, brutality, and barbarism of war. But Wicki, she observes, does not: as her column title indicates ("Die Jungen fressen sich auf" [the young devour themselves]), Wicki allows his boys to utterly renounce the humanity normally allowed to abide amid the well-worn hell of war.

In her title and her critical approach to the genre as it existed, Niehoff is pointing to a generational logic to the genre in its 1950s inflection, a logic, I think, integral to the demythification that the film undertakes and to the resonance it found. As I have argued elsewhere, in the early years of the postwar period, discussions, debates, and general discourse about "die deutsche Jugend" allowed (adult) Germans to engage with the recent past without admitting to a more thoroughgoing and widespread guilt.[31] Recognizing such discourse about young people within Germany's memory culture is part of a recent reconsideration of postwar collective memory in general. As Robert Moeller and others have argued, contrary to common assumption, the early postwar years were not so much marked by silence about the past as diversionary and deliberately distracting modes of working through that past. In this recent reconsideration of the putative postwar silence about the past, various scholars have emphasized the sundry aspects of this diversionary working through. For example, as Moeller as well as Omer Bartov have detailed, such modes of working through the past often highlighted Germans' own (highly constructed and clearly self-serving) victimhood at the hands of the Nazis. Moeller has furthermore highlighted attention given to wartime expellees

---

[31] See the introduction in Jaimey Fisher, *Disciplining Germany: Youth, Reconstruction, and Reeducation after the Second World War* (Detroit: Wayne State, 2007).

and postwar refugees; Elisabeth Heinemann has emphasized the images of women in this period; Frank Biess has focused on the discussions around returning veterans, and in my work I have explored how discussions about youth functioned similarly for early postwar memory and its working through the past.[32] From all of this it becomes clear that the early postwar years were marked not so much by a silence via repression, but rather by deliberate displacement and by the consolidation of self-serving aspects of the recent past.

This diversionary working through the past with narratives about the young became particularly important in the early postwar films, including many of the so-called rubble films.[33] Some of this, I think, can be attributed to the nature of film narrative, which tends to elaborate and exploit clearly drawn conflicts: with the recent past and challenging present, the struggles with young people provided a convenient and relatively unproblematic means to depict such narrative conflict. This was, after all, the early postwar period, a context in which many such conflicts were overdetermined by politics and many Germans' complicity with Nazis, so the much-touted struggles with young people offered fairly apolitical (or at least apparently apolitical) conflicts to foreground. These rubble films frequently followed traumatized male protagonists in a relationship to a young person, often a literal or figurative son. The young person provided a convenient means of representing the unavoidable but also difficult past: very often the son stood for the ideologically convinced Nazis who would be successfully converted to postwar democracy. These narratives consistently suggest that the young, not the adults, were the most gullible about Nazi ideology, such that struggles with the son and (sometimes) the family generally stood for a confrontation with the (Nazi) past and crimes. Such discourses were operative both in the western zones (which would become West Germany) and in the Soviet zone (which would become East Germany), although in somewhat different and subsequently diverging ways.

For the generic context of *Die Brücke*, it is of particular interest to note how many of these early postwar rubble films depicted the intersection of youth with the last stages of the war and the futile fighting that marked it. Although many of the early postwar films are family dramas more than combat films, many did represent combat in one way

---

[32] Robert Moeller, *War Stories*; Elizabeth Heineman, "The Hour of the Woman: Memories of Germany's 'Crisis Years' and West German National Identity," *American Historical Review* (1996): 354–95; Frank Biess, *Homecomings: Returning Pows and the Legacies of Defeat in Postwar Germany* (Princeton, NJ: Princeton University Press, 2006).

[33] Discussed in chapters 5 and 6 of Fisher, *Disciplining Germany*, as well as in Jaimey Fisher, "Who's watching the Rubble-Kids? Youth, Pedagogy and Politics in Early DEFA Films," *New German Critique* 82 (Winter 2001): 91–125.

or another. In fact, in a way not often remarked upon by the few essays about 1950s war films, many of the rubble films of the late 1940s already deployed aspects of the combat film, including combat scenes at key narrative moments and the mise-en-scène of the combat film in uniforms and weapons. And in these rubble films, these elements of the war film often intersect the recurring figure of the young person as central to its narration and its working through the recent past. In Wolfgang Staudte's *Rotation*, for instance, the son Helmuth goes from school directly into combat in what seems an explicit foreshadow of the trajectory that *Die Brücke* addresses. In *Rotation*, it is not until Helmuth sees his teacher drop his military uniform for civilian clothes to conceal his service that Helmuth realizes the mendacity of Nazi ideology and returns to his anti-fascist father. The original end of the film had Helmuth's father declaring of his son's uniform "this is the last uniform [he] will wear" and burning the uniform, an anti-military conclusion that was changed under pressure to vaguer internationalist lessons by the Soviet authorities. In the western zones, in lesser known films as well, such as *Wege im Zwielicht* (Paths into Twilight, 1947) and *Und finden dereinst wir uns wieder* (We'll Find Each Other Again, 1947), young people in uniform occupy the position of the gullible dupes, while their generational superiors teach them that there is a world beyond that created by the Nazis.

With this series of early postwar "Jugendfilme" in mind, one can appreciate that Wicki revived this mode of dealing with the past to demythify the 1950s war film. As noted above, there is a distinct generational discourse to films like *Canaris*, *Stauffenberg*, and *Der 20. Juli*, in which the older and wiser military men, as in the early postwar films mentioned above, have a sense of both the true nature of, and better alternatives to, the Nazis. Although the heroes of those popular films might not have succeeded in resisting the Nazis during the war, they offered postwar audiences paradigmatically older soldiers who did understand and resist while the young around them tended to devote themselves dangerously to Nazi ideology. Whether or not such a generational analysis of complicity with Nazism is actually valid, it served clear purposes in the postwar public sphere. One can speak of a generational logic to the 1950s films that set out to depict the Wehrmacht more positively or at least neutrally: the older, wiser hands in the military were able to recognize the Nazi movement for what it was while the young people around them were too often indoctrinated and thereby rendered more complicit. This false image of the untainted Wehrmacht became a cornerstone of West German political culture, one whose foundations were revealed in the fever-pitch controversy around the Wehrmacht exhibit in the mid-1990s.

As opposed to *Canaris* and *20. Juli*, *Die Brücke* seemed to take the 1950s war picture in a different generational direction entirely: certainly *Die Brücke*, in addition to being received as a war film, was understood as a *Jugendfilm*, that is, a film about and directed at young people. In this regard it extended Wicki's interest in young people from his first film, *Warum sind sie gegen uns?* (Why Are They Against Us? 1958). Besides the many reports of youth responses to the film, another good example of the film's status as a *Jugendfilm* was an announcement just two months after its premiere that the film was to be the centerpiece of the newly founded "Jugend Filmwoche" in West Berlin. The Filmwoche was geared to recognize and realize a culmination of the previous decade of work done by the city governmnet around youth film, including the recommendation of films that were considered especially appropriate for young people and the announcement of ticket subsidies for young people to attend films deemed educationally useful.[34] *Die Brücke* won the first prize at the Filmwoche as "Best Film of the Year for the Young," and Wicki was presented with a ceremonial (white porcelain) Berlin Bear by one of the city senators. The prize commission praised the film for representing the war "schonungslos and ehrlich, ohne Kompromisse und Konzession an den Pubkliumsgeschmack" (unsparing and sincere, without compromise or concession to the taste of the general public), another clear reference to the many popular war films of the 1950s.[35] The Filmwoche was coordinated with a Kongreßhalle exhibit of 150 posters and 400 photos from films deemed appropriate for young people, up to and including *Die Brücke*. The event was intended to bring together the various film clubs, underscoring again how the young were at the forefront of a development of a wider film culture. The film went on, of course, to become a regular part of the curriculum in schools, and so on, but its reception should underscore how it was a product of its moment, a moment defined by the trajectory of the 1950s war film genre and this film's deliberate demythification of that genre with a discourse about youth and the older generation.

Die Brücke's Narrative and Stylistic Transformation of the War Film

In terms of the wider film culture, then, the film is entwined in the generational discourse of the memory culture of both the 1940s and the 1950s and the recoding of the war. But how did this discourse and its intersection with its contemporary production trend impact the film and its agenda of demythifying the previous genre? In analyzing the combat film, there has been much recent and rich theorizing of a militaristic gaze and perceptual regimes that emphasize the privileged (often aerial) perspectives

---

[34] Estr, "Auch Berlin ehrt Wicki, 10 Jahre Berliner Jugendfilmarbeit," *Der Tag*, 26 Jan. 1960.
[35] "Wicki-Film Die Brücke ausgezeichtnet (dpa)," *Abendpost*, 25 Jan. 1960.

that war films afford (cf. Kaplan, Saint-Amour, Schivelbusch, Virilio, and Weber), but these theories have tended to deemphasize the narrative forms in which such notable perspectives and perceptions are embedded.[36] Particularly in discussing the (fictional) film genre as it unfolds over time, these contexts for such perceptual regimes evolve more than the militarist gaze itself. This is particularly true, I would emphasize, for a film that sets out to demythify a dominant genre of its time: *Die Brücke* aims to recontextualize and reframe the combat even as that combat still takes center stage. In considering the film and its demythification of the war genre, it is particularly important to underscore what seems to constitute the narrative core of the majority of war films, namely, the recurring form of the unit, squad, or platoon as the context for combat. As Dana Polan has detailed, one of the important distinguishing features (for him, the most significant distinguishing feature) of the war film is the consistently collective nature of its protagonist.[37] Although Polan's case seems a little overstated—many unit-, squad-, or platoon-based war films still have a central protagonist—it does point to one of the key narrative variations of the war film—what Altman would call a key aspect of its generic syntax. The narrative preeminence of the unit, squad, or platoon as a kind of collective protagonist in the war film was established at least as early as the 1920s: one critic sees it as emerging by 1925 in the US-made *Big Parade*, and certainly it was present, in a high-profile way, in German cinema by the time of Pabst's *Westfront 1918*, as I have detailed elsewhere.[38] The unit, squad, or platoon form is used consistently in war-film narrative for a number of reasons. It stands in, in a manageable narrative form, for the collective nature of war as a social activity. Above all, it affords war films a narratively productive way to stage the integration of individuals into a larger collective that stands for the army and the nation as a whole, with combat and its militaristic gaze then deployed in service to this newly forged collective.

Both the highly successful *Westfront 1918* as well as one of the top-grossing Nazi films, *Wunschkonzert*, demonstrate a second aspect of

---

[36] Caren Kaplan, "Precision Targets: GPS and the Militarization of U.S. Consumer Identity," *American Quarterly* 58, no. 3 (2006): 693–714; Paul Saint-Amour, "Airwar Prophecy and Interwar Modernism," *Comparative Literature Studies* 42, no. 2 (2005): 130–60; Wolfgang Schivelbusch, *Railway Journey: The Industrialization of Time and Space in the 19th Century* (Berkeley: University of California Press, 1986); Paul Virilio, *War and Cinema: The Logistics of Perception* (1989; repr., London: Verso, 2000); Samuel Weber, *Targets of Opportunity: On the Militarization of Thinking* (New York: Fordham, 2005).

[37] Discussed in Jeanine Basinger, *The World War II Combat Film: Anatomy of a Genre* (1986; repr., Middletown, CN: Wesleyan University Press, 2003), 68.

[38] Richard Kozarski, *An Evening's Entertainment: The Age of the Silent Feature Picture, 1915–1928* (New York: Scribner, 1990), 186.

the unit, squad, or platoon form, namely, how its narrative form allows the film to foreground a particular diversity of individuals subsequently integrated into the unit/squad/platoon. Beyond the unit's recurring integration of the individual into the (national) collective, there is a conspicuous variety of individuals to be integrated. As Jeanne Basinger has detailed, this form allows for the deployment of a variety of "representative types" in the film's narrative, be they representing different nations, various socioeconomic or educational strata, or even divergent personality types.[39] These representational types yield tension and drama around the vicissitudes of the integration of this unit: although ultimate integration is usually achieved, getting there from a diverse group of individuals allows for rich narrative elaboration. In US films, very often this diversity and debate is staged around ethnic diversity, whereas in German films it is usually, as in *Westfront 1918* and *Wunschkonzert*, more regionally or class based. The films thereby stage the nation and its ability to overcome regional differences, though it is through a constant dynamic of integration and disintegration that the narrative proceeds.

Die Brücke certainly engages this core narrative form of the war film, the story of the diverse unit's integration, but it does so largely in order to dismantle it. Initially the film is careful to depict socioeconomic diversity among the seven boys, including Sigi and his mother, a woman who does the town's (dirty) laundry and whose representation is reminiscent of Weimar worker films (offered in facial close-up as well as in her melodramatic and almost hysterical reaction to Sigi's being drafted); Jürgen and his mother, "Frau Major" Borchert, who run an estate and who hail from a long line of military officers (key props are his dead father's pistol, and military portraits in the well-appointed home); and Walter and his father, a Nazi party "Ortsgruppenleiter" who ships his wife off to "safety" while romancing local women with his many luxury goods (viewers see him packing expensive suits and cigars in one scene while the about-to-be-deployed boys lack for decent shoes and even soap). In this way the film deliberately offers an array of social types, from the struggling working class to the wealthy estate owners steeped in military tradition to the grotesque nouveau riche privileged by the party. In the four other boys, the film offers more diversity in personal, especially adolescent, circumstance: one boy, Klaus, has been sent to the small town away from urban air raids, and has a budding school romance; another boy, Karl, has a crush on his father's assistant, a young woman who is having an affair with his father (one of the only middle-aged men present in the small town, because of a war wound).

Die Brücke is thus careful to cultivate the diversity of the would-be unit that many war films foreground, but there are a couple of notable

[39] Basinger, *The World War II Combat Film*, 26, 68.

Fig. 5.2. Die Brücke *(1959). Screenshot.*

deviations in this particular demythifying depiction. First, there is the sheer number of central characters, all treated nearly equally in terms of screen time. Seven central characters in a film of around one hundred minutes render the individual boys difficult to differentiate, something commented upon by a number of critics.[40] It is rare that a film would offer so many more or less equal characterizations, something itself symptomatic of the youth film (as far as war films go, *Saving Private Ryan* has around that many, but that was unusual; there was a clear leader in the squad, and the film was almost twice as long as *Die Brücke*, which Spielberg's blockbuster conspicuously cites). This deliberate confusion among the individual characterizations is confirmed by the film's narrative structure: it is not until the boys are actually drafted (about half an hour into the film) that the film cuts among all seven boys, one after the other, deliberately confirming the individual characterization and codings it has been subtly cultivating. And at that precise moment the film dissolves from the individual stories to the clichéd basic-training sequence that, under the homogenizing shadow of standard-issue helmets and uniforms, immediately obscures the differences just established (see fig. 5.2). The film thus sets out to sublate the individual differentiation among the too-many central characters. This undercutting of clear differentiation among the boys is likewise emphasized by the major change from the novel on which the film is based. As noted by a few reviews, the film excises the recurring flashback structure of the novel and thereby the strips out much of the individual detail about the boys.[41]

---

[40] Helmut Haffner, "Das Nein zum Krieg: Uraufführung des Films 'Die Brücke' von Bernhard Wicki," *8 Uhr-Blatt*, 23 Oct. 1959.

[41] Haffner, "Das Nein zum Krieg."

Given the way the film only fully individuates the boys at the moment it forcibly integrates them in basic training, it demonstrates social types rather than offering individuals whose arcs viewers are to follow. It recalls, in fact, the kind of sociological cross-section that was common to the rubble films as well as to socially conscious films of the 1920s.[42] This sense of a sociological interest in the film is confirmed by the second narrative peculiarity of the film's first forty-five minutes, namely, that the film's first half (so well beyond the normal first act or usual fifteen or twenty minute setup portion) carefully alternates the individual characterization above with scenes of the boys together in more collective settings such as the schoolyard, the classroom, and the town's public spaces (squares, bridge, river banks). Although it gives a sense of each boy's family (usually their mothers, given that all but two fathers are away or dead), it also, from the very first shots, offers a sense of a collective small-town milieu and emphasizes how the boys already know each other and are, in fact, a group of friends who already spend time together at recess. Of course the schoolyard, the classroom, and open-air public spaces are all clichés of the youth film, the sort of work in which *Die Brücke* is resetting the war film. This youthful backstory, in which the boys know each other well and already have their friendships (and roles in those friendships) well established, undercuts the drama familiar from the war-film genre, in which the members of the unit have to come to terms with one another. There is simply not the sort of tension and drama among the boys that most war films exploit in the unfolding tale of the unit. Resetting the unit in the schoolyard also, of course, ironizes the generic differentiations within it, which here have as much to do with their childhood antics and adolescent anxieties as wartime dynamics, something foregrounded in early postwar films like *Irgendwo in Berlin* (Somewhere in Berlin, 1946) and *Rotation*.

In her book on the Second World War combat film—one of the few monographs to examine the longer history of the war film—Basinger argues that the core narrative mechanism of the war genre is the plot trinity of "hero, group, and objective." But the above should make clear how *Die Brücke* recasts the first two of this recurring triad by dissolving the conventional hero into a preestablished group of difficult-to-differentiate boys. The third element of this triad, the objective, becomes, in most war films, the staged mission for the hero and group. With the military mission as the narrative objective in such films, one can see how well suited the generic syntax of the war film is to mainstream film narrative, whose trajectory is generally goal-driven and usually comprises a series of goal-directed actions, obstacles that get in the way, and subsequent

---

[42] See Fisher, *Disciplining Germany*, 198.

resolutions.[43] For example, in discussing his popular and acclaimed *Inglourious Basterds*, Quentin Tarantino in fact perceptively reduced the 1950s and 1960s US war films to the "men-on-a-mission" genre. Such missions often drive the narrative forward toward some kind of final resolution, often a climactic last battle, in what is known in German as the *Durchhaltenfilm*.[44] It also, of course, frequently demands the final integration of the unit, often in some sacrifice demanded of the hero as well as of the unit as a whole. The mission as the film's narrative objective is to be distinguished from other genres' objectives, I think, by its deliberate mediating of the hero and the unit back to the larger, usually national discourse of the war. The mission materializes the national, and the sacrifices that the national demands, in the lives of the hero and the unit.

In *Die Brücke*, however, this mission itself proves ironic, even absurd—here, too, the film inverts a core aspect of the genre's syntax, one of the genre's key parameters. The film's title cites this ironic mission, the defense of the small-town bridge that holds no strategic import for the war. Just as *Die Brücke* does not mediate effectively back to the wider war, the film's mission fails to meaningfully mediate individuals to the national. The specific introduction of the mission in the plot underscores the way in which Wicki's work recontextualizes the mission and the hero and unit mechanisms within the group of youths and how they become detached from the larger war and nation. Once the boys enter basic training (in scenes that look as if they have influenced the absurdist, sadistic stagings of military training in Herzog's *Woyzeck*), their teacher, Stern, seeks out their commanding officer, a captain ironically (particularly given his dour manner) named Fröhlich. The captain is a former teacher, and Stern tries to prevail upon Captain Fröhlich, colleague to colleague, to spare the sixteen-year-olds any final battle. Fröhlich rejects the teacher's request by reminding him of the way in which teachers were complicit in spreading nationalist, and belligerent, ideals to the young. When the boy's teacher suggests these notions have fallen into the wrong hands, that they are no longer valid ("stimmt das alles nicht mehr"), Captain Fröhlich says his son was just killed in action and demands coldly what exactly is no longer valid ("Was stimmt nicht?"). The boys' teacher leaves, assuming Fröhlich ("ich habe meinen Befehl und habe danach zu handeln!" [I have my orders and have to act on them!]), will send the boys to the front in search of the mythic *Endsieg* and therefore likely death.

---

[43] The classic work on this topic is David Bordwell, *Narration in Fiction Film* (London: Methuen, 1985), which he has updated in his *The Way Hollywood Tells It: Story and Style in Modern Movies* (Berkeley: University of California Press, 2006).

[44] See "Wicki-Film Die Brücke ausgezeichnet (dpa)," *Abendpost*, 25 Jan. 1960.

Figs. 5.3a and 5.3b. Die Brücke *(1959). Screenshots.*

Another sequence shortly thereafter is central to the mission form as well as to the more general coding of the Wehrmacht in the film. After viewers watch the boys cleaning their weapons in the barracks, Wicki cuts to the headquarters of a colonel, (Oberstleutnant) who immediately, at the beginning of the scene, declares the situation terrible ("beschissen") and then asks for a cigar. The image accompanying this declaration and request is a wall map that reinvokes the boys' school map in the second sequence in the film and underscores the gap between the boys' romanticizing the front on the classroom map and the Wehrmacht's own maps of the inoperable situation (figs. 5.3a and 5.3b). The map, of course, is a cliché of many war films, another means, even more material than the mission, of mediating the hero and the unit back to the national. As Siegfried Kracuaer argues in his analysis of Nazi war films, the maps serve to convey the mission while linking it, visually, to national space.[45] But in *Die Brücke* Wicki ironically undercuts the map in service to the war, first via the classroom and second via the collapsing front that the military commanders cartographically understand but do not communicate to the soldiers. Viewers not only know that the Wehrmacht's situation is terrible, but also know that military commanders know the situation is terrible. This viewer knowledge makes the next scene completely ironic, even cynical: the same colonel gives a boiler-plate yet rousing speech to his troops, including the seven young recruits, about defending every bit of German soil. In this scene the boys show that the one day of training (and likely the premilitary training that Borchert references) has yielded the appropriate discipline. They stand in straight rows and at attention in a familiar iconography lifted from Nazi culture and one critically invoked in postwar films about the young like *Rotation*. The speech reminds the troops of their place in history and their duty to defend this territory at the heart of Germany, words

---

[45] Siegfried Kracauer, *From Caligari to Hitler: A Psychological History of German Film* (1947; repr., Princeton, NJ: University of Princeton Press, 2004).

Figs. 5.4a and 5.4b. Die Brücke *(1959). Screenshots.*

that move them, as viewers see in a tracking close-up of the boys that is also familiar from films such as *Triumph of the Will* (figs. 5.4a and 5.4b).

Although this iconography is familiar from the Third Reich, Wicki has deliberately recontextualized it, demythifying its meaning in the ways that Cawelti discusses: the gap between the colonel's private assessment as he looks at the map and his public speech to the one-day soldiers drives home the cynical complicity of Wehrmacht officers in the boys' credulous self-sacrifice.

During the speech, however, the boys' company commander, Captain Fröhlich, stands to the colonel's right, and in the few moments during which he escorts the colonel to his car, he quickly asks him about his seven young recruits, about whether they might be assigned the mission of defending their own local bridge. After the colonel requests another cigar and orders his assistant to bring cognac, he declares the protection of the bridge pointless, as the United States already has a bridge further north, such that the local bridge will be demolished in any case. But Fröhlich persists, and the colonel brusquely relents, telling Fröhlich to do what he wants as the car whisks the colonel away. Fröhlich's sudden, even furtive request, the colonel's careless manner, and the car speeding away to more meaningless meetings and mendacious speeches underscore the arbitrariness of life-changing decisions by those in command. These carelessly taken decisions determine the mission at the narrative core of this demythifying film.

In fact, the absurdity of the mission is what leads to the boys' dogged commitment to defending a meaningless bridge and their deaths. Their immediate commander, Corporal Heilmann, knows the boys are to be ordered away from the bridge when the Wehrmacht demolition team appears, but Heilmann is suddenly, even shockingly, killed by the local military police in the apparently innocuous small town. Heilmann wanders away from the bridge and into the small town to search for coffee, but is stopped and questioned by the military police. Apparently unaware of the collapsing front and the terrible situation the colonel references, they are surprised to see a deployed soldier in their town. When Heilmann tells them his orders are to defend the local bridge, the mission he recounts is so absurd that they do not believe him and accuse him of being a deserter. When they pull a gun on him, he panics and runs, and they kill him summarily. Intended to save the boys, the mission's apparent irrelevance to the wider war ends up dooming the corporal and the boys, who no longer have anyone to tell them to accede to the bridge's demolition. Without their corporal to temper their ideological fervor for self-sacrifice, most of the boys are killed in a lengthy, gruesome battle sequence undercut by the absurdity of the mission and, by implication, of the war in general. So the bridge stands, but as a derisive parody of the mission given the boys and, indeed, Germany generally in the war. The mission form of the war film has been turned inside out. The recurring metaphor of a bridge suggests not, as it did elsewhere, the promise of the successful relation of the local to the more general, of the small town to the nation. In *Die Brücke*, the failed, pathetic defense of a bridge demythifies the linkages between individual and collective missions, just as integration into the unit is demythified in the group of boys. In these ways, *Die Brücke*'s engagement with the core mechanisms of the genre reverse the generic syntax of the war film, demythifying it in such a way that the 1950s production trend quickly faded in the wake of this celebrated yet decidedly generic film.

6: Ironizing Identity: The German Crime Genre and the Edgar Wallace Production Trend of the 1960s

Sascha Gerhards

FROM 1959 TO 1972, Germany sustained a wave of some thirty-eight filmic adaptations of Edgar Wallace's crime novels, most of which were produced by Rialto Film, a Danish-German film company. The Wallace wave paralleled, in many ways, the success of the Karl May adaptations (also produced by Rialto) and remains one of Germany's most popular cultural artifacts of the postwar era. Preben Philipsen, head of the Rialto production company, filmed the first installment, entitled *Der Frosch mit der Maske* (The Frog with the Mask) in 1959, followed by *Der rote Kreis* (The Red Circle) in the same year. Although both films were made in Denmark, they targeted the German film market and were enormous box-office successes.[1] The production was subsequently relocated to Germany, and the German Rialto was founded as a subdivision of Constantin-Film, which then exclusively distributed the Edgar Wallace films. What followed in the next fifteen years was Germany's longest feature-film series, with thirty-two films produced by Rialto.

At first sight, the relatively low production costs of each of the series' films—*Der Frosch mit der Maske* cost only around 600,000 DM—contrasts with the cycle's audience appeal, yet they also help to explain some of the series' generic aspects. Very few scenes and sequences were actually filmed on location in Great Britain and inserted into the films later. A great number of location shots were overdubbed and reused several times throughout the cycle. All the aforementioned characteristics suggest an affiliation with B-movies, as Georg Seeßlen has argued.[2] Despite the few location shots, the unrealistic depictions of Great Britain, and the modest production costs, attendance ranged from 3.2 million for the first

---

[1] Joachim Kramp, *Hallo! Hier spricht Edgar Wallace—Die Geschichte der legendären deutschen Kriminalfilmserie von 1959–1972* (Berlin: Schwarzkopf & Schwarzkopf Verlag, 1997), 66 and 77.

[2] Georg Seeßlen, "Edgar Wallace—Made in Germany," *epd Film* 6 (1986): 1, http://www.filmzentrale.com/rezis/edgarwallacegs.htm.

film, *Der Frosch mit der Maske,* to 3.6 million for several other productions, until the decline of audiences in the early 1970s, when it shrank to
around 800,000 for *Das Rätsel des silbernen Halbmonds* (The Riddle of
the Silver Half-Moon), the last film of the cycle.[3] By 1970 the films of
the cycle had grossed 140 million DM at the box-office with production
costs averaging only 1.4 million DM per film, rendering it not only one
of the longest but also one of the most commercially successful postwar
German film series.[4]

Almost alone in (anglophone) German film scholarship, Tim
Bergfelder has addressed the impact and significance of the Wallace
cycle and its underlying implications for national identity. In his article
"Extraterritorial Fantasies: Edgar Wallace and the German Crime Film,"
and then in his essay "Imagining England: The West German Edgar
Wallace cycle," Bergfelder argues that the "German crime film was indeed
frequently an extraterritorial genre, centred on a transnational imaginary
or fantasy" and links these fantasies to identity formation.[5] According
to Bergfelder, identity is formed through an involvement with a fictitious
idea of the other or foreign. Bergfelder sees "progressive nostalgia" (*EF,*
46) as one of the most crucial elements of the Wallace cycle, which in his
theory indicates the Germans' unwillingness to deal with their immediate
past. He then concludes that instead of foregrounding national contexts,
the cycle focuses on an international or transnational consumer culture.
The cycle's relation to national culture and particularity is, according to
Bergfelder, therefore largely a negative one.

While Bergfelder's argument concerning escapism through another
(imagined) culture is very persuasive, it does not, I argue herein, take
what scholars have termed the generic life cycle of the Wallace cycle into
adequate account. I argue that German identity is more and more articulated over the 1960s by an increasing number of ironic elements in the
Wallace films, thus manifesting increasing irony and self-reflexivity over
the course of an important cycle in an era of largely genre cinemas. Ironic
elements also reappear in a more obvious manifestation in the recent
Wallace parodies. Even more importantly, there is evidence in contemporary reviews and newspaper articles of an increasing awareness and appreciation of these comic elements by audiences and critics, which gives a
distinctly German inflection to the transnational escapism that Bergfelder
foregrounds in the films. Thomas Schatz has argued that elements such
as irony fulfill an aesthetic cultural function and find their way into genre

---

[3] Kramp, *Hallo! Hier spricht Edgar Wallace,* 66.

[4] Florian Pauer, *Die Edgar Wallace-Filme* (Munich: Wilhelm Goldmann Verlag,
1982), 20.

[5] Tim Bergfelder, "Extraterritorial Fantasies: Edgar Wallace and the German
Crime Film," in *The German Cinema Book,* ed. Tim Bergfelder, Erica Carter, and
Deniz Göktürk (London: British Film Institute, 2002), 39 (hereafter cited as *EF*).

cinema as it evolves.[6] Similarly, John G. Cawelti has convincingly linked the end of a genre's life cycle to parody and satire.[7] The late-genre ironic elements must be taken into account when analyzing the cultural function of the Wallace cycle, especially in light of the generic history of crime fiction in Germany and what I foreground as a recurring dialectic of national particularity and transnational influence and imagery in Germany's many crime narratives in both literature and film.

German screenwriter Gerhard F. Hummel had had the idea for filmic adaptations of Wallace novels as early as 1955, when he submitted the draft of a script for *Die toten Augen von London* (The Dead Eyes of London) to Waldfried Barthel, one of the cofounders of Constantin-Film (established in 1950). Barthel, who later significantly contributed to the success of the Wallace cycle, rejected Hummel's idea at first because of the German film industry's general skepticism about crime films. Interestingly, the industry's refusal to produce crime films resulted from a lack of enthusiasm for German crime films in the immediate postwar years.[8] But when Barthel and Preben Philipsen attended a screening of the English Wallace adaptation of *Der Hexer* (The Sorcerer, released in English as *The Ringer*) in 1958 they realized that they could much improve the quality of crime films and decided to commence with a German Wallace cycle.[9] With its thirty-two films, the cycle can be roughly divided into four phases, as Joachim Kramp has suggested.[10] Films 1 (*Der Frosch mit der Maske*) through 11 (*Das Gasthaus an der Themse*, The Guest House on the Thames, 1962), consist of precise adaptations of Wallace's templates. The movies of the second period heavily altered the original novels, sometimes to the point where only the title and names of certain characters were retained in the films. This second phase consists of films 12 (*Der Zinker*, The Cardsharp, 1963) through 18 (*Das Verrätertor*, The Traitor's Gate, 1964).

Despite their use of original Wallace titles, the narratives of the third period of films, numbers 19 (*Der Hexer*, 1964) through 28 (*Der Mann mit dem Glasauge*, The Man with the Glass Eye, 1969), almost entirely diverge from Wallace's novels, instead offering newly invented content. Except for the first two, all of the films of this period were shot in color. The fourth and final stage of the cycle consists of the last five Wallace adaptations, all of which were international coproductions.[11] Like Kramp, Florian Pauer observes an increase of newly invented elements starting

---

[6] Thomas Schatz, *Hollywood Genres: Formulas, Filmmaking and the Studio System* (Philadelphia: Temple University Press, 1981), 41.

[7] John G. Cawelti: *Mystery, Violence & Popular Culture* (Madison: University of Wisconsin Press, 2004), 208; hereafter cited as *MVP*.

[8] Kramp, *Hallo! Hier spricht Edgar Wallace*, 44.

[9] Kramp, *Hallo! Hier spricht Edgar Wallace*, 44.

[10] Kramp, *Hallo! Hier spricht Edgar Wallace*, 44.

[11] Kramp, *Hallo! Hier spricht Edgar Wallace*, 44.

Figs. 6.1a and 6.1b. Der Zinker *(1963). Screenshots.*

with the third phase and additionally links these elements to the horror genre.[12] The Rialto productions ranged from exact adaptations to films mostly offering newly invented content; that is, using the Wallace brand only as a marketing tool. Commonly included in the discourse on the Wallace wave, several other films based on Wallace novels were produced in the 1960s in addition to the thirty-two Rialto productions, although critics and filmmakers alike regard these films as copycats.

The producers and production and distribution companies are not the only players in the Wallace cycle's genrification, however. To borrow a term from Rick Altman for the transmedial and discursive consolidation of a film genre, other institutions played important roles as well. Early on, officials of the organization FSK (Freiwillige Selbstkontrolle; Voluntary Self Regulation of the Movie Industry) began to criticize the cycle for its depiction of violence, its frequent exposure of blood, and its use of eroti-cized images, which certainly helped attract the target audience of eighteen to thirty-five year-olds, as producer Horst Wendlandt explained in an interview with a film journalist in early 1964.[13] A recurring cast, if not really a star system, also helped to establish these as a genre. For example, Comedian Eddie Arent appeared in twenty-three of the cycle's films, Klaus Kinski totaled sixteen, Siegfried Schürenberg reappeared fifteen times (thirteen films as Sir John, head of Scotland Yard), and Joachim Fuchsberger returned to the screen thirteen times (*SJ*, 97–98).

The decline of the German Edgar Wallace productions in the late 1960s dovetailed with what is widely regarded as an important generational shift in postwar culture. The political situation in Germany escalated and culminated in the formation of the RAF; the *Autoren* of the *New German Cinema* declared the old cinema dead and were even making progress toward replacing it; and the self-referential, realistic television series *Tatort* with its nationally more specific qualities aired for the first time. Nevertheless, several generations of Germans have grown

---

[12] Pauer, *Die Edgar Wallace-Filme*, 20.

[13] Andreas Neumann, *Sir John jagd den Hexer—Siegfried Schürenberg und die Edgar-Wallace-Filme* (Berlin: Schwarzkopf & Schwarzkopf, 2005), 129; hereafter cited as *SJ*.

up on the Wallace films since the 1970s, as the movies were repeated frequently on numerous German television stations; in fact, the term Edgar Wallace film has become a ubiquitous cultural reference. In more recent years several attempts have been made to revive the success of Wallace adaptations. Malte Hagener has pointed out that "even today the German film industry holds up the Wallace cycle of the 1960s as a model producers should emulate."[14] In the mid-1990s the German television station RTL aired a new series of Wallace films that were, as in the 1960s, produced by Rialto, but that were shot in London and starred British actors. More prominently and significantly more successful than the aforementioned RTL adaptations, the two movie parodies *Der WiXXer* (2004) and *Neues vom WiXXer* (2007) brought the German Wallace recipe back to the big screen.

The Wallace cycle is part of an unfolding generic history of crime narrative that is highly relevant to the ongoing tension between its transnational influences and national specificity. The crime genre has had a somewhat troubled trajectory in German cultural history since its emergence in the late 1800s, when early German crime-related literature originated in the genres of the *Geheimnisroman* and *Schauerroman*. This complex history demonstrates, in fact, a long-term entanglement with "foreign" forms and influences that foreshadows the Wallace cycle. For example, while the *Geheimnisroman* roughly resembles the anglophone mystery novel, the *Schauerroman* is linked to the English gothic horror novel, an affiliation with traits that reappear in the Wallace films. The genre's twentieth-century ancestors are to be found elsewhere but nonetheless transnationally, especially in Great Britain's classic detectives and the American hard-boiled variety. Although scholars have recently also recognized E. T. A. Hoffmann as one of the genre's forefathers, German critics and scholars have largely, at least until the 1970s, rejected crime literature as pulp fiction and, in doing so, heavily influenced German authors, who consequently looked abroad for suitable models. Instead of developing recognizable nationally specific generic traits, authors of crime fiction tended to mimic anglophone publications well into the twentieth century.

In these and other ways, German crime narrative unfolded for decades within a dialectic of transnational influence and national particularity. For example, as early as the mid-Weimar era, Siegfried Kracauer emphasized the "internationality" of the genre as one of its abiding characteristics in *Der Detektiv-Roman—Ein philosophischer Traktat*, which he completed in 1925, stating:

---

[14] Tim Bergfelder, *International Adventures—German Popular Cinema and European Co-productions* (New York: Berghahn Books, 2005), 162, hereafter cited as *IA*.

> Der Internationalität dieser vom Detektiv-Roman gemeinten
> Gesellschaft entspricht genau sein internationaler Geltungsbereich,
> ihrer Gleichförmigkeit in den verschiedenen Ländern die
> Unabhängigkeit seiner Struktur und Hauptgehalte von nationalen
> Eigentümlichkeiten.[15]

> [The international domain of the crime novel correlates with the
> internationality of the society it addresses. The independence of its
> structure and contents from national particularities matches the uni-
> formity of societies in the various countries.]

In light of this development, it is not surprising that Kracauer praises the
"highly civilized Anglo-Saxons" for the establishment of the genre.[16]
Commenting on Kracauer's assertions, Tim Bergfelder criticizes Kracauer
in "Extraterritorial Fantasies," observing that Kracauer "seems to conceive of an international circulation of thematic motifs and genres, which
are re-interpreted . . . according to specific cultural needs and historical
contexts" (*EF*, 39). Bergfelder rejects Kracauer's argument that German
cinema was incapable of producing a national version of the crime genre,
calling it a "well-worn verdict frequently leveled [*sic*] at many other
European-made genres, seen as inferior copies of their Hollywood counterparts and often castigated for eschewing their duty of properly reflecting their national context" (*IA*, 139). Contrary to Bergfelder's perception
that Kracauer's statement is proof of a German obsession exclusively tar-
geting Britishness, I argue that Germany (re)established native generic
traits much later than other countries in the 1970s, which explains the
mimicking of British literature and films. At the same time, ironic elements in the Wallace cycle provided a loophole that allowed for compensation for the missing nationally specific generic conventions.

Confirming this ongoing tension of the nationally specific and
transnational was the impact of the so-called *Pitaval* stories during the
Weimar Republic. Todd Herzog discusses these semi-realistic publications in his "Crime Stories: Criminal, Society, and the Modernist Case
History," examining them for fiction and facticity. Originating in France,
the *Pitaval* stories were known even to Schiller, but had their heyday in
early twentieth-century Germany. Instead of providing fictional stories,
the crime narrative in Weimar Germany mixed fiction with actual German
cases, such as that of the serial killer Fritz Haarmann. This resulted in a
plethora of criminal-case stories in lieu of crime fiction. Publications such
as *Außenseiter der Gesellschaft: Die Verbrechen der Gegenwart* (Outsiders

---

[15] Siegfried Kracauer, *Der Detektiv-Roman—Ein philosophischer Traktat*
(Frankfurt am Main: Suhrkamp, 1979), 10. All translations in this essay are my
own, except where otherwise credited.

[16] Kracauer, *Der Detektiv-Roman*, 10. See also *EF*, 39.

of Society: The Crimes of Today, a series of criminal case stories) were widely distributed in the Weimar Republic and combined features of crime fiction with historically accurate details from real criminal cases. Herzog describes the *Pitaval* as follows: "Exciting and crisply narrated stories combine with clinical analyses and trial transcripts in the pages of these volumes, developing a genre that *would become increasingly popular later in the century*: the nonfiction documentary crime novel."[17] The success of the *Pitaval* foreshadowed such revolutionary productions as Fritz Lang's masterpiece *M—Eine Stadt sucht einen Mörder* (M—A City Seeks a Murderer, 1931), with its film-noir setting and a plot that documented pathologically the psychosis of a child killer. Both the *Pitaval* stories and *M* were in part based on the psychopathological drive of murderers. They paralleled public paranoia and are but one example of the media's response to this paranoia.[18] Despite celebrated works such as Lang's *M*, and comparable to literary publications, most German crime films nonetheless mimicked anglophone productions instead of foregrounding nationally specific conventions—German crime films in general largely avoided nationally specific references and referentiality. And contrary to common belief, crime films were continuously produced even during Weimar Germany and National Socialism, despite the Nazis' aversion to the genre. Analogously, the demand for crime literature remained stable, even during the Nazi period and despite attempts of the Nazis to prohibit it (*EF*, 41).[19] Like the films of the Wallace cycle, typical crime films from the Nazi era either focus on foreign criminals sabotaging Germany or, like *Der Mann, der Sherlock Holmes war*, are crime-film comedies.

The early postwar years saw some promising crime narratives that did engage deliberately with specifically national discourse, including the recent past. *M*, in fact, became an explicit model for films like *Die Mörder sind unter uns* (The Murderers Are Among Us, 1946) and *Der Verlorene* (The Lost One, 1951), while *Nachts, wenn der Teufel kam* (Nights When the Devil Came, released in English as *The Devil Strikes at Night*, 1957) also used crime—and another serial-killer narrative—to engage the Nazi past. One of the few self-referential postwar detective films to openly address Germany's unloved and often repressed immediate past was *Epilog—Das Geheimnis der Orplid* (Epilogue—the Secret

---

[17] Todd Herzog, "Crime Stories: Criminal, Society, and the Modernist Case History," *Representations* 80 (2002): 43; my emphasis.

[18] For a detailed discussion of the intersections of the various media—that is, fiction and non-fiction—in response to public paranoia, see Todd Herzog, "Crime Stories."

[19] Andreas Neumann provides an extensive discussion of Nazi crime films in *Sir John jagd den Hexer—Siegfried Schürenberg und die Edgar-Wallace-Filme*, albeit focusing exclusively on Siegfried Schürenberg's career as an actor in Nazi Germany.

of the Orplid, 1950). In light of Yogini's Joglekar's analysis of Helmut Käutner's *Epilog*,[20] the "enduring fascination with Britain" (*EF*, 39) on which Bergfelder focuses becomes all the more complicated. In order to explain the film's surprising success, Joglekar establishes the term "anti-detective cinema," which he defines as a genre with distinctly national generic conventions and a close relation to film noir:

> By antidetective cinema I mean films in which the detective's investigation leads not to a successful solution, but instead to a core of doubt enhanced by two means: (1) a questioning of the traditional detective film form, and (2) a commentary on sociopolitical conditions.[21]

The sociopolitical involvement of later German detective films and the *Neuer Deutscher Kriminalroman*, according to Joglekar, was already foreshadowed in Fritz Lang's *M—Eine Stadt such einen Mörder*, which had overcome generic limitations such as the focus on an imaginative Other. Unlike the postwar Wallace cycle, antidetective films addressed Germany's immediate past, although they did so neither in their pre-texts, nor in their texts, but rather in their subtexts. Joglekar shows this in his close analysis of Helmut Käutner's *Epilog*, in which he provides a reading of the film's *mise-en-scène*, frame, and narrative.

By the mid- and late 1950s, however, this kind of nationally oriented German crime genre was mostly faring quite poorly. Audiences and critics alike perceived the few nationally specific crime novels and films of the era as uninventive, unengaging, even boring—they deliberately chose Wallace and similar British, but also American, crime novels instead. In an article from the late 1960s, for example, the weekly magazine *Der Spiegel* addressed the success of the Wallace films, comparing and contrasting the cycle to other German productions. In the article entitled "Luftzug aus dem Jenseits" (A draft from the past), the magazine reminds its readers of successful and, more importantly, suspenseful crime films of the Weimar era that stood in stark contrast to contemporary productions. The article notes, analyzing the current state of the German crime genre in early 1955, that the film distributor Deutsche London Film-Verleih released a statement claiming that nowadays a German crime film is a rare commodity. This rarity, the article further claims, is predominantly based on poor demand. As the *Spiegel* article emphasizes, critics perceived postwar productions such as *Mannequins in Rio* (1954), *Banditen der Autobahn* (Bandits of the Autobahn, 1955),

---

[20] Yogini Joglekar, "Helmut Käutner's *Epilog: Das Geheimnis der Orplid* and the West German Detective Film of the 1950s," in *Take Two—Fifties Cinema in Divided Germany*, ed. John Davidson and Sabine Hake (New York: Berghahn Books, 2007), 63.

[21] Joglekar, "Helmut Käutner's *Epilog*, 63.

Grabenplatz 17 (Burial Plot 17, 1958), and *Der Greifer* (The Grabber, 1958) as naive, unrealistic, tiring, sentimental, and lacking any kind of suspense, national specificity, or social relevance.[22] After concluding that the profit from these films full of moral rectitude was analogously low, the article turns toward the unexpected success of the Wallace cycle that it labeled "apolitical"—that is, nationally and socially irrelevant—but that was more successful than any foreign production.

An article in the weekly newspaper *Die Zeit* written by crime author C. Amery and published in 1963 evaluates the German crime genre in similar terms. Amery states right in the introduction to his article: "Dieser Tage und Wochen beschäftigt sich eine geplagte Jury mit der Frage, ob es *demnächst* einen guten deutschen Kriminalroman gibt" (These days, a jury is preoccupied with the question of whether there *will be* good German crime fiction *some time soon*).[23] In doing so, he is pointing out the nonexistence of a crime genre with nationally specific traits in Germany. Most contemporary reviews decried the lack of social relevance as a problem of the German crime genre in general and not as one of the postwar Wallace series in particular. Amery locates the reason for this lack in an unwillingness to address contemporary issues grounded in ethical sensitivity (sittliches Empfinden):

> Konsequenterweise ist die Welt des deutschen Kriminalromans (soweit es dergleichen gibt) eine Welt der Außenseiter, der dumpfen oder drolligen Ganoven, der exotischen Messerwerfer, der Randmilieus wie etwa des Zirkusses, des Varietés, der Hafenspelunken.[24]

> [Consequently, the world of the German crime novel (as far as it exists, at all) is one of outsiders, of dull or droll crooks, of exotic knife throwers, of subcultures such as circuses, vaudevilles, and sailors' dives.]

These contemporary reviews suggest (and lament) that audience appeal was based much more on thrilling narratives, unusual murder weapons, and peculiar character types rather than on references to particular social circumstances—or, I would emphasize, a marked tendency toward transnational escapism. In other words, the Wallace cycle was a sort of cinema of attractions rather than a fully narrative cinema that "escapism"

---

[22] "Luftzug aus dem Jenseits," *Der Spiegel*, 30 Nov. 1960, 82. "Anfang 1955 konnte der Deutsche London Film-Verleih konstatieren, daß heute ein deutscher Kriminalfilm Seltenheitswert genießt, aber mit dem Unterschied, daß diese Rarität nicht (wie sonst üblich) besonders gefragt ist."

[23] Carl Amery, "Warum zu fernen Verbrechen schweifen?," *Die Zeit*, 7 June 1963, 18; my emphasis.

[24] Amery, "Warum zu fernen Verbrechen schweifen?," 18.

would imply—and the target audience of eighteen- to thirty-five-year-olds reinforces this impression. A *Filmecho/Filmwoche* review of *Zimmer 13* (Room 13, 1964) carries a very similar undertone. Once again the reviewer implies that the Wallace films were not expected to be realistic, or even well produced, but rather audiences expected them to be thrilling and entertaining (*SJ*, 124).

This insight into the films' attractions returns us to Bergfelder's analysis of the films, which I do not regard as incorrect so much as incomplete: his theory on a transnationally oriented identity formation is convincing in addressing the Wallace cycle, yet his approach does not fully place it within the context of German crime narrative in the longer arc of the genre, which these reviews—not least in comparing them unfavorably with the more nationally specific narratives from the Weimar era—invoke. As I have indicated above, a German crime genre with nationally specific generic traits was not much represented in the 1950s and 60s and only overtly emerged with the *Neuer Deutscher Kriminalroman* and the realistic, self-conscious crime film, especially the *Tatort* series in the 1970s. In fact, the rise of both nationally specific traits and of self-conscious television crime series helps explain the diminishing prospects for the Wallace cycle in the 1970s. This suggests that a remarkable generic gap occurred between the 1920s' more indigenous fiction (as discussed by Siegfried Kracauer) and 1970s German crime fiction, a gap that was largely filled by the nationally ambiguous Wallace cycle. Although often lacking in national specificity, these films did not merely represent transnational escapism. As I shall show, critics and audiences alike were well aware of the series' pseudo-Britishness and perceived the films as comic caricatures of British mannerisms, rather than embracing what Bergfelder regards as a "preferred version of Britishness" (*EF*, 43). But to comprehend the operations of such comedy, parody, and irony, it is useful to look at the theories of generic evolution and life cycle, which sketch multiple tonal registers even for conspicuously generic films.

As this criticism of the late 1950s and early 1960s crime narrative suggests, it does not suffice to understand the mimicking of British and American productions as a postwar phenomenon or as one limited to the Wallace cycle. Rather, a generic and generically historical problem seems to be at hand, one located somewhere consistently between national specificity and transnational influence and imagery. Reflecting on the potential for formulaic films to manifest multiple meanings, Jean-Loup Bourget convincingly argues that "whenever an art form is highly conventional, the opportunity for subtle irony or distanciation presents itself all the more readily."[25] This observation becomes crucial when applied

---

[25] Jean-Loup Bourget, "Social Implications in the Hollywood Genres," *Journal of Modern Literature* 3 (1973): 191.

to the crime film, a genre that has been criticized, as noted above, for its strict compositional structure and lack of social relevance. Bourget emphasizes, for instance, that European directors who had immigrated to Hollywood during the Second World War told stories with "implicit ironical meanings" in their movies.[26] Moreover, unlike the *auteur* theory, the iconological approach "assumes that a film is a sequence of images whose real meaning may well be unconscious on the part of its makers."[27] In a related vein, in *Hollywood Genres*, Thomas Schatz has discussed the interdependence of generic evolution and increasing self-consciousness in genre films. Basing his theory in part on Christian Metz's "Textuality and Generality,"[28] Schatz identifies this interdependence as a crucial factor in Metz's approach to a genre's life cycle, suggesting that "both filmmakers and audience grow increasingly self-conscious regarding the genre's formal quality and its initial social function."[29] According to Schatz, a genre's life cycle consists of four phases. It begins with an experimental phase, in which generic conventions are generated. Early Wallace adaptations in Germany can be linked to this initial stage. At the classic stage, audiences and artists alike are familiar with a genre's conventions, which in the case of the German crime genre explains the tradition of a tendency toward Britain as the genre's paragon. During the stage of refinement "certain formal and stylistic details embellish the form."[30] With the final, "baroque" stage, generic conventions become mannerist or self-reflexive, with irony being a crucial element.[31]

Schatz's observations, though focusing on the American-made Hollywood film, are applicable to the Wallace cycle in that they explicate changing perceptions in filmmakers and audiences during a genre's life cycle, something the large number and long history of the Wallace films demonstrates. With the postwar Wallace films, I argue, the cycle must be read as part of a larger generic trajectory in Germany, in terms of both the genre of crime narrative sketched above and the Wallace films themselves. Florian Pauer points out in his discussion of filmic Wallace adaptations that the postwar fascination with Edgar Wallace was by no means the first filmic involvement with the author. One hundred and sixty-eight (!) films based on Wallace's novels were made between 1915 and 1982, many of which were produced in Great Britain, the United States, and Austria. Several adaptations even appeared in Germany in the 1920s and 1930s

---

[26] Bourget, "Social Implications," 192.
[27] Bourget, "Social Implications," 192.
[28] Christian Metz, *Language and Cinema* (New York: Praeger, 1975).
[29] Schatz, *Hollywood Genres*, 37.
[30] Schatz, *Hollywood Genres*, 37.
[31] Schatz, *Hollywood Genres*, 38.

(*EWF*, 18).[32] After *Der große Unbekannte* (The Great Unknown Man, 1927), five more films were produced for the cinema screen before the rise of National Socialism, with *Der Doppelgänger* (1934) being the last movie of this prewar cycle (*IA*, 145–46). Consequently, limiting the analysis of Wallace adaptations to the German Rialto productions in order to explain Germany's supposed postwar obsession with Britishness neither adequately engages the historically longer arc of the genre nor the diverse offerings in German cinemas. The German Rialto productions were, after all, just one cycle within the larger genre. Even though Tim Bergfelder rightfully argues that the German Rialto productions were certainly among the most successful, the British production company Merton Park surpassed Rialto, with forty adaptations filmed in the relatively short time span between 1960 and 1964, many of which ran on German screens (*EWF*, 18). Thus, given the number and history of such productions, it makes sense to consider the 1950s and 1960s Wallace films as a later stage of the lifecycle of the genre. The number of Wallace adaptations in different national cinemas has to be taken into account when discussing the Rialto cycle's tendency to "transform national identity into a generically coded commodity," as argued by Bergfelder (*EF*, 46). Given the multiplicity of Wallace productions available for transnational escapism, there must be something else at work to explain the particular popularity of the (German) Rialto adaptations of the Wallace novels.

Another theorist of genre, John G. Cawelti, has analyzed the later stages of a given genre and uncovered tonal shifts in these later works. Like Schatz's approach, Cawelti's analysis, in this case of Roman Polanksi's *Chinatown* (1974), addresses the use of irony as a crucial element in (late) genre cinema. In "*Chinatown* and Generic Transformation in Recent American Films," Cawelti argues that *Chinatown*, a late hard-boiled detective film is to some extent a parody, in that "a well-established set of conventions or a style is subjected to some form of ironic or humorous exploitation" (*MVP*, 200). Like Schatz's approach, Cawelti's theory can, with the requisite caveats, be applied to the German context. The combination of well-established generic conventions and altered contexts leads him to suggest four categories, two of which become important in analyzing the Wallace cycle. The second category of generic transformation suggested by Cawelti is a cultivation of nostalgia, and parallels in many ways Tim Bergfelder's observation of progressive nostalgia in the Wallace cycle.

More importantly, however, Cawelti divides the previously mentioned mode of burlesque or parody into two subcategories, of which especially the burlesque proper is of special relevance to the Wallace cycle. "In this

---

[32] For an extensive overview of the Rialto cycle, see Joachim Kramp's *Hallo! Hier spricht Edgar Wallace.*

mode," Cawelti argues, "elements of a conventional formula or style are situated in contexts so incongruous or exaggerated that the result is laughter" (*MVP*, 201). When applied to the Wallace cycle, the exaggeration of generic conventions and the increasing use of grotesque and then comic elements underscores the perception of the burlesque proper and the classification of the cycle's films as genre cinema. Audiences and critics alike, as contemporary reviews show, perceived the films in a way that allows for conclusions about their generic familiarity. As Schatz argues, the use of such elements becomes possible only at a point fairly late in a genre's life cycle, when audiences and artists are thoroughly familiar with the generic conventions.[33] While Cawelti concludes his theoretical approach by emphasizing the nonexclusiveness of the four categories, the foundations of his argument parallel those of Schatz:

> One can almost make out a life cycle of genres as they move from an initial period of articulation and discovery, through a phase of conscious self-awareness on the part of both creators and audiences, to a time when the generic patterns have become so well-known that people become tired of their predictability. It is at this point that parodic and satiric treatments proliferate and new genres gradually arise. (*MVP*, 208)

The late stage of this life cycle is pertinent for the Wallace films, because audiences have been exposed for decades to the films' formula with its British aspirations and generic conventions. Although the attempt of the Hitler regime to ban crime fiction led to a significant break in the generic tradition, the postwar Wallace cycle picked up on the author's literary and filmic success of the prewar decades and combined the well-worn recipe with ironic elements. Moreover, given the diverse foreign product available on German screens, this was a familiar genre indeed. It is worth exploring how in the later stages of the genre these tensions are navigated differently and certainly somewhat ironically.

Pauer's exploration of the worldwide Wallace boom reminds us that the genre comprised not merely the German Rialto productions but also foreign productions that also played a role in the German public sphere and German audiences' familiarity with the genre. But the presence of such foreign productions in the German marketplace also raises the important question of why the Rialto productions were so much more popular than, for instance, the great number of Merton productions likewise available to German viewers (*IA*, 149). The answer is, I think, suggested in the reception of the films, which underscores the late- or at least later-stage genre operations that Schatz and Cawelti chart. Audiences and critics were well aware of generic tendencies and conventions. Uwe

---

[33] Schatz, *Hollywood Genres*, 38.

Nettelbeck commented in *Die Zeit* in 1966 on the supposed triviality of the genre, noting how the "English school" in particular accumulated tea-drinking old ladies who hear terrible rumors, observe unusual types of murder, and suffer frowning butlers, all elements frequently recurring in the Wallace cycle.[34] One might perceive these elements as exaggerated or overacted at times in the Wallace cycle, but critics did not, as Bergfelder claims, regard a tendency to fantasize about Great Britain as a function of a transgressive imagination. On the contrary, characters were perceived as caricatures, while the murder methods were increasingly taken as over-the-top, baroque, and even burlesque.

In a 1966 article, *Die Zeit* jumped on the bandwagon of anti-Wallace reviews, reversing the famous claim established by Wallace himself (and repeatedly used to market the Wallace films) by saying that it is absolutely impossible not to be thrilled by Edgar Wallace's pseudo-crime novels.[35] More importantly, Nettelbeck's aforementioned article comments on the success of the Wallace cycle, stating:

> Mit Ironie freilich sind sie (die Wallace-Romane) weiterhin genießbar, wie es das Rezept der Constantin-Filme beweist, mit denen Edgar Wallace nicht nur eine Renaissance in Deutschland erlebte, sondern sogar noch dem kurzatmigen deutschen Film vorübergehend eine Sauerstoffmaske erleichternd aufstülpte.[36]

> [The recipe of the Constantin films proves that they (the Wallace novels) are still enjoyable when approached ironically. The films did not only lead to a renaissance for Wallace in Germany, but they even reanimated the expiring German film by temporarily providing it with an oxygen mask.]

The article emphasizes the irony of the Rialto cycle as well as the series' aforementioned comic caricatures. Such a critical reception of the Wallace cycle foregrounds the ability of audiences to reflect on the series' ironic tendencies. The implication is that audiences understand the difference between "real" Britishness and the cycle's pseudo-Britishness, instead of taking for granted the images on the movie screen in self-forgetting escapism. Furthermore, the necessity to produce films cheaply and to provide thrilling yet funny narratives is addressed in light of the demise of German movie theaters.

The relative lack of critical involvement of the significant German media suggests an understanding of the cycle as genre cinema, a perception that is confirmed by the few reviews available. While serious newspapers and

---

[34] Uwe Nettelbeck, "Legitimer Lesestoff für alle," *Die Zeit*, 18 Nov., 1966, 50.

[35] Wolfgang von Wadkow, "Edgar Wallace's Reißer-Leben," *Die Zeit*, 21 Oct. 1966, 62.

[36] Nettelbeck, "Legitimer Lesestoff," 62.

magazines seldom addressed the cycle, as my discussion has shown, the film magazine *Filmecho/Filmwoche* frequently reviewed the latest Rialto outputs. Tim Bergfelder rightfully finds a "pleasurable fantasy about England and London, a fantasy grounded both in established generic expectations . . . and in the interrelationship with other forms of cultural consumption" (*EF*, 45), in the Wallace films, which assessment derives precisely from the aforementioned market share. Contemporary reviews, however, deemphasize Bergfelder's notion that location and setting are the main attractions of the cycle. The reviews in *Filmecho/Filmwoche* collected by Naumann reflect the understanding of the cycle as genre cinema by emphasizing the credibility of the plot, comic elements, and stagecraft rather than focusing on mise-en-scène, narrative conventions, and social references. On *Das Gasthaus an der Themse* the reviewer wrote:

> Den anhaltenden Erfolg der Wallace-Filme, der sich mit dem Kassenandrang am Berliner Premierentage auch diesmal ankündigt, muss man als ein Phänomen bezeichnen. Die Filme liegen, was Inhalt und Form anbelangt, auf dem Niveau des Romanautors. Während aber nun die große Gemeinde der Krimileser längst zu spannenderer, besser geschriebener und zumeist auch besser übersetzter Lektüre übergegangen ist, gibt das deutsche Kinopublikum den im Vergleich mit einschlägigen Auslandserzeugnissen hausbackenen Wallace-Verfilmungen den Vorzug. (*SJ*, 105)

> [The persistent success of the Wallace films, which can be seen in the recent press of people at the premiere of the latest film, must be considered a phenomenon. The films' content and form stay on Wallace's artistic level. But while readers of crime fiction long since switched to more thrilling, better-written, and mostly better-translated literature, German cinema audiences prefer the Wallace films, which in comparison to corresponding international productions are rather plain.]

The passage points to an intriguing difference between the literary and film genres. The review indicates that cinema audiences remained loyal to Wallace much longer than readers of crime fiction did, which parallels Tim Bergfelder's observation. This loyalty resulted particularly from the films' different approach to the narratives, an approach based not so much on escapism as on ironic and/or comic elements, as indicated in contemporary reviews. In the literary crime genre, then, audiences prefer a more skilled foreign product, but for film genre, something else seems to be at work for the audience—irony, comedy, even camp. More importantly, crime novels were generally foreign, a hint that confirms my argument about the lack of nationally specific traits in the 1960s. With respect to form and content, the production standards of the Wallace films are acknowledged to be low, which allows for conclusions about the poor potential for producing an accurate version of Britishness.

Finally, and perhaps most intriguingly, the audience's tendency to prefer the Wallace cycle to qualitatively better foreign productions derives from a certain star cult that becomes obvious in several other reviews.[37] A recurring cast, a feature that bore a remarkable resemblance to the Hollywood star system, contributed significantly to audience appeal and gave the Rialto Wallace productions a specifically national as well as ironic inflection. Actors Joachim Fuchsberger, Hansjörg Felmy, Heinz Drache, Karin Dor, Uschi Glas, Siegfried Schürenberg and, above all, Klaus Kinski and Eddi Arent guaranteed each episode's success. Furthermore, Harry Wüstenhagen made six appearances as a villain; Siegfried Lowitz, who stayed loyal to the crime genre with his role in the television series *Der Alte*, starred in four films; and even Christopher Lee, who speaks German fluently, played in three films before he became famous internationally.[38] This star system suggests another mode of national specificity in the genre.

A pivotal film in this context is *Der Hexer* (1964), a huge success for Rialto but also one of the first films to foreground ironic elements. One of the most successful of the German Wallace films, *Der Hexer* played self-consciously with the stereotypical generic traits previously discussed, a tendency specifically noticed by critics in later productions of the cycle. The film's ironic undertone is evidence of an audience very well aware of the series' lack of accuracy, according to the film's review in *Filmecho/Filmwoche*:

> Das ist wohl mit Abstand die beste Wallace-Verfilmung der bisherigen Serie. Er sparte weder mit amüsanten Gags noch mit Modernisierungen der Story, die er hier und da sogar zur Persiflage auflockerte. . . . Regisseur Alfred Vohrer und Kameramann Karl Löb können zufrieden auf diese Hexerei blicken—das Publikum tut es auch. (*SJ*, 137–38)

> [This is by far the best adaptation in this series so far. He (playwright Herbert Reinecker) provided amusing gags and a modernization of the story, and from time to time even lightened up the story to the point that it becomes persiflage. Director Alfred Vohrer and cinematographer Karl Löb can be satisfied with this witchery—as are the audience.]

---

[37] Andreas Neumann's *Sir John jagd den Hexer* contains an extensive collection of reviews from *Filmecho/Filmwoche*, most of which emphasize the importance of stars for the success of the cycle. Likewise, the few reviews to be found in *Der Spiegel* address the significance of a recognizable cast, Klaus Kinski and Eddie Arent in particular, for the series.

[38] SPON—Spiegel Online, einestages, "Im Bann des Killer-Froschs," http://einestages.spiegel.de/static/topicalbumbackground/4906/im_bann_des_killer_froschs.html.

Figs. 6.2a and 6.2b. Der Hexer *(1964). Screenshots.*

"Modernizing" and "persiflage" suggest a level of self-consciousness about the genre and its building blocks that is missing from the classical period of the genre. With irony being the crucial element of *Persiflage* among its ingenious, imitating, and mocking characteristics, the review clearly implies that audience appeal specifically derives from comedic factors and satirical elements rather than from the strict observance of genre parameters and the accuracy of inherent social commentary. Because of the transnationalism of the crime genre, the modernizations of the plot are not applicable exclusively to German society but rather to the social norms and morals of contemporary Westernized societies.

Florian Pauer has noted that, except for the British version from 1952, all filmic adaptations of *Der Hexer* produced between 1928 and 1964 were not only box-office successes but also had critics raving about them.[39] Thus it seems illogical to perceive the audience appeal of the pseudo-Britishness of Rialto's Wallace cycle as a postwar phenomenon and exclusively link it to attempts of identity formation by identifying with the Other. Pseudo-Britishness occurs on several levels in Rialto's *Der Hexer*, but it also contributes to the irony inherent in the film's narrative and cinematography. The movie's cast is almost entirely German, which leads to amusing attempts to pronounce, in proper English, the names of people, streets, and places in "German London town." More importantly, the film seems to overstate the established traits of British crime fiction and, in doing so, forecasts the end of the genre's life cycle, as suggested by Thomas Schatz.

Comic and ironic elements occur predominantly in the film's *mise-en-scène,* especially in the deliberately comical use of props, and in its narrative, where dialogue at times even seems to be completely nonsensical. Yet many of the film's ironic references are so subtle that they require an audience familiar with established generic codes and conventions. It is the way the film takes these codes and conventions over the top that creates the aforementioned subtle irony. In the film's credits sequence that infamously ended—in every one of the thirty-two Rialto productions—with Edgar Wallace's name written in bloody letters and the announcement,

---

[39] Pauer, *Die Edgar Wallace-Filme,* 74.

"Hallo, hier spricht Edgar Wallace" (Hello, this is Edgar Wallace speaking), it is not the genre-typical suspenseful sequence itself with its screams and evil laughter, but the score with its mixture of disco, German folk music (including trumpets and marching drums), jazz, and swing music that presents a stark contrast to the film's serious topic. Although the audience is presented with the film's first murder in the opening sequence of the film, even before the credits described above appear on the screen, what follows is a sequence that disregards any generic conventions by creating the impression that we are watching a comedy. Two female characters, who both play a minor role in the film and thus present the audience with gender roles typical for crime films of the 1960s, get involved in a nonsensical conversation about appropriate clothing, when Inspector Higgins's girlfriend reprimands his secretary: "Schicker Pullover, nur'n bißchen stramm, was?" (Nice sweater but isn't it a little too tight?), while she herself is actually wearing a tube-top.[40] The scene degenerates even further when Inspector Higgins and the infamous Sir John become involved in a discussion and embarrass themselves over a nude photo of Higgins's personal secretary. In this first sequence of the film the investigator and his superior are introduced as fools and philanderers, a theme that continues throughout the movie and puts into question the credibility of Scotland Yard itself. Later in the movie Sir John presents himself as a ladies' man, stating: "Männer von Format, zu denen ich mich in aller Bescheidenheit rechnen darf, haben schon immer einen Eindruck auf kluge Frauen gemacht" (Men with style, and I would in all modesty consider myself to be one, have always been able to impress intelligent women).[41] The only problem is that Sir John has just made the first capital mistake in the investigation, just seconds prior to this statement. Similarly, when the investigation finally seems to gain momentum, Sir John kisses the secretary on her head with excessive enthusiasm, only to add ashamedly: "Bitte vergessen Sie diesen Kuss" (Please forget this kiss).[42] The dopiness of Higgins and especially of Sir John presents the audience with an ironic take on the classical British investigator who, by employing his wit and by perfectly combing clues, is expected to solve a case in a gentleman-like manner.

Similarly, in the resolution the dialogue is full of ironic and comical references. Once again Sir John is depicted as the clueless head of investigation who, seemingly surprised and startled, gets involved in a discussion with Inspector Warren (who really is Der Hexer in disguise) about the imminent arrival of Arthur Milton, aka Der Hexer. Carefully staged, this arrival resembles a previous case in which Der Hexer was involved:

---

[40] *Der Hexer*, 00:05:11.
[41] *Der Hexer*, 00:17:05.
[42] *Der Hexer*, 00:25:50.

Sir John: Wir fühlten uns alle vollkommen sicher.
Warren: So wie jetzt, Sir.
Sir John: Richtig ja. Und dann flackerte das Licht.
Warren: So wie jetzt, Sir.
Sir John: Ja. Und dann ging es ganz aus.
Warren: So wie jetzt, Sir.[43]

[We felt completely safe.
Just like now, Sir.
Right, and then the light flickered.
Just like now, Sir.
Yes, and then the light went out.
Just like now, Sir.]

Immediately following this ridiculous exchange of nonsense, Messer, a criminal the Hexer intends to punish, is stabbed to death in the dark, while the filmmakers used a superimposition to address the audience directly: "Wissen Sie jetzt schon, wer der Hexer ist?" (Do you already know who the Hexer is?). Once again, the investigators are clueless and the appearance of the real Inspector Warren and his Australian colleague, Inspector Wesby, adds to their confusion. Generic codes and conventions are ignored and the dialogue is a caricature of a proper investigation. Especially Warren's (Milton's) answer to Sir John's question, "Was fehlt ihm denn?" (What's wrong with him?) shortly after the light has come back on presents, in its casualness, a final ironic element in the narrative, when he says: "Nichts mehr, Sir" (Nothing any more, Sir). In a less obvious fashion, ironic elements appear throughout the film as nonsensical clues, references, and seemingly displaced actions of certain characters. Be it Eddie Arendt as Archibald Finch, who sneezes at a most inappropriate moment when talking about Gwenda Milton's funeral,[44] the very same character who comments on the news headline "Der Hexer in London" (The Hexer in London), saying "Wer will denn so einen Blödsinn glauben?" (What fool would believe rubbish like this?),[45] or the clue that leads to the resolution of the case. Here the narrative suggests that Inspector Wesby found out about the Hexer being disguised as Inspector Warren because the real Warren, as opposed to the disguised Hexer, does not like women; in so doing it plays with stereotypes by suggesting that the character is homosexual.[46]

An important element of *mise-en-scène* that illuminates identity formation in postwar Germany through the Other is the film's props. Notably,

---

[43] *Der Hexer*, 01:16:30.
[44] *Der Hexer*, 00:21:00.
[45] *Der Hexer*, 00:20:00.
[46] *Der Hexer*, 01:19:55.

little is shown of the streets of London throughout the film. In fact, the movie was filmed in Berlin, with a few outdoor shots filmed on location in London that were taken from the production of reedited sequences of Rialto's 1964 adaptation of Wallace's *Der Zinker* and the (non-Wallace) crime film *Wartezimmer zum Jenseits* (Waiting Room for the Great Beyond, 1964). Indoor sequences allow for a deeper insight into Germany's social aspirations in the mid-1960s. Tim Bergfelder suggests that the British netherworlds in Rialto's Wallace adaptations "were inhabited respectively by crude stereotypes of the British working and upper class . . ., whereas modernity was invariably associated with a white-collar middle class" (*EF*, 43). What is really behind Bergfelder's observation is part of the movie's ironic undertone, which reveals the German social aspirations to prosperity of the 1960s, manifested not least through the use of props. What is presented to the viewer as a stereotypical perception of Great Britain and Britishness indeed "displays a great deal of incomprehension of the real dynamics of the British class system," as Bergfelder argues (*EF*, 43) but at the same time indicates an ironic take on the economic miracle (Wirtschaftswunder). Especially Inspector Higgins's apartment must have come across to 1960s German audiences as a collection of must-haves, including an electronically adjustable sofabed that is used as a comic element in the narrative. Higgins girlfriend uses the bed twice in the film to distract the investigator from the case and to attract his attention in an overtly sexual manner.[47] The inspector's reaction is telling in that he welcomes her attempts to some extent, without, however, completely relinquishing his male domination over the situation. The sofa bed and its use as an ironic contrast to investigators typical of the genre is one of many narrative devices in the film that presupposes an audience familiar with generic conventions. More obvious but equally as comical are the circumstances of Gwenda Milton's funeral. Inspector Wesby receives a clue in a letter from a gardener wearing an armband, yellow with three black dots on it, such as blind people wear. Comically, this gardener neatly picks up fallen leaves from the ground with a stick and never misses a stray leaf. When Wesby asks him who had given the letter to the gardener, it turns out he is not only blind but deaf and dumb, too.[48] Ultimately, it is not the use of obvious ironic references but the sheer amount of nonsense and irony sprinkled throughout that marks the film's irony and makes it clear that this is a genre film that breaks with generic conventions, a tendency that clearly indicates the end of the subgenre's life cycle and predicts the establishment of a new, more nationally specific genre.

As the cycle churned on, particularly in the wake of *Der Hexer*'s success, irony seemed to move more and more into the foreground. Rather

---

[47] *Der Hexer*, 00:32:35 and 00:57:45.
[48] *Der Hexer*, 00:22:05.

than criticizing the Wallace cycle's tendency to fantasize about Great Britain, even media critical of the Rialto productions seem to have generally perceived the films's depiction of Great Britain as inaccurate. For example, in the film *Die blaue Hand* (The Blue Hand, 1967), the producers openly played with the cycle's supposed backwardness and accused lack of originality by increasing the number of ironic elements. *Filmecho/Filmwoche* commented on the concept of *Die blaue Hand*:

> Nun ist das alles nicht mehr ganz so neu. Und nach dem x-ten Wallace auch nicht mehr so originell. Und das hat auch Regisseur Alfred Vohrer begriffen, der mit diesem Fall das ganze Genre in schöne Selbstironie anstatt in Realismus tauchte. (*SJ*, 157)

> [Now this all isn't entirely new anymore. And after the umpteenth Wallace there is hardly originality left. And director Vohrer has realized this. Instead of providing realism, he has exposed the entire genre to beautiful self-irony.]

The fact that audiences and critics considered the later Rialto productions to be ironic variations on a well-established genre, which we can see from contemporary media reports, shows the high self-referentiality and irony inherent in the series; this is far from the transnationally fantasized escapism suggested by Bergfelder. While the films were by no means realistic in their approach, as the *Filmecho/Filmwoche* review rightfully points out, their increasing ironic elements and references imply an awareness of such absences in both filmmakers and audiences, who embraced the films despite their unrealistic aura. This tendency has increased even more in the decades since the end of the cycle, while audiences, at the same time, stayed loyal to quasi-British crime and detective fiction and film.

More recently than the 1960s Wallace adaptations, comedians Oliver Welke, Bastian Pastewka, and Oliver Kalkofe have caricatured the series' comic elements in their pseudo-Wallace films *Der WiXXer* (The Rascal) and *Neues vom WiXXer* (Something New from the Rascal), referring in their titles, narratives, and subtexts to the Rialto originals *Der Hexer* and *Neues vom Hexer*. This recent revival confirms what Eric Rentschler has characterized as a 1990s cinema of consensus, but these late-stage Wallace films also demonstrate how specific certain predominantly ironic genre exercises are to Germany. Set in England like the Rialto Wallace films, *Der WiXXer* revolves around the mansion Blackwhite Castle (Blackwood Castle), residence of the Earl of Cockwood. As in *Der Hexer*, the scoundrel Earl is head of a ring trafficking in teenage girls. His existence and that of other criminals is threatened, just like in *Der Hexer*, by the character Der Wixxer. The rascal's goal is to punish the members of a syndicate, who all bear names of criminals of the Wallace cycle. Especially Christoph Maria Herbst's character Alfons Hatler, an obvious reference to Adolf

Fig. 6.3. Der WiXXer *(2004). Screenshot.*

Hitler, exemplifies the films's irony and self-consciousness around national particularity and allows for conclusions about the film's deliberate tribute. In one scene of the movie, for instance, Hatler answers the door and says to the investigators in typical Hitler-esque fashion: "Ich könnte mich als ihr Föhrer [*sic*] anbieten" (I would love to be your Führer).[49]

Remarkably, confirming the pertinence of the star system, members of the original cast reappear in *Der WiXXer*. Wolfgang Völz makes an appearance, as do Grit Bötcher and Eva Ebner. After initial doubts, Joachim Fuchsberger played a role in *Neues vom WiXXer*. These reappearances once again underscore the significance of a star cult in the Wallace series. The *Lexikon des internationalen Films* emphasizes the film's self-consciousness and its debt in its review, highlighting the film's self-mockery, which is based on obvious precursors, the Rialto Wallace films. Concluding that the film is an effortless example of appropriate entertainment with a retro feel, the review expresses a longing for a filmic tradition, a notion that restates Wendlandt's intention to produce genre cinema with audience appeal.[50] As with the Wallace series, the reception of *Der WiXXer* reaffirms Cawelti's notion of audiences having different expectations later in a genre's life cycle.

---

[49] *Der WiXXer*, Constantin Film, 2004.

[50] *Lexikon des internationalen Films*, www.filmenova-z.de.

The reexamination of the German Edgar Wallace films from the perspective of genre theory has focused on several aspects. The Rialto cycle adheres to a tendency toward escapism typical in postwar genre cinema, as Tim Bergfelder has rightfully argued. This escapism is not, however, limited to the Wallace cycle and needs to be considered within the larger historical arc of the crime genre. When one takes into account this longer trajectory, it appears that the overarching tendency to mimic British and American crime fiction and film is tempered somewhat by ironic and comic tonal shifts in the genre's late stages. Rather than assuming this coincidence to be haphazard, Cawelti and Schatz have shown how audiences develop certain expectations toward genre in the different phases of each genre's life cycle. Changing generic expectations generate an increasing number of ironic elements in a genre, elements that were recognized by critics and appreciated by audiences. The end of a genre's life cycle is reached when audiences demand something "more complicated," as Thomas Schatz put it.[51] In Germany the demand for more complicated formal, thematic, and stylistic generic traits called forth the development of the *Neuer Deutscher Kriminalroman* and the self-referential modern German crime film that had, to some extent, been foreshadowed by the Weimar *Pitaval* and Käutner's *Epilog*. Furthermore, the ongoing fascination and continuous re-broadcasting of the Rialto cycle does not invalidate the newly established self-referential native genre with its realistic focus. Rather, this continuing interest in the cycle embodies an appreciation of the films's ironic variations on unrealistic, and to some extent nostalgic, views of the crime genre's British models, a notion that is only reaffirmed by the latest Wallace parodies.

---

[51] Schatz, *Hollywood Genres*, 38.

7: From Siodmak to Schlingensief: The Return of History as Horror

Kris Vander Lugt

IN 2002 KINO VIDEO released a collection of "German Horror Classics." This four-DVD set, boxed in a slick black case with Gothic lettering, includes Robert Wiene's *Das Cabinet des Dr. Caligari* (The Cabinet of Dr. Caligari, 1920), Paul Wegener's *Der Golem und wie er in die Welt kam* (The Golem and How He Came Into the World, 1920), Friedrich Murnau's *Nosferatu: Eine Symphonie des Grauens* (Nosferatu: A Symphony of Horror, 1922), and Paul Leni's *Waxworks* (1924). None of these films would have been considered "horror films" at the time of their release; nor, some would argue, should some of them rightly be considered horror films today. Nonetheless, these films are invariably cited as key entries in the horror-film lexicon. From Lotte Eisner's famous identification of German Expressionist cinema's "haunted screen" to contemporary transnational thrillers that export German history as horror film, German identity has consistently been represented through the lens of the Faustian soul, the haunted Teuton, the mad genius. It is therefore not surprising that film scholars typically cite Germany—"the land of dark forests and darker myths"[1]—as the birthplace of horror. Carlos Clarens, in his definitive history of horror and science-fiction films prior to 1967, includes the first three films in his chapter on German film between 1913 and 1932, arguing that the sharp contrasts and dramatic acting of Expressionism offered precisely the right style "to render in black and white the reawakened fantasies of the darkly romantic German soul" (14). Similarly, S. S. Prawer attributes German filmmakers' attraction to "tales of terror" to their "rich heritage of demonic folklore, Gothic fiction, and black Romanticism."[2] Recalling the influence of Eisner and Kracauer on the characterization of Expressionist films as "morbid, traumatized and full of foreboding," Thomas Elsaesser remarks, "Rarely before or since has a body of films exerted such a pull

---

[1] Carlos Clarens, "Doubles, Demons, and the Devil Himself: Germany, 1913–1932," in Carlos Clarens, *An Illustrated History of Horror and Science Fiction Film* (New York: Da Capo, 1967), 10.

[2] S. S. Prawer, *Caligari's Children: The Film as Tale of Terror* (Oxford: Oxford University Press, 1980), 32.

towards verbal paraphrase, in which epithets like 'dark' and 'demonic,' 'twisted,' 'haunted,' and 'tormented' leap onto the page."[3] Casper Tyberg notes that *Caligari*, often cited as the godfather of modern horror, "has long been the prism through which the horror pictures of the silent period are viewed." At the same time, Tyberg notes that *Caligari's* status as a progenitor of the horror genre "has introduced considerable distortion," not least being the generalization of Expressionist cinema as uniformly concerned with the gothic or the uncanny: "Thus Expressionism ends up being almost synonymous with horror."[4]

Kino Video's "German Horror Classics" tells us a few things about horror and about genre in general. First, genre is created not only through production and distribution practices but also through institutions: through the vagaries of the marketplace, through film catalogues and DVD re-releases, and indeed, through the institutions of academia, through film scholarship, course syllabi, and so on. Second, whether or not we can define a film as "technically" a horror film—does it have a monster or involve the supernatural? Does it elicit bodily reactions of fright and disgust in the viewer? Does it utilize over-the-shoulder tracking shots and killer points-of-view?—these stylistic markers might matter rather little when it comes to the actual reality of the film's generic status: How is it marketed? How is it consumed? How is it remembered?[5]

Accordingly, this essay concerns itself primarily with the cultural memory of horror film. Thus, while there is considerable disagreement about whether *Caligari* should be considered a horror film in the modern sense, or whether *Nosferatu* should be included in a survey of Expressionist film, it cannot be contested that these films have circulated as such in both scholarly and popular discourse. There is relative consensus that the origins of horror film may be traced to Weimar and the chiaroscuro shadow-worlds of German Expressionism. At the same time, however, there has until recently[6] been little discussion of the afterlife of German horror

---

[3] Thomas Elsaesser, *Weimar Cinema and After: Germany's Historical Imaginary* (London: Routledge, 2000), 19.

[4] Furthermore, this equation neglects the extent to which the horror genre developed from the fantastic film genre that predates the Expressionist classics typically cited as horror's breeding ground. See Casper Tyberg, "Shadow Souls and Strange Adventures: Horror and the Supernatural in European Silent Film," in *The Horror Film*, ed. Stephen Prince (New Brunswick, NJ: Rutgers University Press, 2004), 18.

[5] As Prawer argues with respect to generic identification, there is not necessarily "some obligatory set of rules every work in that category much obey," but rather, "What one is asking about, ultimately, is 'common consensus' within a given society, a given culture." Prawer, *Caligari's Children*, 33.

[6] There have been some notable exceptions in recent years that address postwar German horror film, including Steffen Hantke's edited volume *Caligari's Heirs:*

in the postwar period, with the argument being that the horror film was exiled during the Third Reich and subsequently taboo in the postwar period as Germans attempted to grapple with the very real horrors of the Holocaust. The "absence" of horror is partially explicable in terms of how German film history has tended to be written. As Tim Bergfelder has noted, the study of German film has tended to "condense" and "reduce" German film history to "three emblematic moments"—Expressionism, Third Reich, and New German Cinema.[7] This has not only resulted in neglecting films that do not fall neatly into those moments, but it has also produced a considerable amount of retrospective historiography. In terms of horror films, the Nazi period is seen as a rupture in horror-film production from which the (German) genre never fully recovered. Why this rupture occurred is not entirely understood—some have speculated that the Nazi film industry's aversion to modernism may help explain the lack of contributions to the horror genre between 1933 and 1945. As Hantke points out, however, this explanation entails an equation of horror film and Expressionism and, further, would require us to assume that "horror film turned out to be virtually the only cinematic genre that could not be absorbed and co-opted by the Third Reich."[8] Ronald Hahn and Rolf Giesen, in their *Lexikon des Horrorfilms*, offer a more psychologically based explanation: "After 1933, horror films weren't really necessary anymore. Now the monsters were literally roaming the streets

---

The German Cinema of Fear after 1945 (Lanham, MD: Scarecrow, 2007). The chapter "Germans on Top" in Cathal Tohill and Pete Tombs, *Immoral Tales: European Sex Horror Movies, 1956–1984* (New York: St. Martin's Griffin, 1995), 41–52 looks primarily at exploitation and trash, also tracing the "natural birthplace" of the horror film to Germany (41). Prawer's *Caligari's Children* is also helpful for tracing the continued use of horror tropes in the postwar period, although Prawer does not discuss the films explicitly as horror films. For an illuminating discussion of the ways in which contemporary German thrillers offer alternative modes of "working through a past of perpetration" (298), see Brad Prager, "The Haunted Screen (Again): The Historical Unconscious of Contemporary German Thrillers," in *Victims and Perpetrators: 1933–1945 and Beyond; (Re)Presenting the Past in Post-Unification Culture*, ed. Laurel Cohen-Pfister and Dagmar Wienroder-Skinner (Berlin: Walter de Gruyter, 2006), 296–315. On German horror of the 1990s, see Randall Halle, "Unification Horror: Queer Desire and Uncanny Visions," in *Light Motives: German Popular Film in Perspective*, ed. Randall Halle and Margaret McCarthy (Detroit: Wayne State University Press, 2003), 281–303.

[7] Tim Bergfelder, *International Adventures: German Popular Cinema and European Co-productions in the 1960s* (New York: Berghahn Books, 2005), 2–3.

[8] Steffen Hantke, "Postwar German Cinema and the Horror Film: Thoughts on Historical Continuity and Genre Consolidation," in *Caligari's Heirs: The German Cinema of Fear after 1945*, ed. Steffen Hantke (Lanham, MD: Scarecrow: 2007), vii–xxiv.

in brown and black uniforms, giving the Hitler salute."[9] Of course, this fails to explain why the Nazis would not have taken advantage of horror film's rich inventory of monsters to demonize their enemies, a strategy well employed in American horror film in the 1950s to demonstrate the dangers of communism with films such as *The Invasion of the Body Snatchers* (1956). Furthermore, although it seems that horror films in the modernist vein did not exist during the Third Reich, there were certainly films in production that made use of horrific themes, narrative structures, and cinematography. As Claire Sisco King argues in her essay "Imaging the Abject: The Ideological Use of the Dissolve," films such as *Jew Süss* and *The Eternal Jew* "can all be read as horror texts, aiming to produce feelings of terror and disgust."[10]

Another possible explanation for the decline of horror film during the Third Reich is the simple fact that many practitioners of Expressionism moved into exile, their names eventually appearing in the credits of film noir and horror.[11] Whatever the reasons may be for the absence of horror after Expressionism, the historical record shows that it began to return to German film in the 1950s, earlier than some critics have acknowledged. While some research has been done on the proliferation of horror in Germany in the 1980s and 1990s, little attention has been paid to the 1950s and 1960s, and, again, this is likely a matter of how one defines horror, how available these films have been outside of archives, and perhaps also of ideological concerns.[12] To some extent, the genrification of films has prevented serious consideration of them, as certain genres are inevitably more privileged in academic discourse. And certainly, it is important to remember that it is not only academics and fans who determine generic identification, but also—and, indeed, perhaps first and foremost—institutions. As Altman has observed, the consolidation of horror as a genre was

---

[9] Ronald Hahn and Rolf Giesen, *Lexikon des Horrorfilms* (Mülheim, Germany: Luebbe, 1993), 5.

[10] Claire Sisco King, "Imaging the Abject: The Ideological Use of the Dissolve," in *Horror Film: Creating and Marketing Fear*, ed. Steffen Hantke (Jackson: University Press of Mississippi, 2004), 21.

[11] See Hantke, "Postwar German Cinema," xii. For a productive challenge to the argument that film noir was significantly influenced by German cinema, see Edward Dimendberg, "Down These Seen Streets a Man Must Go: Siegfried Kracauer, 'Hollywood's Terror Films,' and the Spatiality of Film Noir," *New German Critique* 89 (2003): 113–43.

[12] Bergfelder argues that film scholarship in German Studies has tended to privilege "the kind of critical approach that perceives films as a direct and mimetic reflection of specific national developments and which only values those films that didactically engage in a critical, or 'progressive,' political discourse *vis-à-vis* the social and political realities of the time." See Bergfelder, *International Adventures*, 4.

significantly aided in Britain by the introduction in 1937 of the "H" ("horrific") rating, which banned children under sixteen and "simultaneously reinforced the coherence of the horror genre."[13] With the introduction fifteen years later of the "X" rating—used for films with both sexual and horrific content—"an important mechanism for the horror genre was cut off, resulting in the genre's dismemberment and distribution into surrounding genres (science fiction, film noir, melodrama and the like)."[14]

Recent scholarship suggests that horror film "reemerged" in the period surrounding reunification, but this is not the whole story.[15] Horror was not so much *absent* in the period between 1945 and 1989 as it was *rendered* absent in film criticism, not least through the development of an aesthetic vocabulary for film that pitted "art" against "trash." Reacting, in part, to Nazism's celluloid "ministry of illusion," as Eric Rentschler has put it, postwar film critics and many filmmakers alike considered the redemption of German cinema as a medium for political engagement and social critique to be dependent in large part on the elevation of film to a high art. Accordingly, part of the cinematic project of German *Vergangenheitsbewältigung* involved not only rejecting the politics and aesthetics of Nazi cinema but also equating that cinema with "low culture." In the postfascist battle—both onscreen and off—to carve out clear distinctions between high and low, "art" and "trash," horror may be considered as a productive, contested space in which filmmakers, critics, audiences, and institutions negotiated the visual terms by which Germany would address the legacy of the Third Reich. In terms of moral policing, horror has certainly been disproportionately subject to censorship in Germany through the rating of films by the *Freiwillige Selbstkontrolle* (FSK) and indexing by the *Bundesprüfstelle für jugendgefährdende Schriften*.[16] The indexing of horror occurs in Germany primarily via Paragraph 131, passed in 1973, which provided a new instrument for censoring representations of violence. With the rise of video in the 1980s and the subsequent increased availability of films for home screening, a number of films were restricted or even forbidden, and described as generally "disorienting to youths," "desensitizing," "endangering morality," or "glorifying violence."[17] Paragraph 131 has in fact elicited an entire cottage industry online devoted to reporting and cataloging the cutting

---

[13] Rick Altman, *Film/Genre* 1999; repr., London: BFI, 2002), 95.

[14] Altman, *Film/Genre*, 95.

[15] See Randall Halle, "Chainsaws and Neo-Nazis: Contemporary German Horror Film Production," *GFL: German as a Foreign Language* 3 (2006): 41.

[16] Since 2002, the *Bundesprüfstelle für jugendgefährdende Medien* also investigates video games.

[17] C. Weinrich, "Zensur und Verbot im Genrefilm: Die große Schnittparade des Horrors- [*sic*] und Splatterfilms," accessed 21 Sept. 2010, http://www.censuriana.de/texte/genrefilm/genre.htm.

of films placed on the so-called "Index" of films forbidden for children under 18. For example, the website "Schnittberichte" devotes itself to reporting which films have been submitted to the FSK and how much of the film has been cut to satisfy German censors.[18]

Beyond the generic consolidation that occurs through institutions and websites, there is considerable disagreement regarding definitions of horror, especially given its close relation to other genres such as film noir, the psychological thriller, the splatter film, and the fantasy or sci-fi film. Further, these definitions have changed over time. Some films that are now regularly cited in histories of horror film, such as *Phantom of the Opera* (1920) or the John Barrymore vehicle *Dr. Jekyll and Mr. Hyde* (1920), in fact predated the term "horror film." Indeed, the term did not appear until around the mid-1930s in the United States with the first cycle of Universal horror films, set in motion by *Dracula* and *Frankenstein* in 1931.[19] Using the German term *Horrorfilm* already assumes, then, a post-1930s genre that was essentially branded in America. Indeed, prior to about the 1970s, films we now consider *Horrorfilme* would most likely have been referred to as *Gruselfilme* within Germany. In a 1946 essay, Siegfried Kracauer used the term "Greuelfilm"—a term used to describe "atrocity films" based on concentration camp footage—to describe a recent spate of what, in his original English-language essay, Kracauer had termed "terror films"—films such as *Shadow of a Doubt* (Hitchcock, 1943) and *Dark Corner* (Henry Hathaway, 1946), now associated with the film noir or thriller.

On the other hand, films now referred to as classic film-noir films were, as Mark Jancovich has pointed out, often understood as horror films when they were released in the 1940s.[20] These included films

---

[18] Ending up on the Index is largely a matter of representation. The law excuses films that can be resuscitated as "art" as well as films that depict "reality," defined in Germany's penal code as plot lines in service of "der Berichterstattung über Vorgänge des Zeitgeschehens oder der Geschichte [reporting contemporary or historical events]" (§ 131 Abs. 4 Nr. 3 StGB). Stated simply, in the eyes of the law, acceptable portrayals of violence are those that are "real," "historical," or "artistic." Horror auteur Jörg Buttgereit's second feature-length film *Nekromantik 2*, was seized by authorities within days of its release. Only after Knut Hickethier submitted a scholarly appraisal of the film was it eventually released from the ban in 1993, having been elevated to the status of "art." The fact that *Nekromantik 2* is considerably less violent than the nightly news and yet more stringently regulated reveals the extent to which matters of law are also matters of taste.

[19] Lincoln Geraghty and Mark Jancovich, "Introduction: Generic Canons," in *The Shifting Definitions of Genre*, ed. Lincoln Geraghty and Mark Jancovich (Jefferson, NC: McFarland, 2008), 1.

[20] For example, Otto Preminger's *Laura* (1944), Robert Siodmak's *Phantom Lady* (1944), Billy Wilder's *Double Indemnity* (1944), and Fritz Lang's *Woman in*

by Fritz Lang and Robert Siodmak, directors who were sought out by Hollywood, Jancovich argues, to capitalize on the success of the horror cycle that had gained momentum since the 1930s and was once again revitalized following the huge release of *Cat People* in 1942. A 1944 New York Times article in fact described Siodmak as a "former director of German horror films."[21]

To some extent, distinctions between "terror films," "horror films," and "films noirs" are important for understanding the subtle implications of generic labeling at critical historical junctures. On the other hand, they tend to gloss over the necessarily hybrid nature of most film production and the mutual exchange of styles and tropes. The 1950s and 1960s are largely uncharted territory for scholarly discussions of German horror film, precisely for this reason. It was during this period that horror was perhaps at its most ambivalent generically speaking, mixing elements of classic horror (monsters, aliens, the supernatural) with elements of the thriller, the science-fiction film, and the emerging sex-hygiene film.[22]

Take, for example, Robert Siodmak's *Nachts, wenn der Teufel kam* (Nights When the Devil Came, released in English as *The Devil Strikes at Night*, 1957), a "noirish thriller"[23] based on the real-life serial killer Bruno Lüdke, which takes place in Nazi-era Germany. Steffen Hantke has noted the "inconsistency" of its generic claims[24]—it begins as a horror film, with sinister music accompanying the fleeing murderer as he hides beneath branches in a swamp, with the credits gradually superimposed in an eerie script. But further on, it shifts to a police investigation in the style of a noir thriller and, as Hantke notes, by the time we reach the final reel, the film has totally lost sight of its monster figure. Bruno Lüdke has been quietly assassinated to save face for the Nazi authorities.

Another prime example from this tumultuous time of redefinition and reorganization within the German film industry is Victor Trivas's 1959 film *Die Nackte und der Satan* (The Naked Woman and Satan) also known as *Des Satans nackte Sklavin* (Satan's Naked Slave) and in English

the Window (1945). Mark Jancovich, "Master of Concentrated Suspense," *Studies in European Cinema* 5, no. 3 (2008): 171–72.

[21] Crowther in Jancovich, "Master of Concentrated Suspense," 172. Bosley Crowther, "Phantom Lady: A Melodrama of Weird Effects, with Ella Raines and Franchot Tone, has Premiere at Loew's State," *New York Times*, 18 Feb. 1944, p. 15.

[22] See Tohill and Tombs, *Immoral Tales.*

[23] Sabine Hake, *German National Cinema*, 2nd ed. (London: Routledge, 2008), 103.

[24] Hantke, "Hollywood Horror Comes to Berlin," 40. Steffen Hantke, "Hollywood Horror Comes to Berlin. A Critical Reassment of Robert Siodmak's *Nachts wenn der Teufel kam*," in Steffen Hantke, ed., *Caligari's Heirs: The German Cinema of Fear after 1945* (Lanham, MD: Scarecrow Press, 2007) 40.

as *The Head*. The film was released in West Germany in 1959. It was produced by Wolf C. Hartwig, who in the same year produced the schlocky
horror flick *Ein Toter hing im Netz* (A Body Hung in the Web) and would
later stake a claim in the developing industry of pornography with his
pseudo-documentary "schoolgirl" series, *Die Schulmädchen-Reporte*.[25]
Films like *The Head* inaugurated what one might call the "pornographic
turn" in German horror film during the late 1950s and early 1960s, the
beginning of a wave of erotic horror films that swept across much of
Europe through the 1970s with directors such as Jess Franco, Jean Rollin,
Jose Larraz, and Mario Bava, often starring one of the two "Barbaras"—
Barbara Steel or Barbara Valentin—and bearing titles such as *Sie tötete
in Ekstase* (She Killed in Ecstacy, 1971), *La Vampire nue* (The Nude
Vampire, 1969), and *Spermula* (1976, starring Udo Kier).

Die *Nackte und der Satan* is a key film in this context, one that could
be seen as a kind of paracinematic bridge halfway between the aesthetic style
of 1920s Expressionism (*Caligari*'s own Hermann Warm designed the set
for *The Head*) and the self-consciously schlocky underground horror of the
1980s. The plot is based on the familiar sci-fi scenario of a bodiless brain—a
head severed from its body, being kept alive through artificial means, usually
by means of some mysterious serum or chemical (superhuman hormones
administered prior to decapitation in the case of *They Saved Hitler's Brain*
[1966] or the rather more elegant solution of electrically charged saline
in *Donovan's Brain* [1953], based on the novel by Curt Siodmak). In *Die
Nackte und der Satan* we have Serum Z, a life-giving formula developed in
experiments with canine decapitation by the kindly Dr. Abel, assisted by his
lovely but tragically disabled nurse Irene. Enter another staple figure of the
genre: the scientist hailing from parts unknown who is bent on stealing the
serum and using it on humans, the sinister Dr. Ood.

When Dr. Abel has a heart attack and Dr. Ood is called in to assist
with a life-saving heart transplant, the stage is set for reanimation. The
heart transplant fails, of course, but Dr. Abel—or, more precisely, a part
of Dr. Abel—survives. Connected to a complex network of wires and
tubes, Dr. Abel's talking head spends the rest of the film affixed to a table
in the lab—like a "mustached walrus-head" as one reviewer described.

Dr. Ood turns his attention to the hunchbacked Irene, for whom he
has found the perfect body, an exotic dancer named Lilly who works at

---

[25] As Tohill and Tombs note in their study of European sex-horror, the
Schulmädchen-Reporte "outstripped even the Edgar Wallace films to become
Germany's highest earning cinematic exports" at the time (44). See also Tim
Bergfelder, "Exotic Thrills and Bedroom Manuals: West German B-Film
Production in the 1960s," in *Light Motives: German Popular Film in Perspective*,
ed. Randall Halle and Margaret McCarthy (Detroit: Wayne State University Press,
2003), here 205–7.

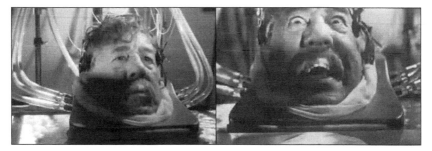

Figs. 7.1a and 7.1b. Die Nackte und der Satan *(1959). Screenshots.*

the local Tam-Tam Club. Lilly has a troubled past that she has sought to escape by having facial reconstructive surgery, which of course turns out to have been performed, with questionable legality, by Dr. Ood himself some years back. The remainder of the movie follows a familiar formula: Lilly is murdered and her body is "grafted" onto the head of the disabled nurse Irene; Irene gradually grows suspicious of her new body that does not seem to belong to her; she enlists the help of her sculptor friend Paul from the Tam-Tam Club and together they eventually manage—with the help of Igor-esque assistant Bert, in consultation with Dr. Abel's brain—to defeat Dr. Ood.

By 1959 the darker side of science was certainly well known and the associations are clearly inextricable from the then recent history of scientific and political abuses of power. The location of power is in fact a primary concern in *Die Nackte und der Satan*—who wields power? Where is it located? How does it reproduce itself? How can it be stopped? Rather than the kind of networked and decentralized power that would be depicted in, for example, a sci-fi movie such as *Bodysnatchers* (1956), *Die Nackte und der Satan* gives us an essentially fascist, dictatorial vision of power: highly centralized and, here is the Nazi twist, essentially biologically bequeathed (the real power lies literally stored within the brain of Dr. Abel, with the secret formula for Serum Z, itself reminiscent of Zyklon B). Bodysnatchers and viruses usually figure as communist and/or feminine threats in horror film—forces that threaten to invade or dissolve a body insufficiently steeled against that threat through heavy armor and heavily patrolled ego boundaries, à la Theweleit. But disembodied brains lend themselves to be read as metaphors for fascism precisely because they insist on the impermeability of those boundaries—fascist bodies have clear borders that are literally clean-cut.[26]

---

[26] One might also note here the unusual reworking of the Metropolis "Hirn und Hand" metaphor ("Mittler zwischen Hirn und Hand muss das Herz sein") figured in strictly literal terms—a brain (Abel) and a body (Lilly)—with the ensuing love story saving the day.

Because it is so closely linked with the body, horror performs a kind of direct working-through of the recent past that is unavailable to other genres. As Brad Prager has argued recently with respect to the thriller genre, "[These films] have a more candid relationship with sex and violence because of their explicit, and expected, connection to the demands of the libido." Indeed, Prager continues, the explicit nature of thrillers "associated with explosive action or grotesque horror . . . have a closer relationship to the truth of historical atrocities than films that would seek to render history digestible or tasteful."[27] Along these lines, coming to terms with the past in *Die Nackte und der Satan* means coming to terms with a fascist model of identity based on essentialism.

These concerns continue in the 1980s, an era that witnessed "a new wave of horror production" in the underground.[28] One of this era's most prominent directors is Jörg Buttgereit. Extolled by Alexander Kluge as a "subversive romantic" and celebrated by Berlin's *Radio Eins* as the "king of the German splatter film," Buttgereit has a large fan following, not only in Germany but also (and perhaps in greater numbers) internationally. He is best known for his first feature film, *Nekromantik* (1987), which virtually explodes generic borders and launches a no-holds-barred assault on bourgeois notions of propriety and decency.

Less a horror film than a bizarre twist on splatter, schlock, or exploitation, with some elements of soft-core porn, *Nekromantik* is, as the title implies, a mixture of death and romance: a lyrical ode to necrophilia for which Buttgereit retrospectively coined the phrase "corpse-fucking art." Serving also as the title of a 1992 documentary that focuses on the making of *Nekromantik* and its sequel *Nekromantik 2*, "corpse-fucking art" situates Buttgereit as a pornographic provocateur—self-styled monarch of his own necrophilic avant-garde. The voice-over to the *Corpse-Fucking Art* trailer sums up the main themes that are woven throughout his work:

> *Nekromantik, der Todesking, Nekromantik 2*: Films about the desecration of corpses, suicide, necrophilic desire, eros, and death—films about loving humans and what remains of them. While the contemporary climate regresses more than ever into Biedermeier idylls, the young Berliner Jörg Buttgereit has been turning out the most disturbing films in the world for several years now. They are 16mm productions. Low, low budget. And realized with a loyal group of friends. The most noteworthy thing about them: Buttgereit's films are neither horror nor splatter, neither art nor commerce. They are all of these simultaneously.[29]

---

[27] Brad Prager, "The Haunted Screen (Again)," 299.
[28] Randall Halle, "Unification Horror," 282.
[29] *Corpse-Fucking Art*, DVD.

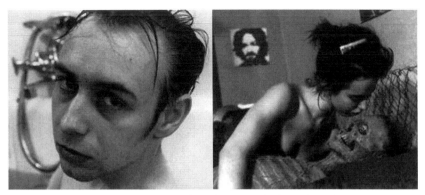

Figs. 7.2a and 7.2b. Nekromantik *(1987) and*
Nekromantik 2 *(1991). Screenshots.*

Here Buttgereit's body of work is characterized in a manner reminiscent of what Jeffrey Sconce has termed "paracinema"[30]—the fact that the films are "low, low budget,"[31] produced independently by a "loyal group of friends," and not easily categorized is part of their appeal.[32] The reference to "Biedermeier idylls" also indicates how German "trash" film consciously constructs itself as the other—and perhaps the antidote—to bourgeois sensibility, represented in *Nekromantik* by a parodic scene in the Schrebergarten of a local gun fetishist, who sits drinking mini-bottles of Jägermeister amid colorful, smiling garden gnomes.

Variously billed as trash, as pornography, as exploitation, but also as art or avant-garde, Buttgereit's films produce a variety of divergent, usually emotional, responses. Anticipating such responses, his first feature-length film *Nekromantik (oder) Die Liebe zu Menschen und was von ihnen übrig bleibt* (Necromantic [or] The Love for People and What Remains of Them, 1987), is preceded by a warning (or an invitation perhaps) that

---

[30] Paracinema has been defined most famously by Jeffrey Sconce as "an extremely elastic textual category [which comprises] less a distinct group of films than a particular reading protocol, a counter-aesthetic turned subcultural sensibility devoted to all manner of cultural detritus . . . The explicit manifesto of paracinematic culture is to valorize all forms of cinematic 'trash' whether such films have been either explicitly rejected or simply ignored by legitimate film culture." See Jeffrey Sconce, "'Trashing' the Academy: Taste, Excess, and an Emerging Politics of Cinematic Style," *Screen* 36, no. 4 (1995): 372.

[31] Further, the fact that the German original deliberately uses the English phrase "low, low budget" (instead of using a German equivalent) also speaks for locating these films within a tradition of paracinema that positions itself self-consciously against both mainstream and *Autorenkino*.

[32] Buttgereit's films are also prominent staples of American horror magazines such as *Shock Cinema* and *Fangoria*.

the film may be seen as "grossly offensive and should not be shown to minors." Inaugurated by this self-imposed interdiction, Buttgereit's "corpse-fucking art" is from the very outset, then, about the legitimacy of representation, in particular the representation of violence, sex, death, and all manner of hybrids thereof. His films have been contradictorily described as "sickening" and "twisted" but also "somber and lyrical,"[33] for some reviewers "boring"[34] but for others "entrancing," "tender," and "surprisingly delicate."[35] Critics of Buttgereit are not exactly sure where (or how) to locate him or his films.

Nekromantik introduces us to Rob, a typical white working-class German male with a rather atypical penchant for collecting specimens from dead bodies. Rob works for "Joe's Säuberungsaktion" (Joe's cleansing agency), a firm that cleans up the blood and gore of accident scenes. Here it is worth noting that the term "säubern" (cleanse) belongs to a specifically Nazi vocabulary used as a euphemism for extermination. Both the terminology, then, and the services rendered ("hygienization" of accident scenes) are coded as fascist. The fascist overtones are further emphasized by the company's symbol: a six-pointed star with a skull and crossbones.

Rob's job at "Joe's" provides him with a convenient way to further his special hobby: human taxidermy. He surreptitiously steals eyes, hearts, intestines, and other body parts from his job for preservation in his lovingly tended anatomical collection, housed in glass jars in the foyer of his one-bedroom apartment in a dilapidated turn-of-the-century apartment building. When an effeminate gardener is accidentally killed by his neighbor in a backyard hunting incident gone awry and is then carried off to a remote marsh in a wheelbarrow, the stage is set for Rob to collect his pièce de résistance: the still-fresh and relatively well preserved body of the dead gardener. Rob takes the corpse home to his girlfriend Betty, and an ill-fated ménage à trois begins. The corpse becomes a sort of proxy body for Rob, standing in for him while he is at work to satisfy Betty's sexual and emotional desires: the corpse listens intently to her as she reads from her romance novels and imagines a blissful future for herself and her new (dead) partner. However, when Rob loses his job and is berated by Betty for his lack of money and manliness, the necrophilic fairy tale ends, and Betty departs with their new "friend." Finally, Rob's emotional and financial impotence is literalized: able to reach orgasm only through autoerotic pain infliction, he commits suicide by stabbing himself repeatedly in the stomach.

---

[33] John Hartl, "*Nekromantik* Features a Grotesque Parade of Gory Obsessions." *Seattle Times*, 31 Jan. 1991, D6.

[34] "Nekromantik (1987)," accessed 8 Nov. 2009, www.stomptokyo.com/otf/Nekro/Nekro.htm.

[35] "Trash City Review: *Der Todesking*," accessed 7 Apr., 2001, www.trshcity.demon.co.uk/BLITZ/BLIT0294.HTM.

While the association of femininity with death is a familiar one in the genre, the partnering of masculinity and death is more surprising.[36] Through Rob, masculinity is styled from the outset as a sort of necrophilic configuration, a self-cannibalizing identity. He is soft-spoken and cowardly, sexually dysfunctional, scrawny, and weak—a real loser, metaphorically othered by the loss of his job, of his girlfriend, of his sex-drive, and, finally, of his will to live. As he revels in the pleasure of his self-inflicted wounds at the end of the film, Rob enters the position of the prototypical Freudian woman, the masochist who finally submits to the self-destructive drive that has marked him from the start. The narrative structure of the film thus draws a straight line from "soft" masculinity to masochism to self-annihilation. Betty, on the other hand, is a parody of monstrous femininity. Not only does she contribute to Rob's descent into impotency with her constant nagging, but she is also marked by blood: in a scene reminiscent of Theweleit's nightmare visions of feminine floods, Betty bathes in a tub of bloody water.

The critique of masculinity in *Nekromantik* works mainly through two key elements: first, the equation of the male body with the corpse and, second, Rob's problematic relationship with his father. The central role played by the father—not only in masochistic fantasy, but also in the basic structuring of the ego—is also critical for the discussion of masculinity in *Nekromantik*. Rob's perverted identity begins and ends with the image of his father. While watching a TV report on the relationship between violent youth, phobias, and shock therapy, Rob has a flashback to a farm courtyard where his father is slicing into a rabbit's skin, slowly bleeding it to death, and then crudely ripping the fur and skin from its body.[37] The same scene returns at the end of the film during Rob's autoerotic suicide, but with the skinning played in reverse so that the rabbit is in effect reassembled, reintegrated in the manner of a postmodern Frankenstein: a recombinant body, which retains the trace of fragmentation that marks its coming into being. The fact that Rob's fascination with dead bodies is linked in his memory not only with his father but also with images of skinning suggests two things: first, that Rob's identity is in very essential ways tied up with an internalized monstrous father and two, that "identity trouble" in the film emerges from the trauma of skinned bodies—where surface features (skin) are decorticated from deep features (muscle, tissue, and organs). Here we might note the very nature of horror film as

---

[36] For an illuminating philosophical discussion of the gendering of desire and death in *Nekromantik*, see Patricia MacCormack, "Necrosexuality, Perversion, and *Jouissance*: The Experimental Desires of Jörg Buttgereit's *NekRomantik* Films," in Hantke, *Caligari's Heirs: The German Cinema of Fear after 1945*, 199–215.

[37] The scene is reminiscent of, and most likely a nod to, the infamous rabbit scene of Godard fame (*Weekend*, 1967), during which a rabbit is graphically skinned and disemboweled onscreen.

Fig. 7.3. Das deutsche Kettensägenmassaker *(1990). Screenshot.*

an assault on ego coherence and disciplined bodies. Recalling the Theweleitian feminine flood that threatens to permeate the armor of the male warrior, everything in horror film oozes, bodies are burst open, organs are eviscerated, limbs are dismembered. In place of a fascist aesthetics of containment, horror substitutes an aesthetics of excess (explosion, disembowelment, and so on) that threatens to violate both bodily and psychic integrity.

If horror in the 1980s was primarily concerned with the transgression of bodily borders, German horror films of the 1990s took on the "disruption of once stable borders, boundaries, and limits," both metaphorical and geopolitical, as reunification prompted a reassessment of German history and German self-identification. Christoph Schlingensief's *Das deutsche Kettensägenmassaker* (The German Chainsaw Massacre, 1990) self-consciously appropriates the American horror film in the service of a political critique that frames German reunification as a process of literal cannibalization, whereby a gluttonous and perverse West turned the East into "Wurst" for consumption—Wessis literally eating Ossis. More recent German horror has taken advantage of the turn toward "heritage film" and more directly addressed the legacy of German fascism, for example in films such as *Anatomie* (Anatomy, 2000), which turns to the history of Nazi medical experimentation, or *Tiefgefroren* (Deep-frozen), a fast-paced splatter film that takes a team of East Germans into the haunted bunkers of the Second World War in the days following the fall of the Wall.

These examples illustrate just a few of the ways that German horror film engages with German history. As a genre made for exploring "the dark side," horror is particularly apt for gauging the vicissitudes of both German *cinematic* history and German history in general—here, bodies return from the grave to call us to task as viewers and as scholars to consider the mechanisms of repression and disavowal that horror inevitably flouts and the dark corners of the past it seeks to unearth. While we need to be careful of retrospectively applying generic labels to films that may or may not be properly understood as "horror" in the contemporary sense, we also need to be attuned to the ways in which these generic labels have been transformed by history, by scholarship, and by questions of taste. By attending to the vagaries of genre, we can also attend to the vagaries of history.

8: Producing Adaptations: Bernd Eichinger, *Christiane F.*, and German Film History

Hester Baer

UNTIL HIS SUDDEN DEATH in 2011 at the age of sixty-one, Bernd Eichinger was not only the most significant German film producer, but also a singular figure in German filmmaking, a man who more than anyone else shaped the course of German cinema over the last forty years. An active player since the early 1970s, Eichinger devoted himself to the commercial renewal of German film. As a self-styled mogul who consciously adopted the ideas and habits of classical Hollywood producers, Eichinger was an auteur producer who played a central role in all aspects of the films he made. First acquiring the story, he then also oversaw script development, casting, selection of the crew including the director, location scouting, the shoot, editing, visual effects, and postproduction, as well as advertising, publicity, and distribution. When he was unhappy with these, he regularly intervened. As such, his vision left an indelible imprint on the dominant narrative and stylistic trends in contemporary German and international film.

Eichinger began his career by founding the independent production company Solaris in 1974. In 1979 he took over the moribund German production and distribution company Constantin-Film. At the reinvented Neue Constantin, Eichinger introduced an emphasis on narrative filmmaking and epic stories, at a moment when art cinema held sway in postwar Germany. Eichinger's formula for success involved tailoring his films to the demands of international audiences, while simultaneously creating new expectations at home for a highly commercialized cinema that could compete with the best that global film industries have to offer. Not only did Eichinger excel at creating a nuanced appeal to diverse audience segments, but he was also adept at recognizing and implementing changing technologies of film exhibition and reception in the late twentieth century. Having achieved success in the 1980s with a string of blockbuster international hits, Eichinger became one of the primary initiators of the new popular cinema that flourished in reunified Germany, promoting both a return to genre cinema and the emergence of a new generation of filmmakers. An innovator in the sphere of international coproductions and transnational financing deals, Eichinger founded his success as a producer on a combination of big-budget, star-studded movies shot in English, such as Wolfgang Petersen's *Die unendliche Geschichte* (The Never-Ending Story, 1984) and Jean-Jacques Annaud's *Der Name der Rose* (The Name of the Rose, 1986), and small, nonexportable German-language films tailored to the domestic market, such as Niki List's *Werner—Beinhart* (Werner—Hard as Bone, 1990) and Sönke Wortmann's *Das Superweib* (The Superwoman, 1995). In both realms, Eichinger's strategy for popularity and profitability derived from his unique deployment of adaptation. In the twenty-first century, this parallel production strategy increasingly merged, as Eichinger turned to producing German-language films— again, largely adaptations—such as Oliver Hirschbiegl's *Der Untergang* (Downfall, 2004) and Uli Edel's *Der Baader Meinhof Komplex* (The Baader Meinhof Complex, 2008) that did double duty as blockbusters on the domestic market and as arthouse hits abroad.

Eichinger presents a necessary complement to accounts of "global Hollywood" by exemplifying how a media hegemon located "outside" Hollywood both competes with and cannibalizes its practices, all the while participating fully in the "New International Division of Cultural Labor."[1] Hollywood entered a new period of hegemony over the world film market beginning in the 1980s, and by the turn of the millennium it owned between 40 and 90 percent of films shown worldwide. The term New International Division of Cultural Labor (NICL), coined by Toby Miller and the collective authors of *Global Hollywood*, describes the way Hollywood exerts control over world markets not only via film-marketing campaigns, distribution, exhibition, and consumption, but also through reproducing and regulating intellectual property, labor (not least through its poaching of film professionals from other countries), and international financing schemes. As Miller et al. argue,

> Shifts toward a neo-liberal, multinational investment climate [since the 1980s] have reinforced global Hollywood's strategic power over the NICL through the privatization of media ownership, a unified Western European market, openings in the former Soviet Bloc, and the spread of satellite tv, the Web, and the VCR, combined with deregulation of national broadcasting in Europe and Latin America. (4)

In this climate, international coproductions have been the main template engaged by national film industries to challenge the behemoth of Hollywood, a challenge to the NICL that takes place at the level of work

---

[1] See Toby Miller, Nitin Govil, John McMurria, and Richard Maxwell, *Global Hollywood* (London: bfi, 2000).

(employment opportunities for film professionals) and at the level of culture (regulating film production, aesthetics, politics, and reception).

Eichinger recognized very early the implications for film production of the shifting world political and economic climate that the NICL describes, a neoliberal new world order defined in particular by the privatization of media, the rise of new technologies, and the erosion of the state's role as a sponsor and facilitator of film culture.[2] Indeed, as Georg Seeßlen has suggested, Eichinger was a "prophet of neoliberalism,"[3] who explicitly aimed to dismantle the collective filmmaking enterprise initiated in the 1960s and 1970s by filmmakers associated with the New German Cinema, replacing it with a top-down management style and a model of filmmaking that sustains itself through ties to global capital.[4] In this sense his internationalist production model harked back to long-standing traditions within popular cinema, at home and abroad: Eichinger created "brand-name movies," often relying on serialization, remakes, or sequels as a central element of production and publicity.[5] At the same time, he pioneered a unique cinematic style that succeeded (at least with mass audiences) in overcoming the longstanding distinctions between art and commerce in German cinema. In particular, Eichinger's trademark prestige pictures aestheticize market-driven consumer society, eliminating divisions between art cinema and escapist entertainment by co-opting the styles and themes of the former to enhance the latter, thereby making art cinema obsolete. Walter Uka has described the early 1980s as a "Zeitpunkt, wo mit dem amerikanischen Produzentenkino und dem europäischen Autorenfilm zwei gegensätzliche Filmkulturen aufeinanderstießen" (moment when two different film cultures collided: the American producer's cinema and the European auteur cinema).[6] Over

---

[2] Even before the landmark decision in 1983 by Interior Minister Friedrich Zimmermann to end the federal subvention schemes that had characterized filmmaking in the FRG for two decades, Eichinger had already advocated private and transnational financing schemes as a strategy for renewing the German cinema. See, for example, F. H., "Langfristig für den deutschen Film," interview with Bernd Eichinger, *Filmreport* 1+2 (1979): n.p.

[3] Georg Seeßlen, "Der Neo-Adenauer-Stil," *die tageszeitung*, 12 Jun. 1997.

[4] In 1984 Eichinger struck a deal with the media conglomerate the Kirch-Gruppe, who became a minority partner in Neue Constantin, and in 1991 he opened a subsidiary in Hollywood, Constantin Film Development. Both these decisions were calculated to connect Neue Constantin—the only remaining film production and distribution company entirely in German hands—to global capital and to promote transnational financing deals.

[5] See Rick Altman, *Film/Genre* (1999; repr., London: bfi, 2002), 115.

[6] Walter Uka, "Der deutsche Film *schiebt den Blues*: Kino und Film in der Bundesrepublik in den achtziger Jahren," in *Die Kultur der achtziger Jahre*, ed. Werner Faulstich (Munich: Wilhelm Fink, 2005), 105. All translations in this essay are my own, except where otherwise credited.

the course of his career, Bernd Eichinger in many ways succeeded in reconciling these two models.

To be sure, Eichinger, more than any other filmmaker, made certain that films would continue to be "made in Germany" in the twenty-first century, and that German and international audiences would watch them.[7] Eleven of the top twenty German films of the last thirty years were produced by Neue Constantin, almost all of them by Eichinger himself.[8] In the new millennium, three of Eichinger's German-language productions were nominated for Academy Awards. As Doris Dörrie has written of Eichinger, despite many aesthetic and political differences,

> Er hatte Respekt vor mir, und ich konnte ihm . . . zuhören und schätzen, dass sein Ziel immer dasselbe ist: einen guten Film zu machen, den alle sehen wollen. Den Wolpertinger der Filmindustrie.[9]

> [He respected me, and I could . . . listen to him and appreciate the fact that his goal always remains the same: to make a good film that everyone wants to see. The jackalope of the film industry.]

As Dörrie suggests, Eichinger's remarkable career is emblematic of some of the most pernicious trends in both production style and cultural politics over the last thirty years, yet any attempt to understand popular cinema during this same period must come to terms with his influence.

Given his highly influential status, it is remarkable that so little attention has been paid to Eichinger by scholars. Indeed, reconsidering German film history through the lens of Eichinger's influence means revising a

---

[7] As Randall Halle points out, "rather than German directors making German films, now industry experts speak of a film as 'made in Germany' or from 'location Germany' [*Standort Deutschland*]." Eichinger was a major player in this transformation of German cinema away from the nationally specific *Autorenfilm* and toward a more flexible, national-global hybrid film. See Halle, "German Film, European Film: Transnational Production, Distribution, and Reception," *Screen* 47 (2006): 252.

[8] These are, beginning with the most successful, *Der Schuh des Manitu* (Manitu's Shoe, 2001); *(T)Raumschiff Surprise—Periode 1* (Dreamship Surprise—period 1, 2004); *Der bewegte Mann* (The Moved Man, released in English as *Maybe . . . Maybe Not*, 1994); *Der Name der Rose*; *Das Parfum* (Perfume, 2006); *Werner—Das muss kesseln* (Werner—That's Got to be Fun, released in English as *Eat My Dust!*, 1996); *Wickie und die starken Männer* (Wicky and the Strong Men, 2009); *Werner—Beinhart*; *Die unendliche Geschichte*; *Christiane F.—Wir Kinder vom Bahnhof Zoo* (Christiane F.—We Children from Bahnhof Zoo, 1981); and *Der Untergang*. Eichinger produced all except *(T)Raumschiff Surprise* and *Wickie und die starken Männer*. Box-office data accessed 6 Jul. 2012, http://www.insidekino.de/DJahr/DAlltimeDeutsch50.htm.

[9] Doris Dörrie, "Der Bernd," accessed 1 Jul. 2012 http://www.sueddeutsche.de/kultur/eichingers-lebenswerk-der-bernd-1.18930.

number of commonplace ways of thinking in German film studies. These include a narrowly defined conception of national cinema; a tendency toward conventional historical periodization that follows national political developments; a focus on the *Autorenfilm* at the expense of attention to the commercial, financial, industrial, and intermedial dimensions of film-making; and a neglect of genre as a central facet shaping the production and reception of films.

The career of Bernd Eichinger coincides with, and itself contributed in no small part to, the professionalization and institutionalization of production culture in Germany over the past thirty years. Asked how one becomes a film producer, Eichinger once responded: "1. Indem man nicht Regisseur wird. 2. Indem man nicht Produktionsassistent bleibt. 3. Indem man ein Firmenschild an die Tür schraubt und Briefköpfe drucken läßt" (1. Don't become a director. 2. Don't remain a production assistant. 3. Hang a sign on your door and order some letterhead.)[10] As Diana Iljine and Klaus Keil have noted, since Eichinger's self-invention as Germany's main mogul in the 1970s,

> Sowohl für eine marktgerechte und dabei qualitativ befriedigende Fernsehproduktion als auch für eine Neuorientierung des deutschen Kinofilms hin zu massenattraktiven, konkurrenzfähigen Einzelereignissen waren *Produktionsfachleute* nötig. (83)
>
> [*Production experts* have become increasingly necessary [in Germany], in order to develop a market-oriented and qualitatively appropriate television production scheme and to foster the new orientation of the German cinema toward competitive films with massive potential to attract audiences.]

In accordance with such developments, John Thornton Caldwell has recently argued that film studies must pay renewed and sustained attention to production culture and production workers, who play an increasingly significant role in today's media world. Today, self-reflexive production artifacts such as outtakes, commentaries, and other DVD extras like making-of "documentaries" are highly integrated into marketing campaigns and multimedia audiovisual products. This sort of reality-based production model, which has predominated since the advent of reality tv, increasingly blurs the lines between "behind the scenes" and diegetic content in creating new "flexible" programming.[11] My analysis of

---

[10] Diana Iljine and Klaus Keil, *Der Produzent: Das Berufsbild des Film- und Fernsehproduzenten in Deutschland* (1997; repr., Munich: TR-Verlagsunion, 2000), 170.

[11] John Thornton Caldwell, *Production Culture: Industrial Reflexivity and Critical Practice in Film and Television* (Durham, NC: Duke University Press, 2008).

Fig. 8.1. Still from Christiane F.—Wir Kinder vom Bahnhof Zoo *(1981). Christiane F. (Natja Brunckhorst) and friends in front of Bahnhof Zoo.*

Bernd Eichinger's immense influence on transnational film history under-scores the insight that only by studying production cultures can we understand better how certain movies get made and how particular styles, genres, and themes may come to pervade popular culture, in Germany and across the globe.

In addition to providing an overview of Bernd Eichinger's career as a producer, this essay takes his breakthrough 1981 film *Christiane F.—Wir Kinder vom Bahnhof Zoo* as a case study to examine adaptation as a central facet of his production model. The top-grossing film of the postwar period after its release in West Germany, and one of the most popular films of all time domestically, *Christiane F.* was also a box-office hit internationally. An underresearched film, *Christiane F.* was one of a number of German-produced blockbusters from the early 1980s that challenge the common perception that this period was characterized by a collapse, or at least a nadir, of the German film. It is certainly the case that 1980 represented a major turning point in German film history, which Eichinger helped to initiate and for which his career is emblematic. However, far from repre-senting a collapse, this period saw a paradigm shift in German filmmaking whose long-term effects are still at play in the German cinema of today.

In addition to the turn away from the *Autorenfilm* and the move already taking place in the early 1980s toward a renewal of genre cinema, the transformation of German cinema during this period was driven by major revisions to the film subvention laws to reward *publikumswirksame Filme* (films with audience appeal). Also significant was the founding of regional film boards with the express purpose of improving the aesthetic quality of German films and strengthening the economy of Germany as a film location.[12] Moreover, this era saw a massive increase in and diversification of modes of audiovisual exhibition, distribution, and reception. In the early 1980s these transformations led to a brief decline in ticket sales, one reason for the perception of (West) German film's overall decline. Not only was this decline partly offset by home-video sales,[13] but significantly this era also saw a massive increase both in the number of German films produced (from forty-nine in 1980 to sixty-eight in 1989) and in the domestic market share of German films (from 9.3 percent in 1980 to 23.4 percent in 1988).[14]

As these figures suggest, the commercial renewal of German cinema usually attributed to the 1990s was already firmly grounded in the West German film culture of the 1980s. This commercial renewal was both driven by and reflective of the neoliberal turn taking shape throughout the West. Characterized by the erosion of autonomous spheres of cultural production, the increasing predominance of corporations and commercial considerations, a growth in income disparity, and a mandate toward privatization, the framework of neoliberalism helps to explain both the production model and the aesthetic vision that have typified (German) cinema since around 1980.[15]

Christiane F. was adapted from a bestselling documentation of teenage heroin use and prostitution in West Berlin, which was first published as a report in the magazine *Stern* and later in book form as *Wir Kinder vom Bahnhof Zoo* (We Children of Bahnhof Zoo, 1978).[16] The film patented the production strategy that paved the way for Eichinger's future success, which hinged on the use of adaptation. An umbrella genre itself, adaptation allowed Eichinger to capitalize on generic associations raised by the original texts he adapted, while avoiding pigeonholing his films according to restrictive film-genre categories. Taking a very flexible approach to adaptation allowed Eichinger to embrace opportunities for genre mixing in order to create multivalent, polygeneric films that would maximize a film's marketability, helping it to reach the widest possible

---

[12] See Uka, "Der deutsche Film *schiebt den Blues*," 111.

[13] Regarding home video sales, Uka cites statistics suggesting that in 1984 in the Federal Republic there were 112 million visits to the movies and 108 million video rentals ("Der deutsche Film *schiebt den Blues*," 111).

[14] See Uka, "Der deutsche Film *schiebt den Blues*," 110–11.

[15] For more on neoliberalism and German filmmaking, see Hester Baer, "*Das Boot* and the German Cinema of Neoliberalism," *German Quarterly* 85, no. 1 (2012): 18–39.

[16] Christiane F., *Wir Kinder vom Bahnhof Zoo: Nach Tonbandprotokollen aufgeschrieben von Kai Hermann und Horst Rieck* (1978; repr., Hamburg: Carlsen Verlag, 2010).

audiences.[17] Furthermore, adaptation provided a cost-effective way of garnering both prestige and "event character," a quality that Eichinger sought to capture in all of his films. Event character—capitalizing on the *Zeitgeist* to generate interest in a film regardless of its merits—is one facet of the aesthetic and political multivalency that inheres in Eichinger's films, which combine sensationalism with conservative values, offering an ultimately affirmative vision of Germany that generates popular interest both at home and abroad.

Eichinger as Producer

In 1974 Eichinger completed film school at the Hochschule für Film und Fernsehen in Munich and founded the independent production company Solaris. There he worked with auteur directors of the New German Cinema such as Alexander Kluge and Edgar Reitz, and produced some of the most noteworthy German films of the 1970s, including Wim Wenders's *Falsche Bewegung* (Wrong Move, 1975) and Hans Jürgen Syberberg's *Hitler—Ein Film aus Deutschland* (Hitler—A Film from Germany, 1977). Not yet thirty when he took over Constantin, Eichinger went on to transform it into the leading production and distribution company in the Federal Republic, achieving widespread popularity with a string of international blockbusters. In addition to *Die unendliche Geschichte* and *Der Name der Rose*, Eichinger's international successes included Uli Edel's *Letzte Ausfahrt Brooklyn* (Last Exit to Brooklyn, 1989), Bille August's *Das Geisterhaus* (The House of the Spirits, 1993) and *Fräulein Smillas Gespür für Schnee* (Miss Smilla's Sense of Snow, 1997), Caroline Link's *Nirgendwo in Afrika* (Nowhere in Africa, 2001), Oskar Roehler's *Elementarteilchen* (Elementary Particles, 2005), Tom Tykwer's *Das Parfum*, and the immensely popular series of *Resident Evil* films (2002; 2004; 2007; 2010).

Domestically, Eichinger was largely responsible for the renewal of commercial German cinema in the 1980s and 1990s, helping to initiate the comedy wave characteristic of these decades. In addition to working with Doris Dörrie over many years (he produced four of her films), in 1993 Eichinger contracted Sönke Wortmann to direct three films for Neue Constantin, beginning with *Der bewegte Mann* (The Moved Man, released in English as *Maybe. . . Maybe Not*), a film whose immense success kicked off the genre of the *Beziehungskomödie* (relationship comedy, see Antje Ascheid's essay later in this volume) that dominated postunification Germany. Eichinger also achieved popular success at home with a

---

[17] In this sense Eichinger's oeuvre provides a case study for Altman's argument that "Studio proclivity towards mixed genres differs markedly from the critical tendency towards pure genres because of the difference in purpose and audience between studios and critics." Altman, *Film/Genre*, 142.

wide range of comic spoofs, including *Manta, Manta* (1990); the *Werner* series of animated films (1990; 1996; 2003); and a popular film cycle starring the television comic Tom Gerhard. Most significantly, Eichinger fostered the transition to filmmaking of the radio and television comic Michael "Bully" Herbig, and his decision to produce the epically popular *Der Schuh des Manitu* (Manitou's Shoe), which broke all box-office records in Germany, paved the way for Herbig's ascent as the most commercially successful contemporary German filmmaker.

In 2003 Eichinger resigned as CEO of Constantin, giving up control of financial matters in the company, which had gone public in 1999. Retaining his position as head of the board of directors, Eichinger maintained his substantial involvement in the creative business of the company, devoting himself not only to production but increasingly to writing screenplays as well, including those for *Der Untergang, Das Parfum, Der Baader Meinhof Komplex,* and *Zeiten ändern dich* (Times Change You, 2010). When he died, Eichinger was working on a screenplay for his next project, a biopic of Natascha Kampusch.[18]

As this brief resume of Eichinger's international and domestic films attests, Eichinger's approach to adaptation is the thread that unites his diverse productions and grounds his success as a filmmaker. Adaptation functions in his body of work as a production strategy that effectively spans different forms of industrial organization, different filmmaking practices, and different reception contexts, and it has proved both prestigious and remarkably lucrative.

Producing Adaptations

A substantial number of films produced across national borders since the beginning of cinema have been adaptations. One tally suggests that more than a third of classical Hollywood films were adapted from novels,[19] while another notes that 85 percent of the winners of Best Picture Oscars have been adaptations.[20] In the German context, Eric Rentschler's 1985 survey counted nearly 800 well-known literary adaptations from all periods of German film history.[21] Yet as Kyle Edwards has noted, there is

---

[18] Now an Austrian media personality, Kampusch was abducted at the age of ten and held hostage for eight years in her kidnapper's basement before she was able to escape in 2006.

[19] Carolyn Anderson, "Film and Literature," in *Film and the Arts in Symbiosis*, ed. Gary R. Edgerton (New York: Greenwood, 1988), 97–132. Quoted in Kyle Edwards, "Brand-Name Literature: Film Adaptation and Selznick International Pictures' *Rebecca* (1940)," *Cinema Journal* 45, no. 3 (2006): 32.

[20] Linda Hutcheon, *A Theory of Adaptation* (New York: Routledge, 2006), 4.

[21] Even the number 800 is low, since Rentschler did not conduct an entirely systematic or exhaustive count. See Rentschler, "Adaptations in German Film

a surprising dearth of scholarship addressing adaptation from the stand-point of production—that is, "factors that led studios to obtain the rights to certain literary properties and to adapt those properties for the screen in a particular way."[22]

The standard work on adaptation has long focused on questions of fidelity, originality, intentionality, agency, and intertextuality, examining the transposition, translation, and artistry of adaptation largely from the perspective of authorship and, to a lesser degree, reception. In her 2006 book *A Theory of Adaptation*, for example, Linda Hutcheon condenses a great deal of previous work from both film and literary studies to outline a systematic approach to adaptation. In answering the question "Who is the adapter?," she suggests that this role might be filled by the composer or music director, the costume and set designers, the cinematographer, the actors, and the editor, but she ultimately concludes that "in a film the director and the screenwriter share the primary task of adaptation."[23]

The producer is notably absent from Hutcheon's extended list of potential adapters. Yet as Edwards's research on Hollywood studios in the classical era suggests, adaptation has long functioned as a strategy whereby individual production companies sought to differentiate them-selves in the marketplace through a particular style of interpretation and retelling. Not only does the examination of adaptation as a collaborative industrial process help to explain how and why certain movies get made, but approaching adaptation from the standpoint of production also sheds new light on questions of transposition and transformation, helping to explain why particular elements of a given text are emphasized or elided in the adaptation.

In his analysis of the historical development of film genres, *Film/Genre*, Rick Altman similarly emphasizes the significant role played by producers in determining the content and style of movies. Altman sug-gests that, at least in Hollywood, genre logic has not been a significant determinant for producers, who favor series, cycles, and remakes rather than genres per se, and who "systematically stress *proprietary* character-istics (star, director and related successful films by the same studio) over *sharable* determinants like genre" (117). Seeking to produce brand-name movies that create capital that can not easily be shared, producers have eschewed genre purity in favor of seeking out a felicitous mix of charac-teristics that will appeal to the widest possible range of viewers. As Altman puts it, "publicity determines product design" (132). In this sense, adap-tation has much to offer producers: not only does it easily facilitate genre

---

History: A Basic Guide (1913–1985)," in *German Film & Literature: Adaptations and Transformations*, ed. Rentschler (New York: Methuen, 1986), 336–65.

[22] Edwards, "Brand-Name Literature," 32.

[23] Hutcheon, *Theory of Adaptation*, 85.

mixing to reach a wide audience, but adapted material generally comes with its own ready-made publicity and a certain level of prepackaged legitimacy and prestige derived from the original text.

In the classical Hollywood era, using adapted works enabled studios to more easily develop the cultural capital and brand recognition to attract both talent and audiences, and thus to increase profitability. In the case of Selznick International Pictures, Edwards notes, "Adapting internationally renowned literary sources [for its immensely successful big-budget pictures *Gone With the Wind* (1939) and *Rebecca* (1940)] enabled SIP to streamline the story development process, promise a built-in audience to distributors and exhibitors, and fulfill its goal of producing 'prestige' pictures" (34).

While the model of Selznick International Pictures offers one effective example of the profitability of adaptation, the German production and distribution company Constantin, originally founded in 1949, presents a different model. By the 1960s Constantin had become the top distributor in Germany, in large part because of its immensely successful coproduced adaptations of popular genre literature, including the Karl May and Edgar Wallace cycles of films. As Tim Bergfelder notes, the mode of production followed by Constantin was tailored specifically to the exploitation of genre series:

> Sequelisation of one-off box office hits and the creation of generic cycles, which characterises not just West German film production during the 1960s but European cinema more generally, were . . . more rigidly adhered to at Constantin than by any other German distributor. Nearly all of the successful genre series in the West German market of the 1960s were distributed and cofinanced by Constantin.[24]

For the original Constantin corporation, adaptation was the key to creating a streamlined process of production and distribution that capitalized on integrating specialized production units from across Europe and within Germany to create the coproduced genre films that were the bread and butter of German cinema in the 1960s.

The examples of Selznick International Pictures and Constantin-Film are instructive here, not only as case studies in examining adaptation from the perspective of production, but also because they present a necessary backdrop to understanding the example of Bernd Eichinger, who self-consciously modeled himself after David O. Selznick as the head of Neue Constantin.[25] Eichinger reinvented the failing Constantin largely by combining two

[24] Tim Bergfelder, *International Adventures: German Popular Cinema and European Co-productions in the 1960s* (New York: Berghahn Books, 2005), 85.
[25] See Andreas M. Rauch, *Bernd Eichinger und seine Filme* (Frankfurt am Main: Haag + Herchen, 2000), 16.

patented strategies of adaptation. Bringing to the screen internationally renowned literary texts, he created prestige pictures for Neue Constantin that reached a built-in global audience familiar with the original literary properties, thereby guaranteeing profitability. At the same time, by updating the original Constantin corporation's strategy, Eichinger also maintained a dedicated German audience with nonexportable genre films, relying strongly on sequelization and the production of series to maximize returns.

During his years working with New German Cinema auteurs, Eichinger had already produced adaptations of well-known literary works by Goethe, Ibsen, Fontane, Eichendorff, Brentano, Ödon von Horvath, and Patricia Highsmith, among others. At Solaris, his popular breakthrough came with *Christiane F.*, material that he selected himself and carefully shepherded through the process of adaptation. At Neue Constantin he went on to make a series of adaptations of bestselling novels by Michael Ende, Umberto Eco, Hubert Selby, Isabel Allende, and Peter Høeg, all of them shot in English, that cemented his reputation as a producer of blockbuster international prestige films. In the 2000s Eichinger continued to produce literary adaptations, working with young German auteur directors, including Oskar Roehler, to adapt Michel Houellebecq's *Les Particules élémentaires*, and Tom Tykwer, to adapt Patrick Süsskind's *Das Parfum*.[26]

In addition to producing adaptations of popular bestsellers, throughout his career Eichinger capitalized on global audiences' ongoing interest in German history of the twentieth century with a series of adaptations of autobiographies, memoirs, and war stories. One of his first business decisions as the CEO of Neue Constantin had been to invest DM 2 million in the struggling production *Das Boot*, at the time the most expensive German film ever made, in exchange for its domestic distribution rights.[27] The success of *Das Boot* not only allowed Eichinger to consolidate his position at Neue Constantin and offset some of his early losses as he learned the ropes there but also helped to set Eichinger's future course both commercially and aesthetically. A number of his most successful films follow the model of *Das Boot*, combining an affirmative message with a familiar image of German history. These include *Nirgendwo in Afrika*, adapted from Stefanie Zweig's autobiographical novel about German-Jewish refugees from Nazi Germany in Kenya, which won an Oscar; *Der Untergang*, nominated for an Oscar, for which Eichinger wrote the screenplay based on both Joachim Fest's history of the last days in Hitler's bunker and the memoir of Hitler's last secretary Traudl Junge;

---

[26] Eichinger had pursued Süßkind about purchasing the rights to the novel *Das Parfum* for more than fifteen years before Süßkind finally relented and Eichinger succeeded in acquiring the novel in 2001 for ten million euros. See Detlef Dreßlein and Anne Lehwald, *Bernd Eichinger: Die Biografie* (Munich: Heyne, 2011), 286–87.

[27] See Baer, "*Das Boot* and the German Cinema of Neoliberalism," 3–4.

and *Der Baader Meinhof Komplex*, also nominated for an Oscar, which Eichinger adapted from the bestselling account by Stefan Aust about the German domestic terrorist group RAF. At the outset of his career Eichinger shot his adaptation of *Die unendliche Geschichte* in English on the premise that a German-language film would not be able to attract a large enough audience at home or abroad to earn back the production costs for the kind of big-budget spectacle he had in mind. By the twenty-first century, however, Eichinger succeeded in creating a kind of nationally branded German-language film that is popular with domestic audiences while also appealing to global markets through its ostensible national-cultural specificity. German history films such as *Der Untergang* and *Nirgendwo in Afrika* are hits abroad precisely because they are shot in German and cater to international expectations of "German" cinema. Notably, while adaptation often figures centrally in the appeal of these films to German audiences, international multiplex crowds may not even be aware that the films they are watching were adapted from well-known texts (for example, *Der Baader Meinhof Komplex*).

Over the last two decades of his life, Eichinger expanded his use of adaptation to produce numerous highly popular intermedial genre films. These include films based on comic books: the German-language animated series of *Werner* films; the paradigm-shifting domestic hit *Der bewegte Mann*; and the English-language blockbuster *Fantastic Four* (2005). Even more successful was Eichinger's filmic adaptation of the video game *Resident Evil*, in four blockbuster films shot in English with Hollywood stars. Eichinger's flexible use of adaptation also extended to remakes (both faithful and satirical) of films and television shows. In addition to introducing popular television comedians such as Gerhard and Herbig to the big screen, Eichinger also remade cinema films for television, for example in the series "German Classics," consisting of popular German films from the 1950s and 1960s adapted for the private television station SAT1.

Eichinger's reliance on adaptation can be understood not only as a cost-effective means of streamlining all aspects of the production process but also as a self-conscious strategy for transferring creative control away from auteurist director-producers, whose efforts at establishing a cinema autonomous from the market were epitomized by the collective distribution project "Filmverlag der Autoren." In their place, Eichinger notoriously promoted commercial directors such as Uli Edel, whose career reflects the transnational and intermedial landscape of neoliberal filmmaking today, in that he moves seamlessly between Germany and Hollywood and between television and the movies, directing almost exclusively adaptations. For Eichinger, then, adaptation functions quite literally as a means of adapting to the demands of the domestic and global markets.

Eichinger's adaptations have often been targeted by critics for their lack of fidelity to the original texts, whose authors have also almost unanimously rejected Eichinger's adaptations of their works. Yet for Eichinger these critiques were beside the point.

Michael Wedel has pointed out that a shift took place around 1965 in the mode of literary adaptations made in Germany. While filmmakers continued to adapt a range of classic and popular texts,

> What changed with the advent of the New German Cinema was a new self-confidence of the director as author, claiming a certain independence vis-à-vis the literary source, and thus not afraid to give "interpretations" of a literary text, without any pretence at rendering its essence in a more transparent or accessible medium.[28]

Eichinger capitalized on this shift in many of his prestige adaptations shot by auteur directors, while continuing to insist that, "Die Geschmäcker sind verschieden. Ich verfilme doch keine Literatur, wo kommen wir denn da hin? Ich ziehe mir meine Filmgeschichten da raus, wo ich sie brauche" (Taste varies. I don't film literature—what good would that bring? I take my film stories where I can get them).[29]

Eichinger described his work as a producer as taking place in three central phases (development, shooting, and postproduction), of which the first—choice and acquisition of the story, development of the script, and choice of the director—was the most important.[30] In its focus on story development and event character, Eichinger's own account of his production model supports Altman's argument that producers function as critics, playing a "producer's game" to assess previous box-office successes, discover their formula, and recalibrate this formula in revising new material for the market.[31] As Altman points out, this market-driven approach to film production has little to do with preordained purity of genre, which from a production perspective may pigeonhole a film rather than helping it reach a wider audience. Indeed, after a career based on internationally successful literary adaptations, and after helping to pioneer the comedy wave in postunification Germany, Eichinger exclaimed in a 2002 interview about *Resident Evil*, "Dies ist mein erster Genrefilm. In fünfundzwanzig Jahren Berufserfahrung habe ich mich zum ersten Mal an ein solches Genre herangetraut" (This is my first genre film. After twenty-five years of professional experience, I decided to have a go at a genre film for the first time.)[32] Yet *Resident Evil*, like all of Eichinger's films from *Christiane F.* on, is in fact

[28] Michael Wedel, "Literaturverfilmung," in *The BFI Companion to German Cinema*, ed. Thomas Elsaesser and Michael Wedel (London: BFI, 1999), 166.
[29] Cited in Dreßlein and Lehwald, *Bernd Eichinger*, 137.
[30] Rauch, *Bernd Eichinger und seine Filme*, 20–23.
[31] Altman, *Film/Genre*, 38.
[32] Cited in Dreßlein and Lehwald, *Bernd Eichinger*, 264. In the case of *Resident Evil*, an adaptation of a popular video game, choosing to align the film with genres—specifically the thriller and the zombie movie—was a calculated publicity

the result of a targeted mix of genres, a "Hollywood cocktail,"[33] carefully shaken *and* stirred to appeal to the widest possible public.

Eichinger's Multivalent Cinema

From the inception to the realization of each film, Eichinger's cinema is characterized most significantly by its market-driven production model, driven by and reflecting the neoliberal quest to transform cultures across the globe into market cultures.[34] In addition to the transnational production and distribution deals that finance most of his films and help guarantee their widespread marketability, this model is also reflected on artistic and social levels in Eichinger's films, which are characterized by a trademark production style. For example, Eichinger routinely shot coverage (to create a more panoramic, immediate, and "believable" cinematic experience), which is not a standard practice for German filmmakers because of its expense. Similarly, he relied strongly on stars (and the concomitant marketing campaigns to promote those stars) to encourage audience identification and to underpin his style of, in Randall Halle's words, foregrounding "representation over reflection."[35] Finally, in choosing stories, Eichinger always sought to create films with event character that would capture the public imagination (often because they are adaptations of familiar texts, or because they address controversial subject matter, or both). By emphasizing event character, Eichinger sought to make going to the movies into an event again in an era when cinema was competing with a range of rival entertainments (not least the home-video market). At the same time, his strategy harked back to Hollywood mogul Darryl Zanuck's focus at Warner Brothers on making "headliners," movies that have the "punch and the smash" to make headlines because they relate to the top stories dominating major newspapers of the day.[36]

Headliners, or movies with event character, are the perfect vehicles for genre mixing. As Altman has argued, genre mixing has long been a standard practice for Hollywood, since it maximizes the marketability of films, but the increasing sophistication of market research about audience demographics, in combination with the drive toward producing ever-larger blockbusters, has led contemporary media corporations "to still greater dependence on and self-consciousness about genre mixing"

---

decision to increase the movie's prestige and market it to viewers unfamiliar with the game.

[33] See Altman, *Film/Genre*, 132.

[34] See Lisa Duggan, *The Twilight of Equality? Neoliberalism, Cultural Politics, and the Attack on Democracy* (Boston: Beacon, 2003), 12.

[35] Randall Halle, *German Film after Germany: Towards a Transnational Aesthetic* (Chicago: University of Illinois Press, 2008), 119.

[36] See Altman, *Film/Genre*, 44–46.

(142). Thus producers like Eichinger strive to create multivalent films, characterized by a formal-aesthetic hybridity and a co-optation of progressive styles and politics for an ultimately affirmative worldview. These ideologically promiscuous films allow viewers to indulge in the thrills offered by countercinema, alternative lifestyles, or leftist politics, while ultimately foreclosing on the critique they offer by incorporating them fully into consumer-driven market culture.

Inasmuch as Eichinger's stylistic trademarks are all self-consciously adapted from Hollywood to some degree, they align his productions with the production values and extradiegetic expectations of global Hollywood. At the same time, his films fulfill a double function as big-budget domestic successes that could also be marketed to arthouse audiences abroad as specifically German or European cinema, in a kind of reverse-engineered version of the global Hollywood strategy that draws huge foreign profits from blockbusters such as James Cameron's *Avatar* (2009).

On a social level, this kind of national-global hybrid cinema certainly has an impact on representations of nation, gender, and sexuality in Eichinger's films. For example, the films routinely resort to clichés of Germanness that appeal to the expectations of international audiences while often generating controversy at home, thus proving profitable in both contexts. Eichinger's perception of Hitler as a charismatic pop star, which he discussed at length in interviews, and his concomitant attempt to represent the dictator's humanity in *Der Untergang* is emblematic of this tendency. Similarly, Eichinger routinely thematized homosexuality in his films, from the 1977 adaptation *Die Konsequenz* to the 1994 hit *Der bewegte Mann*. While both films were sold at home and abroad as presenting an enlightened approach to gay rights, they are ultimately more noteworthy for deploying homosexuality as part of a sensationalist international marketing tactic than for breaking new ground in its cinematic representation. Often referred to as *Der Macho aus München*, Eichinger also used his highly publicized relationships with starring actresses such as Corinna Harfouch, Katja Flint, and Hannelore Elsner to achieve media saturation, simultaneously promoting a model of heterosexuality and conventional gender roles that is further reflected in the plots of his films.

Christiane F.—Wir Kinder vom Bahnhof Zoo

A landmark film for Eichinger's production strategy, *Christiane F.—Wir Kinder vom Bahnhof Zoo* already exhibits most of the formal-aesthetic and social-political characteristics that characterized Eichinger's filmmaking throughout his later career. An event film par excellence, *Christiane F.* was adapted from a book that sold 1.3 million copies in Germany and 3 million copies worldwide, having itself been adapted from a report published in the magazine *Stern*. Estimates suggest that approximately twenty million Germans read the story of Christiane F. in either magazine or book form.[37] The newspaper *Die Zeit* referred to the book as the "Bibel der Turnschuhgeneration" (bible of the tennis-shoe generation), even comparing it to Goethe's *Die Leiden des jungen Werther* (*The Sorrows of Young Werther*).[38]

From the outset Eichinger played a central role in the production of *Christiane F.* He chose the source material, overseeing the acquisition of the rights to the book, and he hired Roland Klick to write the screenplay and direct the film. However, after shooting had already begun, Eichinger decided that Klick's vision was not commercially oriented enough, and he fired Klick, a decision that required a new screenplay and the hiring of a new director. Eichinger turned to two of his friends from film school in Munich, the screenwriter Herman Weigel and the director Uli Edel, constituting a team who would work together on many of Eichinger's future films. Working with Weigel and Edel, Eichinger was able to realize his own vision, and he was omnipresent on the set and in pre- and postproduction.[39]

A central aspect of Eichinger's vision for the material was to capitalize on the story's multivalent and polygeneric qualities to create a commercially successful film. An adaptation, a social-problem film, and a "headliner film," *Christiane F.* contains generic traits of the love story, docudrama, musical, and horror film as well. This genre mix is crucial to the film's widespread popular and international appeal, since it creates multiple points of entry, pleasure, and interpretation for the viewer, fluctuating between "opportunities for generic pleasure and eventual return to cultural values."[40] Eichinger used a realist style reminiscent of television documentaries, including the use of handheld cameras; the film also features a soundtrack and cameo appearance by David Bowie. These intermedial dimensions help to account for both *Christiane F.*'s resounding success as one of the first home-video blockbusters in the early 1980s, at the dawn of the MTV era, and for its longstanding status as a cult film ever since.[41]

---

[37] See Rauch, *Bernd Eichinger und seine Filme*, 34.

[38] Hans C. Blumenberg, "Besonders wertvoll," *Die Zeit*, 3 Apr., 1981, accessed 11 Jul. 2012, http://www.zeit.de/1981/15/besonders-wertvoll.

[39] Natja Brunckhorst, the actress who played Christiane F., recalls: "Der Bernd war als Produzent immer anwesend, er war ständig in Kommunikation mit Uli Edel, war die graue Eminenz, die im Hintergrund guckt, ob alles so ist, wie er sich das vorstellt" (As a producer, Bernd was always present—he was in constant communication with Uli Edel and was the eminence grise always lurking in the background and making sure that everything is going according to his plan). Quoted in Dreßlein and Lehwald, *Bernd Eichinger*, 103.

[40] Altman, *Film/Genre*, 156.

[41] Significantly for the production history of *Christiane F.*, Eichinger only chose to add the plotline, scenes, and soundtrack featuring David Bowie during

Fig. 8.2. Still from Christiane F.—Wir Kinder vom Bahnhof
Zoo *(1981). Eichinger's intermedial genre mix: Synthetic
footage from a David Bowie concert.*

The story of Christiane F. was in many ways tailor-made for
Eichinger's double-edged cinema. On the one hand, it caters to a voyeuristic interest in the West Berlin scene of the 1970s, with visions of promiscuous sexuality, drug use, and shrill popular music. This aspect of the
story—strongly foregrounded in the film—plays on longstanding images
of Berlin as the decadent capital of the Weimar Republic, images that had
recently been revived in the public imagination by Bob Fosse's *Cabaret*
(1972), a worldwide blockbuster that won eight Oscars.

As Laurens Straub pointed out already in 1983, *Christiane F.* prof-
ited from the "Rückkoppelung des international gewordenen deutschen
Provinzfilms" (the feedback loop of the German provincial film that has
gone international).[42] Building on the central theme of the New German
Cinema, "Verweigerung an Deutschland" (refusal of Germany), *Christiane
F.* also reflects the paradoxical fact that, to create international appeal, "je

postproduction for the film. Feeling that the first cut came across as "leaden,"
Eichinger decided that the film needed a different approach to music, and he was
able to recruit David Bowie for the project. The cult scene in which Christiane
attends a Bowie concert is actually a synthetic creation conceived in the editing
room, where the filmmakers spliced together footage of Bowie performing in
New York with footage of a Berlin audience attending an AC/DC concert. See
Dreßlein and Lehwald, *Bernd Eichinger*, 104–5.

[42] Laurens Straub, "Zur Lage des deutschen Filmmarktes," in *Bestandsaufnahme:
Utopie Film—Zwanzig Jahre neuer deutscher Film*, ed. Alexander Kluge (Frankfurt
am Main: zweitausendeins, 1983), 354.

provinzieller und genauer lokalisierbar, desto besser" (Straub, 354, 356; the more provincial and precisely localizable, the better). On the other hand, the circumstance that Christiane F. had purportedly quit drugs and gotten clean—a point addressed only very briefly in the framing voice-over—both endowed the film with a happy ending and allowed Eichinger to promote it as an educational *Problemfilm*, with cinemas offering closed screenings for school classes and politicians commenting on the film's thoughtful treatment of the widespread social problem of drug use.[43]

The fact that Christiane F. was a fourteen-year-old girl was a central part of the film's appeal, both for Eichinger himself and for the film's viewers. In fact, a central point of contention between Eichinger and Roland Klick had been over the casting of Christiane, a role for whom Eichinger insisted on choosing a beautiful actress and not someone who looked like a junkie.[44] Screenwriter Herman Weigel referred to Christiane as a "female James Dean," an embodiment of youth rebellion whose gender helped establish the film's crossover success.[45] Given the film's subject matter, it was important to foreground a female character, since female viewers are more likely to choose crossover films with female protagonists. Moreover, in an era when "women rather than men are constituted as ideal neoliberal subjects,"[46] Christiane F. was well suited to embody the multivalence of Eichinger's cinema on aesthetic and social levels as well. Its focus on a young girl facilitates the film's double edged representation of sexuality, a point I will return to below. The fact that Christiane was a child of divorce whose working mother was often absent also dovetailed with Eichinger's gender politics and the overwhelming tendency in his films to locate the origins of social problems in the private sphere. Rather than treating the socioeconomic causes that led to an epidemic of drug use among urban, working-class teenagers in the 1970s, the film locates the origins of Christiane's delinquency squarely with the decline

---

[43] For example, the Federal Minister for Youth, Family, and Health at the time, the SPD politician Antje Huber, spoke out in favor of the film: "Der Film vermeidet einerseits den berühmten 'erhobenen Zeigefinger.' Er verfällt nicht in bekannte Abschreckungsklischees, von denen wir heute wissen, daß sie nichts bewirken, so gut sie auch gemeint sein mögen. Andererseits zeichnet er die Folgen der Drogenabhängigkeit in einer unsensationellen, dokumentarischen und gerade deshalb realistisch wirkenden Weise auf" (On the one hand, the film avoids the famous 'wagging finger' approach. It doesn't fall back on familiar cliches meant to deter similar behavior, which we know by now don't work, even though they are well meant. On the other hand, it portrays the consequences of drug addiction in an unsensational, documentary way that for this reason seems very realistic). Cited in Rauch, *Bernd Eichinger und seine Filme*, 44–45.

[44] See Dreßlein and Lehwald, *Bernd Eichinger*, 99.

[45] Cited in Rauch, *Bernd Eichinger und seine Filme*, 39.

[46] See Rosalind Gill, *Gender and the Media* (Cambridge: Polity, 2007), 249.

of the nuclear family, blaming her mother in particular for focusing more on her own self-actualization than on the well-being of her children.[47] An individualist who ultimately takes charge of her own destiny, Christiane F. embodies the neoliberal call for personal responsibility rather than social welfare as the solution for human dependency needs, but she does so in the guise of a hipster antihero.

Christiane F. begins with a pan to a close-up of the eponymous protagonist's face, accompanied by a voice-over in which she describes the abysmal living conditions, especially for children, in the Gropiusstadt housing project in the Berlin district of Neukölln, where she has lived since she was six. An establishing shot of the dank corridors of the project links Christiane, who enters the frame, with the space of the city, which is figured here as dark, decadent, and dissolute. Christiane exits the building, where her gaze triggers a cut to a poster for "Sound. Europas modernste Diskothek" (Sound. Europe's most contemporary disco), and her voice-over ends, "Da will ich hin" (That's where I want to go). A tracking shot of the city at night establishes a central visual theme of the film, which pictures West Berlin as a ghost town. Repeated long shots of city spaces at night feature buildings in silhouette and trains passing through the city, linking peripheral and central spaces, almost entirely devoid of human figures. A camera mounted on the front of a subway car reveals the perspective of a train traveling through nighttime Berlin, recalling the popular "phantom ride" genre of early cinema. The train arrives at Zoo Station, where passengers disembark to the strains of the Bowie instrumental "V2 Schneider."

Changing from sneakers into high-heeled sandals, Christiane enters Sound for the first time. The music shifts to the uptempo "Look Back in Anger," and we experience the world of the disco through Christiane's eyes. She sees all the characters who will come to play central roles in the film, before her friend Kessi pulls her into the disco's cinema, where George A. Romero's 1968 zombie film *Night of the Living Dead* is playing. The film is a major intertext for *Christiane F.*, which invokes many conventions of horror and zombie films in its depiction of heroin use. In the cinema Christiane is initiated into the world of drugs and sex: she is offered pills and groped by the boy sitting next to her. At the same time, her gaze meets that of Detlef, the junkie and male prostitute who will become her boyfriend in the course of the film. As a beautiful woman is chased by a zombie on screen, Christiane refuses both drugs and sex, but the futility of her refusal is already clear: in the course of the film her brain will be consumed by the zombie drug heroin.

---

[47] By contrast, the book is much more circumspect about exploring the social origins of drug use. The book also allows Christiane's mother to speak, including three extended excerpts of taped interviews in which she gives voice to her side of the story.

Fig. 8.3. Still from Christiane F.—Wir Kinder vom Bahnhof Zoo *(1981).*
The horrors of heroin: A heroin user as "living-dead" zombie.

Throughout *Christiane F.* the filmmakers employ numerous trademarks of the horror genre, including a dark, nighttime setting; chiaroscuro lighting effects; ominous music and scary noises; abject and
revolting bodies; erupting bodily fluids, including blood and vomit;
drug users who are portrayed as "living-dead" zombies; and corpses that
appear unexpectedly. Packaging the horrors of heroin use in a digestible
format via genre logic, this strategy also allowed the filmmakers to appeal
to horror fans and endow the film with a kind of ironic double valence
through metacinematic references to *Night of the Living Dead* and
Murnau's 1921 horror film *Nosferatu* (which the characters also watch in
Sound's cinema, in a later scene). At the same time, references to zombie
and vampire films connect *Christiane F.* to German film history and cater
to expectations of German cinema among international audiences. The
use of horror is only one example of the polygenericism of *Christiane
F.*, which plays with form and perspective in its multivalent appeal to the
widest possible audience.

In *Film/Genre* Altman has described four strategies commonly employed
by contemporary films to create this kind of multivalent appeal: the incor-
poration of "excess material" not integral to the story; multiple framing to
present a given event in a variety of contexts; fertile juxtaposition, involving
interlaced narratives that can be viewed across multiple registers; and multifocalization, to generate multiple points of view and possibilities for identification (134–36). In the case of *Christiane F.*, all four of Altman's strategies of
genre mixing are amply present. Excess material is repeatedly incorporated,
most obviously the footage of a David Bowie concert, as well as a number

of music-video like sequences of young people set to the sounds of Bowie songs. Multiple framing allows the film to be read according to different genre expectations, including as a horror film, social problem film, love story, and tale of youth rebellion. Via fertile juxtapositions, *Christiane F.* constantly reframes its visual and narrative logic, weaving a "multidimensionally reversible fabric" that allows it to be enjoyed and understood along multiple axes, for example by young viewers indulging in the pleasures of rebellion *and* by teachers lauding its moral message. Multifocalization opens up various points of view and possibilities for identification, allowing us to view Christiane herself, for example, as simultaneously virgin/whore, child/woman, innocent/corrupt, and hero/antihero.

For viewers these multivalent strategies proliferate appeal by producing "generic crossroads," situations that open up two paths the spectator can take: the path of generic pleasure, or the return to culturally sanctioned norms or values. As Altman argues, contemporary films operate via a repeated intensification of the generic crossroads, "offering an increasingly intense countercultural genre pleasure experience, only eventually to reverse that pattern and revert to cultural dominance" (155). For Altman, genre mixing is a production strategy that derives from the impulse to create ever more profitable blockbusters. Though Altman does not investigate the ideological effects of polygeneric films, the use of the generic crossroads to create an increasingly market-driven cinema dovetails strongly with the agenda of neoliberalism, which characterizes itself via an illusion of political neutrality while co-opting resistance and difference.

In *Christiane F.* the ideological implications of the generic crossroads are most evident in the film's depiction of sex and sexuality. Often—for example, when Christiane prostitutes herself for the first time—slow motion is employed to alert the viewer on a formal level to an imminent generic crossroads, to a moment of ideological reversal where countercultural pleasure is appropriated for a culturally dominant agenda. From the outset, the film creates an explicit homology between drug use and sex/sexuality. Before Christiane first shoots heroin, her friends tell her that it is better than an orgasm. Inexperienced at either sex or drugs, she attempts to shoot up in a public bathroom, and when she can not manage the injection herself, another user, a strange man, penetrates her vein with the needle. Later, she tells her friends, "Einen sexuellen Höhepunkt habe ich mir schon anders vorgestellt" (I imagined a sexual climax differently); she then turns to Detlef and asks him to have sex with her for the first time on the coming weekend. Before she sleeps with Detlef, he tells her that he turns tricks at Bahnhof Zoo; though he uses sex as a means to earn money for drugs, Detlef explains to Christiane that he regularly sleeps with men. Christiane soon visits Detlef at Bahnhof Zoo, where she is introduced to a taxonomy of sexual desires embodied by the various johns who patronize the male prostitutes there.

Fig. 8.4. Still from Christiane F.—Wir Kinder von Bahnhof Zoo *(1981).*
Generic crossroads: Christiane propositions Detlef.

Christiane F. pictures its protagonist as sexually curious, introducing her to a multivalent space of sexual mobility, where men and women may take on active or passive sexual roles and may sleep with partners of different sexes. Capitalizing on expectations that European cinema will depict a more frank view of sexuality than Hollywood, *Christiane F.* thus exhibits a wide range of gender and sexual performances. Like drug use, sex is presented as an object of curiosity and voyeurism in the film, something that viewers can indulge in through the eyes of Christiane, but which the heteronormative drive of the narrative ultimately forecloses on, not least by ultimately insisting on an equation between drug use and sexuality as deviant activities. The narrative also denies the possibility of sexual pleasure for its protagonists, employing them as mouthpieces for heteronormativity.

When Christiane and Detlef finally sleep together, their sexual encounter is presented as entirely unpleasurable, a missionary-style penetration comparable to Christiane's first injection of heroin, but even less sensual or erotic. Later, the alliance between Christiane and Detlef falters over their mutual insistence on a normative relationship that they are unable to uphold, and their fights give voice to homophobic, misogynist, and even racist rhetoric.[48] Finally, viewers see Christiane whipping a john in an act of sado-masochism that is figured as the penultimate moment

---

[48] For example, Christiane attacks Detlef: "Du lässt dich wohl von jedem schwulen Schwanz im Arsch ficken, was?," to which he replies, "Glaubst du, mir macht es Spaß, dass du dich von jedem Kanacken durchbumsen lässt?"

of her swift spiral downwards—shortly before she discovers that her close friend Babsi has died of an overdose.

In the final sequence of the film viewers see Christiane on a farm and her voice-over explains, "Ich habe es überlebt" (I survived). In this affirmative ending, she is removed entirely from the decadent space of the city that defined her voice-over at the outset of the film and connected her to drugs, sex, and music within the narrative. For the viewer, this ending establishes a closure in which normative values are firmly reinstated after the generic pleasures offered by the film's depiction of Berlin's youth and counterculture. The immense box-office success of *Christiane F.* confirmed the commercial value of Eichinger's polygeneric, multivalent production strategy, setting a standard for producing adaptations that his future films would profitably emulate in the years to come.

9: Exceptional Thrills: Genrification, *Dr. Mabuse*, and *Das Experiment*

Steve Choe

A MAJOR CONTENTION of Rick Altman's sweeping study *Film/Genre* (1999) is that traditional genre criticism all too routinely assumes generic fixity at the expense of generic historicity. "Genre films" are often considered to have fixed narrative patterns and to repeat a relatively unchanging set of codes. Moreover, genre films are thought to be derivative, commercial in both aim and scope, and as a consequence not art. Fritz Lang's *Rancho Notorious* (1952), to take one example, may be read as a "classic" Western in this regard, exhibiting clear-cut and enduring conventions: the mythical settings on the nineteenth-century American frontier, the encounter between law and lawlessness, and the use of stock characters such as cowboys, outlaws, and "noble" Native Americans. While traditional genre criticism has deemed such elements to be timeless and transhistorical, Altman notes that this use of genres overlooks the historical ebb and flow that consolidates not only specific genres but also the concept of genre itself. "Stressing the apparently representative straight stretches of the mighty genre river rather than its tortuous tributaries, its riverbed-defying floods, or its tidewater-dominated estuary, recent genre theory has devoted too little attention to the logic and mechanisms whereby genres become recognizable as such."[1] Traditional genre criticism has not drawn sufficient attention to the varied contestations and negotiations that consolidate genre categorization. Challenging the notion that genre categories exist outside the flow of time, Altman argues that the categories themselves, in close conjunction with the generic cues through which they are constituted, are always already embedded in a historical trajectory, a "mighty genre river," and are thus always in flux.

These explorations into the "tortuous tributaries" of genre consolidation have implications that extend beyond their contextualization

I would like to thank Rick Altman for reading and commenting on an earlier version of this paper. This article was written with support from the International Programs Summer Research Fellowship at the University of Iowa.

[1] Rick Altman, *Film/Genre* (1999; reprint, London: BFI, 2002), 50.

within a linear, progressive history. In the case of the biopic, for instance, Altman explains that the generic conventions commonly associated with it—the depiction of a mythified historical figure or an eccentric genius misunderstood by his or her contemporaries (38–44)—are not simply repeated in the film text. Rather, the genre codes of the biopic are maintained through the shared and often contentious discursive activities of studios, distributors, advertisers, exhibitors, spectators, and critics. Shifting the focus away from the task of matching films with appropriate genres, Altman places greater analytical emphasis on the moment of their articulation, and argues that genres are consolidated through speech acts, through their utilization in context, and are thus materialized in the (re-)iteration of genres and generic cues. Films undergo a process of "genrification"—a dynamic, hermeneutic process that appropriates past uses of genres to place films within the flow of historical change (closely linked, as Altman makes clear, to the logic of capital and product differentiation). In short, genres constitute and are constituted by discursive acts, by individuals who use genres, and by the historical situation in which these individuals find themselves.

Thus the critic does not stand, disinterestedly, on the banks of the mighty genre river. Rather, she is caught within its perpetual movement, for the status of genres upstream as well as down, and their meanings in the past and future, inform genres and the shape of their articulation at any given moment. "Just as producers would assay a successful film, replicating certain aspects in order to initiate a successful cycle," Altman writes, "so critics in all periods assess recent criticism, replicating certain aspects of successful publications in order to initiate a successful critical cycle" (82). While he understands genre criticism as an activity that takes place against the backdrop of a semiotic matrix, Altman astutely notes that these genre performatives have the capacity to both reproduce and shift the very matrix from which they emerge. Because genres are always in contestation, their futures are not predetermined and are thus subject to reconsideration, redefinition, and even misappropriation.

What interests me in Altman's intervention into genre theory is the manner in which his critique allows historicity, the moment of the writing of history, to be implicated in a genre's process of becoming. If genres are consolidated via a multiplicity of sites through contestation, and are the result of regulative discursive acts made by critics, producers, and spectators who appropriate past uses of genres in order to position them for future commercial success, this dynamic approach may be carried over to the discursive practices of the historian, who recovers the past so that it may be stabilized and made meaningful for posterity. Altman's rethinking of genre offers a means of approaching the past that remains critical of precisely these fixed and stable histories, revealing that, as the future of genres remains fluid, the interpretation of the historical past eludes ossification and as such remains open to constant revision. If the historical signifier and its use are both caught within the flow of historicity, then Altman's insights carry profound implications for traditional history writing just as genrification carries profound implications for traditional genre criticism. Instead of stressing "the apparently representative straight stretches" that are often assumed to progressively lead up to the present moment, the historian engages herself in a highly self-reflexive writing process that moves dynamically between past, present, and future.

This essay will build on Rick Altman's explication of film genrification as an approach toward film historicization. My interest is in the "thrills" offered by Oliver Hirschbiegel's first feature-length film, *Das Experiment* (2001), and the genre cues that have been mobilized around this text. Hirschbiegel's film has enjoyed some popular success by recasting tropes associated with the authoritarian personality. My critical reading of this film will take recourse to a broad generic pattern that may be traced back to the early Weimar context. More particularly, this is the logic of sovereignty under exceptional conditions, a logic that I will read through Fritz Lang's *Mabuse* films from 1922. Working with the genrification of Hirschbiegel's popular film, I will show how its genre cues pass over into the realm of historical allegory.

In order to prepare my analysis, I want to further elaborate the terms of the historical approach I will take in this essay. The stakes of Altman's new genre criticism for film historiography may be illuminated further by reading it alongside a key formulation from Siegfried Kracauer's 1927 essay on photography: "The turn to photography is the *go-for-broke game* of history."[2] By this the Weimar critic means two things: one, to point to an epistemological shift that has taken place with historiography and the historical signifier, a shift produced by the transition from memory to photography (and other indexical media such as the cinema). As Kracauer puts it earlier in the essay, "The world itself has taken on a 'photographic face'" (58)—a formulation that identifies a profound epistemological shift put into place by the image in its reproducibility, one that unmoors history from its natural bonds while allowing its realist pretensions to persist in the realm of simulacra. He clearly ponders this unmooring when he writes that the "foundation of nature devoid of meaning arises with modern photography" (61). Second, rather than lament the loss of nature linked to the loss of memory in modernity, Kracauer insists that the turn to photography must stoically and without nostalgia affirm this loss. The age of mechanical reproduction and "nature devoid of meaning" pose profound challenges to the aspirations toward narrative linearity espoused by rational, Hegelian historiography. The "go-for-broke game of history"

---

[2] Siegfried Kracauer, "Photography," in *The Mass Ornament*, ed. and trans. Thomas Y. Levin (Cambridge, MA: Harvard University Press, 1995), 47–63.

challenges the historian to melancholically affirm the archivization of unmoored nature concomitant with the photographic episteme. Writing history through film in a manner that acknowledges its medium-specific capacities means acknowledging film's capacity to "stir up the elements of nature," while providing the opportunity for the spectator to engage in the game of go-for-broke and reflect on her own fragmented, alienated consciousness. "This possibility is realized whenever film combines parts and segments to create strange constructs" (62–63). Montage in the cinema parallels the radical decontextualization of disjointed, photographed nature. Cinema provides the modern subject with the opportunity, not to disavow fragmented nature, but to traverse its ruined landscape in order that the past may finally be redeemed.

The figure that Kracauer invokes to elaborate this redemptive historiography is allegory. The allegorical image does not ossify its content. Rather, it concedes that the medium in which its content is presented remains contingent. Film, as Kracauer puts it, is "assigned to a particular developmental stage of practical and material life" (61), and represents the past in a manner specific to its own formal and material possibilities. The historicity of allegory means that images remain open to the constant possibility of new interpretations, new forms of historical existence. "At the level of allegory," he writes, "thought maintains and employs the image as if consciousness were hesitating to throw off its cocoon" (60). Photographs do not simply embalm their subjects for posterity, as film theorist André Bazin has noted in his essay on photography.[3] If read allegorically, photography returns its subjects to the material, historical world through photography's own materiality, granting the past renewed life in the course of natural history. "It is therefore incumbent on consciousness to establish the *provisional status* of all given configurations, and perhaps even to awaken an inkling of the right order of the inventory of nature."[4] It is precisely because nature remains out of joint in modernity that this redemptive temporality is made possible at all, for the jumble of daily life and the detritus of objects in modernity beg the historian to bring order to this disarray. The past persists through allegory by calling out to future historians for its continued survival through its allegorical reconstruction, reappropriation, and as well, misinterpretation, for a moment yet to come.

Fritz Lang's two-part film, *Dr. Mabuse, der Spieler* (Dr Mabuse, the Gambler, 1922), is subtitled *Ein Bild der Zeit* (A Picture of the Times), a formulation that refers, as Lang has repeatedly remarked in interviews,

---

[3] See André Bazin, "The Ontology of the Photographic Image," in *What is Cinema?*, vol. 1, trans. Hugh Gray (Berkeley: University of California Press, 2005), 9–16.
[4] Kracauer, "Photography," 63.

to its being a document of the early Weimar period. Despite the film's fictional plot, Lang's film presents a realistic picture of a culture morally destitute and shell-shocked immediately following the First World War.[5] Like the frontier depicted in the Western film, the world of *Mabuse* stands at the threshold between law and lawlessness, where crooks carry out their activities in secret gathering places, often in collusion with legitimate institutions. Weimar journalist Kurt Pinthus, in his review of the film, writes that Mabuse's world is "a concentrate of all the excessive stimulation, decadence, sensation, and speculation that have befallen us over the past few years." He was thinking of the excesses of Weimar culture, the engineered crimes, secret gambling rooms, destitute hedonism, black marketeering, the use of cocaine, the unpredictable boom and bust of the stock exchange, Weimar's devastating hyperinflation, "and all the uprooted existences whose unscrupulousness is axiomatic because they have nothing to lose but their lives, which would be even more lost without this lack of scruples."[6] This situation of extraordinary upheaval, Pinthus continues, is connected to Mabuse's authoritarian will to power, for the weakening of political, economic, and societal institutions in Weimar modernity provided opportunities for exploitation by the lawless master criminal.

When it was not generically recognized as a "Kriminalfilm" or "Detektivfilm,"[7] *Mabuse* was also called a "Sensationsfilm" a designation utilized in Weimar film criticism to underscore the sensational thrills provided by the cinema. It was a genre category, moreover, that in the Kino-Debatte[8] pejoratively referred to the gratuitousness of the relatively new mass entertainment of cinema while emphasizing the inherent

---

[5] See Anton Kaes, *Shell Shock Cinema: Weimar Culture and the Wounds of War* (Princeton, NJ: Princeton University Press, 2009). Although Kaes does not provide an extended reading of *Mabuse*, he does mention it in passing on a number of occasions. For example, he compares it to another important film from 1922, Murnau's *Nosferatu*: "As in *Nosferatu*, predator fantasies articulate the vague fears (stemming from the war) of a traumatized community under siege, except that in *Dr. Mabuse* the threat comes more explicitly from inside. . . . And both films reveal a shell-shocked society in search of an enemy who can be blamed for the defeat" (130).

[6] Kurt Pinthus, "The World of Dr. Mabuse," *Das Tage-Buch*, 6 May 1922. Quoted in *Fritz Lang: Leben und Werk, Bilder und Dokumente*, ed. Rolf Aurich, Wolfgang Jacobsen, and Cornelius Schnauber (Berlin: Jovis, 2001), 75.

[7] "Dr. Mabuse" (review), *Der Film* 7, no. 18 (30 Apr. 1922). "Man muß bedenken, daß es im Grunde ein Detektivfilm ist, für den die alles beherrschende Macht des Verbrechers und nicht die gegen ihn eingesetzte Autorität des Staates den Ton angibt."

[8] See Anton Kaes, *Kino-Debatte: Texte zum Verhältnis von Literatur und Film, 1909–1929* (Munich: DTV, 1978).

inability of the cinematic medium to create high art. Lang himself was sensitive to this genre designation, writing in 1924:

> *Mabuse* was a Sensationsfilm *and* a success. But the essential element of its success couldn't even be called "sensational," an aspect that nevertheless remains somewhat timidly in the background. Its success is based on the exploitation of cinema as a picture of its time ["Zeitbild"], or better put, on the interpretative powers of the cinema as a document of its time ["Zeitdokumentes"].[9]

Lang's *Mabuse* is not cheap entertainment but self-reflexive in its engagement with its historical context, responsive to the modern times in which the film was made. Moreover, it not only provides a picture of those volatile times; it also depicts its own depreciatory characterization in the Kino-Debatte. *Mabuse* documents cinema's own association with the masses: sensorial pleasure for a demoralized populace hungry for cheap thrills.

In the opening sequence of the film Mabuse coordinates technologies of modern communication and travel—the telegraph, automobiles, trains, and the telephone—to present and withhold information on the stock exchange. Buying low and selling high, Mabuse defrauds others without their knowing, thrillingly depicting his virtuosic manipulation of time and space. It is however Lang's virtuosity with the cinematic medium and his exploitation of cross-cutting and montage that in the end are showcased.[10] Later Mabuse uses his powers of hypnosis during card games, self-reflexively allegorizing the hypnotic effects of the cinema itself on its viewers.[11] In a world shell-shocked by military loss, Mabuse's authoritarianism is inseparable from a highly cynical, postwar consciousness that has all but abandoned hope in the legitimacy of modern democracy.[12]

---

[9] Fritz Lang, "Kitsch—Sensation—Kultur und Film," in, *Fritz Lang—Die Stimme von Metropolis*, ed. Fred Gehler and Ullrich Kasten (Berlin: Henschel, 1990), 205. All translations in this essay are my own.

[10] For a powerful reading of how crosscutting functions in the opening scene, see Tom Gunning, "Mabuse, Grand Enunciator: Control and Co-ordination," in *The Films of Fritz Lang* (London: BFI, 2000), 87–116.

[11] See Stefan Andriopoulos, *Possessed: Hypnotic Crimes, Corporate Fiction, and the Invention of Cinema*, trans. Peter Jansen and Stefan Andriopoulos (Chicago: University of Chicago Press, 2008).

[12] Here I am thinking of the analysis of Weimar culture performed in the last section of Peter Sloterdijk's *Critique of Cynical Reason*. See Peter Sloterdijk, "The Weimar Symptom: Models of Consciousness in German Modernity," in *Critique of Cynical Reason*, trans. Michael Eldred (Minneapolis: University of Minnesota Press, 1988), 384–528.

Figs. 9.1a and 9.1b. Dr. Mabuse, der Spieler *(1922). Screenshots.*

This cynicism may be corroborated with a moment from part 2 of the film, subtitled *Inferno*, when Mabuse (played by Rudolf Klein-Rogge) receives a phone call from State Prosecutor Norbert von Wenk (Bernhard Goetzke). During a public psychic demonstration, von Wenk had been hypnotized by Mabuse and commanded to commit suicide by driving an automobile over a cliff. The prosecutor was thought to have died in the ensuing crash, but at the last moment he was saved by some of his perceptive colleagues. Speaking on the telephone, he demands that his criminal adversary surrender himself to the law. Mabuse laughs and responds: "I feel as a state within a state with which I have always been at war. If you want me—come and get me!"

Tom Gunning, in his 2009 essay on Lang's film, reads this claim, "a state within a state," as an expression not only of Mabuse's megalomania but one that "also acknowledges the fragmentation of power, especially the control of force and violence in Germany after the Great War."[13] Gunning links the images of mobilized masses and urban violence in *Mabuse* with the political chaos taking place throughout the republic, for these images recall "the battles between Freikorps and revolutionaries in various German cities" (109). *Mabuse* depicts the Weimar citizen who is legally bound to the state and the rule of law, yet cynically refuses to fully recognize this state's political legitimacy. In his paranoia Mabuse becomes a kind of tyrant, yet one circumscribed by state power.

Mabuse's invocation of himself as a "state" also points to his megalomaniac agency as an aggregate person, an individual made up of many "organs" or "employees." Stefan Andriopoulos notes this in his reading of Lang's film, writing that "the intangibility and the autopoetic agency of an opaque complex organization are thus attributed to the extraordinary qualities of a single human being."[14] After von Wenk hangs up the phone, he gathers police and military officers to storm Mabuse's hide-

[13] Tom Gunning, "Fritz Lang's *Dr. Mabuse, the Gambler* (1922): Grand Enunciator of the Weimar Era," in *An Essential Guide to Classic Films of the Era: Weimar Cinema*, ed. Noah Isenberg (New York: Columbia University Press, 2009), 109.

[14] Andriopoulos, *Possessed*, 127.

out, eventually apprehending the master criminal languishing in a pile of counterfeit bills. "The man who was Dr. Mabuse . . ." an intertitle solemnly announces, signaling that the great mastermind is no longer. He has gone mad, conquered by his visions and overcome by the consequences of his crimes.

In suggesting that Mabuse embodies the authoritarian tyrant who enjoys a kind of mythical exercise of power, I am more or less reiterating a canonical argument made first by Kracauer in 1947. In *From Caligari to Hitler* Kracauer argues that the despots, showmen, vampires, mad scientists, and magicians depicted in the films of Weimar Germany are symptomatic of the traumatized German soul. This "soul," more specifically, is that of the disenfranchised Weimar middle class, who sought the security of an authoritarian dictator to lead the people out of the chaos of the times. Referring directly to Lang's film, Kracauer writes: "Chaos breeds tyrants like Mabuse, who for their part, capitalize on chaos. One should not overlook the seemingly harmless word 'and' through which the prospectus chooses to connect the weighty terms 'war' and 'revolution': this 'and' throws a dazzling light on Dr. Mabuse's origin in the middle-class mind."[15] This is an important reading that, while having undergone a good deal of critique, nevertheless remains the touchstone for any subsequent readings of Weimar cinema and its history.

In contrast to the symptomatic analysis offered by Kracauer that diagnoses the hidden psychology of the Weimar soul, the allegorical reading I am pursuing here does not posit such an interiority. It reads this history as a series of images that momentarily brackets their capacity to sociologically reflect "the middle-class mind." If *From Caligari to Hitler* may be read as one of the first studies to have identified and developed the procession of tyrants in Weimar cinema, then this allegorical approach allows us to read Kracauer's analysis as having identified the "generic cues" of the Nazi film. The genrification of Weimar cinema in *From Caligari to Hitler* reveals that not only is the filmic image contingent on its historicity, but the relationships between film, spectator, and critic are historically fluid as well, and any reading of film history must allow for this fluidity. Our reading of Kracauer's text must be informed by our knowledge that he was writing as an exile, living in New York in 1947. On the other hand, reading the Nazi film as a genre does not relinquish the force and ethical urgency of Kracauer's critique. Altman's intervention in *Film/Genre* allows us to see how these generic tyrants may be read today, allowing their proleptic status, as allegorical images, to travel beyond their historical determination in Weimar Germany and toward our contemporary moment.

---

[15] Siegfried Kracauer, *From Caligari to Hitler* (Princeton, NJ: Princeton University Press, 2004), 84.

Kracauer reads Weimar cinema as giving the spectator access to the surface of physical reality, "to those visible phenomena," as film scholar Gertrud Koch puts it, that "film uses as legible hieroglyphs."[16] This is the hermeneutic that has guided Kracauer's reading of mass culture throughout his career, from the Weimar essay on photography to his *Theory of Film* of 1960.[17] While the historical rupture of the Holocaust remains the vanishing point for his 1947 analysis, it is also this rupture that compels his more materialist tendencies in the later writings. Kracauer writes in the epilogue to the *Theory of Film* that cinema functions as "Athena's polished shield,"[18] a reflective surface that allows the spectator to confront horrors too atrocious to be beheld in reality. The notion that film reflects that which cannot be represented, or brings to the surface a hidden reality, seems to operate in tension with his theory of allegory articulated in his "Photography" from 1927. Yet we should remember that Kracauer in his *Theory of Film* also places great emphasis on the spatial and temporal indeterminacy located beyond the frame of the image, and he insists that film must reflect its close affinity with the flux of physical reality. A correlation may be drawn here between the Kracauer of 1927 and that of 1960, which I believe may be put this way: if the go-for-broke game of history is to be played, and in good faith, then it must be allowed to remain open and contingent just as the interpretation of historical reality remains open and contingent. His reading of Weimar film in *Theory of Film* suggests that if the writing of history is to continue in an age dominated by the photographic sign, this act of writing must be thought of as always already embedded in the flow of everyday life, and as partaking in its endlessness.[19]

I would like to turn for a moment to the problem of sovereignty that arose in response to the implementation of parliamentary democracy in early Weimar Germany, in order to provide further contextualization of the "state within a state" and its legacy through concepts of twentieth-century governmentality. Germany's defeat in the First World War galvanized Weimar writers on the right, such as political theorist Carl Schmitt, who tried to preserve the role of the sovereign despite the political uncertainties that accompanied Germany's introduction to modern republicanism. "Sovereign is he who decides on the exception

---

[16] Gertrud Koch, *Siegfried Kracauer: An Introduction*, trans. Jeremy Gaines (Princeton, NJ: Princeton University Press, 2000), 82.

[17] See Miriam Bratu Hansen's 1997 introduction to *Theory of Film* in Siegfried Kracauer, *Theory of Film* (Princeton: Princeton University Press, 1997).

[18] Kracauer, *Theory of Film*, 305.

[19] For an explanation of what Kracauer calls photography's "affinities," which include the fortuitous, endlessness, and the indeterminate, see Kracauer, *Theory of Film*, 18–20.

[Ausnahmezustand],"[20] Schmitt famously wrote in his *Political Theology* from 1922, the year of Lang's film. Through this he underscores the manner in which a crisis, or a state of exception, "confirms not only the rule but also its existence" (15), while putting into relief a general concept of the modern state. With respect to the regulatory effects of the exception, Schmitt the rejects the notion that it may be juridically predetermined, for by definition the exception cannot be subsumed under the normative interdiction of the law. This contradiction becomes particularly illuminating for delineating the structural constraints of modern governmentality, and for the critique of modern political power.

Philosopher Giorgio Agamben, in his discussion of the state of exception, puts into further relief Schmitt's linking of the state of exception with the force of law, placing the word "law" under erasure. He emphasizes that the state of exception does not simply result in the suspension of the norm, but exists in a state of ontological aporia, remaining unlocatable in relation to the juridical field delineated by state power. "In truth," he writes, "the state of exception is neither external nor internal to the juridical order, and the problem of defining it concerns precisely a threshold, or a zone of indifference, where inside and outside do not exclude each other but rather blur with each other."[21] Agamben thus interprets Schmitt's formulation as a suspension of the norm that poses the status of the exception as a question, one constituted by and constitutive of the rule, rather than concretely determining the legality of exceptions to the rule set against the backdrop of a normative legal order. Moreover he points out that for the purposes of state power such aporias cannot be maintained precisely *because of* the manner in which it brings state legitimacy itself into question, and consequently must be excised in the name of law.

Thus, in a state of exception, power is exercised in its pure state precisely because it is deployed in this state of lawless anomie. Agamben is primarily concerned with the articulation of power and the speech act of the sovereign that puts into motion the force of law. This exercise of power is not supported by normative proscriptions issuing from the state, but in its being given over to the sovereign, absolute power (re)emerges legitimized by a sovereign body situated both inside and outside law's jurisdiction.

> That is to say, in extreme situations "force of law" floats as an indeterminate element that can be claimed both by the state authority (which acts as a commissarial dictatorship) and by a revolutionary organization (which acts as a sovereign dictatorship). That state of

---

[20] Carl Schmitt, *Political Theology: Four Chapters on the Concept of Sovereignty*, trans. George Schwab (Cambridge, MA: MIT Press, 1985), 5.
[21] Giorgio Agamben, *State of Exception*, trans. Kevin Attell (Chicago: University of Chicago Press, 2005), 23.

exception is an anomic space in which what is at stake is a force of law without law (which should therefore be written: force-of-~~law~~).[22]

When the sovereign returns through his articulation of the exception, it is not the sovereign father as delineated by law, but the name of the father that is materialized in conjunction with law's withdrawal. In the effort to legitimate and make legible the mystical foundations of the exception, the sovereign asserts itself through the force of ~~law~~ in order to forcefully demand legitimacy from those to whom law is subjected.

This spectral potentiality, according to Agamben, haunts all forms of modern governmentality following the crises of Weimar and other democracies after the First World War. As we know, the Weimar Constitution of 1919 paved the way for the state of exception in Article 48, the infamous *Notverordnung* clause that granted the president certain legal powers under conditions of political emergency. In 1933, without parliamentary approval, Paul von Hindenburg appointed Hitler as chancellor, and one month later the emergency decree allowed the violation of habeas corpus, freedom of expression, and freedom of assembly, as well as the expropriation of property. Hitler's dictatorial regime, Agamben notes, came into being as a "second structure," one contingent upon its exception to the law, at once preserving the legitimacy of the Weimar Constitution while simultaneously bestowing exceptional power on the sovereign.

> As is well known, what characterizes both the Fascist and Nazi regimes is that they allowed the existing constitutions (the Albertine Statute and the Weimar Constitutions, respectively) to subsist, and—according to a paradigm that has been acutely defined as "dual state"—they placed beside the legal constitution a second structure, often not legally formalized, that could exist alongside the other because of the state of exception.[23]

In the name of emergency, legal civil liberties were revoked and given over to the authority of the sovereign. The secondary structure of the state of exception parallels Mabuse's claim that he exists as a "state within a state." Indeed, this structure not only constitutes his power as both inside and outside the law but also underpins his spectral presence throughout the film—a master of disguises who seemingly has no concrete identity of his own.

The state of exception also helps illuminate the metaphysics of the thriller, and the thrills that arise from the transgression of its normative laws. Because the legal exception reveals the authority of the sovereign in its purest form, Schmitt calls the exception "more interesting" than the

---

[22] Agamben, *State of Exception*, 38–39.
[23] Agamben, *State of Exception*, 48.

"torpid" norm, for it delineates a situation that forces the questioning of normality as such. Slightly shifting the terms in which he casts his discussion of sovereignty, he writes:

> The exception is more interesting than the rule. The rule proves nothing; the exception proves everything: It confirms not only the rule but also its existence, which derives only from the exception. In the exception the power of real-life breaks through the crust of a mechanism that has become torpid by repetition.[24]

Several lines later Schmitt quotes Kierkegaard, calling the perennial predictability of the general uninteresting, precisely because it adheres to an already given rule. "Endless talk about the general becomes boring" (15). More interesting are the illicit and the illegitimate that confound inevitability in favor of novelty and thrill: the destitute characters of *Dr. Mabuse*, the hedonists filled with lust and passion, "the aristocratic woman who, from her cultured milieu, desperately longs for the adventure she senses approaching."[25] The bored repetition of the rule produces its own contingent, more "thrilling" negative, indeed the more interesting exception, sought out by the thrill-seekers of the early Weimar Republic and documented in Lang's Sensationsfilm. "We are bored and tired, Mr. von Wenk," the dancer and Mabuse's mistress Cara Carozza (Aud Egede Nissen) tells the state prosecutor, "We need sensations [Sensationen] of a very special kind to keep us alive."

The logic of the exception and the production of thrills also coincide with an important chapter in Altmann's *Film/Genre* that deals with the narrative economy of the genre film. Altman explains that a narrative development that would otherwise horrify and offend were it to take place in the everyday world, a world in which individuals are bound to the laws and norms of their culture, elicits for some viewers, such as Cara Carozza perhaps, precisely the transgressive thrills of the thriller film.

> Each plot twist not only increases the character's danger (and the spectator's thrill), but it also offers a way off the film's crazy ride. At every turn spectators must make an implicit choice: more thrills (in the continued company of an outlaw) or safety at last (under the socially sanctioned protection of the law and its defenders). (154)

Conduct broadly understood as conforming to a norm is contradicted in the genre of the thriller, so as to raise the stakes of perverse, spectatorial pleasure.[26] In *Dr. Mabuse*, the cinema similarly becomes a heterotopic

---

[24] Schmitt, *Political Theology*, 15.
[25] Pinthus, "The World of Dr. Mabuse," 75.
[26] For a detailed discussion of perverse spectatorship and its pleasures, argued against the backdrop of apparatus theory, see Janet Staiger, *Perverse Spectators:*

space for the spectator's experience of legal transgression, allegorized in the film's own vacillation between law and chaos, precisely that which makes the reassertion of modern sovereignty possible. Here my reading of the thriller follows Jacques Derrida's deconstruction of genre purity in his 1980 essay, "The Law of Genre."[27] The transgressive thrills offered up by the thriller speak to the aporias that Derrida discovers at the heart of the law of genre. In its ostensible demand for purity, genre consolidation presupposes a sovereign subject whose discourse is nevertheless circumscribed by language—who speaks through generic conventions and reiterates generic cues.

Indeed, this economy is crucial for Altman, for it offers a critique of traditional genre theorists and critics "who assume that genres serve to level *all* viewers, transforming the entire audience into a single homogeneous block" (151). At the moment the viewer decides to partake in the thrills offered up by the cinema, she partakes in the alternative moral realm presented by the genre film. As they diverge from her everyday cultural norms, the film allows her to engage in a realm of sin, crime, and utopian indiscretion. Depending on the spectator's individual tolerance for such depictions of misdeeds and for conduct that may be considered tyrannical, some will continue to be entertained by such figures who believe themselves to be outside the law, while others will momentarily refuse the depiction of power enjoyed by the sovereign and take up a more critical spectatorial position.[28]

I would like to turn now to Oliver Hirschbiegel's 2001 film *Das Experiment* and propose a parallel reading, one that critiques the thrills offered up by the thriller genre. As I shall show, this critique is closely linked to the genrification of the film figured within an allegorical-historical trajectory and the exception to the law of genre.

Hirschbiegel's *Das Experiment* is based on a novel by the German author Mario Giordano called *Black Box*, first published in 1999. Giordano's novel is in turn based on Philip Zimbardo's well-known Stanford Prison Experiment of 1971. Hirschbiegel's film adaptation tells the story of a group of regular German men, drawn from varying socioeconomic classes, who volunteer for a two-week investigation into prisoner psychology. Eight of the twenty volunteers become prison guards; they are dressed in blue uniforms and equipped with heavy boots and nightsticks, while the remaining twelve are assigned the role of prisoners, dressed only in nightshirts stitched with a number. Individuals on each side are instructed to perform and conform to their designated roles.

The Practices of Film Reception (New York: New York University Press, 2000).

[27] Jacques Derrida, "The Law of Genre," trans. Avital Ronell, *Critical Inquiry* 7, no. 1 (Autumn 1980): 55–81.

[28] I believe the logic of the legal exception and the sensational thrills of the thriller may be carried over into Lang's Mabuse films from 1932 and 1960 as well.

Figs. 9.2a and 9.2b. Das Experiment *(2001). Screenshots.*

To this end, rules are to be strictly enforced for the duration of the experiment: for example, the prisoners are to address each other by their number only, the prisoners address the guards as "Herr Strafvollzugsbeamter" (Mr. Prison Guard), food and drink are to be consumed in their entirety, and with lights out, the prisoners are not allowed to talk. Above all, test subjects are forbidden the use of physical violence. Researchers will observe the behavior of the test subjects through surveillance cameras mounted throughout the prison, of which the participants are well aware. Upon completion of the research experiment each volunteer will receive 4000 DM compensation.

The explication of the rules at the start of the film makes clear the norms that will regulate the test participants' behavior in the prison. As in reality television, such rules exist not only for the researchers within the diegesis of *Das Experiment* but also for the viewer's gaze. Indeed, the rules guide the spectator's judgment, endowing her with the capacity to ascertain distinctions between correct and incorrect behavior during the experiment. On the other hand, Hirschbiegel's thriller film explicitly cites these rules only to anticipate their transgression later in the film. In this the prison space may be characterized as a kind of Mabusian "state within a state," whose existence is neither external nor internal to the juridical norm, or as Michel Foucault puts it in his essay on heterotopias, a "counter-site, a kind of effectively enacted utopia in which the real sites, all the other real sites that can be found within the culture, are simultaneously represented, contested, and inverted."[29]

At the beginning of the research period, the participants have fun with their roles and the arbitrariness of the situation, aware that they are taking part in what is essentially theater. However, as in the real-life Stanford experiment, their assigned roles quickly bring out the sadistic aspects of these otherwise regular personalities, particularly among the guards. They become shameless in their exercise of power, humiliating and eventually torturing their inferiors, seemingly empowered by their position of authority. The inmates, on the other hand, become increasingly anxious

---

[29] Michel Foucault, "Of Other Spaces," *Diacritics* 16, no. 1 (Spring 1986): 24.

and defiant, acting out so as to exasperate and purposefully infuriate their nominal superiors.

In one of the first major outbursts of prisoner disobedience, the Turkish-German taxi driver Tarek (Moritz Bleibtreu) tricks two guards into his cell. When the jailers enter, he rushes out and closes the prison door, locking them in. Taunting the guards and dancing with glee, Tarek demands cable TV, pizza, and porn magazines, while the rest of the inmates cheer him on. Another guard rushes in to release his humiliated colleagues, while Tarek closes a section of the prison behind him and climbs up the bars like an animal. The inmates loudly and excitedly egg him on as chaos ensues. Later that evening the guards punish the inmates in retaliation, switching off the lights and storming into all the prisoners' cells. The guards command the inmates to strip naked and spray them with with fire extinguishers. They do not use their nightsticks but utilize techniques to humiliate and abuse the prisoners psychologically. The blond Berus (Justus von Dohnanyi), who has emerged as the leader of the guards, pays particular attention to Tarek, stripping him of his clothes and handcuffing him to a prison cell bar, leaving him there until the next morning. From this moment the film increases in intensity, as the men on each side progressively humiliate each other with increasingly disturbing acts of psychological, and eventually physical, cruelty. Hirschbiegel's film is for this reason not easy to watch. When the experiment totally spirals out of control, the film concludes with an explosive ending, leaving two volunteers dead and at least one apprehended by the police.

Das Experiment enjoyed some critical and commercial success, and in the German-language criticism it is often referred to, using the American designation, as a "thriller" or "psychothriller."[30] Among critics there is some ambivalence as to whether its Hollywood-style linear narration combined with gratuitous shock and horror are to be criticized or touted. Film critic Thomas Klingenmeier, in a review for the *Stuttgarter Zeitung*, comments, for example: "The conduct of the prisoners and wardens reminds one of Hollywood's prison films. The experiment's test subjects are unremarkable, recruited as they are from everyday life. And ever more Hollywood genre elements seep into the film."[31] Later he remarks that while Hirschbiegel's film demonstrates that the German filmmaker had mastered the basic building blocks of American genre cinema, *Das Experiment* sacrifices the broader relevance of its theme to its run-of-the-mill Hollywood treatment ("Nullachtfünfzehnrezepten der Hollywoodlehrbücher").

For others, the film's seamless continuity editing and fast-paced style is exemplary of the post-Wall style of German genre cinema, proving that

---

[30] See "Der Angstspieler," *Focus Magazin*, 5 Mar. 2001; *Die Welt*, 8 Nov. 2001.
[31] *Stuttgarter Zeitung*, 9 Mar. 2001.

Europe could produce movies that could compete with their American blockbuster counterparts. In 2001 *Das Experiment* was nominated for a number of awards through the European Film Academy, including the coveted European Film Award, best actor (Bleibtreu), and best director. Reporting on the German nominees, the correspondent for *Die Welt* announced: "Among the forty-four films, from a total of 300, that were recommended for the category of European Film were three German productions: *Das Experiment* by Oliver Hirschbiegel, *The Princess and the Warrior* by Tom Tykwer, and *The State I Am In* from Christian Petzold."[32] Of these three, Hirschbiegel's entry is unquestionably the most "generic" of them in its assimilation of Hollywood conventions. The award for Best European Film that year would go to Jean-Pierre Jeunet's *Le Fabuleux destin d'Amélie Poulain*, a romantic comedy starring Audrey Tautou.

Das Experiment was released in the United States one year later, and American film critics followed their German colleagues in reiterating the signifier "thriller," while touting the film's technique. Ed Halter of the *Village Voice* wrote that *Das Experiment* is "a keen, gripping psychodrama with unsettling real-life underpinnings" that "marries German post-fascist soul-searching to the fast-paced voyeuristic pop thrills of reality TV."[33] He notes the way Hirschbiegel's film showcases high technology, singling out the tiny camera mounted on Tarek's glasses, and appreciates its fast-paced cutting and electronic beats. "But after the film's ultraviolent finale," he speculates with some ambivalence, "one wonders whether this sharp bit of fascinating fascism provides a true analysis of television's new mean streak, or simply an engaging indulgence in same." Halter's reference to the title of Susan Sontag's well-known essay[34] follows a seemingly obvious point: that *Das Experiment* is, according to him, "only the most recent example of an actual study of authoritarianism explored cinematically," and thus deals with the "question of how Nazism gained power."

That Hirschbiegel's film is "obviously" about fascism attests to the all-too-easy identification of German films dealing with tyranny, power, and uniformed "Teutons" as belonging to the genre of the Nazi film, or in this case, the Nazi thriller.[35] Similar connections were made in the German press. "Im Rausch der Macht" (The Intoxication of Power),

---

[32] *Die Welt*, 13 Sept. 2001, Feuilleton, Kultur kompakt, 31.

[33] Ed Halter, "Lords of Discipline," *Village Voice*, 17 Sept. 2002.

[34] See Susan Sontag, "Fascinating Fascism," in her *Under the Sign of Saturn* (New York: Picador, 2002).

[35] For most American critics, the link between this German film from 2001 and Germany's fascist history is all but glaring. "The fact that the movie is German inspires thoughts about the Holocaust," film critic Roger Ebert writes in his review. "The Nazi command structure needed only strong leaders at the top for Hitler to find, as one book called them, willing executioners in the ranks." *Chicago Sun Times*, 25 Oct. 2002.

a long article published in *Der Spiegel* in March 2001,[36] begins by describing a number of scenes from *Das Experiment* that depict abuse and humiliation, using them as occasions for addressing the question of power more generally. Moving onto a detailed discussion of Zimbardo's experiments,[37] the article links institutionalized power made manifest in "firms and hospitals, institutions of authority, churches and schools, and also families and couple relationships" to that monstrously exaggerated in Hitler's addiction to power. (The article contains sidebars that trace examples of authoritarian power through figures such as Wolfgang Wagner, sports coach Christoph Daum, the banker Friedel Neuber, and then Cardinal Joseph Ratzinger.) Such diffuse linkages point to the diffuse nature of power itself, and the *Spiegel* article makes an effort to argue that the potential for tyranny is not limited to a particular historical time and place but may arise in everyday conditions involving individuals who recognize themselves as subjects interpellated by a sovereign power.

Film scholar Steffen Hantke largely concurs with this, writing that *Das Experiment* functions as "social allegory" for the fascism of "everyday life in post-industrial capitalism."[38] He avers, moreover, that the experiment depicted in the film envisages a microsociety comprised only of cohabiting men and thus operates in a tense relationship with broader patriarchal interdictions on homosexuality. Drawing from Freud's theory of drives, Handke explains that in the absence of a proper object of heterosexual desire, this system can maintain itself only through the repressive intervention of an authoritarian personality. Thus "fascism, as *Das Experiment* understands it, depends on an absolute and hierarchical social order, which furthermore enforces—and is enforced by—rigidly defined regimes of desire." Hirschbiegel's film plays out fascism's consolidation in allegorical form, allegorizing the social relations that constitute its structure, while inviting the viewer to "recognize this trajectory in Germany's

---

[36] Johann von Grolle, et al., "Im Rausch der Macht," *Der Spiegel*, 12 Mar. 2001.

[37] Zimbardo, in 2002, then president of the American Psychological Association, voiced the opinion that Hirschbiegel's film gives a negative portrayal of research done in the field of psychology. "'What's wrong is they are masquerading the movie as a documentary of a real-life experiment with real people at Stanford University,' says Zimbardo, who has been bombarded with angry e-mails about the movie from the European academic community. 'It makes Stanford and me and psychology look bad. And I resent that, especially at a time when, as APA president, I am trying to work with the media to advance more positive portrayals of psychology.'" Evidently he sees the film as merely providing a realistic portrayal of the experiment he conducted in 1971. He remarks as well that *Das Experiment* "falls into the genre of the mad-scientist films." See "Film Criticized as Irresponsible," *Monitor on Psychology* 33, no. 3 (Mar. 2002): 20.

[38] Steffan Hantke, "The Origins of Violence in a Peaceful Society," May 2003, http://www.kinoeye.org/03/06/hantke06.php.

history, from the rise of fascism in the wake of the Weimar Republic to World War II." Hantke is sensitive to the post-Wall context of *Das Experiment*, a context that has ostensibly "already come to terms with the problematic figures of its past," and which self-consciously evacuates the rule of the authoritarian father in lieu of a neoliberal subject engaged in a war of all against all.

Hirschbiegel is patently aware of how his film has been understood as critically playing out the deep structure of fascism, appropriations that he in large part resists. In a 2001 interview he explained that he did not want *Das Experiment* to be screened at the Berlinale that year because it was "still ideological" when a German film plays at this festival. "Discussions of German films," he explains, "are often understood to be about whether they are ideologically correct. I'm afraid that such discussions will harm my film. It is important to me that the film does not get too caught up with simply providing a perspective on our history, as it is a universal story that could take place anywhere." Hirschbiegel concedes that while the Third Reich "was characterized by horrendous developments such as torture, oppression, racism, and forced submission," he also maintains that, "these are not inventions of the Germans."[39] On another occasion, Hirschbiegel basically reiterates this position, while explicitly distancing *Das Experiment* from Germany's Nazi past:

> As a German storyteller or German filmmaker, of course there is this awareness and that responsibility that our history gives us. Then again, this whole thing is not about concentration camps; it's not about fascism; it's about prisons, basically, as I just said. I think it can help to understand how these barbaric things could happen—how this barbaric system, the Third Reich, got people to behave in this way. But it's not really reflecting on fascism and Nazi Germany.[40]

Hirschbiegel the auteur wants to protect the aesthetic and political autonomy of his work—a German film made by a modern German filmmaker, a subject position that necessarily must negotiate all the political and historical pretensions this position implies. He refuses easy genrification of his film as "Nazi thriller." Torture occurs everywhere, he suggests, and furthermore, echoing the *Spiegel* article, forms of tyranny can emerge anytime institutional power is enforced.

Despite his protestations, Hirschbiegel's disavowal of a direct link between the cruelty depicted in his film and the cruelty of the Nazi regime seems weak and perhaps a bit disingenuous. For if *Das Experiment*

---

[39] "Gespräch mit Oliver Hirschbiegel," *EPD Film* 3 (2001), http://www.epd-film.de/.

[40] Moritz Bleibtreu and Oliver Hirschbiegel, "Das Interview," with Carlo Cavagna, http://www.aboutfilm.com/features/dasexperiment/interview.htm.

is about "torture, oppression, racism, and forced submission," then the film must necessarily, because of its historical situatedness ("a particular stage of practical and material life," to quote Kracauer once more), be about the horrors that took place under Nazism as well. Moreover, Hirschbiegel's comments are open to a more problematic reading than the one he perhaps implies, one that attempts to normalize Germany's history by placing German fascism within the history of torture and cruelty in general. In order to relieve his film of the burden of directly or indirectly dealing with the Nazi past, Hirschbiegel is disconcertingly in danger of overlooking German fascism's historical specificity. This reading insinuates that because the potential for institutional tyranny exists at all levels of society, concepts of torture may be transhistorically detached from their instantiation and grounding in German history.

An allegorical approach toward film and history can responsibly trace the figurations of fascism through *Das Experiment*. For to quickly categorize Hirschbiegel's film as one that *only* deals with Germany's fascist past, and this is where I believe the filmmaker's comments may be more sympathetically read, delimits the narrative and formal elements of the film as teleologically and thus necessarily signifying Nazi Germany, and this ultimately to foreclose critical analysis. If we are to understand genre cinematically, then genrification, as a speech act that performatively categorizes individual films in time, must be understood historically as well, and thus must be understood to be in constant dialogue with the history of film and Germany's national history. Here the analysis of genre as historiography relates to what political theorist Wendy Brown calls "untimely critique"[41]—critique that remains vigilant to the teleological and ossifying tendencies of traditional historiography, while delineating ontological aporias that put the hermeneutics of the past into radical question. The point is not to reveal how film is symptomatic of society, thus averring merely a one-to-one relationship between filmic representation and the deep structure it signifies. Genrification does suggest quite meticulous relationships between film, culture, and history—yet these relationships proceed via the logic of the images themselves, fluid and historically contingent, without positing an unconscious German "soul," or an invisible, transhistorical fact that analysis aims to make visible. Genrification, in other words, attends to the historicity of genres and does not settle on stable meanings in its interpretation of film, instead holding out for another potential meaning to come.

---

[41] See Wendy Brown, "Untimeliness and Punctuality: Critical Theory in Dark Times," in *Edgework: Critical Essays on Knowledge and Politics* (Princeton, NJ: Princeton University Press, 2005), 1–16.

Figs. 9.3a and 9.3b. Das Experiment *(2001). Screenshots.*

With the aim of elucidating this potentiality, I would like to turn to a key moment from *Das Experiment* that takes us back to the state of exception. In a particularly tense scene toward the end of the film, the inmates are being disciplined for their rebellious, infuriating conduct. Their mouths have been covered with duct tape, while one of them, Schütte (Oliver Stokowski) remains tied to a chair, bleeding. Meanwhile, Tarek has been confined to the claustrophobic "black box," a tiny cell that allows no light for the detained and that seems to be conceived as a cross between a safe and coffin. Jutta (Andrea Sawatzki), the female researcher overseeing the experiment, has been apprehended as well. Like the inmates, she has been stripped down, forced to wear a uniform with a number, and placed in a cell. Unlike the male prisoners, however, she has been threatened with sexual assault. Rage and misogyny increasingly determine the conduct of the prison guards, as their behavior departs further from the rules of engagement set out by the terms of the experiment. One of the detained inmates, Steinhoff (Christian Berkel), turns to a surveillance camera above him and declares, "Professor Thon, this is against the law and violates human rights! I demand that we abort this experiment!" Unfortunately no one is at the monitor and his plea goes unheard. Berus turns to all of the detained and asserts his sovereignty: "How long this state of emergency [*Ausnahmezustand*] lasts depends on you!" He then storms off, irritated and driven by fury.

Moments later one of the prison guards questions Berus, challenging his authority and the premise of the experiment itself: "Don't tell me about some stupid test! They said no violence!" Berus turns and retorts: "This is an emergency [*Ausnahmezustand*]. We'll wait until Professor Thon is back." He justifies the violence that has taken place up to this moment, including his own morally suspect actions, by maintaining that all will be judged according to the terms set out by the experiment and that the researchers will want to know of everything that took place.

In both of Berus's utterances, the *Ausnahmezustand* is exploited in a manner to explain the use of physical violence. In the name of social order, the sovereign Berus decides upon the exception to the rules of the experiment, and through his assertion of power inaugurates a second juridical structure, or a state within a state, that resides within the experiment. From here the film spirals out of control, inducing violent thrills and inciting, as in *Mabuse*, a kind of generic enjoyment specific to political theology. The thrill of *Das Experiment* originates from both inside and outside the law of genre, the zone of indifference between licit and illicit visual pleasure that, as Altman has noted, constitutes the basic tension at the heart of the generic thriller. For some spectators the Ausnahmezustand may compel the feeling of being "alive," and as Hirschbiegel's film continues in its depictions of cruelty, such images will grip these viewers in a surplus of excitation and agitation.

Once more, this crossroads presents the spectator with an aporia that has political and ethical consequences. *Das Experiment* may be read as a straightforward thriller haunted by the specters of Germany's Nazi terror. If the sovereign is the one who decides on the exception, then the social laboratory depicted in *Das Experiment* shows us how the aggressive sovereign is produced in this lawless space, at the very moment of the withdrawal of sovereignty. On the other hand, the critical deconstruction of the thrills offered up by Hirschbiegel's film allows us the opportunity to think once more about the heterogeneity of genres, allegorized through the zone of indeterminacy that underpins Berus's authoritarian discourse. Berus's speech acts, in other words, belong to a genre, a jargon of authenticity whose meanings nevertheless remain decentered and unstable. As Altman contends in *Film/Genre*, genres are always already embedded in a history, subject to a continuing process of reiteration and reappropriation. Accordingly, the discourse of the sovereign, far from issuing from a space of metaphysical purity, is always already heterogeneous and caught within the mighty genre river. The continuing critique of Hirschbiegel's film about aggression and male sovereignty may be seen within a circular historiography, whose meanings, beyond those intended by the auteur, are yet to come.[42]

In July 2009 Sony Pictures began filming a remake of *Das Experiment* in Des Moines, Iowa. *The Experiment*, the Hollywood remake directed by Paul Scheuring, features well-known American actors Adrien Brody and Forest Whitaker, among others. The US version, again called a "thriller," reiterates a number of key scenes from Hirschbiegel's film and places a

---

[42] One allegorical connection may be made to Abu Ghraib photos from 2004, some of them uncannily echoing imagery from Hirschbiegel's film. The photos depict Arab bodies dressed in long smocks and hooded with sandbags, like the prisoners in *Das Experiment*. When Berus's white body performs acts of cruelty on Tarek's Arab body, they seem to resonate with the context depicted in the Abu Ghraib photos, whereby white Americans are seen abusing nonwhite Iraqis. These images return as the *Nachträglichkeit* of Hirschbiegel's film, flashing up in a moment of danger, and reanimating the memory of cruelty and atrocity across time and space, from Germany to Iraq.

bit more emphasis on the background of the main characters. A theatrical release of Scheuring's film was planned, but it eventually went straight to DVD. Understood in relation to Hirschbiegel's 2001 *Das Experiment* and against the backdrop of its generic history, Scheuring's *The Experiment* attests to the continuing need for the critique of the thriller as a genre. The political and ethical dimensions of its key conventions, taken over without further thought, should accompany their continued reappropriation, beyond the 2001 German genre film.

That Altman may have been aware of the broad implications of genre theory for historiography may be evidenced in the final pages of *Film/Genre*. His critique will continue to be relevant as long as genre categories are deployed homogeneously and used in a manner that implicitly downplays their heterogeneity across time. But in the final paragraphs of *Film/Genre*, Altman makes a much broader claim, and in so doing betrays the semiotic basis of his critical intervention.

> I would simply point out that what I have just claimed about genre is true of every communicative structure in every language ever devised. Though the social utility of language has forced cultures to downplay this point, every word, every meaningful gesture, every film image makes meaning only through a process of multiple commutation engendered by the multiple usefulness of the sign in question.[43]

Altman's incursion into genre theory is no less a philosophical incursion into the semiotics of language in general. Despite the fundamentally conflicted nature of linguistic signs, we assume that they have clear, concrete, and obvious meanings when utilized in everyday communication. All signifiers constitute and are constituted by categorical genres within discourse, and they are always being negotiated, reworked, and contested with each utterance.

Altman's *Film/Genre* evinces a cinematic inquiry into genre, one that seeks a language that is appropriate to the mobile, temporalized signifier, and yet enables the recognition of cinema's basic ontological indeterminacy. Kracauer in his *Theory of Film* seems to corroborate this, naming the cinema as the allegorical medium par excellence. By experiencing the world through the camera, we discover the material world through its psychophysical correspondence with the film image. It is for this reason

---

[43] Altman, *Film/Genre*, 215. In the very next sentence he writes, "In spite of Saussure's claim to be presenting a *Course in GENERAL Linguistics*, our theories of language have always been theories of the exception, of the socially stabilized case." By the "exception" Altman means the exception to the notion that language use is constantly in contestation, "contradictory usage, constant repurposing and systematic miscommunication."

that "the cinema can be defined as a medium particularly equipped to promote the redemption of physical reality. Its imagery permits us, for the first time, to take away with us the objects and occurrences that comprise the flow of material life."[44] Kracauer articulates a line of cinematic inquiry that stretches back to his 1927 essay on photography. Looked at from this perspective, we may see how Altman's critique of genre, together with its application to Hirschbiegel's thriller film, allows for a reading of history that carries profound ethical and political implications, for the past as well as the future of the cinema.

---

[44] Kracauer, *Theory of Film*, 300.

10: The Heimat Film in the Twenty-First Century: Negotiating the New German Cinema to Return to *Papas Kino*

Paul Cooke

POINT OF VIEW SHOT: an aerial camera flying through the clouds toward what looks like a large mountaintop observatory, accompanied by a blues-rock soundtrack. Cut to the inside of the building, where the camera pans across a series of iconic images of dead pop stars, from Elvis and Otis Redding to Janis Joplin and Kurt Cobain. Cut to a clothing rack filled with rock-inspired costumes, behind which we glimpse a man swapping an "Uncle Sam" topper for a black cowboy hat. Cut to an extreme close-up of the same man lighting a cigarette, fading down the music on a mixing desk and opening his mouth to speak. So begins Marcus H. Rosenmüller's surprise hit of 2006, *Wer früher stirbt, ist länger tot* (released in English as *Grave Decisions*), an opening sequence awash with intertextual references that encapsulate many of the tensions present in the genre films discussed throughout this volume. The first shot from a camera descending onto the mountain recalls the famous opening of Leni Riefenstahl's *Triumph des Willens* (Triumph of the Will, 1935) and its depiction of Hitler's approach to the 1934 Nuremburg Rally.[1] This echo of Germany's problematic cinematic legacy is then juxtaposed with the presentation of the inside of the building that, it transpires, is a radio station with far more in common with George Lucas's classic nostalgia film *American Graffiti* (1973) than with Riefenstahl: the man we see on the screen before us seems to recall that archetypal American DJ Wolfman Jack, who acts as mythical seer to the teenagers of Lucas's film. However, the echoes of Lucas's Americana are immediately shattered as Rosenmüller's DJ utters his first words in a thick Bavarian dialect. The camera pulls back to reveal a vista of the Bavarian Alps and sets off again on its airborne course, through the station window into the clouds, before beginning its descent to the verdant countryside below.

---

[1] Alexandra Ludewig, *Screening Nostalgia: 100 Years of Heimat Film* (Bielefeld: transcript, 2011), 372.

222 ◆ PAUL COOKE

This shift of focus from American rock to Bavarian country(side) in turn signals to the spectator the key generic affiliation of Rosenmüller's movie. This is to be a Heimat film (homeland film), a genre most famous in its 1950s incarnation, when West German audiences flocked to cinemas to watch escapist, brightly-colored images of Germany and Austria as provincial rural idyll, where dirndl-clad women and trachten-wearing men fell in love to a soundtrack of German *Volksmusik*, providing a cinematic embodiment of idealized German family values. As Thomas Elsaesser suggests, the Heimat film is "Germany's only indigenous and historically most enduring genre."[2] However, it has also, until recently, received scant critical attention, its zenith being reached during a decade that remains, in Johannes von Moltke's words, "the quintessential 'bad object' of German film historiography."[3] And as Anton Kaes notes, the Heimat film itself has generally received particular opprobrium, its "cliché-ridden, Agfa-colored images" being dismissed by its critics, most notably that cultural product of the "68er" protest generation, the New German Cinema, as the worst form of "Papas Kino" (Daddy's cinema), a cinema they viewed as both aesthetically and ideologically defunct.[4] The last decade has seen rapidly growing critical interest in the Heimat film, as well as in German popular cinema more generally.[5] *Wer früher stirbt* has a complex relationship with the Heimat-film tradition, as might be deduced from the brief description of its opening above. Nonetheless, its success has led Rosenmüller to be styled by the German media as the "poster boy" of a new Heimat-film movement, popular with critics and audiences alike.[6]

What is particularly noteworthy about Rosenmüller's work is its national appeal beyond the Bavarian province of its setting, selling 1.8 million tickets during its theatrical release across Germany.[7] However,

---

[2] Thomas Elsaesser, *New German Cinema* (Basingstoke: Macmillan, 1989), 141.

[3] Johannes von Moltke, *No Place like Home: Locations of* Heimat *in German Cinema* (Berkeley: University of California Press, 2005), 21.

[4] Anton Kaes, *From Heimat to Hitler: The Return of History as Film* (Cambridge, MA: Harvard University Press, 1989), 15.

[5] See, for example, Tim Bergfelder, *International Adventures: Popular German Cinema and European Co-productions in the 1960s* (New York: Berghahn, 2005); Jürgen Trimborn, *Der deutsche Heimatfilm der fünfziger Jahre: Motive, Symbole und Handlungsmuster* (Cologne: Teiresias Verlag, 1998); Randall Halle and Margaret McCarthy, eds., *Light Motives: German Popular Film in Perspective* (Detroit: Wayne State University Press, 2003); John Davidson and Sabine Hake, eds, *Framing the Fifties: Cinema in a Divided Germany* (New York: Berghahn Books, 2007).

[6] See, for example, Nikolaus von Festenberg, "Die neue Alm," *Der Spiegel*, 30 Jul. 2007, 136.

[7] Figures taken from the Filmförderungsanstalt website, accessed 8 Nov. 2009, http://www.ffa.de/index.php?page=filmhitlisten.

Wer früher stirbt is only the tip of a very large iceberg of films that have been linked in a variety of ways to the Heimat-film tradition in recent years. To see the hugely diverse list of titles that have been defined as Heimat films as part of a unified corpus brings to mind numerous questions, not least that of how to define the word Heimat itself, a term that is notoriously difficult to translate into English. However, before discussing this term in more detail, let alone its relationship to German film culture, I should first outline how I understand the notion of Heimat film as a genre in this chapter. Following Andrew Tudor, I wish to avoid the search for an "indefinable 'X'" that encapsulates the essence of the Heimat film, an approach, Tudor rightly notes, that can lead to an over-determining form of "genre imperialism," where all aspects of any given film text are subordinated to the reading of a film as part of a specific genre cycle.[8] Instead, I draw on the work of Rick Altman, Steve Neale, and others, who view genres "not as formal patterns or textual canons, but as system and process . . . made up of an interconnected network of user groups and their supporting institutions, each using the genre to satisfy its own needs and desires."[9] Genres exist at the interface of numerous competing discourses, defined by a whole host of stakeholders, changing over time, discourses that in turn are both constructed by, and help to construct, the broader social and historical context within which they exist.

The nature of defining the Heimat genre, specifically, as "system and process" is, however, complicated by the difficulty of defining the word Heimat itself. The first problem, as Elizabeth Boa and Rachel Palfreyman outline in their examination of the historical trajectory of the term, is that Heimat is an extraordinarily heterogeneous concept, used to reflect a wide range of positions in discussions over the years around the role of place, belonging, and identification in the German-speaking world.[10] Second, it is invariably emotionally loaded, thus always escaping the words used to define it.[11] Coming into widespread use in the nineteenth century, as Germany began to negotiate the challenges of modernity and nationhood, Heimat came to denote in the literature and art of the time the rural province, the Bavarian Alps, the Black Forest, or the Lüneburger Heath. It stood for tradition and family, for cultural roots that seemed to

---

[8] Andrew Tudor, *Theories of Film* (New York: Viking, 1974), 133.

[9] Rick Altman, *Film/Genre* (1999; repr., London: British Film Institute, 2002), 195. See also Steve Neale, *Genre and Hollywood* (1999; repr., London: Routledge, 2000).

[10] Elizabeth Boa and Rachel Palfreyman, *Heimat—a German Dream: Regional Loyalties and National Identity in German Culture, 1890–1990* (Oxford: Oxford University Press, 2000).

[11] For a discussion of this aspect of Heimat see Celia Applegate, *A Nation of Provincials: The German Idea of* Heimat (Berkeley: University of California Press, 1990), 4–5.

resist urban cosmopolitanism, foreignness, and progress.[12] Heimat was a place beyond time, and certainly beyond critique. It was, as Peter Blickle puts it, "a space free from irony," a utopia shrouded in nostalgia and thus also always elsewhere, always already lost, but nonetheless longed for, often framed as a return to the childhood home and in particular to the love of a mother.[13]

That said, and in order to prove the impossible heterogeneity of the concept, when we come to the history of the Heimat film it is very clear that this is, at best, only a partial explanation of a term that is at times as much about negotiating and incorporating the process of modernity into tradition, the national and ultimately the global within the local, as it is about protecting the inhabitants of the mythical Heimat from such forces. Rather than seeing Heimat, as it is presented in film, simply as a refuge from modernity, and, following von Moltke in his study of the genre, I argue that Heimat must be understood dialectically. Drawing on Freud's reading of the uncanny, von Moltke highlights the ways Heimat always implicitly references, indeed is defined by and thus inextricably linked to, its "others." Consequently, the type of binaries described above (modernity versus tradition, the local versus the national and so on) should not ultimately be seen to be in opposition within the term, but rather "mutually contingent on one another."[14]

In this chapter I wish to extend previous explorations of the genre by examining the competing ways the term circulates in contemporary German film culture. How does the iconography of the Heimat genre that has built and developed over time, its affective language, or what Altman terms the "semantic" elements of a genre, currently play against its "syntactic" elements, that is, the ideas this language seeks to convey? How does the interplay of syntax and semantics impact upon the aesthetics of contemporary German film as well as the stories and issues it seeks to present?[15] Specifically, I am interested in the way much of this new wave of filmmaking engages the dialectical relationship between modernity and tradition discussed by von Moltke that has always existed within the term, the present moment in the genre's development pointing to a widespread recuperation of the Heimat province, such as we find in the 1950s cycle, in the face of the New German Cinema's critique of the 1960s and 1970s. In so doing, I focus on how contemporary popular films self-consciously reconfigure the genre's semantic iconography, at times evoking the critical tradition of the New German Cinema, only ultimately to find a way

---

[12] Boa and Palfreyman, "*Heimat—a German Dream*," 2.

[13] Peter Blickle, *Heimat: A Critical Theory of the German Idea of Homeland* (Rochester, NY: Camden House, 2002), 40. See also Boa and Palfreyman, "*Heimat—a German Dream*," 26–30.

[14] Von Moltke, *No Place like Home*, 13.

[15] Altman, *Film/Genre*, 216–26.

back to the far more affirmative syntactic world of the 1950s and the construction of the nation as a timeless, yet modern, rural idyll; negotiating the legacy of New German Cinema, to return, as it were, to *Papas Kino*, updated for the twenty-first-century Berlin Republic. This contrasts starkly, as I shall also discuss in my conclusion, with a number of less popular, smaller scale, productions in which contemporary society, specifically the continuing economic and social asymmetries between the eastern and western regions of the country, are explored in terms that reconfigure the genre's iconography into a syntactic landscape of "anti-Heimat" despair. However, in order to give some context to my discussion of contemporary Heimat films, I would first like to give an overview of the genre's development, and in particular of the ways in which the changing dialectical relationship between modernity and tradition has unfolded both politically and aesthetically across the genre's history.

Locating the Heimat Film

From its roots in Peter Ostermayr's hugely successful adaptations of Ludwig Ganghofer's nineteenth-century Alpine Heimat novels (for example, *Der Edelweißkönig* [The Edelweiss King, 1920, remade 1939 and 1957]) and the mountain films of the late 1920s, 1930s, and 1940s (Arnold Fanck, *Die weiße Hölle vom Piz Palü* [The White Hell of Piz Palu, 1929]; and Leni Riefenstahl, *Das blaue Licht* [The Blue Light, 1932]), Heimat is constructed as a space that must negotiate tradition within modernity and the needs of the local in the face of the national and global, rather than ignore the pressures of the outside world. Over time, one finds the various tensions implicit within the concept of Heimat differently inflected to reflect the changing historical context. For the Nazis, Carl Froelich's *Heimat* (1938) or Veit Harlan's *Die goldene Stadt* (The Golden City, 1942) helped underline their industry-based, exclusionary ideology and the need to create a visceral link between the land and Germanness. In the 1950s West Germany wave, by contrast, films such as Hans Deppe's *Schwarzwaldmädel* (The Black Forest Girl, 1950) and *Grün ist die Heide* (Green is the Heath, 1951) or Hans Wolff's *Am Brunnen vor dem Tore* (At the Spring outside the Gate, 1952) created escapist fantasies in which the 12 million Germans who had been expelled from their homes east of the Oder-Neisse line could find a new sense of belonging, the trauma of the mass bombing of German cities and the ravages of occupation could be resolved, and the modernity of the burgeoning *Wirtschaftswunder* (economic miracle) could be celebrated.

Throughout such films one finds the rural landscape presented as a "semantic" space, to return to Altman's terminology, configured "syntactically" to exist, seemingly paradoxically, both beyond, and yet subject to, the forces of modernity. This is reflected, for example, in the easy

Figs. 10.1a and 10.1b. Grün ist die Heide *(1951). Screenshots.*

integration of the aspirational accouterments of 1950s consumerism into the timeless, nostalgic kitsch of the all-singing, all-dancing provincial landscape found in Deppe and Wolff's films, where BP petrol pumps and motor cars can comfortably coexist with horse-drawn carts and *Volksmusik* groups, modernity and tradition working together in a productive dialectic.[16] Indeed, the very existence of these films reflects this same dialectic. The vividness of the rural idyll was, after all, only made possible by the use of the latest color film technology. Moreover, Tim Bergfelder points out that the Austrian Tourist Board was eager to fund Heimat films during the 1950s boom in the hope of fueling a thoroughly modern domestic holiday market.[17] Within the films themselves the potential for progress within a fundamentally unchanging rural world is often reflected in the long lingering shots of the countryside one finds throughout the genre. As Eric Rentschler notes in his discussion of the mountain film, the images of billowing clouds set against the immutable mountains, caught using time-lapse photography, owe a great deal to the romantic iconography of Caspar David Friedrich and his depictions of the sublime power of nature beyond civilization, updated to take account of the visual innovations of Weimar Expressionism and particularly the poetic realism of F. W. Murnau.[18] These images present moments of what Gilles Deleuze would call "becoming," utilizing shots that exemplify the kind of "time-image" he most often associates with postwar European avant-garde cinema. Such films, Deleuze argues, employ the camera to present the infinite possibilities of time and space, rather than to limit both to the logic of a specific narrative.[19] Although such films do invariably limit the potential of such

[16] See Boa and Palfreyman, *Heimat—a German Dream*, 130–49.

[17] Bergfelder, *International Adventures*, 41–44. That said, the relationship between Heimat films and the tourist industry, however primitive, has been in existence for a long time. See Eric Rentschler, *The Ministry of Illusion: Nazi Cinema and Its Afterlife* (Cambridge, MA: University of Harvard Press, 1996), 32–38.

[18] Rentschler, *Ministry of Illusion*, 32–38.

[19] Gilles Deleuze, *Cinema 2: The Time-Image* (London: Continuum, 1989), 1–41.

shots in their final narrative resolution, we nonetheless catch glimpses of the time-image being used to highlight the ever-changing nature of the ostensibly permanent, and thus the dialectical quality of Heimat as a place that might be a haven from, and yet also subject to, the progression of time and with it the concomitant processes of modernity.

By the 1950s, while we continue to be presented with shots of the West German and Austrian countryside, which allow the spectator to identify with its seemingly timeless and yet also changing beauty, Heimat is now as much about people and community as it is about regional specificity. As a result, even in its escapist fantasies, the Heimat idyll is haunted by the trauma of the recent past. This might manifest itself implicitly, as in Kurt Hoffmann's *Ich denke oft an Piroschka* (I Often Think of Piroschka, 1955), a nostalgic story of innocent lost love set in eastern Europe. At times, however, the uncanny underbelly of this trauma is made more explicit, most obviously in Hans H. König's *Rosen blühen auf dem Heidegrab* (Roses Bloom on the Moorland Grave, 1952), which evokes the gothic horror tradition in its story of the rape and death of a young woman during the Thirty Years War, a not-so-veiled reminder of the postwar rape of German women by the Allies. In the GDR, on the other hand, there was less of a straightforward continuation of the Heimat tradition, not least because the artists who had made these films in the 1930s and 1940s, such as Ostermayr or Luis Trenker, found work in the West German film industry.[20] Nonetheless, as von Moltke, Ludewig, and Boa and Palfreyman have noted, the Heimat tradition still engaged filmmakers, either through the direct reworking of the successful West German genre, such as in Konrad Wolf's *Einmal ist Keinmal* (One Time is No Time, 1955), or more obliquely in the Berlin films of the 1960s, banned by the SED until unification in 1990 (Gerhard Klein's *Berlin um die Ecke* [Berlin around the Corner, 1965], or Frank Vogel's *Denk bloß nicht, ich heule* [Just Don't Think I'm Crying, 1965]).[21] Here the link to the genre is largely syntactic. Heimat reflects the need to build a new sense of a local community, based in this case on a socialist rereading of traditional German humanist values. Once again the trappings of modern life can be negotiated, although this was a far more complicated affair for filmmakers in the East, where the population had little prospect of acquiring the consumer goods that helped to drive the Federal Republic's *Wirtschaftswunder*.

---

[20] For further discussion, see Leonie Naughton, *That Was the Wild East: Film Culture, Unification, and the "New" Germany* (Ann Arbor: University of Michigan Press, 2002), 125–38.

[21] Von Molkte, *No Place like Home*, 170–200; Boa and Palfreyman, *Heimat—a German Dream*, 130–43; Ludewig, *Screening Nostalgia: 100 Years of Heimat Film*, 298–310.

By the end of the decade the Heimat films were becoming less popular. With regard to film production, the kitsch of the 1950s began to draw ever more heavily on a variety of genres, from the musical to soft porn. Indeed, the erotic *Lederhosenfilme* were a staple of the German soft-porn boom of the late 1960s and 1970s, producing films that had, for better or worse, far more international impact than the cycle of the previous decade, a moment in German film history that has been revisited recently in Marc Rothemund's romantic comedy *Pornorama* (2007). Titles such as *Liebesgrüße aus der Lederhose* (Love Greetings from his Lederhosen, 1973) and *Unterm Dirndl wird gejodelt* (There's Yodelling under her Dirndl, released in English as *How Sweet is her Valley*, 1974) perhaps give a clear enough flavor of how this particular trend sought to commodify the Heimat film.

With regard to mainstream German audiences, while the population as a whole still preferred domestic productions to the Hollywood product that largely filled its cinema screens, the Heimat film increasingly became a genre for the older generation, while the young were more likely to want to watch Marlon Brando and Jane Russell than Sonja Ziemann and Rudolf Prack.[22] Nonetheless, it was the younger generation that would be crucial to the next stage in the system and process of the genre. As they came of age in the 1960s and began making films themselves, the "68ers," as they have become known, were also drawn to the Heimat genre, even as they decried the likes of Ostermayr and Trenker as "Papas Kino." However, in Peter Fleischmann's *Jagdszenen aus Niederbayern* (Hunting Scenes from Lower Bavaria, 1969), Rainer Werner Fassbinder's *Katzelmacher* (1969), Volker Schlöndorff's *Der plötzliche Reichtum der armen Leute von Kombach* (The Sudden Wealth of the Poor People of Kombach, 1970) or Werner Herzog's *Herz aus Glas* (Heart of Glass, 1976), we find none of the earlier images of the German and Austrian provinces as timeless idylls.

Reflecting growing social concerns at the time as well as open suspicion about the communities formerly celebrated, we are now presented with a world of bigotry and violence, often drawing inspiration from other European critical film traditions, not least the Italian Westerns of Sergio Leone.[23] In these so-called anti-Heimat films, one once again finds numerous examples of the Deleuzian "time-image." Yet unlike its usage in the mountain films of the 1930s, where such images connote the

---

[22] For further discussion see Heide Fehrenbach, *Cinema in Democratizing Germany: Reconstructing National Identity after Hitler* (Chapel Hill: University of North Carolina Press, 1995), 151–67.

[23] See Rachel Palfreyman, "Once upon a Time in the Critical Heimat Film," in *German Monitor: Local/Global Narratives*, ed. Renate Rechtien and Karoline von Oppen (Amsterdam: Rodopi, 2007), 40.

Figs. 10.2a and 10.2b. Jagdszenen aus Niederbayern *(1969). Screenshots.*

potential of the Heimat to integrate time and place in a moment of "becoming," here they tend to undermine any sublime potential of the province. Working against Deleuze's own notion of the time-image, here the unity of time and space that is central to the idyllic Heimat film is fractured; the semantic iconography of the Heimat genre, as it functioned in previous decades, works against any syntactic logic that would indulge traditional Heimat sensibilities. Through the use of a quasi-documentary mode, the province is presented in all its raw filth, with the idyllic Heimat appearing only in moments of irony, which, as we can see from Blickle's definition of Heimat as "a space free from irony," underlines the impossibility of its very existence. In *Der plötzliche Reichtum der armen Leute von Kombach*, for example, Schlondorff's account of the true story of a group of peasants who rob a money transport on its way from von Gladenbach to Gießen, one such idyllic "Heimat moment" is evoked when the thieves finally manage to steal their booty after numerous failed attempts. They capture the wagon in the forest. Suddenly they are bathed in light, in a moment that directly, if imperfectly, evokes the Agfa gaudiness of the 1950s Heimat cycle. This imperfection is due to Schlöndorff's use of black and white film stock, deliberately chosen to distance his work from that of the earlier West German films. For a moment here the narrative seems intent upon breaking through its own distancing device. However, in its failure to do so, the film instead highlights the assumed affluence that underpinned the Heimat idyll of these earlier films, an affluence that is impossible for the thieves of Krombach to sustain, all but one of whom is hanged.

Similarly ironic invocations of the Heimat tradition are to be found in Edgar Reitz's three-part epic *Heimat*, the first installment of which was shown on television around the world in 1984. Reitz's main impetus for making the film was the screening in Germany of NBC's television miniseries *Holocaust* (directed by Marvin J. Chomsky, written by Gerald Green) in 1979. *Heimat* was to be a corrective to what Reitz saw as Chomsky and Green's Americanization of German history,[24] and is part of a trend since the 1980s that has seen the Heimat genre move predominantly to the television screen. As I shall discuss below, the connection of Reitz's

---

[24] See Kaes, *From Heimat to Hitler*, 183–84.

film to anti-Heimat, however, distances his work from the majority of television Heimat output. Instead, his story of life in the fictional village of Schabbach from 1919 to the early 1980s, like Schlöndorff's film, critically and self-consciously engages the Heimat tradition as visual spectacle, using a mixture of film styles to challenge the notion of Heimat as timeless idyllic space, in particular forcing the spectator to reflect critically on the use of the concept in Nazi visual culture. Nonetheless, Reitz offers a far less abrasive image of rural life than is to be found in the earlier anti-Heimat films, a development for which he was heavily criticized at the time, in particular for his lack of engagement with questions of German culpability for the Holocaust.[25] For better or worse, Reitz's film points the way toward developments in the use of Heimat that I will pick up in the second part of this chapter, where we see the continued critical engagement with Heimat as a means of revisiting Germany's problematic past, exploring in more detail the anti-Heimat films' fracturing of the ostensible timelessness of Heimat. At the same time we begin to see the recuperation of Heimat, a trend not lost on the Hunsrück Tourist Board, which has been keen to rekindle the relationship already mentioned between tourism and the Heimat film.[26]

In the decades since Reitz's film the Heimat genre has continued to find favor with both audiences and filmmakers. There has been a massive explosion in television Heimat film production. While the remakes of Ganghofer's work have become more sporadic since the 1970s, the most recent being Bernhard Helfrich's *Der Jäger von Fall* (The Hunter from Fall) in 1993, other staples of the genre from earlier decades continue to flourish, most notably *Die Geierwally* (Vulture Wally), first made by Ewald André Dupont in 1921 and remade on five subsequent occasions, including Peter Sämann's 2005 production for *Bayerischer Rundfunk*. Heritage drama series, including fifty-seven adaptations since 1993 of Rosamunde Pilcher's romantic fiction, along with a number of long-running soap operas such as *Die Schwarzwaldklinik* (The Black Forest Clinic) also adopt semantic elements from the tradition.[27] *Volksmusik* shows drenched in the iconography of the Heimat film remain popular, not to mention the reruns of classics from the 1950s, all of which has

---

[25] For a summary of the reception of the film see Miriam Hansen, Karsten Witte, J. Hoberman, Thomas Elsaesser, Gertrud Koch, Friedrich P. Kahlenberg, Klaus Kreimeier, and Heide Schlüpmann, "Dossier on Heimat," *New German Critique* 36 (1985): 3–24.

[26] See *Heimat is Hunsrück*, accessed 15 Sept. 2009, http://www.hunsrueck touristik.de/en/.

[27] For a discussion of the Pilcher adaptations see Eckart Voigts Virchow, "Heritage and Literature on Screen: Heimat and Heritage," in *The Cambridge Companion to Literature on Screen*, ed. Deborah Cartmell and Imelda Whelehan (Cambridge: Cambridge University Press, 2009), 123–37.

been fueled by an aging population attracted to such fare and culminating recently in the creation of the *Heimatkanal* for German cable.[28] In the cinema there has been less volume of production. However, the films made have often been popular, particularly the work of Joseph Vilsmaier, who along with producing a series of successful war films has also been a regular maker of Heimat-inspired dramas (*Schlafes Bruder* [The Brother of Sleep, 1995], *Bergkristall* [Mountain Crystal, 2004], *Die Geschichte vom Brandner Kaspar* [The Story of Brandner Kasper, 2008]). Throughout such productions we find an uncritical and nostalgic reappropriation of the Heimat-film tradition that, most notably, seems to airbrush the mores of anti-Heimat from the genre's history.

Recuperating Heimat Traditions in the New Millennium

The new wave of Heimat films since the turn of the millennium has continued the process of reappropriation outlined above. However, in the work of Hans Steinbichler (*Hierankl*, 2003; *Winterreise* [Winter Journey, 2006]), Thomas Kronthaler (*Die Scheinheiligen* [The Hypocrites, 2001]), and Rosenmüller, as well as that of their northern colleagues Detlev Buck (*Liebes Luder* [Dear Little Minx, released in English as *Bundle of Joy*, 2000]) and Sven Taddicken (*Emmas Glück* [Emma's Bliss, 2006]), we find films that attempt to recuperate the power of the Heimat province in the face of anti-Heimat critique rather than simply trying to ignore the existence of an anti-Heimat tradition. Instead of the ironic invocation of a rural province being used to challenge the very existence of Heimat values in the present, as it had been in the work of the New German Cinema, irony is now often used to reinvest Heimat with meaning for the contemporary spectator. Returning to Rosenmüller, for the most part he would seem to be working in the Vilsmaier mold. His coming-of-age romantic comedies *Beste Zeit* (The Best of Times, released in English as *Good Times*, 2007) and *Beste Gegend* (The Best of Regions, 2008), for example, engage straightforwardly with the Heimat tradition's celebration of the regional and the function of the rural idyll as a sanctuary, where its inhabitants can learn to negotiate the pressures of the modern world. However, his greatest success to date came with his first feature, *Wer früher stirbt, ist länger tot*, a film that offers a more complex engagement with the Heimat tradition than the rest of his oeuvre.

Rosenmüller's surprise hit tells the story of eleven-year-old Sebastian (Fritz Karl), who believes himself responsible for the death of his mother, who died giving birth to him. Fearing the fires of purgatory, this young

---

[28] See Sandy Pletz, *Die Phänomene Heimatfilme und Volksmusiksendungen in Deutschland* (Saarbrücken: VDM, 2008), 38–63.

Figs. 10.3a and 10.3b. Wer früher stirbt,
ist länger tot *(2006). Screenshots.*

Catholic boy spends the film looking for a way to redeem himself for this
"crime," as well as for other grievous sins, such as the accidental killing
of his brother's rabbits, and spitting in the soup of a guest in his father's
hostelry for failing to give the boy a tip. Or if salvation is impossible, he
will find a way of becoming immortal and so similarly avoid the pains of
the afterlife. *Wer früher stirbt* is a comedy Heimat film. However, as can
be seen from its opening described above, it engages with a network of
allusions through which it reflects, to an extent like Reitz's *Heimat*, self-
consciously on its generic status.

Once we move beyond the cinematic aerial acrobatics of Leni
Riefenstahl and George Lucas and are introduced to life on the ground,
the idyllic innocence of the Heimat vista is almost immediately challenged
by the attitude of the drayman, Sepp (Johann Schuler), whom we see
ogling the local primary-school teacher, Veronika (Jule Ronstedt) from
the inside of his truck. Sepp is a figure who could have appeared in a
Heimat sex film, if it were thirty years earlier and he were thirty years
younger. However, this lascivious portrayal of him persists throughout
the film, as he explains to Sebastian how best to approach a woman—"Du
beißt sie ins Ohrläppchen und dann flüsterst 'Willst Du mit mir vögeln?'"
(nibble her earlobe and ask her "Do you want to screw me?"). We first
meet Sebastian soon after seeing the drayman. Here the film shifts from
the softest of porn into a children's film, in the tradition of Gerhard
Lamprecht's *Emil und die Detektive* (Emil and the Detectives, 1931), as
we see a precocious boy drive his father to distraction, as he rides his
bicycle through the bar, only to be knocked down by the drayman's
truck. The spectator is stunned by this event, and the genre seems to shift
again, as we are presented with an overhead shot of the motionless child,
whom we assume to be dead, lying on the ground. The camera pauses
for the first time and the title appears, a title that has all the cadence of a
Fritz Lang film noir (the German translates as "The Earlier You Die, the
Longer You are Dead"). Fortunately the boy survives. "Glück gehabt"
(that was lucky), says an offscreen voice, either the boy's or that of a spiritual guide, perhaps his mother who, we will shortly learn, died bringing
him into the world, an event for which he is, of course, blameless. Back

in the hostelry the regulars are preparing a traditional *Volksstück*, a morality play about the Day of Judgment. The play's nightly rehearsals invade Sebastian's sleep, attempting, in vain, to turn the film into a grotesque horror movie reminiscent, as Rachel Palfreyman notes, of *Rosen blühen auf dem Heidegrab* in its evocation of a spirit world returning to haunt the living.[29] Finally, against this whirlwind of allusions to a variety of cinematic fantasy worlds, Rosenmüller sets up a realistic mise-en-scène that has more in common with 1960s anti-Heimat than it does with the lurid colors found in *Grün ist die Heide*. This is a real village, where we see the mud of the farmyards and the blood of the pigs that are slaughtered, where we know that rabbits are food, not pets, and that even if Sebastian had not killed them by accident, they were due to be eaten. It is a world where life is defined by death and where all the characters are acutely aware of their own mortality.

Despite its self-conscious allusion to the entire history of the Heimat genre, unified into a single cinematic moment, the kind of nostalgic innocence to be found in the 1950s Heimat cycle dominates, communicated to the spectator through our identification with Sebastian. While the mise-en-scène evokes semantic elements of the anti-Heimat world, there is none of its cynicism. The fracturing of time and place, introduced through the anti-Heimat's use of realism, is papered over. Life might be defined by dirt and death. Nonetheless, we also know that life will go on in this little upper-Bavarian community. The regulars at the village hostelry might eventually pass on, but the pub itself will remain forever. Thus the invocation of the anti-Heimat merely allows the 1950s Heimat fantasy to be updated slightly and given more credibility. The rural idyll is challenged by Sebastian's attempt to redeem himself. He decides that he must find a new wife for his father and, ostensibly following his mother's signals from the spirit world, is led to the primary-school teacher, Veronika. Unfortunately she is already married, to the DJ Alfred (Jürgen Tonkel). Despite this barrier, the romantic subplot of the film is eventually resolved, with Veronika and Sebastian's father falling in love. However, this resolution is far from comfortable, leaving Alfred out in the cold and contemplating suicide. In the final sequence of the film, Alfred seems to have gotten over his former wife. We see him playing air-guitar in his radio station as he broadcasts Sebastian's musical debut, the boy at last appearing to be on the way to finding immortality, having learned the guitar, thereby following in the footsteps of the rock heroes that adorn the walls of the radio station, all of whom, he is assured by Alfred, life forever in their music. As Alfred and Sebastian disappear into

---

[29] Rachel Palfreyman, "Links and Chains: Trauma between the Generations in the Heimat Mode," in *Screening War: Perspectives on German Suffering*, ed. Paul Cooke and Marc Silberman (Rochester, NY: Camden House, 2010), 145–64.

their fantasy world of rock, we are given an inkling of the reasons why Veronika left her husband, preferring the domestic stability of life with Sebastian's family to Alfred's permanent adolescence. Nonetheless, we are not wholly convinced of her insistence to Sebastian that Alfred is now fine. The neat resolution demanded of the traditional Heimat film is withheld. That said, the power of the Heimat idyll is maintained. As with the use of a realist mise-en-scène, the evocation of real world problems, such as marriages that do not necessarily end "happily ever after," merely seeks to enhance the authenticity of the fantasy. This is a postmodern Heimat that assumes a cine-literate audience who will have an inbuilt "ironic distance" from this tradition. At the same time, it exploits the knowingness of its audience to overcome any cynicism the viewers might have toward the Heimat genre and to indulge their perhaps unavowed desires for the nostalgic innocence the Heimat space always represents.

Heritage, Heimat, and the Historical "Back Story"

The self-conscious deconstruction of the Heimat genre in order to enact its recuperation is found in numerous contemporary films, both in the type of explicit engagement discussed above and in other more oblique invocations, such as Til Schweiger's romantic comedy *Keinohrhasen* (Rabbit Without Ears, 2007). Schweiger mixes "backstage comedy" with Heimat schmaltz in his mainstream, highly successful romantic comedy that astoundingly sold more than 6 million tickets on its theatrical release (see Antje Ascheid's essay in this volume).[30] Of particular interest to the present discussion is his depiction of the "back story" to an outwardly idyllic couple who present a *Volksmusik* show, but who are barely able to refrain from screaming at each other off camera long enough to film their links between songs. While the staging of the Heimat "back story" seems to deconstruct the Heimat illusion, ultimately this simply provides an authenticating contrast to the "true" Heimat idyll encapsulated in the film's central romantic narrative.

A similar use of a Heimat "back story" can found in a number of history films, films that are part of the recent "heritage film" boom in Germany, which, as Rentschler notes, has been a mainstay of the German industry since the late 1990s.[31] The affinities between the Heimat genre and the heritage film, a key element of contemporary European filmmaking more broadly, have been discussed by several critics, with the Heimat

[30] Figures taken from the *Filmförderungsanstalt*, accessed 15 Sept. 2009, http://www.ffa.de/.
[31] Eric Rentschler, "Postwall Prospects: An Introduction," *New German Critique* 87 (2002): 4.

Figs. 10.4a and 10.4b. Nordwand *(2008). Screenshots.*

film appearing "ready made," as von Moltke puts it, for the "postwall revisionist impulses" German heritage cinema often encapsulates.[32] This connection becomes particularly clear in films such as Sönke Wortmann's story set around West Germany's Soccer World Cup win in 1954, *Das Wunder von Bern* (The Miracle of Bern, 2003), or Philipp Stölzl's account of the race to be the first to climb the north face of the Eiger, *Nordwand* (North Face, 2008). Here we find films exploring specific moments in German national history that intersect with important moments in the development of the Heimat genre. Through a sustained engagement with the historical "back story" to the worldview found in the 1930s mountain film and the 1950s Heimat cycle respectively, these films ostensibly seem to deconstruct the cinematic images of the time, showing the historical reality behind the celluloid. However, in both cases this deconstruction is used, once again, to recuperate the Heimat tradition.

Wortmann's film *Das Wunder von Bern*, for example, tells the story of the former Wehrmacht soldier Richard Lubanski (Peter Lohmeyer), who returns to his home and family in the Ruhr in 1954 after having spent twelve years in a Soviet POW camp. Adopting a standard Heimat trope of the lost family member returning to the fold, we see the difficulties Richard faces trying to find a place in a family that has learned to manage without him and a society that he does not recognize. The story of the family trying to readjust to the postwar reality is then mirrored in the story of the German national football team winning the World Cup in 1954. The fraught relationship between Richard and his children, in particular his football-obsessed son Matthias (Louis Klamroth), gradually eases, as do the tensions between the German national coach, Sepp Herberger, and his high-spirited striker Helmut Rahn (Sascha Göpel). Both father and coach learn that the authoritarian ways of the German past are out of step with the present and that discipline must be tempered with love and compassion. At the same time, their respective "children" begin to understand the world from their fathers' point of view, and, most importantly, that it is not their elders' fault that they act in the way they do.

---

[32] Von Moltke, *No Place like Home*, 233. See also Voigts Virchow, "Heritage and Literature on Screen."

This journey of intergenerational reconciliation is further reflected in the film's mise-en-scène. Richard returns to a bombed-out grey world of rubble, reminiscent of the early postwar *Trümmerfilme* (rubble films). These films, shot amid the destruction of the German cities, tended to be highly introspective in tone, their setting offering an external reflection of the inner turmoil of their protagonists. Richard could be a figure from such a film, his alienation from the world around him recalling, for example, the traumatized protagonist of Wolfgang Staudte's *Die Mörder sind unter uns* (The Murderers Are Among Us, 1946) or, given its generational themes, Gerhard Lamprecht's *Irgendwo in Berlin* (Somewhere in Berlin, 1946). The muted tones of the Ruhr sequences are subsequently contrasted starkly with the vibrant colors of the football training camp in Switzerland. Here we are presented with the chocolate-box semantics of the 1950s Heimat film, full of idyllic mountainscapes bathed in sunlight overlooking the lush green fields where the team trains. This is a world unsustainable in the Germany of the time. However, as both team and family learn to trust each other, and Germany progresses to World Cup victory, the Heimat semantic begins to spread. We see green shoots appear on the muddy field where the children play their own football matches. And finally, as the German team returns home victorious, the transformation from *Trümmer* to Heimat film is completed. We join the train that is taking the team to Germany, along with Robert and Matthias, who have also managed to sneak on, as it travels off into the sunset through a picturesque rural landscape that could be straight out of the 1950s genre cycle, populated by country folk driving hay-carts and waving their team on its way.

As in *Wer früher stirbt*, there are brief moments where the world of anti-Heimat is recalled. However, unlike Rosenmüller's film, here the syntactic configuration of this moment in the genre's history is only evoked in order for it to be rejected. Once again, rabbits are used to communicate the tension between Heimat idyll and anti-Heimat reality. Richard slaughters his son's pets in order to provide a meal for his wife's birthday, a meal Matthias thoroughly enjoys until he realizes that he is eating his beloved "Karnickel" (bunnies). While we understand Richard's motives, we sympathize most strongly with Matthias. The shot of the bloody rabbit carcasses covered in flies is out of step with the film's dominant Heimat/ heritage aesthetic, thereby highlighting the inappropriate nature of the father's actions. These were Heimat "Karnickel," not anti-Heimat food. The intrusion of this anti-Heimat moment in turn reflects the relationship of the film to the critical agenda of this moment in the genre's history. As already discussed, anti-Heimat was a product of the 1960s critique by the generation who had grown up after the war of their parents, whom their children accused of not only having been complicit with National Socialism but of subsequently not having accepted their guilt for this compliance. This is a view reflected most obviously by Richard's eldest son Bruno (Mirko Lang), a character who prefigures the confrontational attitudes that would dominate in the late 1960s. Ultimately Bruno leaves the family for the GDR, where he believes he will find a better, more open society. Of course, the spectator knows that this is a deeply naive and ultimately self-destructive view. Bruno will eventually be walled in, cut off from his family for decades. The potentially real "68er" in the film is Matthias. He would be old enough to be a student at the time and able to take to the streets. However, Matthias will not be amongst the protestors. The tensions that will come to the fore a decade later have already been resolved in the film. History is telescoped and we can move directly from postwar trauma and questions of guilt to contemporary declarations of German "normality," and the nation's right to move on from its past and be treated like any other Western democracy.[33] It would seem that the famous newspaper headline of 1954 "Wir sind wieder wer!" (We are someone again!) is, in 2003, at last allowed to come to fruition. Crucially, however, this is not to be understood as a statement of a problematic version of German nationalism. Interestingly the film does not, for example, show the crowd singing the outlawed first verse of the national anthem, as the actual crowd in Bern famously did, an omission that sparked a strong reaction among many of the film's reviewers.[34] Instead, this is an image of a harmonious, mature German nation that has already confronted its authoritarian ways and put them behind it, where the generational conflicts that would dominate the 1960s have already been overcome. The tensions of history are resolved and a timeless Heimat idyll is put in their place, where the past can recirculate in the present as consumable heritage culture, signaled most obviously in the boom in sales of replica football shirts from the 1954 team the film helped to promote.

East-West Relations and the Limits of Heimat Space

Beyond offering an escape from the legacy of National Socialism and the question of German guilt, football would also seem to offer a resolution to German division, as we see Bruno and his new friends in the East also enjoying the West German World Cup win. As Jutta Braun and René Wiese discuss, football was indeed important to the populations across the two Germanys at the time, allowing a unified point of identification

---

[33] For further discussion of recent "normalization" debates, see Stuart Taberner and Paul Cooke, eds., *German Culture, Politics, and Literature into the Twenty-First Century: Beyond Normalization* (Rochester, NY: Camden House, 2006).

[34] See, for example, Dietrich Kuhlbrodt, "Papa ist der Größte," *taz*, 15 Oct. 2003.

for Germans in the East and West.[35] And it played a role during the fall
of the Berlin Wall and German unification, of course, as the West German
team won the World Cup in the summer of 1990 for the third time in
the country's history. The timing could not have been better, the win
seeming to confirm the status of the population as "das glücklichste Volk
auf der Welt" (the happiest people in the world), as the mayor of Berlin
Walter Momper famously declared them at the time.[36] This is a motif
that plays a key role in a number of films that examine the question of
German unification, films that often also offer a further engagement with
the notion of German Heimat. Reitz's *Heimat 3*, a notable exception
among the otherwise generally affirmative reproduction of the Heimat
tradition on television, for example, makes reference to the World Cup
win as he reconfigures the provincial Heimat from his first film as a unified German space where Easterners and Westerners meet. In so doing,
he ironizes the celebration of German unity under the sign of the West
German team. Heimat is a space fraught with tensions as the film's central couple, Hermann (Henry Arnold) and Clarissa (Salome Kammer),
employ cheap East German labor to renovate their house. The celebration of the football victory is only able to elide briefly a view of unification
as a neocolonial takeover of the East by the West, in which citizens of the
former GDR exchange Soviet domination for capitalist exploitation.

Reitz's film is one of many that have reconfigured semantic elements
of the genre into a syntax that can explore the changing relationship
between East and West since unification. In the immediate aftermath of
unification a whole series of road movies were produced by West German
production companies, including the so-called "Trabi Comedies" (Peter
Timm's *Go Trabi Go*, 1991 and Wolfgang Büld and Reinhard Klooss's
Das war der wilde Osten [That Was the Wild East, 1992]), which tell of
the humorous adventures of the plucky but naive Struutz family, or Detlev
Buck's *Wir können auch anders* (We Can Do It Differently, released in
English as *No more Mr. Nice Guy*, 1993), the comic story of two brothers who travel to the former GDR to claim their family inheritance. Such
films have been read by critics as a new form of Heimat film. Leonie
Naughton, for example, sees these road movies as a revisitation of the
1950s cycle, nostalgically reconfiguring the former GDR as a rural fantasy
world with the same power of integration we find in the earlier films.[37]
Here, the East is "discovered" by the West, presenting the so-called "*neue*

[35] For further discussion see Jutta Braun and René Wiese, "DDR-Fußball und
gesamtdeutsche Identität im Kalten Krieg," *Historical Social Research* 30 (2005):
191–210.

[36] Quoted in Siegfried Schiele, ed., *Deutschland wächst zusammen: Eine
Zwischenbilanz nach zehn Jahren* (Stuttgart: Landeszentrale für politische Bildung
Baden-Württemberg, 2000), 17.

[37] Leonie Naughton, *That Was the Wild East*, 125–38.

Länder" (new states), as they are popularly described, as a narcissistic, orientalist vision that helps to define Germanness in the unified nation on western terms.[38]

In the last decade, as we can see from Reitz's film, the construction of the East as a proto-western Heimat space has been challenged in a variety of ways. Most obviously, we find the deconstruction of the nostalgia that is at the heart of these early comedies. On the one hand, films such as Wolfgang Becker's hugely successful *Good Bye, Lenin!* (2003), along with numerous other nostalgia films, including Leander Haußmann's *Sonnenallee* (Sun Alley, 1999) and *Herr Lehmann* (2003), Stefan Krohmer's *Sie haben Knut* (They've Got Knut, 2003), Benjamin Quabeck's *Verschwende deine Jugend* (Waste Your Youth, released in English as *Play it Loud*, 2003), and Carsten Fiebeler's *Kleinruppin forever* (2004), examine the extent to which unification brought about a genuinely *new* Germany that meant the end of both the GDR *and* the old Federal Republic, and which has, in turn, engendered nostalgic recollections, for better or worse, of both as lost Heimat.[39] In so doing, such films at times play to, at times challenge, the role of the heritage film discussed above in the transformation of Germany's past into a consumable present. On the other, films such as Vanessa Jopp's *Vergiss Amerika* (Forget America, 2000), Andreas Dresen's *Halbe Treppe* (Half a Staircase, released in English as *Grille Point*, 2002), Susanne Irina Zacharias's *Hallesche Kometen* (Halle Comets, 2005), Valeska Grisebach's *Sehnsucht* (Longing, 2006), and Christian Klandt's *Weltstadt* (Cosmopolitan City, 2008) continue the kind of engagement with the genre, albeit mixed with New German Cinema social critique, that we find in some earlier GDR films. Such films, which are generally produced on much smaller budgets than the more popular heritage films, reject all notions of nostalgic longing, drawing directly on the syntax of an anti-Heimat mode to present the former GDR as a space where Heimat as a rural idyll is impossible in the face of the continuing economic and social hardships to which the population has been subjected in the rapid transition since unification to a "modern" market economy.

Christian Klandt's debut feature, *Weltstadt* (2008), styled in its tagline a "Heimatfilm," for example, depicts the events that lead up to a violent attack on a homeless beggar (Jürgen A. Verch) by two teenagers in the provincial Brandenburg town of Beeskow. Based on a true event, this ex-GDR, anti-Heimat film also draws on a tradition of social-realist filmmaking, from Ken Loach (*Raining Stones*, 1993) and Mathieu Kassovitz (*La Haine* [Hate, 1995]) to Larry Clark (*Kids*, 1995), and Gus Van

---

[38] For further discussion see Paul Cooke, *Representing East Germany: From Colonization to Nostalgia* (Oxford: Berg, 2005), 27–59.

[39] For further discussion see Ludewig, *Screening Nostalgia*, 311–60.

Sant (*Elephant*, 2003) in order to contextualize this brutal and unprovoked attack. In so doing, Klandt presents us with a decaying, postindustrial landscape, where the population has lost everything, the town's older inhabitants live in fear of a youth they cannot understand, and the young have little chance of escape. Karsten (Gerdy Zint) and Till (Florian Bartholmäi) spend their days drinking and smoking dope, their anger with the world erupting into violence against themselves, each other, and ultimately the homeless tramp. In *Weltstadt* Klandt explodes the clichés of the Heimat film. In a similar fashion to earlier moments in the genre's development, the narrative is punctuated with long takes of the local countryside. Set during a crisp winter's day, the film offers shots of the Spree in all its tranquil splendor, or of a bright winter sky, its light breaking through the dilapidated estates of prefabricated housing that fill the town's suburbs. While in the 1950s such landscapes would have been a means through which the rural community could come together and find a common point of identification, here the population of the town is entirely dislocated from the natural world around it. Echoes of Caspar David Friedrich reemerge as we see the film's protagonists stare into the landscape that surrounds them. However, their brief moments of contemplation simply underline their dislocation, as well as the lack of any real sense of community in the town, which can only be mustered when a few people come together occasionally to drown their sorrows in alcohol or drugs. Heinrich (Hendrik Arnst), a failed business man who is being forced to close his snack bar to make way for a car park, stares at the Spree in one such moment. Rather than finding peace in the sublime beauty of the river, he is focusing on his own reflection. He is unable to find a way out of his own misery. This sequence is then immediately followed by shots of the other protagonists in the film, caught in similarly self-reflexive moments of isolation. If this provincial town has the timeless quality associated with earlier visions of Heimat, then it is a dystopian timelessness rooted in the certainty that its population has no prospect of a better future.

The films discussed in this chapter highlight just a few of the ways in which contemporary filmmakers are engaging with and developing the Heimat film. Overwhelmingly, we find filmmakers mining the history of the genre to recuperate the idyllic innocence of the 1950s, using the tradition of Heimat to validate the modern nation, in this case reappropriating aspects of so-called *Papas Kino* to set the seal on the Berlin Republic as having overcome not only the traumas of the Nazi past but also the critical legacy of the 68ers and the New German Cinema. That said, at times one also still finds echoes of the New German Cinema's anti-Heimat tradition, particularly in a number of low-budget socially critical films that examine the state of unification, with a particular emphasis on the difficulties faced by the former GDR. However, these are not the only ways in which the Heimat genre impacts contemporary German film. Elsewhere we find productions that use the idea of Heimat syntactically to explore the international boundaries of the new Germany, and its relationship with its western and eastern "Others." These include films by Fatih Akin (*Gegen die Wand* [Against the Wall, 2004], *Auf der anderen Seite* [On the Other Side, released in English as *The Edge of Heaven*, 2007], and *Soul Kitchen*, 2009), which examine the concept of Heimat from the perspective of the German-Turkish diaspora. Akin is a self-declared maker of Heimat films, adopting elements of both German and Turkish film traditions to capture what he views as the dynamic, hybrid notion of Germanness in the age of globalization.[40] Or we find films that transpose the "other"—conceptualised in the early 1990s as the former GDR—to the eastern border of the country with Poland, which until 2004 was also the eastern border of the European Union. In Henner Winckler's *Klassenfahrt* (Class Trip, 2002), Jan Krüger's *Unterwegs* (En Route, 2004) and *Milchwald* (released in English as *In this Very Moment*, 2003), Hans-Christian Schmid's *Lichter* (Lights, 2003), and Robert Thalheim's *Am Ende kommen Touristen* (In the End Tourists Come, released as *And Along Come the Tourists*, 2007), the Polish borderland is used as a self-reflexive device to offer a critical assessment of Germany's changing role in the new Europe and the continuing problems of defining the limits of the German Heimat. Of course, if one explores contemporary German film solely in syntactic terms, an extraordinarily broad range of films can be defined as part of a Heimat corpus, as the nation's filmmakers continue to examine the tensions between "traditional" conceptions of Germanness and the imperatives of contemporary society. However, as is evident in the films discussed throughout this chapter, along with numerous others, from Tom Tykwer's reworking of the mountain film, *Winterschläfer* (Winter Sleepers, 1997), to Esther Gronenborn's Bavarian gothic horror, *Hinter Kaifeck* (Behind Kaifeck, 2009), it is both the ideas and the iconography of the Heimat film tradition that continue to be explored. The semantics of the genre remain an important part of the language of German cinema, working in conjunction with a variety of other more international traditions as filmmakers continue to engage with the German-speaking world's unique contribution to global film culture.

---

[40] Anke Westphal, "Wer zuletzt lacht in Venedig: Goldener Löwe für israelischen Antikriegsfilm, Spezialpreis für Komödie von Fatih Akin," *Berliner Zeitung*, 14 Sept. 2009.

11: The Romantic Comedy and Its Other: Representations of Romance in German Cinema since 1990

Antje Ascheid

TIL SCHWEIGER'S 2007 hit romantic comedy *Keinohrhasen* (Rabbit Without Ears) opens with a spoof on Hollywood stardom. In its first scene, German art-cinema actor Jürgen Vogel, playing himself, pretends to have undergone a ridiculous transformation, or rather, Americanization. Bragging about his supposedly improved appearance, which includes exaggerated dental work, a deep tan, substantial hair replacements, and silicone butt implants, Vogel announces that his previous work doing "arthouse shit" like *Das Leben ist eine Baustelle* (Life is a Construction Site, released in English as *Life is All You Get*, 1997) appealed only to an audience of "pseudo-intellectual pop culture idiots from Berlin," but left him dissatisfied and depressed. While these statements are later revealed as a parody staged to make fun of gullible paparazzi journalists, this opening also reflexively contrasts films such as the humorous *Keinohrhasen* with arguably more "alternative" arthouse productions, which are favored by critics but frustrate general audiences. Schweiger's petulant response to not being considered for the German Film Prize in 2008 (he left the German Film Academy and announced that he would establish his own award[1]), despite the film's overwhelming popularity (by 2008 6.3 million Germans had seen the film, which put it ahead at the box office, surpassing all other cinematic releases, including big Hollywood blockbusters, that year), while Fatih Akin's much less successful *Auf der anderen Seite* (On the Other Side, released in English as *The Edge of Heaven*, 2007), which barely drew 500,000 viewers, went home with the coveted *Lola*

---

[1] See Marin Zips, "Die Rache des Keinohrhasen," *Süddeutsche Zeitung*, 4 Nov. 2008, http://www.sueddeutsche.de/kultur/980/439723/text/. The German film academy responded that they were not able to consider the film, as the producers had failed to officially submit it (see http://www.deutschefilmakademie. de/auswahl.0.html). Also see: *Der Spiegel*, 30 Nov. 2009, "Ist doch nur ein Film," interview with Til Schweiger, by Lars-Olav Beier und Wolfgang Höbel, http:// www.spiegel.de/spiegel/0,1518,664363–3,00.html.

244   ◆   ANTJE ASCHEID

award, recalls familiar tensions between high and low art biases towards the cinema.

Indeed, Schweiger's apparent irritation at the notion that in order to be considered valuable films have to be "serious" (ernst) rather then "entertaining" (unterhaltend) rearticulates the traditional dichotomy of art and genre cinema, an oppositional pairing in no way particular to a German context. American critics similarly lamented the decline of the New Hollywood of the 70s in favor of generic blockbusters, just as French scholars dismissively labeled France's stylish genre thrillers of the 1980s the *Cinema du Look*, implying that surface had replaced substance. In 2000 Eric Rentschler followed suit by labeling post-Wall German cinema the "cinema of consensus," which he contrasted with its more cerebral and overtly political predecessor, the New German Cinema.[2] A cinema popular with critics thus tends to be artsy and socially critical, formally experimental, and politically challenging.

By now these contentions are long familiar. Indeed, fundamentally I agree with Rentschler's assessment that the German romantic comedies of the early 1990s "have no depth of despair, no true suffering, no real joy." And yes, "with their triangulated desires and mismatched partners, their schematic constellations and formulaic trajectories, these yuppie comedies of errors [do] follow strictly codified patterns."[3] On the other hand, all genre films rehearse expected patterns; they are by definition formulaic, repetitive, and conventional. I also concur with Rentschler's contention that, even as genre pictures, these films were not very well executed, thus limiting their capacity to compete with their Hollywood counterparts both domestically and abroad. That said, I do find that any analysis that dismisses genre cinema as too generic fails to deal with what is actually well worth detailed consideration. What is at stake here is a popular cinema that relentlessly repeats variations of particular narrative constellations because audiences continually consume them. Such constellations must resonate socially for certain reasons. Indeed, criticism directed at Hollywood genres has long engaged in a variety of analytical models ranging from structuralism to psychoanalysis to figure out what kind of underlying social or psychological questions motivate the perpetuation of certain themes and styles. I would like to continue in this tradition by investigating the representation of romance in post-Wall German cinema, not only in terms of its place within a national cinema but in an international framework as well. My interest in the generic treatment of

---

[2] Eric Rentschler, "From New German Cinema to the Post-Wall Cinema of Consensus," in *Cinema and Nation*, ed. Mette Hjort and Scott Mackenzie (London: Routledge, 2000), 260.

[3] Rentschler, "From New German Cinema to the Post-Wall Cinema of Consensus," in *Cinema and Nation*, ed. Mette Hjort and Scott Mackenzie (New York: Routledge, 2000), 263.

romance narratives in German cinema since 1990 comes from a variety of sources, which in turn invite several at times disparate considerations.

The commercial success and overall popularity of the post-Wall comedy clearly invites critical scrutiny. Next to what is now commonly referred to as *Arthaus-Kino* in Germany, the majority of German-produced cinematic releases are comedies and children's films, while other film genres are pursued almost exclusively by German television. German-made political thrillers, police dramas, action pictures, and science-fiction films are all strikingly absent from German movie screens.[4] To date, *Keinohrhasen* is the tenth-highest grossing German film since 1968 (the only film among the top ten that is not a comedy is the 1970 film *Schulmädchenreport* [Schoolgirl Report], which featured sexual content considered shocking at the time).[5] Moreover, in the last decade the market share of German films has increased steadily, indicating a substantial shift in consumer behavior since German reunification. In 1995, only 9.4 percent of all films seen in German cinemas were German productions (including international coproductions). Since the early 2000s, however, the market share of German films has risen to levels between 20 and 40 percent, depending on how many hit films were released any given year. Interestingly, arthouse films constitute around 10 to 15 percent of the general box office in Germany, yet are made up of a considerably higher percentage of German films. In 2010, 40.15 percent of all films categorized as arthouse by the *Filmförderungsanstalt* (FFA, German Federal Film Board) that were seen on German screens were of German origin.[6] Given that audiences vastly favor German-made comedies over other German films, it comes as no surprise that the majority of films with romantic content also contain comedic elements. In addition, we must note that the distinction between mainstream and arthouse cinema in Germany is relatively soft, as budgets rarely reach the level of Hollywood blockbusters (except for large-scale productions that are German-financed English-language films). Yet while both the romantic comedy and German arthouse productions tend to concentrate on romance and relationships, they often do so in dramatically different ways, thus provoking comparison.

What complicates this analysis, however, is that neither art cinema nor the romantic comedy is exclusively tied to German national cinema. Moreover, genre cinema is frequently associated with Hollywood, while non-American genre films are often looked at as derivative. Thus only film genres that do not seem to have a direct Hollywood counterpart— the Heimat film, German Expressionist drama, or the various genre films

---

[4] See *Inside Kino* for box-office analysis: http://www.insidekino.com/DBO.htm#JAHRES_&_ALL-TIME_CHARTS_

[5] http://www.insidekino.com/DJahr/DAlltimeDeutsch50.htm, 3 Sept. 2012.

[6] Very detailed market analyses are published by the FFA (Filmförderungsanstalt) and are available online at http://www.ffa.de.

of Nazi cinema, for instance—have received significant attention within a German national frame. In turn, American remakes of European films tend to be dismissed as shamelessly commercial, stripped of the originals' art-cinema texture and national specificity. The US remake *No Reservations* (2007), for example, is seen to function within the frame of the romantic comedy, whereas Sandra Nettelbeck's original *Bella Martha* (2001) is seen as an art film. The concomitant push to center any analysis of German genre films on what marks them as particularly German can at times be useful, but it can also hinder insightful commentary. Indeed, the distinction between the European art film and Hollywood cinema has become increasingly blurred in what is now often referred to as transnational cinema. Along these lines European art-cinema traditions have found their way into what Jeffrey Sconce has labeled the "new American smart film," where biting satire meets social realism in the form of "cold melodrama," while national versions of the romantic comedy have triumphed on British, French, and German screens.[7] It follows that because neither romantic comedies nor relationship dramas are generically exclusive to German cinema, German genre films of that nature must be seen in a broad international context. Within that spectrum, their generic variations, their specific codes and narrative concerns, must be delineated and placed into a historical context specific to the time period under discussion. And second, we must ask what, if anything, is specifically German or speaks to a particular German context in these productions.

Consequently, I will first investigate the developments within genres of romance in general, then place these developments within a German context, and finally use three case studies (*Das Leben ist eine Baustelle*, *Keinohrhasen*, and Andreas Dresen's *Sommer vorm Balkon* [Summer in Front of the Balcony, released in English as *Summer in Berlin*, 2005]) to illustrate my arguments.

The Demographics of Romance

To situate representations of romance within the contemporary social context, let me first introduce some statistics. In charting recent demographic changes in the West, one of the key terms invoked by both the media and politicians is the "singles" society, or singularization (a phrase coined by French literary enfant terrible Michel Houllebecque, whose 1998 novel *Les Particules élémentaires* was incidentally adapted as a German film by Oskar Roehler in 2006 [*Elementarteilchen*]). This term indicates the spectacular increase in single adults, a dramatic decline in birth rates, and the extended life spans of Europeans and North Americans. Particularly in Germany,

---

[7] Jeffrey Sconce, "Irony, Nihilism and the New American 'Smart' Film," *Screen* 43, no. 4 (Winter 2002): 349–69.

worries about the generational contract requiring population growth to ensure continuing retirement benefits have exacerbated the anxieties about the so-called collapse of the family: with rising divorce rates and reproductive reluctance, it has, in fact, become an important political issue in the last two decades. In the United States, a similar trend toward "backlash" rhetoric, particularly the Republican emphasis on "family values," must be seen as a response to dramatic social changes regarding the organization of private lives. Notwithstanding this political appeal to return to the family, the demographic shift toward single households continues. In 2004 there were 95.7 million unmarried Americans. This group comprised 43 percent of all US residents aged 15 and over.[8] Fifty-four percent of single Americans were women.[9] The US divorce rate in 2007 stood at 49 percent. The divorce rate in Germany in 2011 was over 39 percent. Twenty percent of the overall German population lived alone in 2011.[10] Nineteen percent of all households with children were single-parent homes.[11] Similar data exist for most industrialized nations.

Frequently held accountable for these shifts, particularly by conservatives, are the increasing independence and economic self-sufficiency of women in the wake of the second wave of feminism in the 1960s and 70s, which includes reproductive control, an increased emphasis on personal happiness and self-realization over social and familial responsibility (the collective "selfishness" of what the Germans have dubbed the *Spaßgesellschaft* [fun society]), and "unrealistic" expectations regarding the nature of love, sex, and romance. The data assembled by the *National Marriage Project* at Rutger's University in 2002 indicates that the young Americans surveyed tend to be skeptical about the marriages they observe. "52% agree that one sees so few good, happy marriages that one questions it as a way of life." At the same time, however, an impressive 88 percent believe that "there is a special person, a soul mate, waiting for you somewhere out there."[12] The ideal of the soul-mate marriage, according to the *Project*'s findings, is inevitably connected to the high level of divorce: marriage is less and less child-centered and less connected to larger social or religious institutions. The research clearly shows a wid-

---

[8] All data released by the United States Census bureau (19 Jul. 2004), http://factfinder.census.gov/servlet/DatasetMainPageServlet?_program=ACS&_lang=en&_ts=100621288252.

[9] http://factfinder.census.gov/servlet/DatasetMainPageServlet?_program=ACS&_lang=en&_ts=100621288252.

[10] http://www.spiegel.de/panorama/gesellschaft/mikrozensus-zahlen-dokumentieren-veraenderung-der-lebensstile-a-843891.html.

[11] https://www.destatis.de/DE/Publikationen/Thematisch/Bevoelkerung/HaushalteMikrozensus/Alleinerziehende.html.

[12] The National Marriage Project, "The State of our Unions," Rutgers University, 2002, http://marriage.rutgers.edu.

ening gap between what individuals hope for, indeed may deem necessary for their personal happiness, and what they ultimately find.

Representing Relationships

Concurrently, films that feature love and sex as the central question driving the narrative have significantly increased since the late 1980s, going along with the altered social environment and the audiences it produces. Independent sociologist Bernd Kittlaus's German website on the "singles generation," for instance, runs comprehensive updates on every aspect of single life and its treatment in the media, including an expansive filmography of related films and television programs.[13] Obviously, contemporary representations of romance interact with the conceptual changes in attitude and demographic shifts in populations across various generic fields. When trying to map romance in an era of "post"s, particularly postfeminism and postmodernism, various developments within the field of literary, film, and popular culture appear relevant. Three particularly generic modes of romance representation in contemporary film emerge as prominent: the nostalgic, the utopian, and the dystopian modes. The first is the costume drama, which I will not discuss further here, especially as the romantic period drama or heritage film is particularly prominent in British Cinema.[14] The utopian mode is the romantic comedy, or *Beziehungskomödie*. The dystopian mode (what I will label the postromance) represents issues of dating, love, sex, and romance, along with modern urbanity, "singularization," and isolation in a fundamentally pessimistic or at least highly skeptical fashion. It is this dystopian mode that I will discuss in greater detail in this essay.

As early as 1998, *LA Times* critic Kenneth Turan pointed to a new trend toward immorality and nihilistic darkness in US independent cinema, diagnosing in films such as *Happiness* (1998) or *Your Friends and Neighbors* (1998) an inappropriate "lust for the grim."[15] Like-minded critics suggested the emergence of a "new cinema of hate."[16] Jeffrey Sconce countered that even though these films depict scenarios of postmodern disaffection and alienation and favor a dark cynical tone and narrative distance, they

---

[13] The website is run by sociologist Bernd Kittlaus, who sees himself as an activist on behalf of singles. See http://www.single-generation.de.

[14] I have previously written on romance and the heritage film. See Antje Ascheid, "Safe Rebellions: Romantic Emancipation in the 'Women's Heritage Film,'" *Scope: An Online Journal of Film Studies* (Feb. 2006), http://www.scope. nottingham.ac.uk/article.php?issue=4&id=124. See also Andrew Higson, *English Heritage, English Cinema* (Oxford: Oxford University Press, 2003).

[15] Kenneth Turan, "Fade to Pitch Black," *Los Angeles Times*, 22 Nov. 1998.

[16] Manohla Dargis, "Whatever: The New Nihilism," *LA Weekly*. 1998.

ultimately engage in social critique.[17] Since then there has been a marked increase in this generic development, identifiable in art films across an international spectrum. Indeed, when we explore the work of art-film directors internationally, it quickly emerges that a pronounced focus on postromantic narratives, which stress the destructive aspects of romantic relationships, has gained significant momentum over the last fifteen years. Postromantic tendencies thus unify the work of otherwise dissimilar "auteur" directors, making it possible to argue for a thematic generic movement within international art-cinema practice; the work of directors as diverse as Neil La Bute, Todd Solondz, Oskar Roehler, Andreas Dresen, François Ozon, Gregg Araki, Pedro Almadovar, and Wong Kar Wai, as well as many others, comes to mind. As Marco Abel explains:

> The characters populating such postromance environments could be argued to enact the "success" of the feminist intervention since the 1960s. They have grown up with the awareness that marriage is neither the necessary nor the "normal" framework one needs in postadolescent life, and they share the post-1968 skepticism of the traditional "ideal" of lifelong, monogamous relationships. Indeed, these characters might also be regarded as symptomatic of the age of neoliberal finance capitalism, with its imperative for citizens to be hypermobile workaholics, which induces a permanent state of fear of unemployment and an attendant emotional, psychological, and physical restlessness. As a result, these socioeconomic pressures manifest themselves on the private level, where the demands of fast-paced contemporary *social* life hinder one's ability to maintain the different temporality required for developing and sustaining romantic relationships.[18]

At the same time, the ultimately optimistic romantic comedy, or chick flick, is one of today's most enduringly successful commercial film genres. Beginning with the comedies of the late 1980s and 1990s (*When Harry Met Sally . . .* [1989], *Sleepless in Seattle* [1993], *You've Got Mail* [1998], and so on), comedic romances have promised, as Peter William Evans has suggested "that rather than lead to alienation, humiliation or entrapment, heterosexual romance can result instead in the fulfillment of desire."[19] Moreover, a wide range of German directors whose films deal with relationships may be considered under this umbrella; Neele Volmar, Til

[17] Jeffrey Sconce, "Irony, Nihilism and the New American 'Smart' Film," 369.

[18] Marco Abel, "Failing to Connect: Itineraries of Desire in Oskar Roehler's Post-Romance Films," *New German Critique* 109 (Winter 2010): 77. While I first introduced the term postromance to Abel, this article elaborates considerably on the concept and its expression in Roehler's work.

[19] Peter William Evans, "Meg Ryan, Megastar," in *Terms of Endearment: Hollywood Romantic Comedy of the 1980s and 1990s*, ed. Peter William Evans and Celestino Deleyto (Edinburgh: Edinburgh University Press, 1998), 188–208.

Schweiger, Doris Dörrie, Ralf Huetter, Ralf Westhof, Gregor Schnitzler, and Leander Haussmann, to name but a few.

I would further like to suggest that when we are looking at films called "comedies" or "romantic comedies" by their distributors, we *may* be looking at films that deal with romance and relationships in a way that is exclusively romantic, but more often than not these films are actually also anti-romantic simultaneously, thus sabotaging their mission. Frequently there is a very thin line between utopian and dystopian content in these films, as many of the so-called "comedies" contain story elements that are cynical and cruel rather than light-hearted and funny. In my opinion, the romantic comedy of the 1980s began to give birth to its evil twin, the postromance, in the 1990s, and by now the two often merge into two-faced hybrids. This phenomenon, just like the other generic trends I stressed earlier, is by no means unique or specific to German national cinema but prominent in popular genre as well as arthouse productions. What is specific to a German context, however, is how the films deal with characters, locations, and cultural context—in other words, the way these films work as German films within a given generic framework. Particularly the use of Berlin as a romantic or postromantic location is significant here, as is an interest in various social milieus. In order to flesh out these issues in detail, let me now turn to a few representative examples.

Mapping the Field: Three Case Studies

Das Leben ist eine Baustelle

Das Leben ist eine Baustelle, written by Tom Tykwer and Wolfgang Becker and directed by the latter, explicitly contrasts itself with Hollywood genre films and implicitly also with Germany's popular *Beziehungskomödien*. When the film opened at the Berlin Film Festival in 1997, many critics praised its art-cinema realism. The film received several prizes, including an honorable mention at the festival as well as the *Bundesfilmpreis in Silber* (second place) for best picture and first prizes for best actor Jürgen Vogel and best supporting actress Martina Gedeck. "Becker is an *Autorenfilmer* (film auteur)" wrote *Der Spiegel*, "[and] those who see his work understand why *auteur* cinema was once seen as the medium's new hope: Becker develops the same hunger for the present that also drove Fassbinder, this lust for the here and now, this curiosity about how people live and think and talk."[20] Even critical voices admitted that despite its flaws the film was a "ray of light" after three years of comedic "bliss,"[21]

---

[20] Susanne Weingarten, "Was nun, Jan?," *Der Spiegel*, 17 Mar. 1997, 217.

[21] Andreas Kilb, "Nebel: Ein Leben," *Die Zeit*, 21 Mar. 1997, http://www.zeit. de/1997/13/Nebel_Ein_Leben.

constituting a glimpse of hope, as *Die Zeit* argued, within a German cinema that was otherwise headed toward the "lukewarm catastrophe of ridiculousness," a national embarrassment because of its mediocrity.[22]

Baustelle opens with a sex scene, albeit interrupted. Jan (Jürgen Vogel) fails to perform with Sylvia (Andrea Sawatzki) and escapes to the bathroom. Slouched on the toilet he ponders a film poster depicting Tom Cruise on Sylvia's wall, a comparison that foregrounds Jan's status as an impotent working-class loser, the antihero of art cinema. Trying to make his way to his job at a slaughterhouse, Jan unwittingly gets caught up in a Kreuzberg riot, where he meets Vera (Christiane Paul) with whom he tries to evade the police. Things become worse and worse: first Jan is arrested and then he is fired from his job. Next he learns from a former lover that she may have infected him with HIV. The film follows Jan's subsequent efforts to cope with these problems, while pursuing a relationship with the somewhat flighty Vera. Jan's life, as the film's title suggests, is a building site, just as Berlin, where the film is set, was literally a place under construction in 1997. Yet while *Baustelle* aspires to social realism chronicling episodes of family dysfunction shot in gritty streets, alienating shopping centers, and cramped apartments, it is also deeply romantic. As Martin Schwickert complains:

> *Das Leben ist eine Baustelle* is a production by *X-Filme creative pool*, a company run jointly by directors Wolfgang Becker, Tom Tykwer, Dani Levy, and producer Stefan Arndt. They see their work as a counter-movement to the romantic-comedy boom. And thus *Das Leben ist eine Baustelle* does not take place in polished apartments peopled by bourgeois roommates, or in light-flooded Munich penthouses. Becker dives deeply into the proletarian milieu, where people still eat breakfast wearing wife-beaters . . . [but] Becker solves the problems he raises rather quickly. The motto is "let's not get into a bad mood," which returns us to what makes the German comedy so problematic. As much as the film claims to participate in social realism, it still reaches for those audiences that have made the romantic comedy so successful at the box office.[23]

The film thus straddles utopian and dystopian elements that invoke the kind of generic fusion suggested earlier, while also positioning itself as an antidote to the comedies of consensus. If the cinema of consensus stressed yuppie trends and featured urban fashionistas in expensive clothing, thus underlining that Germans have fully re-entered a trendy designer world

---

[22] Andreas Kilb, "Wollt ihr den totalen Film?" *Die Zeit*, 6 Jun. 1997, http://www.zeit.de/1997/24/Wollt_ihr_den_totalen_Film_UZ_Das_deutsche.

[23] Martin Schwickert, "Voll in Ravioli: Der neue Trend; Proll-Comedy," http://www.ultimo-bielefeld.de/kr-film/f-baust.htm. All translations in this essay are my own.

Figs. 11.1a and 11.1b. Das Leben ist eine Baustelle *(1997). Screenshots.*

after reunification, then *Baustelle* celebrates the kind of underground scene associated with Berlin's subculture. The plot implies solidarity with the Kreuzberg rioters, assumed to be the kind of discontented radical anarchists who year after year damage cars and buildings, ransack stores, and fight with the police on Mayday. Indeed, when Jan first encounters Vera, she seems to be carrying looted groceries. All the characters in the film suffer from poverty and struggle in a variety of dead-end jobs to make ends meet. They also are not sure just who they really are. "Who is Jan Nebel?" asks Vera, whose true identity in turn remains nebulous to him. Jan is intrigued but also confused by Vera's offbeat attitude.

Vera's social rebellion stresses getting something for nothing: she steals food, crashes a fancy reception to partake in the buffet, and checks into a hotel room then leaves without paying, yet these unlawful actions are not meant to depict her as either desperate or criminal. They celebrate an "alternative" culture marked by a profound disdain for the contemporary social order: for capitalism and those it benefits. That said, Vera is no proletarian rebel but an artsy musician who participates in magical avant-garde performance pieces and charms Jan with her bohemian irreverence. Indeed, even Jan, who is solidly working class, soon moves toward adopting a hipster lifestyle. His uncomfortable living situation as an unwanted guest in his sister's tiny flat ironically improves when his father dies, his head dropping into a plate of ravioli. This allows Jan and his rock-n'-roll-obsessed friend Buddy (Rick Tomlinson, a British actor known for his roles in Ken Loach's realist dramas) to move into his late father's apartment, which is soon transformed into a funky party pad, where various roommates form an alternative family for Jan and his neglected niece Jenni.

The film thus stresses an aesthetics of cool that—while not interested in the kind of consensus Rentschler has identified, one marked by materialism and consumer culture—allows for both hope and underground hipness. It acknowledges urban blight, loneliness, and isolation, but it is not truly cynical like some other postromantic or social-realist films. Becker and Tykwer are careful to include many unsuccessful romances and dysfunctional families: Jan's sister Lilo (Martina Gedeck) has a sleazy lover who does not get along with Jenni; Jan's parents are divorced and alienated from their children; Buddy falls in love with Greek immigrant Kristina (Christina Papamichou), only to find her in bed with Jan; Jan does not return Sylvia's feelings, and his casual fling with a colleague has exposed him to the AIDS-virus. But Jan and Vera also fall in love at first sight. The characters may be poor, but they are not truly desperate. Films like *Baustelle* thus stress social realism while preserving utopian moments. The film depicts working-class people living in underprivileged yet bohemian Berlin-Kreuzberg, which turns out to be a romantic location despite, or perhaps even because of, its dilapidated charm. The film's conclusion is ambiguous (we do not find out about Jan's HIV status), as befitting an arthouse movie, but it also allows for the possibility of a happy ending, thus rendering the film both romantic and realistic at the same time. The film celebrates "alternative" lifestyle models, a phrase loaded with oppositional political meaning since the early 1980s, pointing back to a Berlin subculture that precedes post-Wall aspirations. The narrative's union of a blue-collar boy and a funky girl (whom Jan sometimes accuses of behaving like a spoiled dentist's daughter, which she may indeed be) envisions a leveling of class divisions worked out in the sphere of bohemian urbanity.

With just under 500,000 viewers *Baustelle* proved to be a successful arthouse production—very few art films released in the Germany attract a larger audience—which ranked twelfth among the most popular German films released that year.

Keinohrhasen

In contrast, Til Schweiger's hit film *Keinohrhasen* is a bona fide romantic comedy in every way. The film is not interested in supplying a socially critical subtext or in spending time on anything but what the romantic comedy proper has always been about: the battle between the sexes. We are initially introduced to paparazzo journalist Ludo (Til Schweiger) during the interview with Jürgen Vogel mentioned earlier, where Vogel claims to have been damaged by his art-cinema roles, only to be reborn as an Americanized star. In fact, it is Ludo himself who is the opposite of Vogel's character Jan in *Baustelle*, while Vogel is later revealed to have stayed true to himself. Attractive and ruthless, Ludo chases after stars and scandals, all the while enjoying continuous sexual success with various women. His playboy persona, the superficial man-about-town who is interested only in casual sex and phobic of serious commitment, indeed perfectly mirrors male characters well-known from the international romantic comedy.

Many of the genre's leading men are, at least initially, sexy and unavailable and thus in desperate need of change. Along these lines, male characters (think, for instance, of Hugh Grant in *Bridget Jones's Diary* [Maguire, 2001], *About a Boy* [Weitz, 2002] or *Two Weeks Notice*

Fig. 11.2. Keinohrhasen *(2007). Screenshot.*

[Lawrence, 2002]) typically get a psychological makeover. The fictional maturation of "adult boys" brings about the happy ending. Moreover, the romantic comedy frequently offers up the city (New York, London, Paris) as a glamorous and romantic space for the well-to-do, without concern for verisimilitude or social realism. Well-known stars are typically cast and connote both glamour and privilege, while plotlines rarely undermine the image of the films' star personae. Unlike Jürgen Vogel, Til Schweiger conforms to the paradigm of the romantic comedy's nonchalant cute guy, who feels at home in trendy restaurants, drives a Mercedes, and exudes sexual confidence. In *Keinohrhasen* Berlin is also finally on a par with other romantic capitals. City shots never suggest social inequality but instead communicate the lively glamour of the stylish metropolis, a bright lights and big-city aesthetic that forms the backdrop for seemingly upwardly mobile characters with modish careers (jobs in media, journalism, art, publishing, fashion, and music dominate the romantic comedy). Even the day-care center where Ludo undergoes his inevitable transformation is located in a beautiful bourgeois home. Likewise, the apartment shared by the two young teachers, love interest Anna (Nora Tschirner) and her friend Miriam (Alwara Höfels), is just as unrealistic as the equally spacious New York apartments inhabited by desirable urban singles in Hollywood comedies. In this sense, then, *Keinohrhasen* is like the classic comedies of consensus that Rentschler describes, marked by the celebration of an apolitical yuppie lifestyle, perhaps with the single exception that it is just as well executed as other successful romantic comedies worldwide.

Ludo needs to learn how not to be an "asshole," and over the course of the plot he is taught how to give women sexual pleasure, how to be a caring father-figure, and, finally, how to love. The film reiterates the cliché of the sexually carnivorous seducer, both an incorrigible ladies' man

Figs. 11.3a and 11.3b. Keinohrhasen *(2007). Screenshots.*

and a confirmed bachelor. His reformation is initially brought about by a court order, which condemns him to several weeks of community service in a local day-care center. There he finds both his true love, Anna, and a truly meaningful occupation as a kindergarten teacher. While this metamorphosis from jerk into husband material is the staple of the contemporary romantic comedy, the execution of the plot and particularly the dialogue are unusually biting for a German *Beziehungkomödie.* For instance, when Anna and Miriam compare lousy lovers and bad pizza, the pizza wins because first, it does not demand instant reassurance "that you really, really liked it," and second, "at the very least, once you've eaten it, it's gone . . ." *Keinohrhasen*'s immense box-office success, despite its critical failure, is clearly due to the fact that the film successfully stages the generic conventions of the romantic comedy and surprises with witty writing. And, of course, it provides a happy ending, ironically one in which Anna's new boyfriend Jürgen Vogel tactfully withdraws to make room for Til Schweiger's romantic lead, Ludo. Genre cinema thus literally wins over "arthouse shit" in *Keinohrhasen.*

However, even if the appeal of the romantic comedy essentially derives from its entertaining escapism, this does not mean that the genre does not respond to fantasies and desires rooted in the social real. The romantic comedy concentrates on the manufacture of gender compatibility and stages the formation of the heterosexual couple as the starting point for a utopian "happily ever after," but the initial dichotomization of the sexes, which is the starting point for subsequent narrative reversals, also acknowledges fundamental social conflict. Feminist critics have complained that the representations of women that romantic comedies offer essentially limit female characters to wanting to find the right guy. Following Tania Modleski's condemnation of postfeminism as a posture that ultimately undermines feminist activism against oppression, many feminist scholars have read recent filmic articulations of postfeminism as problematic.[24] Diane Negra, for instance, argues that the post-9/11 romantic comedy—for instance, *Kate and Leopold* (2001), *How to Lose a*

---

[24] See Tania Modleski, *Feminism without Women: Culture and Criticism in a "Post-Feminist Age"* (New York: Routledge, 1991).

Guy in Ten Days (2003), and *Two Weeks Notice*—repeatedly stages dramas of mis- and rewanting "in which the heroine comes to realize that her professional aspirations are misplaced."[25] In a similar vein, feminist critics have suggested a conservative media conspiracy that pathologizes single women, threatens them with declining fertility statistics, and promises romantic bliss in exchange for a traditional marriage-oriented lifestyle.

One could also argue, however, that many romantic comedies are actually just as interested in reorienting male identities and motivations. In *Keinohrhasen*, for instance, the drama of mis-wanting is centered on Ludo, while Anna is fine just the way she is. Eric Rentschler rejects the German romantic comedies of the 1990s as either Peter Pan narratives or anti-feminist fantasies featuring men in arrested development and women who predominantly look for love and bourgeois security.[26] This may also be true in this case, but is this not precisely one of the dominating themes of the postfeminist generation, where many women find themselves challenged by men unwilling to commit, couple, and procreate? Indeed, if the major question contemporary German media consistently throws at German women of childbearing age is "why are you not having any, or more, children?," this question is reframed by German films like *Keinohrhasen*, which instead interrogates why it is that many men do not care to participate at all. And perhaps the recurring reenactment of male transformation that the romantic comedy repeatedly rehearses points to emotional motivations of an audience (largely female) that is part of the singles generation; spectators whose real lives, as statistics show, are often marked by the failure of relationships and unfulfilled desire. The escapist utopia of the romantic comedy is thus just as connected to the very issues that postromantic art films address more openly.

Keinohrhasen's unproblematic status as a romantic comedy and its investment in mobilizing the generic traditions that have made both British and American romcoms so successful, however, succeeded in assuring the film's impressive popularity. In fact, it allowed for a sequel, *Zweiohrküken* (Chicks with Two Ears, released in English as *Rabbit without Ears 2*, 2009), which in turn attracted over 4.2 million viewers.

Sommer vorm Balkon

Andreas Dresen's *Sommer vorm Balkon* was also marketed as a comedy, even though its social realism dominates the plot and the story is fundamentally postromantic. Set in Prenzlauer Berg, a district located in the former East Berlin that has since been radically gentrified, the film centers on two female friends living in the same apartment building. Katrin (Inka

---

[25] Diane Negra, "Structural Integrity, Historical Reversion, and the Post-9/11 Chick Flick," *Feminist Media Studies* 8, no. 1 (2008): 51–68.

[26] Rentschler, "From New German Cinema," 273.

Friedrich), who is about to turn forty, is a single mother to Max (Vincent Redetzki) and unemployed. Nike (Nadja Uhl) works doing housework for senior citizens. *Der Spiegel* called the film a "melancholy comedy" whose characters' "courage for living and will-power enables them to defy life's *tristesse*." The review continued: "With astonishing ease Dresen and screenwriter Wolgang Kohlhaase (*Solo Sunny*) repeatedly manage to extract comedic moments from the grey reality of everyday life."[27]

The film opens as the two friends spend a night drinking and talking on Nike's small balcony overlooking a city square. They tease the pharmacist on night duty in the apothecary down below with prank calls and philosophize about the men they would like to meet. "I need a man who gets along with Max," Katrin laments. "I just need one who gets along with me . . ." counters Nike. She is skeptical about the longevity of love. "It's all about hormones in the brain," she argues, "and eventually they'll stop working, suddenly and without warning." Nike was raised in an East German children's home, while Katrin came to Berlin from the West German South, for a love long-gone. Now the two women find themselves together in a changed Germany. The grey façade of their building becomes the subject for Katrin's paintings. She wants to preserve her impressions on canvas, now that everything is being repainted. "Perhaps," argued Christian Buß, "*Sommer vorm Balkon* is the first true reunification film—precisely because reunification is not being treated explicitly."[28] Günter Reisch sees the film "as a description of transition: from a socialist state toward the state of the individual, from a society of public welfare to one that asks everyone to take care of themselves."[29]

We observe Nike at her job, where she is repeatedly reminded not to linger with the isolated seniors she takes care of, as she is not paid just to talk or read from the Harlequin romances that one old lady enjoys. But her profound humanity and her love for the elderly in her care rejects depersonalized labor. In one instant, when one of her patients is about to be robbed by burglars hoping to take advantage of his old age to grab his meager possessions, Nike even defends him with a knife. Katrin, in contrast, is deeply frustrated with her inability to find new employment. "Frankly," a job agent is at pains to explain, "we like to place younger people . . . you have no idea how hard it is to have to tell people this

[27] Lars-Olaf Beier, "Grauer Alltag, kunterbund, *Der Spiegel*, 2 Jan. 2006, 139.

[28] Christian Buß, "'Sommer vorm Balkon': Wo der Mülltonnen-Duft verfliegt," *Spiegel Online*—Nachrichten—Kultur 12/29/09 5:34 PM, http://www.spiegel.de/kultur/kino/0,1518,druck-393291,00.html.

[29] Cited in Christoph Dieckmann, "Einsamkeit hat viele Namen: Andreas Dresens sonniger Milieu-Film Sommer vorm Balkon," *Die Zeit*, 29 Dec. 2005, http://www.zeit.de/2005/01/Einsamkeit_hat_viele_Namen.

Figs. 11.4a and 11.4b. Sommer vorm Balkon *(2005). Screenshots.*

every day. You're not yet old." Thus Katrin cannot afford the expensive sneakers Max wants so he can impress a girl, and she drinks heavily.

The film fuses the concerns of a social milieu study and an interest in the marginalized groups of the post-Wall Hartz IV generation (a phrase associated with unemployment benefits) with a postromantic discourse on modern relationships. When Nike and Katrin encounter Ronald, a truck driver, both women find themselves attracted to him, which challenges their friendship. Prior to his arrival the women had enjoyed deep platonic intimacy that included physical tenderness, but Ronald's entry into the relationship becomes divisive. Nike begins to neglect Katrin, who ends up spending her evenings drinking alone. Her efforts to meet someone in a nightclub even lead to an attempted rape. Katrin consoles herself with more vodka and is hospitalized. While she spends some days in a rehabilitation facility, Nike's relationship is by no means happy. Depictions of the young couple having sex concentrate on Nike's face, which shows her enduring rather than enjoying Ronald's efforts. Ronald is a macho poser who uses Nike for free food and rent. If the local barmaid, who also has her eye on Ronald, is to be believed, he also calls her a whore who can cook. He criticizes Nike for not fulfilling her potential, only "wiping other people's arses," while he aspires to "move up" from delivering carpets to delivering electronics because "it's more modern." When Nike discovers that he also has three children with different women, we witness her falling out of love. "Do you think that just because we have sex you can act like an ass?" she asks, first locking him out on the balcony for the night, then dropping him altogether. Ronald, despite his working-class charm, turns out to be the very "asshole" Til Schweiger's Ludo starts out as. Yet Ronald never reforms and quickly moves on to the barmaid. Here, rather than achieving narrative resolution through the formation of the heterosexual couple, the film offers restoration between the two girlfriends whose friendship has suffered. Nike cries over her estrangement from Katrin, while tearlessly dismissing Ronald, stating that "that man has been used up." Katrin in turn has to console Max, who is heartbroken because the girl he likes has chosen another boy. The film closes with another scene showing the women on the balcony, now sipping tea. A few months later, a final shot informs us, their building is also undergoing renovation.

"A beautiful power flows through the films of Andreas Dresen," argues *Die Zeit*, "a realism of a higher order. He sketches his characters to an extreme, but he does not surrender them to fate. He has mercy. He shows love. He understands old people as well as children."[30] And while Andreas Dresen's *Sommer vorm Balkon* appears to be a comedy, it ultimately portrays characters who struggle with alcoholism, unemployment, and failed relationships. What is perhaps not immediately obvious, however, is that the film is also not unlike the postfeminist US television series *Sex and the City* (albeit without the money and the glamour), which is in many ways equally cynical, ultimately celebrating the comfort of female companionship over the bliss of heterosexual coupling.

Sommer vorm Balkon proved to be successful with both critics and audiences, drawing almost a million viewers. Andreas Dresen received the *Bayrischer Filmpreis* (Bavarian film award) for best director in 2005 and the film closed among the top ten most successful German films of 2006.

As these examples demonstrate, the romantic comedy and its other, the postromance, engage with questions of gender, sexuality, and family in different ways. The cinema has always been complicit in shaping spectators' fantasies and desires, yet it is also capable of critically reflecting social realities. In relation to the politics of desire, the romantic comedy centers on utopian models of fantasy production, while the postromance deals with the failure of this fantasy. Life, in other words, is not like the movies, and the postromance film knows it. Moreover, even classic romantic comedies now tend to contain moments that point to the possibility of romantic failure. The films end blissfully, but deep down the genre's narrative conventions concurrently suggest that maybe there really is something wanting in the attitude of many contemporaries. Why do relationships continuously fail? How can one make it work? How to be happy? The contemporary romantic comedy is all about this, and so is its dystopian twin, the postromance. Across both genres and their hybrids a discussion is taking place that has increased relevance in the dramatically altered social environment of the singles generation or postfamily society, one that questions just how individuals should think of themselves and others in the framework of intimate relationships. A society of singles, single-parent homes, and patchwork families necessitates an intellectual reframing of the family as the social norm, and some of this reframing is playing out in cinematic fictions within the romance genres.

German films that deal with romance and relationships thus engage with the kind of romantic and postromantic narrative strategies that have become increasingly prominent on movie screens worldwide, and draw on a variety of generic conventions from both the romantic comedy and art cinema. They find their national specificity through their treatment

---

[30] Dieckmann, "Einsamkeit hat viele Namen."

of city locations, use of character study, and attention to social milieu. The films' investigation of gender conflict and sexual politics, however, is transnational. Within the aesthetics of modernism, romance fiction was often regarded as suspect because of its supposed triviality and sentimentality. Romance as a feminized discourse also seemed suspicious to feminists who feared its ideological force as a repressive control mechanism that sutured women into desiring their own oppression via their psychological investment in heterosexuality and patriarchy. Romance narratives, particularly if focused primarily on romantic fantasy rather than repressive social forces, thus occupied a space that was firmly placed within low culture and was ideologically suspect. However, I do not see the current shift toward films dealing with relationships as an escapist move away from pressing social and political concerns. Instead, in relation to the battle between the sexes, singularization, and the postfamily environment, the personal is once again political and alive and well in genres of romance, German or otherwise.

12: Yearning for Genre: The Films of Dominik Graf

Marco Abel

> *I think that it does not make much sense to demand, as [Dominik Graf] does, genre cinema in Germany because genre cinema requires existing genres; you cannot artificially make it or revive it as a retro-event . . . Graf's Sisyphus work is to keep making a film here and there that reminds us of how wonderful streets used to look in cinema, of how great nights used to look, and of how awesome women looked.*
>
> —Christian Petzold[1]

> *I never harbored the hope, as Petzold describes it, to create once again the prototype that would somehow ignite once more an entire industry. But I suppose he is right that . . . I am in hell, where all those old films roast, and I try to inhale some vitality into them, but this is admittedly a difficult task, since the whole system is one that prevents a particular vitality in films.*
>
> —Dominik Graf[2]

WHEN TAKING STOCK OF German film culture since the demise of its famous *Autorenkino*, which attracted international attention in the 1970s and reestablished West German cinema as "legitimate," one could do worse than consider the singular case of Dominik Graf.[3] For over the last thirty years Graf—who is almost completely unknown outside Germany and whose status at home does not nearly approach the level

---

[1] Marco Abel, "'The Cinema of Identification Goes on My Nerves': An Interview with Christian Petzold," *Cineaste* online 33, no. 3 (Summer 2008), http://www.cineaste.com/articles/an-interview-with-christian-petzold.htm.

[2] Marco Abel, "'I Build a Jigsaw Puzzle of a Dream-Germany': An Interview with German Filmmaker Dominik Graf," *Senses of Cinema* 55 (2010): http://www.sensesofcinema.com/2010/feature-articles/"'i-build-a-jigsaw-puzzle-of-a-dream-germany'-an-interview-with-german filmmaker-dominik-graf"-2/

[3] In the mid-1970s, Werner Herzog frequently referred to the films of the New German Cinema as "legitimate German cinema" (*legitimer deutscher Film*). See "Lorbeer für die Wunderkinder," *Der Spiegel*, 17 Nov. 1975, 188.

of recognition enjoyed by post-*Autorenkino* filmmakers such as Wolfgang Petersen, Roland Emmerich, and Doris Dörrie, nor that of the better-known post-*Wende* directors such as Sönke Wortmann, Tom Tykwer, and Florian Henckel von Donnersmarck—has been one of German film's most productive filmmakers. Of the more than sixty productions to his credit thus far, however, Graf made only seven for big-screen release: *Die Katze* (The Cat, 1988), *Spieler* (Gambler, 1990), *Die Sieger* (The Victors, released in English as *The Invincibles*, 1994), *Der Felsen* (The Rock, released in English as *A Map of the Heart*, 2002), *Der rote Kakadu* (The Red Cockatoo, 2006), *Das Gelübde* (The Vow, 2007), and *Komm mir nicht nach* (Don't Follow Me Around), part of the *Dreileben* (Three Lives) trilogy (2011) made by him, Christian Petzold, and Christoph Hochhäusler.[4] Three additional films, which were initially produced for television, were given a theatrical release: *Treffer* (Winner, 1984), *Drei gegen drei* (Three Against Three, 1985), and *Tiger, Löwe, Panther* (Tiger, Lion, Panther, 1989).[5] The rest of his oeuvre encompasses stand-alone made-for-TV feature films such as, for example, his remarkable trio of melodramas, *Deine besten Jahre* (Your Best Years, 1999), *Bittere Unschuld* (Bitter Innocence, 1999), and *Kalter Frühling* (Cold Spring, 2003), which all take a cold, hard look at the ghostly lives lived in bourgeois living rooms around the turn of the millennium in unified Germany, as well as episodes for some of German television's best-known and highly praised crime series: two each for *Tatort* (Crime Scene) and *Sperling*, three for *Polizeiruf 110* (Police Call 110) and thirteen for *Der Fahnder* (The Investigator).

During these three decades then, Graf has forged a career that resembles, albeit without the attending international fame, that of a director such as Anthony Mann, who made films during the "Golden Age" of Hollywood with a regularity of which filmmakers in Germany usually can only dream.[6] Graf's filmmaking career—beginning with his debut fea-

---

[4] The last two are associated with the so-called "Berlin School"—a contemporary German filmmaking movement of which Graf has repeatedly been critical. See, for example, Dominik Graf, "Unerlebte Filme," *Schnitt* 43 (2006): 62–65. For a detailed account of the movement, see Marco Abel, "Intensifying Life: The Cinema of the 'Berlin School'" *Cineaste* online 33, no. 4 (Fall 2008), http://cineaste.com/articles/the-berlin-school.htm. And for a fascinating *Streitgespräch* [disputation] between Graf, Hochhäusler, and Petzold, see their "Mailwechsel 'Berliner Schule,'" *Revolver* 16 (May 2007): 7–39.

[5] Graf also contributed episodes to two omnibus films produced for the big screen, *Neonstadt* (Neon City, 1982) and *Deutschland 09: 13 kurze Filme zur Lage der Nation* (Germany 09: 13 Short Films about the State of the Nation, 2009).

[6] "Ich wollte nach meinen ersten Filmen eine Filmographie wie Anthony Mann erwerben, das heißt: Filmen mit dem Schrotgewehr, also im Schnitt ungefähr drei Western pro Jahr, denn irgendeiner wird dann schon dabei sein, der was taugt und

ture, *Der kostbare Gast* (The Precious Guest, 1979), which earned him Bavaria's *Nachwuchsfilmpreis* (Newcomer Award)—is in many ways a perfect reflection of the fate German national cinema has suffered over the course of the last three decades.[7] For I can think of no other contemporary German director during this time period who has embodied what Andreas Kilb (derisively) calls the "abgeklärten, hochprofessionellen Genrefilmregisseur" (serene, highly professional genre-film director) more than Graf has.[8] Despite, or perhaps because of, his status as a supreme professional, however, Graf has essentially remained a lonely fighter in German film—a Sisyphus, as Petzold suggests in this essay's epigraph. Throughout his career, Graf has been pushing the boulder of genre filmmaking up the hill of a German film industry that has generally been unwilling to carve out a generic niche in which Graf might have been able to rest his films so that his efforts could have acquired a degree of consistency with those of other filmmakers, thus fashioning the very "neighborhood" that is essential to any genre. As Petzold argues, such a genre "neighborhood" is produced by and organized according to a logic of scriality, repetition, similarities, and differences and usually has appeal for larger audiences precisely because they tend to associate with such a "neighborhood" a desirable feeling of familiarity (and, occasionally, of surprise)[9] Because there is no such neighborhood consistency in the context of contemporary German film culture, however, the results of Graf's Sisyphean labor remain lonely probes exploring the possibilities of genre filmmaking; he was never to enjoy the luxury of making such films for a preexisting, preconstituted audience that would await the latest results of his explorations with anticipation and curiosity, which would ultimately render such filmmaking commercially viable.[10]

---

mal ins Schwarze trifft" (After my first films I wanted to acquire a filmography like Anthony Mann, to wit: to film with a pellet gun, that is, on average three Westerns per year, in the belief that one or the other will be good and hit the bull's eye). Graf, Hochhäusler, Petzold, "Mailwechsel," 12.

[7] Graf's first filmic effort was the self-scripted short film *Carlas Briefe* (Carla's Letters, 1975). Among the many awards Graf received are ten Adolf-Grimme prizes (Germany's most important television award), as well as the German film prize (until 1999, "Bundesfilmpreis," now "Deutscher Filmpreis"), the country's most highly endowed cultural award.

[8] Andreas Kilb, "Tiger, Löwe, Polizist," *Die Zeit*, 23 Sept. 1994, http://www.zeit.de/1994/39/Tiger-Loewe-Polizist.

[9] Graf, Hochhäusler, and Petzold, "Mailwechsel," 9.

[10] The only genres the German film industry steadfastly supports are children's films and especially comedies, the latter being the *de facto* "financial backbone of the German film industry throughout its history." See Michael Wedel and Thomas Elsaesser, "German Film Comedy," in *The BFI Companion to German Cinema*, ed. Thomas Elsaesser and Michael Wedel (London: BFI, 1999), 55. For an interesting assessment of German film comedies, see also Jan-Christopher Horak,

Differently put, the lack of recognition of Dominik Graf abroad and at home[11]—which corresponds to his own filmmaking ideal of being a craftsman rather than auteur[12]—results from the German film industry's failure to invest more in the production of genre films. Conversely, the failure of the German film industry to produce with greater frequency and regularity films (other than comedies and films about the country's totalitarian past) that manage to attract larger audiences can be considered symptomatic of the indifference, if not hostility, that meets Graf's efforts. Throughout his career he has tried to generate a viable genre-film culture in Germany, specifically, a genre-film culture drawing more on police films, crime films, thrillers, science-fiction films, and horror films (film genres that rose to their earliest artistic heights during the years of the Weimar Republic) than on comedies, which are notoriously difficult to export, but his attempts have consistently been met with indifference at best. It is, then, perhaps not too great an exaggeration to say that Graf's career, more than that of any other director, points to the conclusion that the very idea of a German film "industry" is a misnomer: although Graf has made some of the best noncomedic German genre films since the days of Fritz Lang, F. W. Murnau, and, later, Max Ophüls, his career has been marked by many missed opportunities (films he was unable to make due to the industry's lack of support) and, in the case of *Die Sieger*, a box office failure the magnitude of which may very well have killed any desire the industry might have ever harbored to develop a *big-screen* genre film culture.[13]

"German Film Comedy," in *The German Cinema Book*, ed. Tim Bergfelder, Erica Carter, and Deniz Göktürk (London: BFI, 2002), 29–38, in which he argues that the roots of the "German bias against film comedy [are] buried in the intellectual disdain *for genre cinema in general*" (29, my italics).

[11] It is telling that Graf, unlike Petersen, Emmerich, Tykwer, and Wortmann, did not even receive an entry in *The BFI Companion to German Cinema*.

[12] Marco Abel, "'I Build a Jigsaw Puzzle of a Dream-Germany'."

[13] According to www.insidekino.com, *Die Sieger* opened with 155 copies in September 1994, attracted slightly over 60,000 viewers in its first week of release, and by year's end had fizzled out at approximately 170,000 viewers. At a production cost of twelve million DM (www.imdb.com), Graf's attempt at realizing his *grossen Wurf* (grand slam) became one of the more significant commercial failures of German cinema since unification, which, according to Graf, had "sicher einen fatalen Einfluß gehabt, weil alle meinten, daß Polizeithriller nach diesem Film erst mal fürs deutsche Kino gestorben sind" (certainly a fatal impact because everyone believed that after this film the police thriller would be dead for the foreseeable future for German cinema). Quoted in Katja Nicodemus, "Film der neunziger Jahre: Neues Sein und altes Bewußtsein," in *Geschichte des deutschen Films*, ed. Wolfgang Jacobsen, Anton Kaes, and Hans Helmut Prinzler, 2nd ed. (Stuttgart: J. B. Metzler, 2004), 330.

I emphasize "big screen" here because it is important to note that noncomedic genre filmmaking does in fact exist in Germany—on television; especially *Krimis* (crime films in the largest sense) have been almost completely relegated to the small screen, where the genre is successful. Katja Nicodemus speculates that the thriller genre is almost totally absent from German cinema because the crime film, holding up a mirror to German culture, increasingly migrated to the small screen after the success of the Edgar Wallace films of the 1960s.[14] That is, the very fact that genre filmmaking takes place almost exclusively on German television directly reflects the now-decades-long struggles of the German film "industry" to become a proper *industry* despite the absence of the very structures that would enable and ensure the successful existence of industrial film production. Or, as Graf remarks: "Ein grosser Kinomarkt wie unserer [trägt] eine eigene Kinoindustrie (nach der die Branche ja lechzt seit ich denken kann) nur dann . . . wenn dabei auch die Genres gut und schlau und fantasievoll bedient werden" (a large cinema market like ours can support a film industry [for which the functionaries have been thirsting since I have been able to think] only if it serves the genres well and intelligently and with imagination).[15]

Graf is an outspoken critic of the German *Autorenkino*. He prefers a tradition of filmmaking influenced by the New Hollywood of Sam Peckinpah, Robert Altmann, and early Martin Scorsese, as well as directors such as Nicholas Roeg, Mike Figgis, Sam Fuller, Jean-Pierre Melville, and, in Germany, Klaus Lemke. He has doggedly worked within the limitations imposed on him by the German film production system over the years.[16] Doing so enabled him to consistently find directorial work within the confines of German television productions while being granted

---

[14] Nicodemus, "Film der neunziger Jahre," 328. See also Sascha Gerhards's essay in this volume.

[15] Dominik Graf, "RAF-Vampire beim Erfurter Blutbad," *Die Zeit*, 9 Jan. 2003, Feuilleton 31.

[16] Graf has a long history of expressing his opposition to the German *Autorenfilm*. He argues, for example, that its characters are too abstract: Dominik Graf, "Man spürt die Schläge im Gebälk," Interview with Katja Nicodemus, *Die Zeit*, 18 Jul. 2002, http://www.zeit.de/2002/30/Man_spuert_die_Schlaege_im_Gebaelk; that, unlike the American cinema of the 1970s, it never tried to reinvent genres: Dominik Graf, Interview mit Martin Farkas, *Revolver* 7 (September 2002): 24; and that the excessive desire of the *Autoren* generation in the 1970s exerted a somewhat oppressive force on the following generation: Dominik Graf, *Schläft ein Lied in allen Dingen: Texte zum Film* (Berlin: Alexander Verlag, 2009). In the promotional material for *Deutschland 09* he suggests that his antagonism may be due to the fact that he does not belong to the generation of "68" but is, rather, a "Hinterher-68er" (post-68er), not having been born until 1952. Dominik Graf, "Der Weg, den wir nicht zusammen gehen," Presseheft *Deutschland 09*, accessed 1 Dec.2009, http://deutschland09-der-film.de/downloads, 11, my italics.

only scant opportunities to work on big-screen productions. In fact, Nicodemus suggests that the traumatic experience of shooting *Die Sieger* made Graf shrink back from seeking out new cinema projects for many years[17]; once he returned to the big screen eight years later, it was with *Der Felsen*, a small-scale production shot on DV, which was considerably less demanding logistically than the production of *Die Sieger*.

However, Graf himself puts a positive spin on the fact that as one of Germany's most talented directors he had only rarely the chance to prove what he can do when given a larger filmmaking canvas to work on; looking back on his career, he claims that television in general, but especially *Der Fahnder*, was his safe home to which he could return whenever he got beaten up for a big cinema production.[18] Given the circumstances he has found himself working in throughout his career—that is, in the absence of the kind of "neighborhood" that Petzold posits as essential to any viable genre filmmaking—what is ultimately remarkable about what Ekkehard Knörer calls the "singular position" of Dominik Graf in German film is the fact that he has consistently mobilized his specific working conditions in order to develop just such a "neighborhood" within his own *oeuvre*.[19] Indeed his films can be regarded as a multiplicity of iterations, indeed, *itinerations*, of genre filmmaking that collectively amount to a "neighborhood" (of one), which we might describe as a singular counter-tradition of contemporary German filmmaking taking place *within* the confines of the industry's television-based production structures.[20] By embracing, for example, the formats of German (crime) television shows such as, most significantly, *Der Fahnder* but also *Tatort*, *Polizeiruf 110*, *Sperling*, *Kommissar Süden* (Detective Süden), and *Morlock*, he managed to hone his skills as a genre filmmaker;[21] furthermore, doing so also enabled him both to redefine the very formats within which he found himself working and, over time, to stretch the borders of the genre "neighborhood"—so much so that Graf and his collaborators might genuinely have felt that a German audience would (finally) be ready to participate in Graf's "Traum

---

[17] Nicodemus, "Film der neunziger Jahre," 329.

[18] Dominik Graf. "Wo die Straßen keine Namen haben," *Süddeutsche Zeitung*, 11 May 2005, 17.

[19] Ekkehard Knörer, "Fighter im System: Dominik Graf im Gespräch," accessed 14 Dec.2009, http://www.cargo-film.de/artikel/fighter-im-system-dominik-graf-im-gesprach-teil-1/.

[20] Gilles Deleuze and Félix Guattari call *itinerative* a form of repetition that *in* its serial articulation intensifies that which is repeated to such a degree that it generates internal difference—that it becomes different from itself. Gilles Deleuze and Félix Guattari, *A Thousand Plateaus: Capitalism and Schizophrenia*, trans. Brian Massumi (Minneapolis: University of Minnesota Press, 1987), 372.

[21] Even earlier, Graf shot six episodes for *Köberle kommt* (1983), in which a juridical archivist helps a female detective solve cases.

vom unbekannten deutschen Film" (dream of the unknown German film)[22] of which *Die Sieger* ended up becoming his first, perhaps to this day still most significant, albeit compromised and commercially unsuccessful, instantiation.[23]

Graf, who frequently composes his own film scores, has worked in various genres—comedy, melodrama, and, in the case of *Das zweite Gesicht* (The Second Face, 1982), even psychic-horror—but what stands out in the end is his efforts to develop one specific genre more than any other, the police thriller or *policier*.[24] Indeed, Graf (who in Hitchcockian fashion frequently appears in his own films, albeit often merely through his disembodied voice on, say, a police radio) himself admits that he is primarily interested in police films rather than crime films in general, that is, in films "die diesen Apparat schildern, der sich über eine Stadt oder eine Gegend legt" (that depict this apparatus that holds sway over a city or area).[25] His efforts over the years to develop this specific genre in Germany have been characterized by a dynamic of repetition and difference—that is, by the very law of genre par excellence as articulated by Raphaëlle Moine, who argues that

> spectators can . . . classify a new film in a genre through two different approaches: either they can refer directly to the features that

---

[22] Graf, "Wo die Straßen." Graf continues: "Wir träumten das deutsche Kino anders, und wir träumten es im Fernsehen. So, wie es das in Wahrheit niemals gab und wie es das wohl so auch niemals geben wird. Außer im Fernsehen . . . Es war eine Art Anrufung einer anderen Art von Filmen, die zwar keine Preise für Deutschland im Ausland gewinnen würden, die aber vielleicht genau die richtigen Filme zur rechten Zeit gewesen wären, um solides Vertrauen beim deutschen Publikum zu erwerben. Vertrauen in eine Kontinuität von guter Erzählung, von unprätentiösem Humor, von Spannung und ab und zu auch von überraschender Härte" (We dreamt German cinema differently, and we dreamt it in television. As it never really existed and likely never will. Except for on TV . . . It was a sort of invocation of a different kind of film, which would not win any awards for Germany abroad, but perhaps would have been the right films at the right time to gain the solid trust of German audiences.Trust in consistently good story-telling, of unpretentious humor, of tension, and occasionally even of a surprising hard-hitting quality).

[23] Graf's collaborators include a host of actors who regularly appear in his films. Most significant, however, is Graf's reliance on a small number of screenwriters, especially Christoph Fromm, Bernd Schwamm, Rolf Basedow, Markus Busch, and Günter Schütter, who collectively have authored more than half of Graf's films.

[24] I refer to the particular French inflection of this genre because of Graf's admiration for filmmakers such as Jean-Pierre Melville, arguably the undisputed master of this particular subgenre of the thriller.

[25] Rainer Gansera, "'Ich versuche, die Luft zu filmen': Begegnungen mit dem Regisseur Dominik Graf," accessed 29 Nov. 2009, http://www.kath-akademie-bayern.de/contentserv/www.katholische.de/index.php?StoryID=427.

characterize a genre without reference to other films that constitute it, or they can compare this new film with other films in the genre, discuss the resemblances, and then either reinforce the generic quality, perhaps adding a new element, or else question its adequacy in the light of the new case.[26]

In Germany, however, this law is generally prevented from functioning. Christoph Fromm, for instance, agrees with Graf that German cinema is in dire need of rejuvenating the thriller genre, among others. But, he claims, this is impossible in Germany because the restrictions enforced by the conventions of German prime-time television are not compatible with the demands of proper genre filmmaking; simply put, German television, which is almost always the primary sponsor of German cinema films, is only interested in producing films that meet the demands of the 8:15 p.m. time slot, which, according to Fromm, essentially excludes suspenseful thrillers.[27] Nicodemus concurs with Fromm's assessment, adding that the influence exerted by Germany's private cable channels often yields films that have little connection to social reality and are instead driven by the demand that they be easily consumable, which often means that anything unwieldy and unresolved—realistic—is eliminated from a script even before it goes into production. What remains, says Nicodemus, are the two German tax-funded public networks (ARD and ZDF), which occasionally allow for a degree of experimentation with the possibilities of genre filmmaking, of which Graf has probably made use better than any other German genre filmmaker in the last two decades.[28] In fact, Graf himself claims that he loves working for prime time, because almost all his favorite films are marked by their direct engagement with their respective national film industries—by how these films work with rather than in opposition to the rules and structures of those industries.[29] In any case, the creation and development of genre thrillers—in Graf's case, more specifically the police film—is in Germany possible only within the preset

---

[26] Raphaëlle Moine, *Cinema Genre*, trans. Alistair Fox and Hilary Radner (Oxford: Blackwell, 2008), 3. Rick Altman's *Film/Genre* (199; repr., London: BFI, 2002) offers what is probably still the most complex approach to the subject. His "semantic/syntactic/pragmatic" genre theory proposes genre as "a site of struggle and co-operation among multiple users" (211). Genres, according to Altman, neither preexist spectators nor guide their reception; rather, genre is the site of a "cross-fertilization process whereby the interests of one group [say, viewers] may appear in the actions of another [say, producers]" and thus involves a "feedback system" (211).

[27] "Interview mit Christoph Fromm," *Vierundzwanzig.de: Das Wissensportal der Deutschen Filmakademie*, accessed 20 Nov. 2009 www.vierundzwanzig.de/drehbuch/interview_mit_christoph_fromm.

[28] Nicodemus, "Film der neunziger Jahre," 329.

[29] Graf, Hochhäusler, and Petzold, "Mailwechsel," 12.

formats of television series, which demand precisely the kind of repetition and, occasionally, modest differences for which the conditions of big-screen film production in Germany are not designed.

But by having been able to work repeatedly within the *policier* format for television, Graf, when eventually given the opportunity to apply his filmmaking skills to big-screen material, managed to make what are arguably two of the greatest German police films since Fritz Lang made his *Großstadtthrillers* (metropolitan thrillers) in the 1920s and early 1930s. Graf's *Die Katze*, the commercially more successful, can be considered a big-screen dry run for his masterpiece, *Die Sieger*.[30] To demonstrate, then, how Graf's yearning for a viable genre filmmaking tradition in Germany—specifically, for the *policier*—manifests itself in and as a fight within the system of television-based German film production, I will focus in the rest of this essay on *Die Sieger*—arguably the closest that postunification German cinema has come to making a film akin to Michael Mann's crime-genre masterpiece, *Heat* (1995). I will do so, however, by embedding my discussion of *Die Sieger*, which according to Nicodemus set the standards for German genre filmmaking,[31] in the context of four additional films, all of which fall, like *Die Sieger*, into the category of the police film: namely, two of his early *Fahnder* episodes, *Über dem Abgrund* (Above the Abyss, 1987) and *Glückliche Zeiten* (Happy Times, 1987); his first made-for-the-big-screen thriller, *Die Katze*; and the made-for-TV feature *Eine Stadt wird erpresst* (A City is Blackmailed, 2006).

Die Sieger hit the German big screens in fall 1994, during the height of post-Wall Germany's *Spaßkultur* (fun culture), of which the commercially successful yuppie comedies—"cinema of consensus" films that eagerly participated in the then prevailing German *Zeitgeist* of "party, not politics"—symptomatically constituted the perfect cinematic articulation.[32] This 135-minute film was, as Graf claims, "consciously a film that lacked any basis"[33]—an untimely film, if you will, which even twenty years later is still awaiting its match within the German film-production context. The plot—which according to Graf is the skeleton of any genre film, akin to a piece of wood that prevents one from drowning

[30] *Die Katze* attracted more than 1.3 million viewers to the big screen (www.ffa.de), making it the fourteenth biggest hit at the German box office in 1988. Graf qualifies this success, however, by pointing out that the casting of Götz George, who was at the time one of Germany's biggest stars, essentially ensured a large audience. See Marco Abel, "'I Build a Jigsaw Puzzle of a Dream-Germany'."
[31] Nicodemus, "Film der neunziger Jahre," 329.
[32] Eric Rentschler, "From New German Cinema to the Post-Wall Cinema of Consensus," in *Cinema and Nation*, ed. Mette Hjort and Scott Mackenzie (New York: Routledge, 2000), 260–77.
[33] Marco Abel, "'I Build a Jigsaw Puzzle of a Dream-Germany'."

in a river—follows the exploits of a tightly knit group of special police (*Sondereinsatzkommando* or SEK). Its leader, Karl Simon (Herbert Knaup in his first major big-screen role), believes that he has recognized a former colleague and friend, Heinz Schäfer (Hannes Jaenicke in his fourth and last role to date in a film by Graf) in a sting operation. Schäfer had allegedly committed suicide after killing his severely handicapped newborn baby. Simon gradually discovers that Schäfer did not in fact die but instead became a V-Mann (contact person) who is now involved in criminal operations involving higher-level politicians who used their political power to block anti-money-laundering legislation. In order to protect his cover, Schäfer raises suspicions against Simon with the latter's superiors. The V-Man is eventually instructed to abduct another politician who got wind of the goings-on and unwisely decided to gain political capital from his knowledge. Schäfer, however, pursues his own ends together with one of Simon's men (the film features many "doubles": Simon and Schäfer; not one but two betrayals; the dynamics among both the SEK men and the higher-ups; the wives of Simon and Schäfer; and so on) and plans to extort a large sum of money from the government in exchange for his hostage. Their status threatened by the suspicions raised against Simon (and thus the group at large), "die Helden der inneren Sicherheit" (heroes of internal state security), as Peter Körte aptly calls them,[34] decide to ignore the orders of their superiors and take matters into their own hands—an act of group solidarity that, as Graf suggests, "demonstrates the absurdity of the entire police apparatus.[35]

Until this point the film oscillates between carefully orchestrated set-action pieces showcasing the kind of work the SEK does (sting operations; providing protection for politicians, and so on); nuanced observational moments revealing the workings of the police apparatus; and detours into the private lives of the *Sieger*, their superiors, and their opponents. With the SEK group finally affirming their "winner" status to the fullest extent—abnegating any responsibilities to the ostensibly democratic system that gave birth to them as supermen, as "invincibles"—the film, the title of which is undoubtedly meant ironically rather than affirmatively, enters its final third. At this moment Graf transforms what has thus far been a metropolitan *policier* into a chase-action thriller that forces Simon's men to drive south on the *Autobahn* from Düsseldorf to the Bavarian Alps, where they meet Schäfer for one of the more elaborately explosive showdowns in the history of German film production. More specifically, in an ingeniously conceived and staged transitional set piece

---

[34] Peter Körte, "Verstörte Helden der inneren Sicherheit: Zu Dominik Grafs Film *Die Sieger*," in *Dominik Graf, Verstörung im Kino: Der Regisseur von Die Sieger im Gespräch mit Stefan Stosch über die Arbeit am Film* (Hanover: Werhahn Verlag, 1998), 7.

[35] Marco Abel, "'I Build a Jigsaw Puzzle of a Dream-Germany'."

(to which I will turn in a moment), Graf pushes his film through a generic porthole, with the effect that what has up until now been essentially a *Großstadtthriller* is being transformed into a road-/chase-movie plot that irreversibly races towards its deadly telos high up on the Karwendel. In the process the film eliminates various members of the group, thus both foregrounding the V-Man's considerable skills at anticipating his pursuers' moves and preparing us for the final confrontation between the erstwhile colleagues and friends, Simon and Schäfer, whom we had first encountered in the film's opening scene in which Simon drives his friend to the hospital where he eventually murders his baby.[36]

This plot summary, convoluted as it already is, does not fully do justice to everything that is going on in the film. Remarkably, Graf actually had to shorten his original cut from three hours to the contractually stipulated 135 minutes. In his extended conversation about the film with Stefan Stosch, Graf expresses his regrets for having been forced to cut so much material; he feels that much of it would have both lightened up the film with scenes depicting the humor and lightheartedness of his SEK protagonists and revealed more about life in the Federal Republic.[37] Indeed, as Graf told me, he felt the material he was given from real SEK people (whom he had gotten to know when shooting *Die Katze* and who served as production advisors for *Die Sieger* and even assumed small roles in it) would have been enough for twenty different stories. In the end, he and Schütter tried to make a "Mega-Ober-Fernsehfilm" (mega-mega television film), well aware that in essence their material would lend itself better to a television series than a movie.[38]

Notwithstanding these apparently substantial cuts, what lifts the final version of the film above the multitude of middle-of-the-road thrillers is the fact that Graf, as he is wont to do in all of his work, still manages to lavish much attention on the context within which the main plot unfolds: *Die Sieger* spends considerable time shedding light on the protagonists' private lives and their affairs and petit-bourgeois family values; it offers up atmospheric interludes that reveal much about the Federal Republic through its spaces and architecture (rarely has Düsseldorf looked more interesting, not least because the film affords viewers numerous lovingly

---

[36] This scene, which has a dream-like quality to it, constitutes in fact a flashback, but the film does not clearly mark off the subsequent scene as taking place years later. On the DVD's commentary track Graf speculates that the failure to provide a clear temporal marker might have been confusing to viewers (*Die Sieger*, DVD, Euro Video, 2002); this, together with the shock effect provoked by how Graf stages Schäfer's infanticide likely caused some viewers to leave the film early, possibly contributing to the bad publicity that ultimately hurt the film's box-office chances.

[37] Dominik Graf, *Verstörung im Kino*, 32–33, 16.

[38] Marco Abel, "'I Build a Jigsaw Puzzle of a Dream-Germany'."

composed bird's-eye-view shots, which render the petit-bourgeois design of this medium-sized German city intriguing while abstaining from the temptation to "Manhattanize" it); and it bitingly comments on postunification Germany's political culture—a culture that likes to congratulate itself for its ostensible liberalism, democratic stability, and tolerance, but that, if but slightly pushed, quickly exhibits tendencies reminiscent of the country's less democratic past(s).[39] In this context, what Melba (Katja Flint, playing in a star-making performance the wife of the abducted politician) casually remarks to Simon, with whom she is about to enjoy a brief yet intense sexual affair, is hardly a throw-away line: "Wenn Wahlen wirklich etwas bewirken könnten, wären sie in diesem Land verboten" (if elections could really bring something about they would be forbidden in this country)! This cultural-political pessimism—which Graf first evoked in his *Morlock* episode *Die Verflechtung* (The Entanglement, 1993), which dramatizes the *Abwicklung* (liquidation) of the German Democratic Republic—is lent its perhaps most glorious cinematic articulation in *Eine Stadt wird erpresst*. In this film, Graf's own deeply felt alienation from postunified Germany comes to a climax with the literal blowup of both the compromised but sympathetic (and authentic) detective Kalinke (Uwe Kockisch) and Günter Naumann, Kalinke's antagonist from their mutual "Eastern" past, who, notwithstanding his criminal actions, has earned the detective's respect because of how he affirms the very sense of solidarity that postunified, neoliberal Germany has completely abnegated.[40]

Offering an earlier expression of the same sentiment, *Die Sieger* is in the end, to use the words of Michael Althen,

> ein Aktionfilm, der von so etwas Flüchtigem wie Gefühlen handelt; ein Männerfilm, der am liebsten von Frauen erzählt; ein "amerikanischer" Film, der so nur in Deutschland möglich ist. Dominik

---

[39] In his interview with me, Graf explained that originally Günter Schütter had Schäfer forge contacts in the terrorist milieu. Before handing in the final script, however, they were asked to eliminate any references to terrorism, lest the film were to get involved in the then ongoing RAF-amnesty debate. Shortly thereafter, just weeks before shooting for the film commenced, the events in Bad Kleinen took place: the GSG 9 (a special police force not unlike the one depicted in *Die Sieger*) tried to arrest Werner Grams, a member of the RAF, at a train station; resisting arrest, Grams shot two policemen (one fatally) and is said to have shot himself before falling off the station platform.

[40] Graf feels that since unification Germany is becoming a country that has little to do with what he wants from a homeland: Dominik Graf, "Der Weg, den wir nicht zusammen gehen." Specifically, the cultural openness he experienced during the 1970s and 1980s gradually vanished after the fall of the Wall, so much so that, according to Graf, today people refuse once again to look each other in the eye: Dominik Graf, "Lernt schlechte Filme," *Die Zeit*, 8 Nov. 2007, Feuilleton 58.

Graf hält sich an die Konventionen, um sie immer wieder verletzen zu können.[41]

[an action film that is about something as fleeting as feelings; a men's film that prefers to tell of women; an "American" film that in this way is possible only in Germany. Dominik Graf heeds conventions in order to violate them over and over again.]

That is, *Die Sieger* is a film that could have been made only in Germany, because of the way the film draws its characters, because of how it images its locations, and because of its specific political outlook that, as Nicodemus suggests, comments on a corrupt society that is exclusively preoccupied with securing its standard of living.[42] It is this combination of an untimely political attitude (which in the context of the *Spaßkulturgesellschaft* could not but be received as being out of step), together with the fact that Graf might have misjudged his audience's readiness for the specific genre "violations" he committed, that likely doomed the film to failure at the time.

Considered within the context of Graf's oeuvre, however, the film was timely, standing tall as both the culmination of Graf's previous efforts and the impetus to keep fighting within the system—that is, to continue making *policiers* on the small screen, not least in order to pursue genre in television "auf eine andere, reduziertere Weise . . . auch um zu zeigen, was damit gemeint ist" (in a different, more reduced manner . . . also in order to show what is meant by this).[43] In fact, *Die Sieger* is the upscale villa in the otherwise humble genre "neighborhood" Graf has been developing through his prior work in television as well as his previous big-screen effort, *Die Katze*. Indeed, it seems to me that *Die Sieger* marks precisely the moment when Graf's skills were honed enough for him to drop this kind of film into a big-screen environment that had otherwise little or no established *policier* genre lineage that could have prepared audiences for his biggest production to date.

What, then, are the specific connections between *Die Sieger* and its surrounding "neighborhood"? To begin, we can point out how the film

---

[41] Michael Althen, "Der Preis des Glücks," *Süddeutsche Zeitung*, 22 Sept.1994, accessed through www.filmportal.de, entry for *Die Sieger*. Althen codirected two documentary/essay films with Graf: *Das Wispern im Berg der Dinge* (The Whispering in the Mountain of Things, 1997), Graf's film essay about his famous father, actor Robert Graf (who had starring roles in *Jonas*, dir. Ottomar Domnick, 1957 and *Wir Wunderkinder* [We Wonder-Children, dir. Kurt Hoffmann, 1958]); and *München: Geheimnisse einer Stadt* (Munich: Secrets of a City, 2000).

[42] Nicodemus, "Film der neunziger Jahre," 330.

[43] Dominik Graf, "Man spürt die Schläge im Gebälk," interview with Katja Nicodemus, *Die Zeit,* 18 Jul. 2002, http://www.zeit.de/2002/30/Man_spuert_die_Schlaege_im_Gebaelk.

draws directly upon Graf's previous work in concrete ways: most significantly, it utilizes a plot idea around which Graf's *Fahnder* episode *Über dem Abgrund* already structured its story line and furthermore almost literally repeats dialogue moments from the scene in which the titular protagonist, Faber (the late, great Klaus Wennemann), is being interrogated by his superiors because they suspect that he simply made up the story of having recognized a former policeman in a sting operation only to prevent discovery of his own illegal activities. Moreover, what I just called *Die Sieger*'s "porthole" scene is a restaging of a scene from Graf's *Fahnder* episode *Glückliche Zeiten*: Faber, like Simon, trails a woman through a shopping arcade, which in both films is literally the same arcade (and which really existed in Munich). Finally, the way Graf renders the capital of North Rhine Westphalia, Düsseldorf, in *Die Sieger* is directly reminiscent of how he shows it in *Die Katze*. However, in both cases the way Graf's mise-en-scène stages the metropolis differs significantly from how he visualizes Munich (which is known only as "G" for *Großstadt* or metropolitan area) in *Fahnder* but at the same time it also anticipates the almost-Michael-Mann-like images Graf wrests away for the television screen from the East German city of Leipzig in *Eine Stadt wird erpresst* more than a decade later.[44]

We can add other aspects to these explicit connections, including how Graf handles dialogue in his work for both *Der Fahnder* and *Die Sieger*, with the former's innovation setting the stage for the latter's big-screen "application." Explaining how his work on the early episodes of *Der Fahnder* constituted a small revolution in German television acting, Graf points out that actors, who usually come from the theater, used to deliver their lines consecutively without interrupting each other; rarely would two or more characters speak at the same time. Not so in *Der Fahnder*: from its first season, on which Graf's direction left an indelible mark,[45] the show's dialogues

---

[44] To point out but one other pronounced moment of "recycling" in Graf's oeuvre, for *Die Katze* Graf relied on a basic plot element he had already used in the *Fahnder* episode *Glückliche Zeiten*. In both films the bank robber makes use of inside information he gained from a woman: in the latter case, the robber has an affair with a woman who works at the bank he proceeds to rob (with her knowledge); in the former, the robber has an affair with the wife of a bank manager. Unlike in *Glückliche Zeiten*, where the robber is a regular guy, the big-screen version depicts him as a master criminal who, like a puppeteer, orchestrates the robbery executed by two lackeys while he himself observes and intervenes in the police response by using the latest high-tech surveillance technology. Götz George's character likely has a military or special police force background, as may be appropriate for a big-screen character in a thriller, whereas in the *Fahnder* episode he is an immigrant, working-class stiff merely looking for an easy paycheck.

[45] Graf directed episodes 2, 4, 6, 13, and 14. For an episode guide see "Der Fahnder," *Wikipedia*, accessed 9 Dec. 2009, http://de.wikipedia.org/wiki/Der_Fahnder#Episodenguide.

were characterized by the actors delivering their lines in a way more akin to real-life conversations, with multiple interlocutors often talking simultaneously; and even more astonishingly, these characters would speak at a breakneck speed, something that was essentially completely unheard of in German filmmaking, which at the time was largely dominated by theater-actors and, of course, the legacy of the *Autorenkino*, in which characters often spoke deliberately and slowly, if at all. That is, the cadence of everyday speech, the successful use of which Graf accredits to Wennemann's acting genius, made its entry into German filmmaking with *Der Fahnder*. As a result, viewers were forced to get used to a different way of delivering information and frequently had to accept that they might not be able to catch all the intricacies revealed in the dialogue. This being a television series, however, the scripts always featured explanatory scenes in which one or more characters, engaging each other, had to explain the case to the audience; although Wennemann races through these dialogue moments as fast as he can, such scenes still allow viewers to catch up in ways that they are not able to in *Die Sieger*, which does not feature such explanatory dialogues. I suspect that the singular case of *Die Sieger* also manifests the expressed hope that German audiences, after going through a decade-long *Fahnder* "boot camp," in which they were afforded the chance to habituate themselves to a new style of acting and speaking—to a new way of delivering information—would be ready to encounter a big-screen *policier* that instilled in them the same degree of confusion by which the characters on screen are affected themselves. This, of course, was not the case.

Graf's work for *Der Fahnder* had yet another near-revolutionary impact on German television productions and thus on audiences' viewing habits. Conventional television grammar stages dialogue scenes so that a carefully delineated distance separates two characters, a spatial arrangement that is then shot in evenly paced shot/reverse-shot sequences. These static scenes almost always take place in interior locations; movement, that is, occurs only outside and is generally unaccompanied by much speech. Graf's *Fahnder* episodes, as Petzold recalls, revealed fundamentally new possibilities in this respect, as his characters tend to speak while moving on the street, falling silent when entering a room: "Das war damals ziemlich sensationell, so was überhaupt im Fernsehen zu sehen" (Back then it was rather astounding to see something like that on television).[46] This fundamental alteration of conventional German television grammar and speech patterns, which Graf initiated with his work on *Fahnder*, and which he intensified through its serialization, would affect all Graf's subsequent work, including *Die Katze*, the comedy *Spieler*, and *Die Sieger*, as

---

[46] Christian Petzold in his interview with Felix von Boehm and Sebastian Seidler, "Wenn das Kino zu spät kommt," *Schnitt* online, accessed 1 Dec. 2009, http://www.schnitt.de/233,5392,01.

well as his subsequent television work, to which he retreated for almost a decade, such as *Frau Bu lacht* (Mrs. Bu Laughs, 1995), *Hotte im Paradies* (Hotte in Paradise, 2002), *Der scharlachrote Engel* (The Scarlet Angel, 2004), and *Er sollte tot* (He Supposed Dead, 2006).[47]

Throughout his work, then, Graf reiterates not merely content but also the form through which he delivers it—whether in terms of mise-en-scène or the rendering of speech. What this recycling marks is Graf's attempt to create the neighborhood consistency required for genre film-making to work: he repeats elements as large as an entire plot setup, as functional as an entire scene, as specific as a single shot, and even as amorphous as the way he handles the look of a city or the way characters speak to each other—all in the service of habituating his viewers to a film language (in the broadest sense) that they are not used to from home-grown big- or small-screen productions. Significantly, the force of difference always sits at the heart of Graf's repetitive gestures—gestures that add up to a new German genre cinema. So while Graf may indeed never have desired to invent a new prototype as the match that could spark an entire industry, he nevertheless ended up engineering a prototype for his own (policier) films. This prototype turned out to be tremendously productive, not least because he continually managed to tweak it; specifically, he developed and altered it through inhabiting the very serial-ized production conditions of German television with such intensity that through this conventionally iterative process he and his collaborators were able to effect moments of itineration, moments of difference that affect the repetition-based structures of a genre from within. In doing so Graf adds to the possibilities inhering in the given relations constituting the genre, including formal relations, the feedback loop between produc-tions and audiences, and the genealogical relations immanent to a series of films that constitute the genre as much as that genre marks those films as belonging to it.

Take, as but one significant example, the "porthole" scene from *Die Sieger* and compare its staging and purpose to its predecessor in *Glückliche Zeiten*. In the television blueprint, the scene occurs about a third of the way into the forty-seven minute episode. A bank robbery has taken place, and the robber has ingeniously managed to elude the police. The surveillance camera, however, provides clues as to the robber's iden-tity and his relationship with a female bank clerk. Faber is asked to help find the man, and after an interior-location dialogue scene in which both

---

[47] The unique place Graf occupies in the context of contemporary German film and television was recently emphasized by the fact that Petzold and Hochhäusler created a film essay in which they deconstruct frame by frame the first interrogation scene of *Er sollte tot*. This fifteen-minute-long exercise in close reading of a film scene with the help of cinematic means is included in Alexander Kluge's eleven hour-long DVD project *Früchte des Vertrauens* (Filmedition Suhrkamp, 2009).

Faber and the audience are brought up to speed with regard to the story's developments, Graf shows Faber, eating a hotdog, walking on a sidewalk, while Max Kühn (Hans-Jürgen Schatz), the straight-laced sidekick to Faber's unconventional *Bulle* (cop), follows him in Faber's iconic green Ford Granada, also eating a hotdog. The diegetic sound features a simple, somewhat humorous two-way radio conversation between Kühn and their boss, Rick (Dietrich Mattausch), which is clearly designed to inform the audience of the goings-on; concurrently, various well-centered, unobstructed tracking shots—in each shot we see at most one passer-by fleetingly crossing through the frame—show that Faber is trailing the female bank clerk, who walks briskly, as if suspecting that she is being observed. Continuing his pursuit by himself through a shopping arcade into which the woman has turned, Faber finds her lingering in front of a shop window and is thus forced to stop as well. After momentarily feigning interest in a window display, he bluntly looks at the woman, who suddenly returns his gaze. Faber immediately turns away from her in such exaggerated manner that she cannot help but realize his true intentions (this brief moment is one of many that lighten up the mood of Graf's *Fahnder* episodes, for Wennemann's acting here is rather slapstick-like and not intended to be "realistic").

The next shot, set up like all others at eye-level, shows us Faber still looking at the window display, while we already hear the sound of feet running away. Hearing the noise, Faber turns back to where the woman was before she ran away. A subsequent shot reveals the woman hurrying through the arcades, followed by a shot of Faber passing by the same shop windows. The next shot shows us Faber running around a corner in one of the arcade's passageways toward a street, but the woman is nowhere in sight. He stops to pick up the woman's scarf, which a quick close-up highlights, before continuing his movement toward the street, from which bright light shines into the passageway. Having reached the end of the arcade, Faber looks to both sides, not seeing the woman anymore. In the final shot of the scene, Faber returns to Max and complains that he is rusty. In the next scene Faber and his colleagues discover that the woman has been brutally murdered, causing Faber to feel guilty for having taken his surveillance job too lightly. In this episode, then, this "porthole" scene functions to link the subgenre of a bank-robbery film to that of a (sadistic, as we discover) murder story: the solving of the bank robbery becomes the vehicle to solving the more serious crime of murder.

Seven years later, working on a considerably larger canvas, Graf repeats this scene but stages it differently and ultimately uses this "porthole" to different effect. Whereas the blueprint impresses through its sheer economy of shot selection (a mere handful of shot setups suffice to stage the scene), the "recycled" version in *Die Sieger* stirs us by virtue of the complexity of the *découpage*. Too complex to be described in full

Figs. 12.1a and 12.1b. Faber chasing woman in an arcade in Glückliche Zeiten *(left) and Simon's p.o.v. of woman he is chasing in* Die Sieger *(right). Screenshots.*

here, the entire scene lasts considerably longer (four minutes rather than ninety-five seconds) and consists of a substantially higher number of shots (fifty rather than twenty-four). Graf structures this interval so that in the first twenty-three shots viewers are not even aware that Simon, who together with his group has been put on ice by their superiors, is on location together with the police force, who are trying to cover Melba's every move as she walks from the Munich central station into a shopping street and subsequently into an arcade, waiting for one of Schäfer's helpers to make contact with her (she is carrying the ransom for her husband, whom Schäfer kidnapped). Unlike in the *Fahnder* scene, which is rendered in an invisible style, here Graf takes great pleasure in using, and making visible, the entire filmmaking arsenal at his disposal: extreme close-ups on one hand and extreme long shots on the other; the use of extreme zooms to bridge significant distances across a mass of people, many of whom are real, others extras hired for the scene, while yet others are the characters with whom we are familiar; high-angle shots, low-angle shots, partial-object shots, stationary fetishistic star shots, and smoothly moving tracking shots. The soundtrack is a mix of original sound and the police communicating via radio; some shots are in deep focus while most rely on shallow focus to foreground a specific aspect of the frame, of the action.

Three and a half minutes into the scene, after Melba meets a girl who provides her with a pair of sunglasses with an ear piece through which Schäfer's accomplice instructs her so that she can shake off the police (we never can tell how many agents are on her trail), she emerges from a café, with some agents following her; However, Simon, who has been only in two shots thus far, recognizes in shot 38 that this woman, wearing the red raincoat Melba was instructed to wear, is not Melba at all (echoes of Hitchcock's *Vertigo* [1958]!)—not least because he, unlike the rest of the police, is intimately familiar with Melba's body from their prior heated sexual encounter. The last twelve shots, amounting to the scene's final thirty seconds, then show us Simon running in the direction of where he thinks Melba must have disappeared, soon seeing her walking through the very same arcade passageway through which the female bank clerk in *Glückliche Zeiten* walked—the difference, of course, being that unlike Faber, Simon is closing in on his object of desire, ultimately chasing her down as she exits the arcade (shot 45: fig. 2) and pushing her into a Mercedes in which her guide (Schäfer's accomplice who has been instructing her) has been waiting for her.

Die Sieger, in other words, itinerates what was in *Fahnder* an economically yet fairly leisurely paced scene, ultimately highlighting the fact that Faber underestimated his job of trailing the bank clerk. The "recycled" scene, in contrast, uses the big-screen to its full advantage to depict the enormous power of the police apparatus and the complexity of the orchestration with which Schäfer tries to outfox his former employers. It also functions to emphasize that Simon is in the end not like Faber at all, although both hold similar petit-bourgeois values when shown in their private sphere. Rather, Simon is a superman trained by the special police force, whose professional training, with the crucial help of his privately gained insights (which he came by, in turn, because of the macho sex appeal conferred by his profession, which is clearly what attracted Melba to him in the first place), allows him to both match wits with his immediate opponent, Schäfer, and outdo the assembled police apparatus. He sees through the elaborately staged identity hoax that derives much of its tension and visual effectiveness from how Graf pulls out all the stops of the (genre) trade. So the porthole scene in *Die Sieger* clearly iterates that of *Glückliche Zeiten*; however, in the end this generic recycling of police-film grammar (the chase) becomes a moment of *itineration*, as the newly staged scene is considerably more complex and ends differently, propelling the plot forward and transforming it into a road-chase movie. Even more, it also appears to *speed up* the proceedings, even though they *de facto* take considerably longer to transpire. That is, Graf's masterly, highly professional command of the grammar of the *policier* ends up affectively altering our perception of temporality. Through the scene's complex *découpage*, Graf effects a sensation of time in our minds and bodies that compresses the actual temporal duration constituting this scene to its virtual core.[48] Consequently, viewers not only feel excitement but also are forced to adjust their relation to the possibilities of the genre as based on their exposure to and expectations derived from those provided by the *German* film-production context.

---

[48] For more on the relation of actual and virtual, see Gilles Deleuze, *Cinema 2: The Time-Image*, trans. Hugh Tomlinson and Robert Galeta (Minneapolis: University of Minnesota Press, 1989).

Evidently viewers were not yet ready for the challenge issued by *Die Sieger*—one posed not merely by this scene but also by the overall darkness of the film's tone, which is set right away by the infanticide and is subsequently furthered by the political outlook verbalized for the film as a whole by Melba; by the complexity of the plot that undoubtedly makes it difficult for viewers to follow the events upon first viewing; by the nuanced attention to the action's context, which at times seems to take over from the action itself and thus might test the patience of an audience expecting nothing but a good old action thriller (though Graf would argue that a good old action or police thriller *does* feature such "digressions," which indeed often function as the real heart of such films, rather than constituting mere scenic detours); and also by the film's unresolved, ambiguous ending that leaves us with Simon, who has quit the SEK and is seen back in the fold of his family, possibly (but perhaps not likely) getting ready to testify in a court case Melba wants to initiate in order to publicize the dirty games played by the political status quo. At a moment when in Germany citizens were preoccupied with their *Spaßkultur* while simultaneously being nearly paralyzed by the seemingly never-ending reign of the always optimistic chancellor Helmut Kohl (1982–98), *Die Sieger* was clearly not the right film for its era—perhaps, as Graf believes, ultimately having been too serious to have served as a genre "Folie, die man über die BRD legen kann, um sie besser zu ertragen" (foil that you can lay on top of the BRD in order better to endure it).[49]

Further analysis of *Die Sieger* shows how the film uses the other blueprint moments I mentioned above. For instance, it uses dialogue sequences from *Über dem Abgrund* verbatim, such as the moment when a high-ranking police bureaucrat assures Faber and Simon, respectively: "ich kenne die Biographie meines V-Mannes" (I am familiar with the biography of my V-Man). Noteworthy is that the two identical dialogue moments are visually differentiated ever so slightly: while the camera set-ups essentially perfectly match each other, and while the police bureaucrats could almost be played by the same actor and certainly could have stepped from one film into the other (similar physique, glasses, ties, suits, posture, condescending tone, and camera's attitude towards them), the fact that in *Die Sieger* the shot is a two-shot inevitably puts greater pressure on the mise-en-scène, crowding the frame with, crucially, an additional layer of the state apparatus in the form of the politician who will eventually be abducted.

Consider also how Graf's *Die Sieger* re-stages, and in so doing alters, the scene in which Faber faces his interrogator. In *Fahnder: Über dem Abgrund* the interrogation is staged in the form of a sequence of shot/reverse-shot close-ups of Faber, a slimy DA, and, at the very moment

---

[49] Graf, Hochhäusler, and Petzold, "Mailwechsel," 8.

*Figs. 12.2a and 12.2b. "I know the biography of my
V-Man" from* Über dem Abgrund *and* Die Sieger,
respectively. Screenshots.

*Figs. 12.3a, 12.3b, 12.3c. Shot (Faber); Reverse Shot (the DA); Shot 3
(Faber's boss, Rick, as the witness) in* Über dem Abgrund. *Screenshots.*

when Faber's temper is about to get the better of him, Faber's boss, Rick,
who has been witnessing the testy exchange offscreen. The scene's intensity feeds off Wennemann's acting and the near cliché-like presentation of
a slick, careerist DA (with the scene's witness, Rick, offering comic relief
by virtue of his awkwardly enacted attempt to appease Faber).

Reusing the dialogue between Faber and the DA in *Über dem
Abgrund* almost verbatim, *Die Sieger* transforms the content expressed by
the classically rendered shot/reverse-shot scene into one single image, in
which the smoke-filled interrogation room's icy blue-greens increase the
tension manifest in the spatial arrangement of Simon sitting on the near
right, opposite the other six men in the room. Whereas in *Fahnder* the
level of corruption is by and large kept on the level of a few *individuals*,
which Graf formally foregrounds by using shot/reverse-shot close-ups—
of the police bureaucrat claiming to know the biography of his V-Man
as well as of the DA—in *Die Sieger* Graf makes it clear that corruption

Fig. 12.4. Interrogation of Simon from Die Sieger. *Screenshot.*

now exists on a supra-individual, *systemic* plane, having permeated all levels of the postunified *state itself*—that of the police, the bureaucracy, and the political; this, in fact, is why elections, according to Melba's quip, do indeed not change anything.

This, in the end, is what makes *Die Sieger* one of Graf's most radical films—indeed, one of postunification Germany's most radical films, perhaps matched, in Graf's oeuvre at least, only by *Eine Stadt wird erpresst*, in which Graf refuses to give German television viewers even the mere hint of the possibility of a "happy end," which one may still locate in *Die Sieger*'s ambiguous, open ending. For in *Eine Stadt wird erpresst*, the problem is not even the fact of state corruption as such anymore; rather, the effects of all-pervasive state corruption have now affected life itself to such a degree that dying appears preferable to living in a society in which its constitutive element—that of the social—has been replaced by the coldly calculating forces of neoliberal economic imperatives.

Die Sieger, then, is a made-for-the-big-screen production that ultimately consists of a series of set pieces and staging decisions taken from Graf's prior films made for TV and *Die Katze*. On all levels, that is, *Die Sieger* appeals to the logic of repetition, seriality, and similarity immanent to the notion and functionality of genre; in its deployment of the law of genre, the film, because it assumed its audience's familiarity with these *Versatzstücke* [set pieces] from Graf's own oeuvre, ultimately went beyond its various blueprints, becoming different from them in significant ways—so significantly, apparently, that audiences were alienated by the film and turned it into a box-office failure with consequences that affect the German film industry to this day, in that it continues to refuse to invest in the *systematic* production of *policiers* (or crime films in general). So while *Die Sieger* can be understood as the most significant of the industry's sporadic attempts in the last two decades to reestablish the crime genre as a cinematic form in Germany, it ultimately failed, not just because it might have been too challenging for viewers or out of tune with the *Zeitgeist* but also, as Hochhäusler suggests, because "kein Genre [ist denkbar] ohne Wiederholung, die die Regeln in das öffentliche Bewusstsein einbrennt" (no genre is imaginable without the very repetition that burns the rules [of genre] into public consciousness).[50]

That said, over the course of his career to date, Dominik Graf could still be said to have accomplished the seemingly impossible, at least within the confines of his own oeuvre: to create a genre "neighborhood." That this oeuvre-immanent success has not yet effected a larger scale emergence of German police-genre cinema, indeed of genre filmmaking structures at large, can hardly be held against him. The problem, perhaps, is that German film culture continues to be too hung up on the issue of "legitimacy," which was proudly reintroduced by Werner Herzog in the early 1970s. Graf's relentless demand for genre filmmaking and his affirmation that "Das Schöne beim Genre ist ja, dass Du nicht dauernd Deinen Film legitimieren musst" (The nice thing about genre is that you do not constantly have to legitimize your film)[51] marks his resistance to Germany's *Kunstkino* (art-cinema) tradition. Instead, he stubbornly continues to produce a counter-discourse within the structures of the German film industry. As Petzold argues, Graf makes films that, because they go against the sociopolitical status quo without necessarily mark(et)ing themselves as counter-films, have a difficult time in Germany precisely because they do not derive their identity merely from their oppositional attitude but are, instead, characterized by a certain composure and openness, by a relaxed attitude that gives them the impression of being *aus-dem-Ärmel-geschüttelte* films (films produced casually, just like that)—arguably Graf's aesthetic filmmaking ideal.[52]

Because Graf nevertheless endeavors to produce just such counter-films, he continues paying the price of relative isolation. But judging from his output over the last fifteen years—which reached new heights in the form of *Im Angesicht des Verbrechens* (In the Face of Crime, 2010), his eight-part television series set in the Russian mafia milieu in Berlin—he remains willing to roll the police genre stone up the hill of the amassed history of German cinema, gradually influencing from within it the very question of *legitimate* German cinema. With

---

[50] Graf, Hochhäusler, and Petzold, "Mailwechsel," 10.

[51] Graf, Hochhäusler, and Petzold, "Mailwechsel," 9.

[52] Christian Petzold in an interview with Margrit Fröhlich, "Uns fehlt eine Filmwirtschaft," *epd Film*, Dec. 2009, accessed 13 Dec. 2009, http://www.epd-film.de/33178_69894.php.

each additional film, Graf delineates a counter-genealogy whose virtual potential continues to await its actualization. Given the many gems one can discover in Graf's filmography (which is woefully underrepresented on DVD even in Germany and essentially nonexistent anywhere else), one can only hope the future arrives soon.

Bibliography

Abel, Marco. "'The Cinema of Identification Goes on My Nerves': An Interview with Christian Petzold." *Cineaste* online 33, no. 3 (Summer 2008). http://www.cineaste.com/articles/an-interview-with-christian-petzold.htm.

———. "Failing to Connect: Itinerations of Desire in Oskar Roehler's Post-Romance Films." *New German Critique* 109 (Winter 2010): 75–98.

———. "'I Build a Jigsaw Puzzle of a Dream-Germany': An Interview with German Filmmaker Dominik Graf." *Senses of Cinema* 55 (2010). http://www.sensesofcinema.com/2010/feature-articles/"'i-build-a-jigsaw-puzzle-of-a-dream-germany'-an-interview-with-german-filmmaker-dominik-graf'"-2/.

———. "Intensifying Life: The Cinema of the 'Berlin School.'" *Cineaste* online 33, no. 4 (Fall 2008). http://cineaste.com/articles/the-berlin-school.htm.

Adorno, Theodor W. "Essay as Form." In *Notes to Literature*, vol. 1, translated by Shierry Weber Nicholsen, 3–21. New York: Columbia University Press, 1991.

———. "Transparencies on Film." *New German Critique* 24/25 (1981): 199–205.

Adorno, Theodor W., and Max Horkheimer. *Dialectic of Enlightenment: Philosophical Fragments*. Translated by Edmund Jephcott. Stanford, CA: Stanford University Press, 2002.

Agamben, Giorgio. *State of Exception*. Translated by Kevin Attell. Chicago: University of Chicago Press, 2005.

Aitken, Ian. *Film Reform: John Grierson and the Documentary Film Movement*. London: Routledge, 1990.

Albrecht, Donald. *Designing Dreams: Modern Architecture in the Movies*. New York: Harper & Row, 1986.

Alloway, Lawrence. "On the Iconography of the Movies." *Movie* 7 (1963): 4–6.

Alpi, Deborah Lazaroff. *Robert Siodmak*. Jefferson, NC: McFarland, 1998.

Altenloh, Emilie. *Zur Soziologie des Kinos: Die Kino-Unternehmung und die sozialen Schichten ihrer Besucher*, diss. Heidelberg (Jena: Eugen Diederichs, 1914).

Alter, Nora. "Framing Terrorism: Beyond the Borders." In *Projecting History: German Nonfiction Cinema, 1967–2000*, 43–76 (Ann Arbor: University of Michigan Press, 2002).

———. "Hans Richter in Exile: Translating the Avant-Garde." In *Caught by Politics*, edited by Sabine Eckmann and Lutz Koepnick, 223–43. New York: Palgrave, 2007.

Altman, Rick. *Film/Genre*. 1999. Reprint, London: BFI, 2002.

Andriopoulos, Stefan. *Possessed: Hypnotic Crimes, Corporate Fiction, and the Invention of Cinema*. Translated by Peter Jansen and Stefan Andriopoulos. Chicago: University of Chicago Press, 2008.

Applegate, Celia. *A Nation of Provincials: The German Idea of* Heimat. Berkeley: University of California Press, 1990.

Arnheim, Rudolf. "Escape into the Scenery (1932)." In *Film Essays and Criticism*, 187–89.

———. *Film*. Translated by L. M. Sieveking and Ian F. D. Morrow. London: Faber & Faber, 1933.

———. *Film Essays and Criticism*. Translated by Brenda Benthien. Madison: University of Wisconsin Press, 1997.

———. "Hans Albers (1931)." In *Film Essays and Criticism*.

———. "Partly Expensive, Partly Good (1931)." In *Film Essays and Criticism*.

———. "Sound Film Gone Astray (1932)." In *Film Essays and Criticism*.

Ascheid, Antje. "Safe Rebellions: Romantic Emancipation in the 'Women's Heritage Film.'" *Scope: An Online Journal of Film Studies* (January 2006).

Baer, Hester. "*Das Boot* and the German Cinema of Neoliberalism." *German Quarterly* 85, no. 1 (2012): 18–39.

Balázs, Béla. *Theory of the Film*. Translated by Edith Bone. New York: Dover, 1970. First published in 1945.

Balio, Tino. *History of American Cinema*. Vol. 5, *Grand Design: Hollywood as a Modern Business Enterprise*. New York: Scribner, 1993.

Basinger, Jeanine. *The World War II Combat Film: Anatomy of a Genre*. 1986. Reprint, Middletown, CN: Wesleyan University Press, 2003.

Bazin, André. "The Ontology of the Photographic Image." In *What Is Cinema?*, vol. 1, translated by Hugh Gray, 9–16. Berkeley: University of California Press, 2005.

Beier, Lars-Olaf. "Grauer Alltag, kunterbund," *Der Spiegel*, 2. Jan. 2006, 139.

Belton, John. "Edgar G. Ulmer: A Reassessment." In Belton, *Cinema Stylists*. Metuchen, NJ: Scarecrow, 1983.

Benjamin, Walter. "The Author as Producer." In Benjamin, *Reflections*, edited by Peter Demetz, 220–38. New York: Schocken Books, 1986.

———. "The Task of the Translator." In *Illuminations*, translated by Harry Zohn, edited by Hannah Arendt, 69–82. New York: Schocken Books, 1969.

Bergfelder, Tim. "Exotic Thrills and Bedroom Manuals: West German B-Film Production in the 1960s." In *Light Motives: German Popular Film in Perspective*, edited by Randall Halle and Margaret McCarthy, 197–219. Detroit: Wayne State University Press, 2003.

———. "Extraterratorial Fantasies: Edgar Wallace and the German Crime Film." In Bergfelder, Carter, and Göktürk, *The German Cinema Book*.

———. *International Adventures—German Popular Cinema and European Co-productions in the 1960s*. New York: Berghahn Books, 2005.

Bergfelder, Tim, Erica Carter, and Deniz Göktürk, eds. *The German Cinema Book*. London: British Film Institute, 2002.

Berghahn, Daniela. "The Re-evaluation of Goethe and the Classical Tradition in the Films of Egon Günther and Siegfried Kühn." In *Defa East German Cinema, 1946–1992*, edited by Seán Allen and John Sandford, 222–44. 2001. Reprint, New York: Berghahn Books, 2006.

Biess, Frank. *Homecomings: Returning POWs and the Legacies of Defeat in Postwar Germany*. Princeton, NJ: Princeton University Press, 2006.

Bleibtreu, Moritz, and Oliver Hirschbiegel. "Das Interview," with Carlo Cavagna. http://www.aboutfilm.com/features/dasexperiment/interview.htm.

Blickle, Peter. *Heimat: A Critical Theory of the German Idea of Homeland*. Rochester, NY: Camden House, 2002.

Bloch, Ernst. *Erbschaft dieser Zeit*. Zurich: Oprecht & Helbling, 1935; In English, *Heritage of Our Times*, translated by Neville Plaice and Stephen Plaice. Berkeley: University of California Press, 1991.

Blümlinger, Christa, and Constantin Wulff, eds. *Schreiben Bilder Sprechen: Texte zum essayistischen Film*. Vienna: Sonderzahl, 1992.

Boa, Elizabeth, and Rachel Palfreyman. *Heimat—a German Dream: Regional Loyalties and National Identity in German Culture, 1890–1990*. Oxford: Oxford University Press, 2000.

Bordwell, David. *Narration in Fiction Film*. London: Methuen, 1985.

———. *The Way Hollywood Tells It: Story and Style in Modern Movies*. Berkeley: University of California Press, 2006.

Bourget, Jean-Loup. "Social Implications in the Hollywood Genres." *Journal of Modern Literature* 3 (1973).

Braun, Jutta, and René Wiese. "DDR-Fußball und gesamtdeutsche Identität im Kalten Krieg." *Historical Social Research* 30 (2005): 191–210.

Brockmann, Stephen. *A Critical History of German Film*. Rochester, NY: Camden House, 2010.

Brook, Peter. *The Melodramatic Imagination: Balzac, Henry James, Melodrama and the Mode of Excess*. New Haven, CT: Yale University Press, 1995.

Brown, Wendy. "Untimeliness and Punctuality: Critical Theory in Dark Times." In *Edgework: Critical Essays on Knowledge and Politics*, 1–16. Princeton, NJ: Princeton University Press, 2005.

Browne, Nick, ed. *Refiguring American Film Genres*. Berkeley: University of California Press, 1989.

Burch, Noël. *Theory of Film Practice*. New York: Praeger, 1973.

Buscombe, Edward. "The Idea of Genre in the American Cinema." *Screen* 2, no. 2 (March-April 1970): 30–45.

Buß, Christian. "'Sommer vorm Balkon': Wo der Mülltonnen-Duft verfliegt." *Spiegel Online*—Nachrichten—Kultur, 29 December 2009, 5:34 p.m. http://www.spiegel.de/kultur/kino/0,1518,druck-393291,00.html.

Caldwell, John Thornton. *Production Culture: Industrial Reflexivity and Critical Practice in Film and Television*. Durham, NC: Duke University Press, 2008.

Carter, Erica. "Men in Cardigans: *Canaris* (1954) and the 1950s West German Good Soldier." In *War-Torn Tales: Representing Gender and World War II in Literature and Film,* edited by Danielle Hipkins and Gill Plain, 5–29. Oxford: Peter Lang, 2007.

Cawelti, John G. *Adventure, Mystery and Romance: Formula Stories as Art and Popular Culture.* Chicago: University of Chicago Press, 1976.

———. "Chinatown and Generic Transformation in Recent American Film." In Grant, *Film Genre Reader III,* 243–61.

———. *Mystery, Violence & Popular Culture.* Madison: University of Wisconsin Press, 2004.

Clarens, Carlos. "Doubles, Demons, and the Devil Himself: Germany, 1913–1932." In Carlos Clarens, *An Illustrated History of Horror and Science Fiction Films,* 9–36. New York: Da Capo, 1967.

Confino, Alon. *The Nation as a Local Metaphor: Württemberg, Imperial Germany, and National Memory, 1871–1918.* Chapel Hill: University of North Carolina Press, 1997.

Confino, Alon, and Peter Fritzsche, eds. *The Work of Memory: New Directions in the Study of German Society and Culture.* Urbana: University of Illinois Press, 2002.

Cooke, Paul. *Representing East Germany: From Colonization to Nostalgia.* Oxford: Berg, 2005.

Corrigan, Timothy, and Patricia White, with Meta Mazaj. *Critical Visions in Film Theory: Classic and Contemporary Readings.* Boston: Bedford/St. Martin's, 2010.

Crowther, Bosley. "Phantom Lady: A Melodrama of Weird Effects, with Ella Raines and Franchot Tone, has Premiere at Loew's State." *New York Times,* 18 Feb. 1944.

Davidson, John, and Sabine Hake. *Framing the Fifties: Fifties Cinema in a Divided Germany.* New York: Berghahn Books, 2007.

Deleuze, Gilles. *Cinema 2: The Time-Image.* London: Continuum, 1989.

Deleuze, Gilles, and Félix Guattari, *A Thousand Plateaus: Capitalism and Schizophrenia.* Translated by Brian Massumi. Minneapolis: University of Minnesota Press, 1987.

Derrida, Jacques. "The Law of Genre." Translated by Avital Ronell. *Critical Inquiry* 7, no. 1 (Autumn 1980): 55–81.

Dillmann, Claudia. "Die Wirkung der Architektur ist eine magische: Hans Poelzig und der Film." In *Hans Poelzig: Bauten für den Film,* 20–75. Frankfurt am Main: Deutsches Filmmuseum, 1997.

Dimendberg, Edward. "Down These Seen Streets a Man Must Go: Siegfried Kracauer, 'Hollywood's Terror Films,' and the Spatiality of Film Noir." *New German Critique* 89 (2003): 113–43.

"Dr. Mabuse." *Der Film* 7, no. 18 (30 Apr. 1922).

Dreßlein, Detlef, and Anne Lehwald. *Bernd Eichinger: Die Biografie.* Munich: Heyne, 2011.

Duggan, Lisa. *The Twilight of Equality?: Neoliberalism, Cultural Politics, and the Attack on Democracy.* Boston: Beacon, 2003.

Dyer, Richard, and Ginette Vincendeau, eds. *Popular European Cinema*. New York: Routledge, 1992.

Edwards, Kyle. "Brand-Name Literature: Film Adaptation and Selznick International Pictures' *Rebecca* (1940)." *Cinema Journal* 45, no. 3 (2006): 32–58.

Eggeling, Viking, and Hans Richter. *Universelle Sprache*. Fort in der Lausitz, Germany: Eigenverlag, 1920.

Ehrenburg, Ilje. *Die Traumfabrik: Chronik des Films / The Dream Factory*. Berlin: Malik, 1931.

Eisenschitz, Bernard, and Jean-Claude Romer. "Entretien avec Edgar G. Ulmer." *Midi-Minuit Fantastique* 13 (1965): 1–14.

Eisner, Lotte H. *The Haunted Screen: Expressionism in the German Cinema and the Influence of Max Reinhardt*. Translated by Roger Greaves. Berkeley: University of California Press, 1973.

Elsaesser, Thomas. *Fassbinder's Germany: History Identity Subject*. Amsterdam: University of Amsterdam Press, 1996.

———. "Film History and Visual Pleasure." In *Cinema Histories, Cinema Practices*, edited by Patricia Mellencamp and Philip Rosen (Frederick, MD: University Publications of America, 1984).

———. "It's the End of the Song: Walter Reisch, Operetta, and the Double Negative." In Elsaesser, *Weimar Cinema and After: Germany's Historical Imaginary*, 330–58.

———. *New German Cinema*. Basingstoke, UK: Macmillan, 1989.

———. *Weimar Cinema and After: Germany's Historical Imaginary*. London: Routledge, 2000.

Elsaesser, Thomas, and Michael Wedel, eds. *The BFI Companion to German Cinema*. London: BFI, 1999.

Evans, Peter William. "Meg Ryan, Megastar." In *Terms of Endearment: Hollywood Romantic Comedy of the 1980s and 1990s*, edited by Peter William Evans and Celestino Deleyto, 188–208. Edinburgh: Edinburgh University Press, 1998).

Everson, William K. *Classics of the Horror Film*. Seacaucus, NJ: Citadell, 1974.

F., Christiane. *Wir Kinder vom Bahnhof Zoo: Nach Tonbandprotokollen aufgeschrieben von Kai Hermann und Horst Rieck*. 1978. Reprint, Hamburg: Carlsen Verlag, 2010.

Fehrenbach, Heide. *Cinema in Democratizing Germany: Reconstructing National Identity after Hitler*. Chapel Hill: University of North Carolina Press, 1995.

———. "Rehabilitating Fatherland: Race and German Remasculinization." *Signs* 24 (1998): 107–28.

Festenberg, Nikolaus von. "Die neue Alm." *Der Spiegel*, 30 July 2007, 136–37.

F. H. "Langfristig für den deutschen Film." Interview with Bernd Eichinger. *Filmreport* 1+2 (1979): n.p.

"Film Criticized as Irresponsible." *Monitor on Psychology* 33, no. 3 (March 2002): 20.

Fisher, Jaimey. *Disciplining Germany: Youth, Reconstruction, and Reeducation after the Second World War*. Detroit: Wayne State, 2007.

———. "Landscapes of Death: Space and the Mobilization Genre in G. W. Pabst's *Westfront 1918* (1930)" In *The Many Faces of Weimar Cinema: Rediscovering Germany's Filmic Legacy*, edited by Christian Rogowski, 268–85. Rochester, NY: Camden House, 2010.

———. "Who's Watching the Rubble-Kids? Youth, Pedagogy and Politics in Early DEFA Films." *New German Critique* 82 (Winter 2001): 91–125.

Foucault, Michel. "Of Other Spaces." *Diacritics* 16, no. 1 (Spring 1986): 22–27.

Frei, Norbert. *1945 und wir*. Munich: C. H. Beck, 2005.

———. *Vergangenheitspolitik: Die Anfänge der Bundesrepublik und die NS-Vergangenheit*. Munich: DTV, 2003.

Fritzsche, Sonja. "A Natural and Artificial Homeland: East German Science-Fiction Film Responds to Kubrick and Tarkovsky." *Film & History* 40, no. 2 (2010): 80–101.

———. *Science Fiction Literature in East Germany*. Oxford: Peter Lang, 2006.

Fülöp-Miller, René. *Die Phantasiemaschine / The Fantasy Machine*. Berlin: Zsolnay, 1931.

Gallagher, Tag,."All Lost in Wonder: Edgar G. Ulmer." In *Screening the Past* (March 2001). http://www.latrobe.edu.au/screeningthepast/firstrelease/fr0301/tgafr12a.htm.

Gansera, Rainer. "'Ich versuche, die Luft zu filmen': Begegnungen mit dem Regisseur Dominik Graf." Accessed 29 November 2009. http://www.kath-akademie-bayern.de/contentserv/www.katholische.de/index.php?StoryID=427.

Garwood, Ian. "The *Autorenfilm* in Contemporary German Cinema." In Bergfelder, Carter, and Göktürk, *The German Cinema Book*, 202–10.

Gemünden, Gerd. *A Foreign Affair: Billy Wilder's American Films*. New York: Berghahn, 2008.

Geraghty, Lincoln, and Mark Jancovich. "Introduction: Generic Canons." In *The Shifting Definitions of Genre*, edited by Lincoln Geraghty and Mark Jancovich, 1–12. Jefferson, NC: McFarland, 2008.

"Gespräch mit Oliver Hirschbiegel." *EPD Film* 3 (2001). http://www.epd-film.de/.

Gill, Rosalind. *Gender and the Media*. Cambridge: Polity, 2007.

Goergen, Jeanpaul, ed. *Walter Ruttmann: Eine Dokumentation*. Berlin: Freunde der Deutschen Kinemathek, 1990.

Graf, Dominik. "Interview mit Christoph Fromm." *Vierundzwanzig.de: Das Wissensportal der Deutschen Filmakademie*. Accessed 20 November 2009. www.vierundzwanzig.de/drehbuch/interview_mit_christoph_fromm,

———. Interview mit Martin Farkas. *Revolver* 7 (September 2002): 10–31.

———. *Schläft ein Lied in allen Dingen: Texte zum Film* (Berlin: Alexander Verlag, 2009).

———. "Unerlebte Filme." *Schnitt* 43 (2006): 62–65.

———. "Der Weg, den wir nicht zusammen gehen." Presseheft *Deutschland 09.* Accessed 1 December 2009. http://deutschland09-der-film.de/downloads.

Graf, Dominik, Christoph Hochhäusler, and Christian Petzold. "Mailwechsel." *Revolver* 16 (2007): 7–39.

Grant, Barry Keith, ed. *Film Genre Reader III.* Austin: University of Texas Press, 2003.

Grissemann, Stefan. *Mann im Schatten.* Vienna: Paul Zsonlay, 2003.

Grolle, Johann von, Philip Betghe, Markus Dettmer, Konstantin von Hammerstein, Susanne Koelbl, Johannes Saltzwedel, Klaus Umbach, Alfred Weinzierl, MarianneWellershoff, and Peter Wensierski. "Im Rausch der Macht." *Der Spiegel,* 12 March 2001.

Gunning, Tom. "Fritz Lang's *Dr. Mabuse, the Gambler* (1922): Grand Enunciator of the Weimar Era." In *An Essential Guide to Classic Films of the Era: Weimar Cinema,* edited by Noah Isenberg, 95–114. New York: Columbia University Press, 2009.

———. "Mabuse, Grand Enunciator: Control and Co-ordination." In *The Films of Fritz Lang,* 87–116. London, BFI: 2000.

Haase, Christine. *When Heimat Meets Hollywood: German Filmmakers and America, 1985–2005.* Rochester, NY: Camden House, 2007.

Haffner, Helmut. "Das Nein zum Krieg: Uraufführung des Films 'Die Brucke' von Bernhard Wicki." *8 Uhr Blatt,* 23 Oct. 1959.

Hahn, Ronald, and Rolf Giesen. *Lexikon des Horrorfilms.* Mülheim, Germany: Luebbe, 1993.

Hake, Sabine. *German National Cinema.* London: Routledge, 2002.

Halle, Randall. "Chainsaws and Neo-Nazis: Contemporary German Horror Film Production," *GFL: German as a Foreign Language* 3 (2006): 40–61.

———. "German Film, European Film: Transnational Production, Distribution, and Reception." *Screen* 47 (2006): 251–61.

———. *German Film after Germany: Towards a Transnational Aesthetic.* Chicago: University of Illinois Press, 2008.

———. "Unification Horror: Queer Desire and Uncanny Visions." In Halle and McCarthy, *Light Motives: German Popular Film in Perspective,* 281–303.

Halle, Randall, and Margaret McCarthy, eds. *Light Motives: German Popular Film in Perspective.* Detroit: Wayne State University Press, 2003.

Hansen, Miriam. "Early Silent Cinema: Whose Public Sphere?" *New German Critique* 29 (Spring 1983): 147–84.

———. Introduction to Kracauer, *Theory of Film,* vii–xlvi.

Hansen, Miriam, Karsten Witte, J. Hoberman, Thomas Elsaesser, Gertrud Koch, Friedrich P. Kahlenberg, Klaus Kreimeier, and Heide Schlüpmann. "Dossier on *Heimat.*" *New German Critique* 36 (1985): 3–24.

Hantke, Steffen, ed. *Caligari's Heirs: The German Cinema of Fear after 1945.* Lanham, MD: Scarecrow, 2007.

———. "Hollywood Horror Comes to Berlin: A Critical Reassment of Robert Siodmak's *Nachts wenn der Teufel kam.*" In Hantke, *Caligari's Heirs: The German Cinema of Fear after 1945,* 37–54.

————. "The Origins of Violence in a Peaceful Society." May 2003. http://www.kinoeye.org/03/06/hantke06.php.

————. "Postwar German Cinema and the Horror Film: Thoughts on Historical Continuity and Genre Consolidation," In Hantke, *Caligari's Heirs: The German Cinema of Fear after 1945*, vii–xxiv.

Heineman, Elizabeth. "The Hour of the Woman: Memories of Germany's 'Crisis Years' and West German National Identity." *American Historical Review* (1996): 354–95.

Hembus, Joe. *Der deutsche Film kann gar nicht besser sein*. Bremen: Carl Schünemann Verlag, 1961.

Herzog, Todd. "Crime Stories: Criminal, Society, and the Modernist Case History." *Representations* 80 (2002): 34–61.

Herzogenrath, Bernhard. *Edgar G. Ulmer: Essays on the King of B's*, edited by Bernd Herzogenrath. Jefferson, NC: McFarland, 2009.

————, ed. "Ulmer and Cult/ure." In *Edgar G. Ulmer: Essays on the King of B's*.

Hickethier, Knut. "The Restructuring of the West German Film Industry in the 1950s." In *Framing the Fifties: Fifties Cinema in Divided Germany*, edited by John Davidson and Sabine Hake, 194–209. New York: Berghahn Books, 2007.

Higson, Andrew. *English Heritage, English Cinema*. Oxford: Oxford University Press, 2003.

Hirschborn, Clive. *The Universal Story*. New York: Crown, 1983.

Horak, Jan-Christopher. "German Film Comedy." In Bergfelder, Carter, and Göktürk, *The German Cinema Book*, 29–38.

Hutcheon, Linda. *A Theory of Adaptation*. New York: Routledge, 2006.

Iljine, Diana, and Klaus Keil. *Der Produzent: Das Berufsbild des Film- und Fernsehproduzenten in Deutschland*. 1997. Reprint, Munich: TR-Verlagsunion, 2000.

Jancovich, Mark. Horror: *The Film Reader*. London: Routledge, 2002.

————. "Master of Concentrated Suspense," *Studies in European Cinema* 5, no. 3 (2008): 171–72.

Jaspers, Karl. *Die geistige Situation der Zeit* (Berlin: de Gruyter, 1931). In English, *Man in the Modern Age*, translated by Eden Paul and Cedar Paul. New York: Anchor, 1957.

Joglekar, Yogini. "Helmut Käutner's *Epilog: Das Geheimnis der Orplid* and the West German Detective Film of the 1950s." In *Take Two—Fifties Cinema in Divided Germany*, edited by John Davidson and Sabine Hake, 63. New York: Berghahn Books, 2007.

Kaes, Anton. "Film in der Weimarer Republik: Motor der Moderne." In *Geschichte des deutschen Films*, edited by Wolfgang Jacobsen, 2nd rev. ed., 39–98. Stuttgart: Metzler, 2004.

————. *From Heimat to Hitler: The Return of History as Film*. Cambridge, MA: Harvard University Press, 1989.

————, ed. *Kino-Debatte: Texte zum Verhältnis von Literatur und Film, 1909–1929*. Munich: DTV, 1978.

————. *Shell Shock Cinema: Weimar Culture and the Wounds of War.* Princeton, NJ: Princeton University Press, 2009.

Kapczynski, Jennifer M. "Armchair Warriors: Heroic Postures in the West German War Film." In *Screening War: Perspectives on German Suffering*, edited by Paul Cooke and Marc Silberman, 17–35. Rochester, NY: Camden House, 2010.

Kaplan, Caren. "Precision Targets: GPS and the Militarization of U.S. Consumer Identity." *American Quarterly* 58, no. 3 (2006): 693–714.

Kasten, Jürgen. *Der expressionistische Film: Abgefilmtes Theater oder avantgardistisches Erzählkino? Eine stil-, produktions-, und rezeptionsgeschichtliche Untersuchung* (Münster: MAkS, 1990).

Kawin, Bruce. "The Mummy's Pool." In *Planks of Reason: Essays on the Horror Film*, edited by Barry Keith Grant, 3–20. Metuchen, NJ: Scarecrow, 1984.

King, Claire Sisco. "Imaging the Abject: The Ideological Use of the Dissolve." In *Horror Film: Creating and Marketing Fear*, edited by Steffen Hantke, 21–34. Jackson: University Press of Mississippi, 2004.

Kitses, Jim. *Horizons West.* London: Thames & Hudson, 1969.

Kittel, Manfred. *Legende von der "zweiten Schuld": Die Vergangenheitsbewältigung in der Ära Adenauer.* Berlin: Ullstein, 1993.

Knörer, Ekkehard. "Fighter im System: Dominik Graf im Gespräch." Accessed 14 December 2009. http://www.cargo-film.de/artikel/fighter-im-system-dominik-graf-im-gesprach-teil-1/.

Koch, Gertrud. *Siegfried Kracauer: An Introduction.* Translated by Jeremy Gaines. Princeton, NJ: Princeton University Press, 2000.

Koebner, Thomas, ed. *Diesseits der "Dämonischen Leinwand": Neue Perspektiven auf das späte Weimarer Kino.* Munich: edition text + kritik, 2003.

Koepnick, Lutz. "Mad Love: Re-Membering Berlin in Hollywood Exile." In *Caught By Politics: Hitler Exiles and American Visual Culture*, edited by Sabine Eckmann and Lutz Koepnick, 195–222. New York: Palgrave MacMillan, 2007.

————. "Screening Fascism's Underground: Kurt Bernhardt's *The Tunnel*," *New German Critique* 74 (Spring/Summer 1998): 151–78.

Körte, Peter. "Verstörte Helden der inneren Sicherheit: Zu Dominik Grafs Film *Die Sieger*." In *Dominik Graf, Verstörung im Kino: Der Regisseur von* Die Sieger *im Gespräch mit Stefan Stosch über die Arbeit am Film*, 5–10. Hanover: Werhahn Verlag, 1998.

Kozarski, Richard. *An Evening's Entertainment: The Age of the Silent Feature Picture, 1915–1928.* New York: Scribner, 1990.

Kracauer, Siegfried. "Cult of Distraction: On Berlin's Picture Palaces." In *The Mass Ornament: Weimar Essays*, translated and edited by Thomas Y. Levin. Cambridge, MA: Harvard University Press, 1995.

————. *Der Detektiv-Roman—ein philosophischer Traktat.* Frankfurt am Main: Suhrkamp, 1979.

————. *From Caligari to Hitler: A Psychological History of German Film.* 1947. Reprint, Princeton, NJ: Princeton University Press, 2004.

————. "Photography." In *The Mass Ornament*, edited and translated by Thomas Y. Levin, 47–63. Cambridge, MA: Harvard University Press, 1995.

————. *Theory of Film*. Oxford: Oxford University Press, 1960.

Kramp, Joachim. *Hallo! Hier spricht Edgar Wallace—Die Geschichte der legendären deutschen Kriminalfilmserie von 1959–1972*. Berlin: Schwarzkopf & Schwarzkopf Verlag, 1997.

Kraus, Karl. *Erlaubt ist, was missfällt: Karl Kraus zum Vergnügen*. Edited by Günter Baumann. Ditzingen, Germany: Reclam, 2007.

Kreimeier, Klaus. *Die Ufa-Story: Geschichte eines Filmkonzerns*. Munich: Hanser, 1992.

Lang, Fritz. "Kitsch—Sensation—Kultur und Film." In *Fritz Lang—Die Stimme von Metropolis*, edited by Fred Gehler and Ullrich Kasten, 202–6. Berlin: Henschel, 1990.

Langford, Barry. *Film Genre: Hollywood and Beyond*. Edinburgh: Edinburgh University Press, 2005.

Lenning, Arthur. *The Count: The Life and Films of Bela "Dracula" Lugosi*. New York: G. P. Putnam's Sons, 1974.

Leyda, Jay. *Films Beget Films*. London: George Allen & Unwin, 1964.

Lewis, Sinclair. *It Can't Happen Here*. New York: Signet, 2005.

"Lorbeer für die Wunderkinder." *Der Spiegel*, 17 November 1975, 182–92.

Ludewig, Alexandra. *Screening Nostalgia: 100 Years of Heimat Film*. Bielefeld: transcript, 2011).

"Luftzug aus dem Jenseits." *Der Spiegel*, 30 Nov. 1960.

Lukacs, Georg. "On the Nature and Form of the Essay (1910)." In *Soul and Form*, 1–18. Cambridge, MA: MIT Press, 1980.

Maase, Kaspar. *Bravo Amerika: Erkundungen zur Jugendkultur der Bundesrepublik in den fünfziger Jahren*. Hamburg: Junius Verlag, 2000.

MacCormack, Patricia. "Necrosexuality, Perversion, and *Jouissance*: The Experimental Desires of Jörg Buttgereit's *NekRomantik* Films." In Hantke, *Caligari's Heirs: The German Cinema of Fear after 1945*, 199–215.

Maland, Charles. "'Film Gris': Crime, Critique and Cold War Culture 1951." *Film Criticism* 26, no. 3 (2002): 1–30.

Mandell, Paul. "Edgar Ulmer and *The Black Cat*." *American Cinematographer* (October 1984): 34–47.

Mank, Gregory William. *Karloff and Lugosi: The Story of a Haunting Collaboration*. Jefferson, NC: McFarland, 1990.

Marker, Chris. "Croix de bois et chemin de fer." *Esprit* 175 (January 1951): 88–90.

Marston, Sallie. "The Social Construction of Scale." *Progress in Human Geography* 24, no. 2 (2000): 219–42.

Matthews, J. B., and R. E. Shallcross. "Must America Go Fascist?" *Harpers Magazine*, June 1934, 1–15.

McArthur, Colin. *Underworld USA*. London: Secker & Warburg, 1972.

Metz, Christian. *Language and Cinema*. New York: Praeger, 1975.

Miller, Toby, Nitin Govil, John McMurria, and Richard Maxwell. *Global Hollywood*. London: bfi, 2001.

Modleski, Tania. *Feminism without Women: Culture and Criticism in a "Post-Feminist Age."* New York: Routledge, 1991.

Moeller, Robert. "The Politics of the Past in the 1950s: Rhetorics of Victimisation in East and West Germany." In Niven, *Germans as Victims: Remembering the Past in Contemporary Germany*, 26–42.

———. "Victims in Uniform: West German Combat Movies from the 1950s." In Niven, *Germans as Victims*, 43–61.

———. *War Stories: The Search for a Usable Past in the Federal Republic of Germany*. Berkeley: University of California Press, 2001.

Moine, Raphaëlle. *Cinema Genre*. Translated by Alistair Fox and Hilary Radner. Oxford: Blackwell, 2008.

Moltke, Johannes von. *No Place like Home: Locations of* Heimat *in German Cinema*. Berkeley: University of California Press, 2005.

Müller, Corinna. *Vom Stummfilm zum Tonfilm*. Munich: Fink, 2003.

Naremore, James. *More Than Night: Film Noir and Its Contexts*. Berkeley: University of California Press, 1998.

Naughton, Leonie. *That Was the Wild East: Film Culture, Unification, and the "New" Germany*. Ann Arbor: University of Michigan Press, 2002.

Neale, Steve. *Genre*. London: BFI, 1980.

———. *Genre and Hollywood*. 1999. Reprint, New York: Routledge, 2000.

Negra, Diane. "Structural Integrity, Historical Reversion, and the Post-9/11 Chick Flick." *Feminist Media Studies* 8, no. 1 (2008): 51–68.

"Nekromantik (1987)." Accessed 8 November 2009. www.stomptokyo. com/otf/Nekro/Nekro.htm.

Neumann, Andreas. *Sir John jagd den Hexer—Siegfried Schürenberg und die Edgar-Wallace-Filme*. Berlin: Schwarzkopf & Schwarzkopf, 2005.

Nicodemus, Katja. "Film der neunziger Jahre: Neues Sein und altes Bewußtsein." In *Geschichte des deutschen Films*, edited by Wolfgang Jacobsen, Anton Kaes, and Hans Helmut Prinzler, 2nd ed., 219–356. Stuttgart: J. B. Metzler, 2004.

Niven, Bill, ed. *Germans as Victims: Remembering the Past in Contemporary Germany*. Basingstoke, UK: Palgrave Macmillan, 2006.

O'Brien, Charles. "Film Noir in France: Before the Liberation." *iris* 21 (Spring 1996): 7–20.

Palfreyman, Rachel. "Links and Chains: Trauma between the Generations in the Heimat Mode." In *Screening War: Perspectives on German Suffering*, edited by Paul Cooke and Marc Silberman, 145–64. Rochester, NY: Camden House, 2010.

———. "Once upon a Time in the Critical Heimat Film." In *German Monitor: Local/Global Narratives*, edited by Renate Rechtien and Karoline von Oppen, 39–61. Amsterdam: Rodopi, 2007.

Pauer, Florian. *Die Edgar Wallace-Filme*. Munich: Wilhelm Goldmann Verlag, 1982.

"Wolfgang Petersen: Eichinger war ein Freund." Accessed 21 June 2011. http://www.dw.de/wolfgang-petersen-eichinger-war-ein-freund/a-6420125.

Petzold, Christian. Interview with Felix von Boehm and Sebastian Seidler, "Wenn das Kino zu spät kommt." *Schnitt* online. Accessed 1 December 2009. http://www.schnitt.de/233,5392,01.

———. Interview with Margrit Fröhlich, "Uns fehlt eine Filmwirtschaft." *epd Film* Dec. 2009. Accessed 13 December 2009. http://www.epd-film.de/33178_69894.php.

Pinthus, Kurt. "The World of Dr. Mabuse," *Das Tage-Buch*, 6 May 1922. Quoted in *Fritz Lang: Leben und Werk; Bilder und Dokumente*, edited by Rolf Aurich, Wolfgang Jacobsen, and Cornelius Schnauber. Berlin: Jovis, 2001.

Pletz, Sandy. *Die Phänomene Heimatfilme und Volksmusiksendungen in Deutschland*. Saarbrücken: VDM, 2008.

Poe, Edgar Allan. *Selected Writings*. Baltimore: Penguin, 1967.

Poiger, Ute. *Jazz, Rock, and Rebels: Cold War Politics and American Culture in a Divided Germany*. Berkeley: University of California Press, 2000.

Polan, Dana. "*Detour*'s History/History's *Detour*." In Herzogenrath, *Edgar G. Ulmer: Essays on the King of B's*, 137–49.

Prager, Brad. "The Haunted Screen (Again): The Historical Unconscious of Contemporary German Thrillers." In *Victims and Perpetrators: 1933–1945 and Beyond; (Re)Presenting the Past in Post-Unification Culture*, edited by Laurel Cohen-Pfister and Dagmar Wienroder-Skinner, 296–315. Berlin: Walter de Gruyter, 2006.

Prawer, S. S. *Caligari's Children: The Film as Tale of Terror*. Oxford: Oxford University Press, 1980.

Rauch, Andreas M. *Bernd Eichinger und seine Filme*. Frankfurt am Main: Haag + Herchen, 2000.

Ree, A. L. "Foreword." In Richter, *The Struggle for the Film: Towards a Socially Responsible Cinema*, 3–10.

Reimer, Robert C., and Carol J. Reimer. *A Historical Dictionary of German Cinema*. Lanham, MD: Scarecrow, 2008.

Rentschler, Eric. "Adaptations in German Film History: A Basic Guide (1913–1985)." In *German Film & Literature: Adaptations and Transformations*, edited by Rentschler, 336–65. New York: Methuen, 1986.

———. "From New German Cinema to the Post-Wall Cinema of Consensus." In *Cinema and Nation*, edited by Mette Hjort and Scott Mackenzie, 260–77. New York: Routledge, 2000.

———. *The Ministry of Illusion: Nazi Cinema and Its Afterlife*. Cambridge, MA: Harvard University Press, 1996.

———. "Postwall Prospects: An Introduction." *New German Critique* 87 (2002): 3–5.

———. "Remembering Not to Forget: A Retrospective Reading of Kluge's *Brutality in Stone*." Special issue on Alexander Kluge, *New German Critique* 49 (Winter 1990): 23–41.

Richter, Hans. "Der Filmessay: Eine neue Form des Dokumentarfilms." In Blümlinger and Wulff, *Schreiben Bilder Sprechen: Texte zum essayistischen Film*, 195–98.

———. "Film von morgen." In *Hans Richter: Film ist Rhythmus*, edited by Ulrich Gregor, special issue of *Kinemathek* 95 (July 2003).

———. *The Struggle for the Film: Towards a Socially Responsible Cinema.* Translated by Ben Brewster. Edited by Jürgen Römhild. New York: St. Martin's, 1986.

Riess, Curt. *Das gab's nur einmal: Das Buch der schönsten Filme unseres Lebens.* 2nd ed. Hamburg: Verlag der Sternbücher, 1957.

Rosar, William H. "Music for the Monsters: Universal Pictures' Horror Film Scores of the Thirties." *Quarterly Journal of the Library of Congress* 40, no. 4 (1983): 391–421.

Ruttmann, Walter. "Kunst und Kino." In Goergen, *Walter Ruttmann: Eine Dokumentation*, 73.

———. "Malerei mit Zeit." In Goergen, *Walter Ruttmann: Eine Dokumentation*, 74.

Ryan, Michael, and Douglas Kellner. "Technophobia." In *Alien Zone*, edited by Annette Kuhn, 58–65. London: Verso, 1990.

Sahl, Hans. "Zapfenstreich bei der Ufa." In *"Und doch . . ." Essays und Kritiken aus zwei Kontinenten*, edited by Klaus Blanc. Frankfurt am Main: Luchterhand, 1991.

Said, Edward. "Reflections on Exile." In *Altogether Elsewhere: Writers on Exile*, edited by Marc Robinson, 137–49. New York: Harcourt Brace, 1994.

Saint-Amour, Paul. "Airwar Prophecy and Interwar Modernism." *Comparative Literature Studies* 42, no. 2 (2005): 130–60.

Sarris, Andrew. *The American Cinema: Directors and Directions, 1929–1968.* New York: Dutton, 1968.

Schatz, Thomas. *Hollywood Genres: Formulas, Filmmaking and the Studio System.* New York: McGraw-Hill, 1981.

Schiele, Siegfried, ed. *Deutschland wächst zusammen: Eine Zwischenbilanz nach zehn Jahren.* Stuttgart: Landeszentrale für politische Bildung Baden-Württemberg, 2000.

Schissler, Hanna, ed. *The Miracle Years: A Cultural History of West Germany, 1949–1968.* Princeton, NJ: Princeton University Press, 2001.

Schivelbusch, Wolfgang. *Railway Journey: The Industrialization of Time and Space in the 19th Century.* Berkeley: University of California Press, 1986.

Schmitt, Carl. *Political Theology: Four Chapters on the Concept of Sovereignty.* Translated by George Schwab. Cambridge, MA: MIT, 1985.

Scholz, Anne-Marie. "The *Bridge on the River Kwai* (1957) Revisited: Combat Cinema, American Culture and the German Past." *German History* 26, no. 2 (2008): 219–50.

Schweiger, Til. "Ist doch nur ein Film." Interview with Til Schweiger, by Lars-Olav Beier und Wolfgang Höbel. *Der Spiegel*, 30 November 2009.

Schweinitz, Jörg. "'Wie im Kino!': Die autothematische Welle im frühen Tonfilm." In Koebner, *Diesseits der "Dämonischen Leinwand": Neue Perspektiven auf das späte Weimarer Kino,* 373–92.

Sconce, Jeffrey. "Irony, Nihilism and the New American 'Smart' Film," *Screen* 43, no. 4 (Winter 2002): 349–69.

———. "'Trashing' the Academy: Taste, Excess, and an Emerging Politics of Cinematic Style." *Screen* 36, no. 4 (1995): 371–93.

Seeßlen, Georg. "Edgar Wallace—Made in Germany." *epd Film* 6 (1986). http://www.filmzentrale.com/rezis/edgarwallacegs.htm.

———. "Das Unterhaltungskino II: Das Spiel mit der Liebe—Aspekte der deutschen Stummfilmkomödie." In *Die Perfektionierung des Scheins: Das Kino der Weimarer Republik im Kontext der Künste,* edited by Harro Segeberg, 95–96. Munich: Fink, 2000.

Silverman, Kaja, and Harun Farocki. *Speaking about Godard.* New York: NYU Press, 1998.

Simpson, Philip, Andrew Utterson, and K. J. Shepherdson, eds. *Film Theory: Critical Concepts in Media and Cultural Studies,* 4 vols. London: Routledge, 2003.

Slocum, J. David, ed. "General Introduction: Seeing through American War Cinema." In *Hollywood and War: The Film Reader,* edited by David J. Slocum, 1–22. London: Routledge, 2006.

———. *Hollywood and War: The Film Reader.* London: Routledge, 2006.

Sloterdijk, Peter. *Critique of Cynical Reason.* Translated by Michael Eldred. Minneapolis: University of Minnesota Press, 1988.

———. "The Weimar Symptom: Models of Consciousness in German Modernity." In *Critique of Cynical Reason,* 384–528.

Small, Edward S. *Experimental Film/Video as Major Genre.* Carbondale: Southern Illinois University Press, 1994.

Sontag, Susan. "Fascinating Fascism." In *Under the Sign of Saturn.* New York: Picador, 2002.

Staiger, Janet. "Hybrid or Inbred: The Purity Hypothesis and Hollywood Genre History." In Grant, *Film Genre Reader III,* 185–201.

———. *Perverse Spectators: The Practices of Film Reception.* New York: New York University Press, 2000.

Stern, Frank. "Film in the 1950s: Passing Images of Guilt and Responsibility." In Schissler, *Miracle Years: A Cultural History of West Germany, 1949–1968,* 266–80.

Straub, Laurens. "Zur Lage des deutschen Filmmarktes." In *Bestandsaufnahme: Utopie Film—zwanzig Jahre neuer deutscher Film,* edited by Alexander Kluge, 349–56. Frankfurt am Main: zweitausendeins, 1983.

Taberner, Stuart, and Paul Cooke, eds. *German Culture, Politics, and Literature into the Twenty-First Century: Beyond Normalization.* Rochester, NY: Camden House, 2006.

Telotte, J. P. *A Distant Technology: Science Fiction Film and the Machine Age.* Middletown, CN: Wesleyan University Press, 1999.

Tohill, Cathal, and Pete Tombs. *Immoral Tales: European Sex Horror Movies, 1956–1984.* New York: St. Martin's Griffin, 1995.

"Trash City Review: *Der Todesking.*" Accessed 7 April 2001. www.trshcity. demon.co.uk/BLITZ/BLIT0294.htm.

Trimborn, Jürgen. *Der deutsche Heimatfilm der fünfziger Jahre: Motive, Symbole und Handlungsmuster.* Cologne: Teiresias Verlag, 1998.

Tudor, Andrew. "Genre." In Grant, *Film Genre Reader III,* 3–11.

———. *Theories of Film.* New York: Viking, 1974.

Tyberg, Casper. "Shadow Souls and Strange Adventures: Horror and the Supernatural in European Silent Film." In *The Horror Film,* edited by Stephen Prince, 15–39. New Brunswick, NJ: Rutgers University Press, 2004).

Uka, Walter. "Der deutsche Film *schiebt den Blues*: Kino und Film in der Bundesrepublik in den achtziger Jahren." In *Die Kultur der achtziger Jahre,* ed. Werner Faulstich, 105–21. Munich: Wilhelm Fink, 2005.

Ulmer, Edgar G. "Interview with Peter Bogdanovich." In Peter Bogdanovich, *Who the Devil Made It: Conversations with Legendary Film Directors,* 558–604. New York: Ballantine, 1997.

Virchow, Eckart Voigts. "Heritage and Literature on Screen: Heimat and Heritage." In *The Cambridge Companion to Literature on Screen,* edited by Deborah Cartmell and Imelda Whelehan, 123–37. Cambridge: Cambridge University Press, 2009.

Virilio, Paul. *War and Cinema: The Logistics of Perception.* 1989. Reprint, London: Verso, 2000.

Weaver, Tom. "An Interview with Shirley Ulmer." In *The Films of Edgar G. Ulmer,* edited by Bernd Herzogenrath, 265–87. Metuchen, NJ: Scarecrow, 2009.

Weber, Samuel. *Targets of Opportunity: On the Militarization of Thinking.* New York: Fordham, 2005.

Wedel, Michael. *Der deutsche Musikfilm: Archäologie eines Genres, 1914–1945.* Munich: edition text + kritik, 2007.

———. "Literaturverfilmung." In Elsaesser and Wedel, *The BFI Companion to German Cinema,* 163–67.

Wedel, Michael, and Thomas Elsaesser. "German Film Comedy." In Elsaesser and Wedel, *The BFI Companion to German Cinema,* 55–56.

Wehrstedt, Norbert. "Das Genre-Kino der Defa." In *Der geteilte Himmel: Hohepunkte der Defa-Kinos, 1946–1992,* edited by Fritz Raimund, 91–106. Vienna: Filmarchiv Austrian, 2001.

Weingarten, Susanne. "Was nun, Jan?" *Der Spiegel,* 17 March 1997, 217.

Weinrich, C. "Zensur und Verbot im Genrefilm: Die große Schnittparade des Horrors- [*sic*] und Splatterfilms." http://www.censuriana.de/texte/ genrefilm/genre.htm. Accessed 21 September 2010.

"Will Fascism Come to America?" *Modern Monthly,* September 1934, 464–66.

Williams, Linda. "Melodrama Revisited." In *Refiguring American Film Genres,* edited by Nick Browne, 42–88. Berkeley: University of California Press, 1998.

Witte, Karsten. "Too Beautiful to Be True: Lilian Harvey." Translated by Eric Rentschler. *New German Critique* 74 (Spring–Summer 1998).

———. "Visual Pleasure Inhibited: Aspects of the German Revue Film." Translated by J. D. Steakley and Gabriele Hoover. *New German Critique* 24/25 (Fall–Winter 1981–82).

———. "Wie Filmgeschichte schreiben?" *epd Kirche und Film* 34, no. 12 (December 1981).

Wood, Robin. "The American Nightmare: Horror in the 1970s." In *Horror: The Film Reader*, edited by Mark Jancovich, 25–32. London: Routledge, 2002.

Wright, Judith Hess. "Genre Films and the Status Quo." In Grant, *Film Genre Reader III*, 42–50.

Wright, Will. *Sixguns and Society: A Structural Study of the Western*. Berkeley: University of California Press, 1977.

Contributors

Marco Abel is an associate professor of English and film studies at the University of Nebraska-Lincoln. Author of *Violent Affect: Literature, Cinema, and Critique After Representation* (University of Nebraska Press, 2007), he has published widely on contemporary German cinema in journals including *Cineaste, Quarterly Review of Film and Video, New German Critique, Senses of Cinema*, and *German Studies Review*, as well as in a number of edited collection. He also co-edited *Im Angesicht des Fernsehens: Der Filmemacher Dominik Graf* (text + kritik, 2012), the first volume of critical essays on contemporary German cinema's most important genre filmmaker. His second monograph, *The Counter-Cinema of the Berlin School*, is forthcoming with Camden House (2013).

Nora M. Alter is professor of film and media arts at Temple University. She is author of *Vietnam Protest Theatre. The Television War on Stage* (1996); *Projecting History: Non-Fiction German Film* (2002); *Chris Marker* (2006); and co-editor with Lutz Koepnick of *Sound Matters: Essays on the Acoustics of Modern German Culture* (2004). She has published essays on German and European studies, film and media studies, cultural and visual studies, and contemporary art. She has been awarded year-long research fellowships from the National Endowment for the Humanities, the Howard Foundation, and the Alexander von Humboldt Foundation.

Antje Ascheid is associate professor of film studies at the department of theatre and film studies at the University of Georgia. She received her PhD in Cinema Studies at New York University in 1999. Her academic research focuses on women and film, German Cinema, and film genres. Her first book, *Hitler's Heroines: Stardom, Womanhood and the Popular in Nazi Cinema*, was published with Temple University Press in 2003. She has also published numerous articles and book chapters. Prior to coming to UGA, she was professionally active in the field of documentary and independent film production in New York City and has taught at Smith College and SUNY New Paltz.

Hester Baer is associate professor of German at the University of Maryland—College Park. Her research focuses on how popular culture responds to social and political change in Germany in the twentieth and twenty-first centuries. She is the author of *Dismantling the Dream Factory: Gender, German Cinema, and the Postwar Quest for a New Film Language* (2009) and the editor of a special issue of the journal *Studies in 20th and 21st Century Literature*, "Contemporary Women's Writing and the Return of Feminism in Germany" (2011). She is currently at work on a new book, *German Cinema in the Age of Neoliberalism*.

Steve Choe is an assistant professor in the department of cinema and comparative literature at the University of Iowa. His research revolves around film theory and philosophy as well as the cinemas of Germany and South Korea. His book, *Afterlives: Allegories of Film and Mortality in Early Weimar Germany*, is forthcoming with Continuum.

Paul Cooke is Centenary Chair in World Cinemas at the University of Leeds, UK and has published widely on contemporary German culture. He is the author of *Speaking the Taboo: A Study of the Work of Wolfgang Hilbig* (2000); *The Pocket Essential to German Expressionist Film* (2002); *Representing East Germany: From Colonization to Nostalgia* (2005); and *Contemporary German Cinema* (2012). His edited books include *World Cinema's Dialogues with Hollywood* (2007); *The Lives of Others and Contemporary German Film* (2013); with Stuart Taberner, *German Culture, Politics and Literature into the Twenty-First Century: Beyond Normalization* (2006); with Marc Silberman, *Screening War: Perspectives on German Suffering* (2010); and with Chris Homewood, *New Directions in German Cinema* (2011).

Jaimey Fisher is associate professor of German and cinema and techno-cultural studies as well as director of cinema and technocultural studies at the University of California, Davis. He is the author of the forthcoming *Christian Petzold* (University of Illinois Press, 2013) as well as *Disciplining German: Youth, Reeducation, and Reconstruction after the Second World War* (Wayne State Press, 2007). He also co-edited *Collapse of the Conventional: German Film and its Politics at the Turn of the Twenty-first Century* with Brad Prager (2010); with Barbara Mennel, *Spatial Turns: Space, Place, and Mobility in German Literary and Visual Culture* (2010); and, with Peter Hohendahl, *Critical Theory: Current State and Future Prospects* (2001). His current book-project analyzes war films in Germany from 1914–61.

Gerd Gemünden is the Sherman Fairchild Professor in the Humanities at Dartmouth College, where he teaches in the departments of German studies, film and media studies, and comparative literature. He is the author of *Framed Visions: Popular Culture, Americanization, and the Contemporary German and Austrian Imagination* (1998), *A Foreign Affair: Billy*

Wilder's American Films (2008) and most recently, *Continental Strangers: German Exile Cinema, 1933–1951* (2014). His volumes as editor include *The Cinema of Wim Wenders* (1997); *Dietrich Icon* (2007); and *Culture in the Anteroom: The Legacies of Siegfried Kracauer* (2012). He serves on the editorial board of *New German Critique* and *Film Criticism*. His current project, *A Cinema of Deceleration*, investigates the latest trends in Latin American film.

SASCHA GERHARDS is visiting assistant professor of German at Miami University in Oxford, Ohio. He completed his dissertation, entitled "Zeitgeist of Murder: The Krimi and Social Transformation in Post-1945 Germany" at the University of California, Davis. Sascha received his BA equivalent in English and social sciences from the University of Cologne, Germany, and completed his master of arts degree in comparative literature at the University of Rochester, NY. He has published an interview with acclaimed linguist Claire Kramsch on her book *The Multilingual Subject*, and is currently working on a contribution to the first American Anthology on the German crime genre as well as an essay on crime film in East Germany.

LUTZ KOEPNICK is the Gertrude Conaway Vanderbilt Chair of German at Vanderbilt University in Nashville. He has written widely on German literature, film, media, visual culture, new media aesthetics, and intellectual history from the nineteenth to the twenty-first century. Book publications include *Framing Attention: Windows on Modern German Culture* (2007); *The Dark Mirror: German Cinema between Hitler and Hollywood* (2002); and *Walter Benjamin and the Aesthetics of Power* (1999). Co-edited volumes include *After the Digital Divide? German Aesthetic Theory in the Age of New Media* (2009); *The Cosmopolitan Screen: German Cinema and the Global Imaginary* (2007); *Caught by Politics: Hitler Exiles and American Visual Culture* (2007); and *Sound Matters: Essays on the Acoustics of German Culture* (2004).

ERIC RENTSCHLER is the Arthur Kingsley Porter Professor of Germanic Languages and Literatures and the chair of the film and visual studies program at Harvard University. His publications concentrate on German film history and theory during the Weimar Republic, the Third Reich, and the postwar and postwall eras. His books include *West German Film in the Course of Time* (Redgrave, 1984); *German Film and Literature* (Methuen, 1986); *West German Filmmakers on Film* (Holmes & Meier, 1988); *Augenzeugen* (Verlag der Autoren, 1988; second updated edition 2001, with Hans Helmut Prinzler); *The Films of G. W. Pabst* (Rutgers University Press, 1990); *The Ministry of Illusion* (Harvard University

Press, 1996); and *Neuer Deutscher Film* (Reclam, 2012, with Norbert Grob and Hans Helmut Prinzler).

KRIS VANDER LUGT is an instructional technology specialist at Northern Virginia Community College. Before entering the instructional technology field, she was assistant professor of German at Iowa State University and later taught at George Mason University. Her publications include articles on Elfriede Jelinek's literature of the undead, Christoph Schlingensief's politics of gore, and postwar German horror film. Together with Daniel H. Magilow and Elizabeth Bridges, she co-edited the volume *Nazisploitation! The Nazi Image in Low-Brow Cinema and Culture*.

Index

Neue Sachlichkeit, 40
Neues vom Wixxer (Something New from the Rascal), 137, 153, 154
neunte Tag, Der (The Ninth Day), 110
New German Cinema, 1–3, 24, 50, 64, 78, 109, 114, 118, 136, 159, 175, 222, 224–25, 239–40, 244
New German Critique, 5, 7, 63, 76, 94–95, 122, 160, 230, 234, 249
New Hollywood, 244, 265
New Sobriety, 40
New York, 33, 54, 59, 163, 204, 254
News from Home, 60
newsreels, 49, 53
Nibelungen, Die, 28n2
Nichts neues im Westen (All Quiet on the Western Front), 113
Nicodemus, Katja, 264–65, 273
Niehoff, Karena, 120, 121
Nietzsche, Friedrich, 50
Night of the Living Dead, 192–93
nihilism, 246, 249
Nirgendwo in Afrika (Nowhere in Africa), 180, 184, 185
Nissen, Aud Egede, 147, 177, 208
Niven, Bill, 115
nonfiction film, 49, 50, 53–55, 57–60
Nordwand (North Face), 24, 235
Nosferatu: Eine Symphonie des Grauens (Nosferatu: A Symphony of Terror), 30–32, 44, 52, 91, 157, 158, 193, 201n5
nostalgia and nostalgic, 67, 102, 104, 118, 134, 144, 155, 199, 221, 224 226–27, 231, 233–34, 238–39, 248
Novembertage (November Days), 67
Numero Deux, 68

Oberhausen Manifesto, 63, 115
O'Brien, Charles, 20
Ophüls, Marcel, 67
Ophüls, Max, 264
Opus I–IV, 54n10
Orgelstube, 53
originality, 6, 32, 153, 182
Orlacs Hände (The Hands of Orlac), 76, 86

Oscar (Academy Award), 110, 176, 181, 184–85, 190
Ostermayr, Peter, 225, 227, 228
Ottinger, Ulrike, 50, 67, 68, 70
Ozon, Francois, 249

Pabst, G. W., 76, 91, 97, 99, 109, 113, 119, 125
painting, 51, 55–56, 68–66, 257
Palfreyman, Rachel, 223–24, 226–28, 233
Panofsky, Erwin, 9
panorama, 93
Papamichou, Christina, 253
Papas Kino, 222, 225, 228, 240
paracinema, 164, 167
Parfum, Das, 176, 180–81, 184
Paris, 38, 254
parody, 17, 80, 132, 135, 142, 144, 169, 243
parole (vs. langue), 12
Particules élémentaires, Les (Elementary Particles), 246
Pastewka, Bastian, 153
Patalas, Enno, 62, 63
Pauer, Florian, 134–35, 143, 149
Paul, Christiane, 251
Paul, Eden, 92
Peckinpah, Sam, 265
Penn, Arthur, 119
Peter William Evans, 249
Petzold, Christian, 212, 261–63, 268, 275–76, 280, 283
philosophy, 50, 64
photography, 52, 54, 64, 199–200, 205, 219; Kracauer on, 199
Picabia, Francis, 56
Pilcher, Rosamunde, 230
Pinthus, Kurt, 201, 208n25
Pitaval stories, 138–39
pleasure, 73, 75, 79, 80, 82, 84–85, 89, 91, 95, 101, 103, 169, 189, 194–96, 202, 208, 217, 254, 278
plot, 17–18, 31–33, 36, 38, 58, 81, 87, 89, 103, 119, 128–29, 139, 141, 147, 149, 162, 164, 188–89, 201, 208, 228–29, 233, 252, 254– 56, 269, 271, 274, 276, 279, 280

Soviet Union and Soviet culture/cin-
ema, 66–67, 83, 87
space: and *The Black Cat*, 42; and
Deleuze, 226; and Eichinger, 192,
195; and essay film, 54, 62, 67, 68;
and exhibition, 68; and Foucault,
210; and Graf, 271; and Heimat
film, 224–26, 229 230, 234, 237–
39; and horror, 42; and maps, 130;
and modernity, 42; and museum,
68; and musical operettas, 92,
94, 102, 104; and myth, 14; and
nation, 130; and prison, 210; public space, 128; and romance films,
254, 260; and rural, 104; and science fiction (incl. outer space), 71,
73–75, 78, 82–87; and structuralism, 14; and urban, 67. 91, 102,
104, 106, 193, 195, 196, 254; and
war films, 113n10, 125n36, 128;
and Weimar era, 71, 73–75, 78,
91, 92, 102, 104, 106; and West
Germany, 271. *See also* architecture;
landscape
Spaßkultur and Spaßkulturgesellschaft,
269, 273, 280
special effects, 31, 71–72, 74, 78,
80–82, 88–90
spectacle, 74, 85, 106, 185, 230
spectators, 55–56, 59–60, 68, 78, 103,
105, 107, 194, 198, 200, 204–5,
208–9, 217, 222, 232–33
speech act, 198, 206, 215, 217
Sperling, 262, 266
Spermula, 164
Spielberg, Steven, 127
Spieler (Gambler), 262
splatter film, 162, 166, 170
stabbed in the back myth, 29
Stadt wird erpresst, Eine (Blackmailing
of a City), 269, 272, 274, 282
Stahltier, Das (The Steel Animal), 61
Staiger, Janet, 17, 19, 86–87, 208
Stand der Dinge, Der (The State of
Things), 79
Stanford Prison experiment, 209
star system and stardom, 11, 136, 148,
154, 243

Stargate, 80
Starobinski, Jean, 50
state power, 203, 206
Statues also Die, 63
Staub (Dust), 68
Staudte, Wolfgang, 62, 123, 236
Steinbichler, Hans, 231
Sternberg, Josef von, 41, 97
Steyerl, Hito, 67
Stimmung (atmosphere), 105
Stokowski, Oliver, 216
Stölzl, Philipp, 235
Stosch, Stefan, 270–71
Stosstrupp 1917, 113
Strasse, Die (The Street), 106
Straub, Jean-Marie, 50, 64
Straub, Laurens, 190, 191
street film, 31, 91
Stromlinien (Flow Lines), 53–54
structuralism, 12–13, 15–19, 244
Student von Prag, Der (Student of
Prag), 109
studio era, 86
style: and auteurism, 8, 34, 80; and
Bauhaus, 39, 40; and *The Black
Cat*, 34; and Eichinger, 175, 176,
178, 182, 187–89; and essay film,
57, 59, 64, 68; and genre, 80; and
Graf, 275, 278; and Heimat film,
230, 239; and horror, 157, 163–
64, 169; and late genre, 144–45;
and musical operetta, 91n4; and
paracinema, 167n30; and romance
films, 244; and science fiction, 80;
and thriller, 211; and Ulmer, 34;
and Weimar era, 27, 34, 39, 40,
91n4, 157
sublime, 74, 93, 226, 229, 240
subsidy, 114
subtitle, 58, 60, 200, 203
Suchsland, Rüdiger, 2n3
Sunless, 60
supernatural, 36, 44, 158, 163
Superweib, Das (The Superwoman),
174
surrealists, 56
surveillance, 210, 216, 274, 276–77
Süsskind, Patrick, 184